2nd Revised and
Enlarged Edition 2002

India's Economy in the 21st Century

OPTIONAL

The present edition is also available in Hard-back format accompanied by a CD-ROM comprising full-text of several important Reports, Discussion Papers & Policy Documents.

2nd Revised and Enlarged Edition 2002

India's Economy in the 21st Century

A Collection of Select Articles

Edited by

Raj Kapila & Uma Kapila

- C. Rangarajan
- Montek S. Ahluwalia
- Bimal Jalan
- Vijay L. Kelkar
- Rakesh Mohan
- Shankar Acharya
- V.S. Vyas
- N A Mujumdar
- Y.V. Reddy
- C.H. Hanumantha Rao
- S.S. Tarapore
- K.C. Pant
- Nagesh Kumar
- Uma Kapila

Academic Foundation
www.academicfoundation.com

First Edition : 2001

2nd Revised Edition : 2002

Published by

ACADEMIC FOUNDATION
4772-73 / 23 Bharat Ram Road,
(23 Ansari Road), Darya Ganj,
New Delhi - 110 002.

Phones : 3245001, 02, 03, 04.

Fax : 011-3245005

e-mail : academic@vsnl.com

www : academicfoundation.com

India's Economy in the 21st Century (2nd Revised & Enlarged Edition: 2002)
Raj Kapila & Uma Kapila, ed.

ISBN 81-7188-263-3

Laser-Typeset at AF's DTP Division.
Printed at Print Perfect, Mayapuri, Phase - II, Delhi.

Dedicated To
All Those Engaged In
The Development Of India's Economy

CONTENTS

...Contd....

...Contd....

...Contd....

III. Agriculture

IV. Industry & Infrastructure

...Contd....

...Contd....

V. External Sector

ACKNOWLEDGEMENT

The editors are indeed grateful to the contributors mentioned overleaf, for their papers/articles that have been published in this volume.

AUTHORS / CONTRIBUTORS

C. Rangarajan. .... *Governor, Andhra Pradesh; Ex-Governor, Reserve Bank of India, Mumbai.*

Montek S. Ahluwalia. .... *Director (EvO), IMF, Washington; Ex-Member, Planning Commission; Formerly : Finance Secretary, Govt. of India*

Bimal Jalan. .... *Governor, Reserve Bank of India, Mumbai.*

Shankar Acharya. .... *Hony. Professor, ICRIER, New Delhi; Formerly : Chief Economic Advisor, Ministry of Finance, Government of India, New Delhi*

C.H. Hanumantha Rao. .... *Chairman, Centre for Economic & Social Studies, Hyderabad; Ex-Member, Planning Commission; formerly, Director, Institute of Economic Growth, Delhi*

K.C. Pant. .... *Deputy Chairman, Planning Commission, Government of India, New Delhi*

Rakesh Mohan. .... *Director & Chief Executive , Indian Council for Research in International Economic Relations (ICRIER), New Delhi; Formerly : Economic Advisor to the Finance Minister, Ministry of Finance; Ex-Director General, National Council of Applied Economic Research (NCAER), New Delhi*

...Contd....

..Contd....

V.S. Vyas. .... *Professor Emeritus; Chairman, Governing Board, Institute of Development Studies, Jaipur*

Vijay L. Kelkar. .... *Executive Director, International Monetary Fund (IMF); Ex-Chairman, Tariff Commission; Formerly : Finance Secretary, Government of India, New Delhi*

Y.V. Reddy. .... *Dy. Governor, Reserve Bank of India, Mumbai.*

Nagesh Kumar. .... *Senior Fellow, Centre for Research & Information Systems for the Non-Aligned and other Developing Countries (RIS), New Delhi*

S.S. Tarapore. .... *Ex-Dy. Governor, Reserve Bank of India*

N.A. Mujumdar. .... *Editor, Indian Journal of Agricultural Economics; Ex-Principal Advisor, Reserve Bank of India, Mumbai*

V. Ratna Reddy. .... *Centre for Economic and Social Studies, Hyderabad*

Editors:

Raj Kapila. .... *Director and Chief Editor, Academic Foundation, Delhi*

Uma Kapila. .... *Reader, Department of Economics, Miranda House, University of Delhi*

PREFACE

to the Second Edition

THE first edition of *India's Economy in the 21st Century* was brought out in February 2001. Encouraged by the response of the first edition, it has been decided that instead of bringing out simply a reprint of the book, a revised edition, including **several new chapters** to make it more comprehensive and up-to-date, may be brought out in paperback to make it more affordable and useful for the readers. Hence, all major sectors of the economy have been covered in the present '2nd Revised and Enlarged Edition: 2002.' New section on infrastructure has been added. The present edition has seven new chapters. The edited chapters of the earlier edition have been thoroughly revised and updated — both in analysis as well as data.

The editors sincerely hope that the book, in its present revised format, shall be able to serve far greater number of readers than its predecessor. Comments and suggestions for further improve ment are always welcome. Communications in this respect can be sent via e-mail at: academic@vsnl.com

— *Editors*

OPTIONAL

The present edition is also available in Hard-back format accompanied by a CD-ROM comprising full-text of several important Reports Discussion Papers & Policy Documents.

I

The Economy

EDITORS' INTRODUCTION :

1

India's Economy at the Beginning of the New Millennium : — the 21st Century

Challenges and Opportunities

As we enter the 21st century, we must assess where we are *vis-a-vis* other countries in terms of various economic indicators such as growth, stability and poverty as well as make an introspection as to how far we have achieved the planned objectives of growth with social justice. The articles/papers selected for the purpose, provide a good insight into the current state of the Indian economy, highlighting the challenges of the growth process and the opportunities.

The analysis has been divided into five sections :

I. The Economy
II. Banking and Finance
III. Agriculture
IV. Industry and Infrastructure
V. External Sector.

The process of growth in Indian economy since 1950 is discussed in section I – analysing the constraints on growth, the emerging economic challenges, the economic reforms and policy agenda for the future (chs. 2 to 7). The structural transformation of the Indian Economy in the last decade of the 20th century and the future prospects, have been analysed in chapter eight.

The monetary policy of the Reserve Bank of India; Banking

and Finance in the new millennium covering banking sector reforms; and the future agenda for financial sector reforms, are covered in section II (chs. 9 to 11).

Section III is devoted to agriculture, discussing recent experiences and providing insights into the long term issues of agricultural development and, challenges and opportunities in the new international trade regime in the 21st century (chs. 12 to 14).

The Industrial sector of Indian economy, as it stands today, highlighting the structural transformation, performance and recent policy initiatives, including the infrastructure development, and the issue of corporate governance, have been discussed in section IV (chs. 15 to 17).

The last section (V), is devoted to India's external sector — managing the external economic challenges and lessons for the future, liberalisation and the changing patterns of Foreign Direct Investment, the issue of capital account convertibility, and globalisation *vis-a-vis* the Indian economy (chs. 18 to 21).

How We Progressed

When India was in the midst of an acute economic crisis in 1991, the Government of India introduced a number of measures to improve the working of the economy. These measures had two broad objectives. One was the reorientation of the economy from a statist, centrally directed and highly controlled economy to what is referred to in the current jargon as a 'market-friendly economy'. A reduction in direct controls and physical planning was expected to improve the efficiency of the economy. It was to be made more 'open' to external trade and external flows through a reduction in trade barriers and liberalisation of foreign investment policies. A second objective of the reform measures was macro-economic stabilisation. This was to be achieved by substantially reducing fiscal deficits as well as reducing the government's draft on society's savings.

Compared with the historical trend, the impact of these policies, according to Bimal Jalan, has been positive and significant. The growth rate of the economy during 1992-93 to 1999-2000 was close to 6.5 per cent per annum. The balance of payments position has also substantially improved. Despite several unfavourable external developments, including the imposition of sanctions in 1998 and sharp rise in oil prices more recently, foreign exchange reserves are at a record level. Exports have done well, current account deficits have been moderate, and India's external debt (as a percentage of GDP) and the debt servicing burden have actually come down since the early Nineties. There is also evidence of considerable restructuring in the corporate sector with attention being given to cost-competitiveness and financial viability. Industrial growth increased sharply during the period 1993 to 1996, to over 9 per cent per annum. The industrial growth rate came down to 5.5 per cent per annum in the next two years, but increased again to 8 per cent, upto the end of 1999-2000. The rate of inflation also came down sharply — from 10.3 per cent in 1990-91 to a modest 3.3 per cent in 1999-2000. Fiscal deficit has also come down — from 8.3 per cent in 1990-91 to 5.6 per cent in 1999-2000.

Compared with the record of the first 40 years of development, there is very little doubt that India's economy — by any standard of measurement — is stronger and more resilient today than was the case a decade ago, reiterates Bimal Jalan. There is also little doubt that India's "potential" for growth combined with external and domestic financial stability is greater today — *at the beginning of the twenty-first Century* — than was the case 20, 50 or 100 years ago.

The New Economy

A most remarkable feature of the so-called "New Economy" is the role of the services sector (including the Information Technology) in generating growth of income and employment, says Jalan. The focus of attention in conventional economics, including development economics, was on production of goods — manufactured products and agricultural commodities. It was, of course, recognised that the services sector (which includes transport, communication, trade, banking, construction and public administration, etc.) was an important source of income and employment in most economies. However, the growth of services was perceived at best as a byproduct of developments in the primary and secondary sectors, and at worst as a drag on the prospects for long-term economic growth. Services were believed to be mainly non-tradable activities with slow productivity growth and low employment potential. In developing countries the conventional view of the growth of the services sector was even worse. It was seen to divert scarce resources away from production of goods, and instead contribute to the accentuation of income inequalities.

In the last few years, however, there has been a phenomenal change in the conventional view of services and their role in the economy. The development of certain services is now regarded as one of the preconditions of economic growth, and not as one of its consequences. The boundary between goods and services is also disappearing, as services of various kinds are delinked from the manufacturing process. Many industrial products are not only manufactured — they are also designed, marketed, advertised, distributed, leased and serviced. Thus, in the changed scenario, India does not necessarily have to be a low-cost producer of certain types of goods (e.g., computers or discs) before it can become an efficient supplier of services embodied in them (e.g., software or music). There are very few developing countries which are as well placed as India to take advantage of the phenomenal changes that have occurred in production technologies, international trade, capital movements, and the deployment of skilled manpower. India today has the knowledge and the skills to produce and process a wide variety of industrial and consumer products and services.

It must be recognised that the *death of distance* and the growing integration of global production, services and financial markets in recent years has presented new challenges for management of the national economy — not only in India but all over the world, remarks Bimal Jalan. Thus, *at the beginning of the new century*, the challenge before us is in two directions — how to seize the new opportunities, while at the same time, protecting ourselves against unanticipated risks. We must keep some safety nets handy by building a diversified and efficient financial system which can aid and protect the development process at all times, good and bad.

In terms of rate of growth, we have done better in the latter half of the 20th century than during the first half, and far better in the final two decades, says Y.V. Reddy (ch. 4). Over the period, fluctuations in growth of output have been reduced. The resilience to withstand shocks has progressively increased. External sector has become comfortable in the sense that there is no foreign currency constraint on growth now. Yet, we have pervading poverty, high illiteracy and poor condition of health and sanitation. There are islands of excellence, like information technology experts, amidst a sea of deprivation and misery. Clearly, economic policy, especially of the "nineties" has removed several constraints on economic growth, which is in itself an achievement and a necessary condition for the rest of the goals of a civil society. But, there are lurking doubts on whether we are systematically building a system that would ensure continued high level of growth and also the achievement of minimum social objectives associated with such growth. The end product of all economic policy is social well being, and admittedly the long term prospects for economic growth depend crucially on the social well being. The social indicators in regard to our country do not give us too much of comfort. Literacy levels are low, though public expenditure as a percentage of GDP is comparable to many other countries. The picture in regard to health and sanitation is not encouraging, and it is unfortunate that we spent in this area a much lower proportion of GDP than others. Overall, we rank rather low in human development and high in human deprivation. One notices relatively low levels of public expenditures in health, and in primary education. There seems to be a very disturbing insensitivity among many of us to human suffering and needs of the poor, laments Reddy.

The medium term challenge relating to institutions and infrastructure as well as the longer term one relating to social development, demand a more focused government i.e., a government that efficiently delivers the essential services that it is supposed to deliver. What we need is not less government and more market, but better government and genuine market. So far, perhaps, the reality in our country was often the State and market versus poor people, but effort should now be to aim for State and market for the people, or better government and genuine market for the people. Y.V. Reddy rightly remarks, "the refocused role of government demands both professional skills and personal integrity among all leading participants. Tomorrow's problems cannot be solved with yesterday's strategies, and cannot even be understood with day before yesterday's knowledge".

As we enter into the new century, the Indian economy stands at cross roads. Either it can take the "business as usual" road which means continued poverty and a low growth trap or take the high road to prosperity through accelerated reforms. If we take this road, then there is no reason why India, by the year 2020, cannot achieve a per capita income of more than one thousand dollars (i.e., 50,000 rupees) and wipe out the poverty and illiteracy and also increase life expectancy by ten years or more and become an Economic Super Power. Presently, we are in the bottom twenty amongst all the countries in terms of Human Development Index. In the year 2020 we should be amongst the first twenty. This is surely possible and it is entirely up to us to build the necessary consensus for accelerated reforms and implement it, opines Vijay Kelkar (ch.4).

Next Phase of Reforms

We need to show greater vigour and greater sense of urgency in implementing the next phase of reforms. The reason for emphasizing the urgency is due to the unique state of our demographic transition. In the next couple of decades India will have, once in a life-time chance, of having a population structure where we will have the largest share of working population. Naturally, after these decades, the process of aging will catch on and the vigour of the working population would decline. "Like a satellite when it is put in the orbit, it requires high velocity to ensure exit from the Earth's gravitational force; if our economy is to exit from the gravitational pull of poverty, it also requires a high exit velocity of double-digit growth rate over the next two decades", says Vijay Kelkar. This kind of high growth is feasible, as other miracle economies achieved it, maintaining high savings and investment rates and also increasing labour supply and productivity.

According to Montek Ahluwalia, "A policy agenda for the future should be determined by looking at existing strength and weaknesses and building on the strength while correcting the weaknesses." *India enters the new millennium* with some important strengths. First, our growth performance is now much better than the frustratingly low 3.5/4 per cent growth which characterised the first three decades after independence. The growth rate has accelerated to 6.5 per cent in the Eighth Plan period and is expected to be maintained. If we focus on the 1980s and 1990s, India has been one of the fastest of the ten fastest growing economies in the world. The literacy level which was a drag on our growth potential has increased from 18.3 per cent in 1951 to 34.4 per cent in 1971 and to 62 per cent in 1996-97. Although it is still low, but it is consistent with achieving growth rates of 7 to 8 per cent. The population growth, which for long remained above 2 per cent, at last appears to be declining. India's population growth in the next decade is expected to slow down to 1.5 per cent.

These positive developments have important implications for our prospects in the next decade. If GDP growth can be pushed up from around 6.5 per cent at present to say 7 per cent at the start of the decade, and then to 8 per cent by the end of the decade, it would give us an average growth of around 7.5 per cent for the decade as a whole. With population growing at 1.5 per cent, this means per capita income would grow at about 6 per cent per year. Growth of this order is much higher than we have experienced in the past and can create many virtuous circles. If it is reasonably well distributed, it would guarantee a sharp reduction in the level of poverty by the end of the next decade. One can go further and say that unless we can achieve growth of this order, we cannot expect to see a significant improvement in the conditions of living of the mass of our people. What are the policies we need to follow to achieve such growth and especially to make it broad-based? According to Montek Ahluwalia (ch. 5), fortunately, a substantial consensus has now emerged in professional and even in political circles on economic policies. There is general agreement that the process of economic reforms must be strengthened and deepened and this is sometimes described as implementing "the second generation of reforms". The first item on this agenda (on which there is a great deal of agreement) must be to restore fiscal discipline. This is actually a first generation reform, which we have not been able to carry out as planned. We must reduce the fiscal deficit to release resources for private investment but we must simultaneously increase public investment in critical areas. This suggests that the scale of fiscal effort needed is very large. It cannot be achieved by acting on one or two instruments. Action will be needed on several fronts like (i) Improving tax administration to raise larger revenues (ii) reducing subsidies (iii) downsizing of government (iv) bolder privatisation and (v) reprioritizing plan schemes.

Montek Singh points out that an area that has not been touched by the reforms thus far, but which must now be addressed urgently, relates to reforms in the labour markets and especially labour laws. The second generation reforms need to be carried out in the legal system as well. If we want to integrate with the world and to benefit from large inflows of foreign investment we need a well functioning legal system in which contractual rights and obligations can be effectively enforced.

Fiscal Predicament

Rakesh Mohan emphasises that it is only through higher economic growth that we can reduce poverty and provide sustainable economic security. No distribution can take place when there is nothing to distribute. The nation cannot be secure without economic strength and economic strength cannot be achieved without substantial economic growth. Ensuring long term economic health of the nation requires acceleration of economic growth on a sustained basis. The main impediment constraining India's growth in the future is the continuing fall in public investment in infrastructure which has been caused by the deteriorating fiscal environment, at both, the central and state government levels. Apart from ensuring higher buoyancy in tax revenues, the key solutions to India's fiscal predicament are bold programmes for improving user charges for all public services amenable to such charges, and the implementation of a crash programme of privatisation. In the absence of such urgent action, the already serious fiscal situation will get worse and will pose a serious threat to economic security in the very near future.

According to Rangarajan, the economy needs to grow at least at 7 per cent per annum, if the employment opportunities are to expand to absorb the additional labour force as well as to reduce the backlog of unemployed. In the early years after Independence a major constraint on economic growth was a low savings rate. In the early fifties, the gross savings rate of the economy was only ten per cent. The savings constraint has been steadily overcome. In recent years the savings rate of the economy has remained between 25 and 26 per cent. If we add to this even a modest current account deficit of two per cent of the GDP, the growth rate of seven per cent becomes possible with the incremental capital-output ratio remaining more or less at four. Thus, the growth rate of seven per cent over the medium term is distinctly possible, says Rangarajan. All efforts should be made to achieve this rate of growth in a sustained way. In fact, there is an urgent need to step up the savings rate, if the economy is to grow at seven per cent comfortably.

As the world moves into the new century and the new millennium, a country like India, with continental dimensions, has to reckon with changes that are occurring in the rest of the world. *The new millennium* is being looked forward to with great hopes and expectations and also with some trepidation. How will this new millennium be different? What are the challenges and opportunities for which we should be prepared? It is difficult to forecast what the future is going to be. Nevertheless, according to Rangarajan, we can perceive three strongly emerging trends. First, technological changes are going to be even faster. It will be no exaggeration to say that the new millennium will be characterised by some fundamental changes in technology. Second, the new millennium will see greater integration of the economies. The process of globalization will gather further momentum. And third, the wave of rising expectations will surge even further. All countries will become aware of the changes happening all over the world and the developing economies will naturally demand that their aspirations are met. Not only different countries, but also different segments within a country, will demand that their rights are fully respected.

"What is the model of economic growth that is appropriate for India? Development has many dimensions. Economic growth is only one aspect. Nevertheless, accelerated economic growth is a necessary condition for achieving many other dimensions of development. Development must ensure equality of opportunities for all. We need, therefore, to stress simultaneously economic development in the conventional sense of accelerating growth rate and social development in the sense of securing for every one the basic needs. The two have a mutually interacting beneficial impact and the two must be pursued together. Any strategy of development which ignores any one of the two legs will be unsustainable. Efficiency and equity should not be posed as opposing considerations. They must be weaved together to produce a coherent pattern of growth" says Rangarajan.

Banking and Finance

Commenting on the monetary policy (ch. 10) Rangarjan remarks "since the inception of development planning, the broad objectives of India's economic policy have been to achieve a faster rate of growth, ensure reasonable degree of price stability and promote distributive justice. Working of monetary policy in India over the past several decades would reveal that the broad objectives of monetary policy have been: (i) to maintain a reasonable degree of price stability and (ii) to help accelerate the rate of economic growth. The emphasis as between the two objectives, according to Rangarajan, has changed from year to year, depending upon the conditions prevailing in that year and in the previous year.

According to Rangarajan, effectiveness of the monetary policy depends, among other factors, on the stance of fiscal policy. The concerns of fiscal policy and monetary policy are at once same and different. Fiscal policy has a much broader spectrum of objectives to achieve. It is quite true that in India, monetary policy has been very much conditioned by the stance of fiscal policy. The system of ad hoc treasury bills facilitated monetisation of the fiscal deficit without limit and without prior approval. The 1990s saw the introduction of the scheme of Ways and Means advance. The Fiscal Responsibility Bill, when enacted, would be a great step forward not only in fiscal but monetary management.

A sound financial sector is a pre-requisite for efficient macroeconomic management. The process of liberalisation of the Indian economy, initiated in 1991, has meant corresponding changes in the financial sector which has witnessed a significant transformation during the 1990s.

According to Mujumdar, not being able to tailor the reforms to suit the specific socio-economic milieu has been our weakness. Furthermore, in the process of implementation of reforms, a number of distortions have also crept in. Correcting such distortions and attending to neglected segments should therefore claim a pre-eminent position on the agenda for future reforms.

Indian Agriculture and Economic Reforms

After a detailed discussion of economic reforms and Indian agriculture — recent experience and long term issues — Vyas and Reddy state that, "in our context agricultural policies have to address three principal objectives. As the primary sector, agriculture has to generate surpluses for financing economic growth. Secondly, it has to ensure productive employment and adequate incomes to the large number of households directly dependent on this sector. Finally, in a poor country where a substantial number of people spend significant proportion of their income on food, agriculture has the pivotal role in ensuring Food Security. In order to achieve the objective of a dynamic surplus generating agriculture, ensure equitable distribution and, provide safety nets for the vulnerable sections, the role of the non-price factors, especially the institutional factors, is important.

In planning for Agriculture *for the 21st Century*, K.C. Pant points out that, "while our past efforts have undoubtedly contributed to the overall growth process, region-specific planning would also be necessary to tackle regional disparities in agricultural productivity and income which have increased perceptibly, and the gulf between developed and underdeveloped regions which has widened. Whereas the northern and western regions have performed remarkably well, the eastern and northeastern regions have lagged behind in agricultural development.

There is also the issue of environmentally sustainable agricultural development. In the past, excessive focus on intensive agricultural growth has resulted in degradation of natural resources. The Green Revolution of the mid-1960s could have also contributed to the over-exploitation of natural resources. To an extent, this exploitation and mismanagement of natural resources was induced by an under-estimation of the capacity of our farmers, and made worse by over-enthusiastic populism. For example, high subsidy on canal waters, electricity, nitrogenous fertilizer, among others, induced farmers to overexploit soil and water resources without recognising the dangers inherent in such behaviour. Problems of soil salinity, waterlogging, declining water table, deteriorating water quality, are often reported in those regions which witnessed the green revolution.

The cumulative effect of degradation of natural resources has led to deceleration of agricultural growth. According to Pant, conserving natural resources to meet the current and future requirements of the growing population would be the biggest challenge in the 21st century. Sustainable agricultural production calls for effective planning and environment-friendly technologies and policies. Further, the emerging trade environment calls for appropriate planning for those regions and groups which we expect will be adversely affected.

The growth and development of our agricultural sector will depend on our clear-sighted pursuit of national interests and our ability to respond swiftly to a rapidly changing international economic environment. Globalisation, Pant points out, is not just a threat; it also throws up a number of opportunities. We are richly endowed with natural resources and climatic variety. We have one of the largest reservoirs and potential for bio-diversity in the world. There is hardly any crop that cannot be grown in our country. Implementation of WTO agreements is expected to increase our access to the world market. Currently, our share in world export is less than one percent. We need to identify commodities where we have a comparative advantage in the global market. We need to improve our quality standards if we have to compete in the world market. We have the advantage of availability of a relatively cheap and extremely hard-working labour force. We need to assess how this important resource can be utilized more productively to promote labour-intensive activities for competing in the global market.

The liberalisation of Indian economy which had commenced from around the mid-1980s and accelerated with the launching of fullfledged macroeconomic reforms since the early 1990s has improved the incentive framework for agriculture, says C.H. Hanumantha Rao. With the liberalisation of exchange rate and opening up of the economy, the terms of trade for agriculture have shown a significant improvement. As a result, private investment in agriculture registered a steep rise in the post-reform period. At 1993-94 prices, private investment in agriculture was over 50 per cent higher in 1999-2000 when compared to 1993-94. The exports of agricultural commodities, particularly foodgrains, accelerated in this period. For example, for the first time since independence, India has been a net exporter of foodgrains consecutively for the last six years, net exports amounting, on an average, to around 1.8 million tonnes per annum. In the light of this evidence, the fears being expressed in certain quarters that import of foodgrains under the new liberalised trade regime is having a dampening effect on the foodgrain prices in the country is totally misplaced. The evidence does not lend credence to the view that trade liberalisation would endanger India's food security. Achievement of effective food security when we can accumulate enough stocks of foodgrains, thanks to our comparative advantage in respect of major cereals, hinges basically on raising the purchasing power of the poor through the generation of employment opportunities. If the prices of foodgrains at the moment are out of reach of the poor, it is not due to the rise in exports but to the steep rise in procurement and issue prices.

Our major effort on the domestic front for ensuring the viability of Indian agriculture has to be focused on raising productivity by stepping up public investment, by accelerating the evolution and adoption of cost-reducing technologies, and by removing restrictions on agricultural trade, marketing and processing within the country. All this requires to be achieved through appropriate policy framework and institutional arrangements, emphasises Hanumantha Rao.

Industry & Infrastructure

In India, industry has been undergoing a significant transformation in the 'nineties. The process of organisational restructuring and the concomitant supportive changes in industrial policy aimed at creating a more competitive and challenging industrial environment are under way. The structural changes have impacted on the generally robust industrial performance. The need for industrial restructuring has raised several issues associated with mergers and acquisitions in the private corporate sector, reforms in the public sector enterprises and policy initiatives for competitiveness and effective working of the corporate sector.

Corporate Governance

In India the question of corporate governance has come up mainly in the wake of economic liberalisation, de-regulation of industry and business and increasing integration of the Indian economy with the rest of the world. According to Rangarajan, the need to conform to internationally accepted standards of corporate governance has become essential, as stakeholders in the Indian industry are no longer confined to this country alone. Also, there have been some important changes in the evolution of the Indian corporate system. Many family owned enterprises have moved from private limited companies to closely held public limited companies and further on to widely held limited companies. The recognition of the need for a code of corporate governance has also moved in line with this trend.

Infrastructure Development

An important conclusion from the review of infrastructure development (ch. 16) is that the demand for infrastructure services continues to outpace supply. Unless these shortfalls are met by creating new capacities in power, telecom, rail, roads and ports, there would be serious constraints on faster industrial and overall economic growth. Social welfare considerations also make it imperative that a minimum supply of water, housing, power and transport services are made available to every citizen. In fact, one of the biggest challenges facing the Indian economy today is to step up infrastructure investment and to upgrade the technology for better services.

Another important lesson is that greater private sector participation in infrastructure development is essential not only due to constraint of government resources but also to improve the quality of services and the delivery system. Although considerable progress has been made in attracting private investment much more needs to be done for sectoral reforms, rationalization of user charges and strengthening of institutional, legal and regulatory framework for ensuring fair competition among private and public operators and protecting consumer interests.

Changing Patterns of FDI

India has sought to increase inflows of foreign direct investment

(FDI) with a much liberal policy since 1991 after four decades of cautious, if not always restrictive, attitude to it. According to Nagesh Kumar, while the magnitudes of inflows have recorded impressive growth, they are still at a small level compared to the country's potential. The policy reforms have enabled the country to widen the sectoral as well as the source-country composition of FDI inflows. Compared to a near total concentration in manufacturing, the bulk of new inflows have come in the energy and services sectors. While the relative importance of European countries as sources of FDI in India has consistently declined, that of the US and some emerging sources in east Asia has increased steadily.

One of the objectives of the current reforms of policies is to remove impediments for export-oriented manufacture in general and to attract MNEs to locate efficiency-seeking FDI in the country. These investments could help India in expanding manufactured exports by using her as an export platform. The majority of the recent approvals of FDI, however, aims to explore India's sizeable and expanding domestic market. The efficiency-seeking FDIs have yet to start flowing into the country in a considerable manner. In an era of stiff competition among developing countries to attract export-oriented FDIs, liberalisation of policies alone may not be enough to win the race. More active negotiations and bargaining with MNEs may often be required, says Nagesh Kumar. India should use her bargaining advantages such as large domestic markets, abundant supply of trained and low wage labour, vast pool of technical professionals, well developed capital markets, etc, more effectively to attract a greater proportion of efficiency-seeking FDI.

The External Sector

The last decade of the 20th century has been an extraordinarily eventful decade for the Indian economy, especially in regard to the external sector. The decade threw several challenges in the external sector. According to Shankar Acharya, there have been mainly six external economic challenges that confronted the economy and economic policy makers during this decade. These challenges are the balance of payments crisis of 1991, the surge in foreign capital inflows in 1993 and 1994, trade liberalisation, external debt management, the risks of contagion from East Asian flu, and options and issues in exchange rate management.

The single greatest challenge that India's external sector is likely to face in *the first decade of the new millennium* will be to enhance the productivity and competitiveness of the Indian economy in an increasingly integrated global environment. This is crucial for assuring sustained growth in exports of goods and services, which, in turn, is central to the long-term health and viability of India's external sector. Higher productivity and greater competitiveness will not happen by themselves. It will require strong and sustained commitment to what has been called the second generation reforms in such difficult areas as fiscal responsibility legislation, labour laws, pricing and distribution of public utility services, deeper tax reforms, effective privatisation of many public enterprises and redirection of scarce public resources towards education, health, and rural infrastructure.

Capital Account Convertibility

According to S.S. Tarapore, there is an erroneous belief that India avoided the East Asian currency contagion as its capital account was closed. The reason for India not facing turbulence at that time was that it followed a sensible exchange rate policy and that its key external parameters were sound with significant reductions, as compared with the position at the time of the crisis of 1990-91, in the current account deficit, the external debt service ratio and the proportion of short-term debt to total external debt. Furthermore, in the capital flows there was a shift from exclusive debt financing to a blend of debt-equity financing with a significant liberalisation of foreign direct investment and portfolio flows. More importantly, India has had a relatively low medium-term inflation rate. Undoubtedly, there should be a proper sequencing of capital account liberalisation and that there must be a strong commitment to maintain macro economic stability and strengthen the domestic financial sector. These thoughts pervade the Indian report on capital account convertibility.

There is considerable discussion of exchange rate stability, monetary policy independence and capital account convertibility and this is labelled as the *holy* or *unholy* trinity depending on one's predilection, says Tarapore. The issue of reconciling these policies is by no means easy but if sound policies are followed it should be possible to attain a satisfactory resolution of the trinity. If a country uses the inflation rate as a nominal domestic anchor, depending on the inflation rate differentials *vis-a-vis* other major countries, the movements in the exchange rate should be acceptable. Now, if a country then subjects itself to the rigours of capital account convertibility it would make secure its basic policy objectives as with a liberalised capital account regime corrective measures would need to be taken expeditiously. Thus, the question whether it is appropriate for a country to move to capital account convertibility is, in a sense, not the issue. Rather, the question which a country has to ask itself is whether it chooses to have a higher or lower inflation rate relative to major industrial countries. Once this policy choice is made the exchange rate and capital flows will fall into place. "A country cannot afford to blame capital account convertibility for the ailments of its economy", remarks Tarapore.

One may ask this question whether there is a real choice for countries between capital account convertibility and capital controls. In an increasingly integrated world, and with current account convertibility, the only choice appears to be between an orderly sequenced capital account liberalisation and a disorderly liberalisation imposed by the international economy. The benefits of a well prepared and gradual integration into the global financial system outweighs the risks; this does not mean that a country should plunge into rapid capital liberalisation without proper preparation to attain the preconditions of fiscal reforms, inflation control and strengthening of the domestic financial system. There is no substitute for sound macro economic policies, emphasises Tarapore, and it is not as if we can follow imprudent policies and protect ourselves with capital controls.

Globalisation

The issue of Globalisation – the fears and opportunities that are associated with it – have been discussed in ch.21. Globalisation involves the increasing interaction of national economic systems — more integrated financial markets, higher factor mobility, and spectacular change in information technology, leading to the spread of knowledge throughout the world. It is a well-known fact that the process of globalization does not evolve equally worldwide. Some countries obtain great benefit from the process, mainly driven by their rapid integration into the global economy relative to other countries. In other words, the integrated global economy does not guarantee that the benefits of globalization are shared equally by all countries involved in the process.

More important, opportunities provided by the globalization process are not always beneficial, as shown by the recent crises. Hence, the process of globalization always carries social, economic, financial, cultural and even political risks in addition to the risk of contagion.

There are several reasons for this situation. Some of them are beyond the control of the countries involved such as external shocks and other unexpected changes in external environment. Indeed, most of these reasons are due to: weak macroeconomic and financial policies; inconsistencies in domestic policies; increased vulnerability of national economies to external shocks; higher international capital mobility; and higher volatility of exchange rates due to integrated financial markets, which hits real sectors of economies.

If India is to reap maximum benefits from globalisation, we have to complete the unfinished agenda of economic reforms. For this, the first thing to be done is to reinvigorate the process of economic reforms and complete its unfinished agenda. The State should also bring radical changes in terms of technological profile of the product through careful building up of technological relations and alliances with other countries. Having an open mind on economic issues is a prerequisite for reaping maximum benefits from globalisation.

2

India's Economy in the Twenty-First Century

BIMAL JALAN

The Post-Independence Development Record, 1950-1990

As we reflect on the history of human civilization in the millennium that has just ended, it is surprising to recall just how recent is the story of economic growth. As Paul Krugman has noted in a recent book, "economic growth, at least economic growth that raises living standards, is a modern invention. From the dawn of history to the Eighteenth century, the world was essentially Malthusian. Improvements in technology and capital investments were always overtaken by population growth; the number of people slowly increased, but their average standards of living did not."[1] Up to about the end of the Nineteenth century, the only countries where per capita incomes were increasing on a sustained basis for any length of time were the Western countries, particularly, England, Germany, France and the United States. During this entire period, the then so-called under-developed or Third World countries continued to be exporters of primary products and importers of industrial products with stagnant, and in some cases, declining per capita incomes. A large number of them were also colonies of the Western powers, and the connection

Parts of this Lecture draw on some of my previous publications, particularly *India's Economic Crisis: The Way Ahead*, (Oxford University Press, 1991); *India's Economic Policy: Preparing for the 21st Century*, (Viking/Penguin, 1996); and *Finance and Development: Which Way Now?* (Administrative Staff College of India, Hyderabad, 1999).

between these two situations — the colonial state and income stagnation — was not missed by their leaders and intellectuals.

The development strategies of the newly independent and developing countries, including India, in mid-Twentieth century were framed against this background. The central and the leading role for breaking away from the colonial legacy and for speeding up the process of industrialisation was assigned to the State. The need for the Government to occupy the commanding heights and to lead from the top received further support from the astounding success of the Soviet Union in emerging as a rival centre of political and industrial power within a very short period. India, at that time, played a pioneering role in giving expression to the aspirations of the newly independent Third World countries in the economic field. Thus, in 1956, India's Second Five Year Plan outlined the goals of development strategy in the following terms:

> "The pattern of development and the structure of socio-economic relations should be so planned that they result not only in appreciable increases in national income and employment but also in greater equality in incomes and wealth. Major decisions regarding production, distribution, consumption and investment — and in fact all significant socio-economic relationships — must be made by agencies informed by social purpose."

In practice, it meant, that all allocation decisions were to be made by the Government or its agencies. The need of raising resources for development was, of course, considered important. However, the primary emphasis was to be on increasing the domestic savings rate by suppressing consumption, high taxation, and appropriating profits through ownership of commercial enterprises. Accelerated capital accumulation through these means was considered to be the key to development. In a celebrated observation which guided many a planner and policy maker in developing countries, Professor W. Arthur Lewis observed that:

> "The central problem in the theory of economic development is to understand the process by which a community which was previously saving and investing 4 to 5 per cent of its national income or less, converts itself to an economy where voluntary saving is running at about 12 to 15 per cent of national income and more. This is the central problem because the central fact of economic development is rapid capital accumulation (including knowledge and skills with capital)".[2]

In the process of capital accumulation, the role of financial system was essentially limited, as allocation decisions were to be made by the central planning authorities and not by the financial markets. To a large extent, financial system also had a limited role in providing incentives for savings and capital accumulation as interest rates were controlled, and generally "repressed", and household savings were pre-empted through high levels of statutory reserve and liquidity ratio. New banks and financial institutions were set up, and old ones were taken over, in order to act primarily as deposit taking agencies and providers of credit and finance for designated and centrally determined purposes.

While the reasons for adopting a centrally directed strategy of development were understandable against the background of the colonial rule, it, however, soon became clear that actual results of this strategy were far below expectations. Instead of showing high growth, high public savings and a high degree of self-reliance, India was actually showing one of the lowest rates of growth in the developing world with rising public deficits and periodic balance of payments crises. According to one calculation, in 30 out of 35 years between 1956 and 1991, India had balance of payment problems of varying intensity. Thankfully, public memories are short! However, looking back, it is hard to believe that for as long as 40 years between 1950 and 1990, India's growth rate averaged less than 4 per cent per annum, and per capita income growth was less than 2 per cent per annum. This was at a time when the developing world, including the Sub-Saharan Africa and other least developed countries, showed a growth rate of 5.2 per cent per annum.

In my view, however, the most striking failure was not in terms of growth, or even in the precarious situation of the balance of payments. Although the argument is not convincing, it could still be argued by some that the low growth outcome was due to a number of factors beyond India's control, such as, the border wars, severe droughts, periodic oil shocks, and — finally — inhospitable global environment! The balance of payments difficulties could also — with some imagination — be attributed to the global woes of primary producers, and the struggle of a poor developing country like India to industrialise and become self-reliant in heavy industry (which hitherto was the monopoly of the rich industrialised countries). The most conspicuous failure, in my view, for which there is no alibi, and the responsibility for which lies squarely and indisputably at our doors, is the erosion in public savings and the inability of the public sector to generate resources for investment or provision of public services.

It will be recalled that an important assumption in the choice of post-independence development strategy was the generation of public savings, which could be used for higher and higher levels of investment. However, this did not happen, and the public sector- instead of being a generator of savings for the community's good — became, over time, a consumer of community's savings. This reversal in roles had become evident by the early Seventies, and the process reached its culmination by the early, Eighties. By then, the Government began to borrow not only to meet its own revenue expenditure but also to finance public sector deficits and investments. During the period 1960-1975, total public sector borrowings (including Government) averaged 4.4 per cent of GDP. These increased to 6 per cent of GDP by 1980-81, and further to 9 per cent by 1989-90. Thus, the public sector, which was supposed to generate resources for the growth of the rest of the economy, gradually became a net drain on the society as a whole. It is interesting to note that the Central Government's total internal public debt by the year 1994-95 was close to Rs.5,00,000 crore, and nearly one-third of it was accounted for by assets held in the public sector. The interest payments on public debt amounted to nearly Rs.40,000 crore, which was financed by new net borrowings, and represented nearly 70 per cent of the Centre's fiscal deficit. In effect, by 1994-95, one-third of the interest payments was on account of the Government's past investment in the public sector. In the last five years since then, the Centre's internal debt has almost doubled to Rs.9,70,000 crore in 1999-2000. This sharp increase in internal debt is partly accounted for by the need to borrow higher and higher amounts to service the past debt.

A large part of the cherished "family silver" has thus been financed out of borrowings, and kept polished with further borrowings by an impoverished family.[3] In the annals of development history, it is hard to find another example of a perfectly sensible idea — the need for higher public investment for greater public good — leading to exactly the opposite result, i.e. higher public consumption with diminishing returns for the public!

The 1990s — The Shift in the Development Paradigm

The State-dominated development paradigm has shifted rather sharply in recent years. Almost all developing countries have moved towards a more market-determined strategy of development. There were several factors which contributed to this change in perception. First and the foremost reason for questioning the earlier strategy, as mentioned above, was the simple fact that actual results in terms of growth of incomes or industrial development were well below expectations. While saving rates were rising, as per the Arthur Lewis model, so were capital-output ratios because of inefficiencies in the allocation and use of resources. Paradoxically, a strategy which was expected to reduce dependency on foreign aid and foreign trade, also resulted in greater dependence on aid and emergency assistance from abroad.

An equally important factor contributing to the change in perceptions was the astonishing success of Japan and the East Asian countries in accelerating their rates of growth by relying on market - oriented pattern of industrialisation (with, of course, varying degrees of "guidance" by the State). Japan's per capita rate of growth of 8 per cent per annum during 1953 - 1973 was unprecedented in the history of economic development. No economy had ever grown at that rate before, and Japan emerged from the ruins of war to become the world's second largest economy. Similar was the record of industrialisation in East Asia particularly in countries like Hong Kong, Singapore, Taiwan and South Korea. In the Fifties, their per capita incomes or the degree of industrialisation was no different from those of the rest of Asia. However, within a period of 30 years, they were able to catch up with the industrialised countries of the West. A final and decisive development leading to the demise of the old strategy was the collapse of the Soviet Union and the acceptance of market-led development strategies by all countries of Eastern Europe.

Beginning in 1991, when India was in the midst of an acute economic crisis, the Government of India also introduced a number of measures to improve the working of the economy. These measures, spread over a number of years, had two broad objectives. One was the reorientation of the economy from a statist, centrally directed and highly controlled economy to what is referred to in the current jargon as a 'market-friendly economy'. A reduction in direct controls and physical planning was expected to improve the efficiency of the economy. It was to be made more 'open' to external trade and external flows through a reduction in trade barriers and liberalisation of foreign investment policies. A second objective of the reform measures was macro-economic stabilisation. This was to be achieved by substantially reducing fiscal deficits and the government's draft on society's savings.

Compared with the historical trend, the impact of these policies has been positive and significant. The growth rate of the economy during 1992-93 to 1999-2000 was close to 6.5 per cent per annum. The balance of payments position has also substantially improved. Despite several unfavourable external developments, including the imposition of sanctions in 1998 and sharp rise in oil prices more recently, foreign exchange reserves are at a record level. Exports have done well, current account deficits have been moderate, and India's external debt (as a percentage of GDP) and the debt servicing burden have actually come down since the early Nineties. There is also evidence of considerable restructuring in the corporate sector with attention being given to cost-competitiveness and financial viability. Industrial growth increased sharply during the period 1993 to 1996 to over 9 per cent per annum. The industrial growth rate came down to 5.5 per cent per annum in the next two years, but increased again to 8 per cent upto the end of 1999-2000. The rate of inflation also came down sharply — from 10.3 per cent in 1990-91 to a modest 3.3 per cent in 1999-2000. Fiscal deficit has also come down somewhat — from 8.3 per cent in 1990-91 to 5.6 per cent in 1999-2000.

There has been considerable debate in the country about the content, the pace and the results of the reform process. I do not propose to enter this particular debate, except to say that compared with the record of the first 40 years of development, there is very little doubt that India's economy — by any standard of measurement — is stronger and more resilient today than was the case a decade ago. I leave you to judge whether this outcome is due to the reform process, astute short-term economic management, favourable external circumstances, or just plain old good luck! There is also little doubt that India's "potential" for growth combined with external and domestic financial stability is greater today — at the beginning of the Twenty-First century than was the case 20, 50 or 100 years ago.

India in the New Global Economy

A most remarkable feature of the so-called "New Economy" is the role of the services sector (of which the IT or Information Technology sector is a part) in generating growth of income and employment. It will be recalled that the focus of attention in conventional economics, including development economics, was on production of goods -manufactured products and agricultural commodities. It was, of course, recognised that the services sector (which includes transport, communication, trade, banking, construction and public administration, etc.) was an important source of income and employment in most economies. However, overall, the growth of services was perceived at best as a byproduct of developments in the primary and secondary sectors, and at worst as a drag on the prospects for long-term economic growth. Services were believed to be mainly non-tradable activities with slow productivity growth and low employment potential. In developing countries, the conventional view of the growth of the services sector was even worse. It was seen to divert scarce resources away from production of goods, and contribute to accentuation of income inequalities.

In the last few years, there has been a phenomenal change in the conventional view of services and their role in the economy. The development of certain services is now regarded as one of the preconditions of economic growth, and not as one of its consequences. The boundary between goods and services is also disappearing, as services of various kinds are delinked from the manufacturing process and become essential elements of the productive structure. Many industrial products are not only manufactured — they are also designed, marketed, advertised, distributed, leased and serviced. A significant and rising part of the value added by manufacturers now consists of services.

The change in the image and role of services has been brought about by unprecedented and unforeseen advances in computer and communication technology in the last two decades. An important aspect of the "services revolution" is that geography and levels of industrialisation are no longer the primary determinants of the location of facilities for production of services. As a result, the traditional role of developing countries is also changing — from mere recipients to important providers of long-distance services.

From India's point of view, some of the recent global developments, which provide opportunities for substantial growth, are the following:

- The fastest growing segment of services is the rapid expansion of knowledge-based services, such as, professional and technical services. India has a tremendous advantage of the supply of such services because of a developed structure of technological and educational institutions, and lower labour costs.
- Progress in information technology is making it increasingly possible to unbundle the production and consumption of information-intensive service activities. These activities — research and development, computing, inventory management, quality control, accounting, personnel administration, secretarial, marketing, advertising, distribution, and legal services - are performed in all economic sectors.
- Unlike most other prices, world prices of transport and communication services have fallen dramatically. By 1960, sea transport costs were less than a third of their 1920 level, and they have continued to fall. The cost of a telephone call fell more than ten-fold between 1970 and 2000. Moreover, the cost of communication is also becoming independent of distance. The most dramatic example in this area is, of course, provided by the 'Internet'. India's geographical distance from several important industrial markets (for instance, North America) is no longer an important element in the cost structure of skill-based services.

- Further, India does not necessarily have to be a low-cost producer of certain types of goods (e.g., computers or discs) before it can become an efficient supplier of services embodied in them (e.g., software or music). It is possible now to provide value added services without waiting to 'catch up' in technology for production of sophisticated equipment or products.
- The decline in the share of manufacturing in the output of rich countries implies a relative decline in their demand for industrial raw materials and fuels. This means that growth in exports of developing countries in the future will depend less on natural resource endowments and more on efficiency in providing services and service-intensive goods.

As a result of the above developments, the sources of comparative advantage of nations are vastly different today from what they were 50 or even 20 years ago. And, there are very few developing countries which are as well placed as India to take advantage of the phenomenal changes that have occurred in production technologies, international trade, capital movement, and deployment of skilled manpower. India today has the knowledge and the skills to produce and process a wide variety of industrial and consumer products and services. Another important factor in India's favour is the international capital mobility and integration of global financial markets. Domestic savings continue to be important for development. However, scarcity of domestic capital is no longer a binding constraint. Increased mobility of capital has ensured that global resources would flow to countries which can show high growth and high returns. It is possible now for India to take advantage of a virtuous circle of higher growth, higher external capital inflows, and higher domestic incomes and savings, which in turn can lead to further growth.

At the same time, it must be recognised that the "death of distance" and the growing integration of global product, services and financial markets in recent years has also presented new challenges for management of the national economy — not only in India but all over the world. The trend towards integration of markets, particularly financial markets, is by no means an unmixed blessing. Unlike the old days, a heavy price may have to be paid by national economies for somnolence, sloth and non-conformity to generally accepted international norms and standards of macro-economic management, disclosure, transparency and financial accountability. If a country does not put its financial house in order, fresh investments, trade and technology are likely to pass it by. Faced with this situation, only a few countries, with certain special advantages and resource endowments, may still manage to grow at an acceptable rate. Other countries which need capital and external flows to meet their trade or current account deficits, are likely to find it increasingly difficult to meet their import requirements of essential commodities (such as, oil), raw materials and machines.

Another consequence of recent global trends is the greater vulnerability of national economies to developments outside their own borders. In addition to the direct effects (which are currently most visible in the volatile stock markets), the indirect effects due to "contagion" can be quite serious. A crisis in any one or a group of countries, can be transmitted to other countries - including countries which may not have any strong economic linkages with crisis-affected countries. Thus, the Nineties have been marked by a large number of currency crises (for example, in Mexico, Russia, Asia and Brazil); substantial swings in exchange rates (including the exchange rate of three leading currencies -the dollar, the Euro and the Yen); and run ups in asset prices followed by sharp collapse (for example, in Japan and East Asia). While the crises initially occurred in one or two specific countries, their adverse effects were felt across the world.

The lessons of recent developments are clear. Advances in IT, the increasing role of services, the integration of financial and capital markets, and the diminished role of distance, provide tremendous new opportunities for countries like India. At the same time, like other countries, we are also likely to be subject to greater vulnerability and new risks. Thus, at the beginning of the new century, the challenge before us is in two directions — how to seize the new opportunities, while at the same time, protecting ourselves against unanticipated risks? Insularity or isolation is not the answer, as such an approach would promote neither growth nor stability.

India has to move vigorously to take advantage of expanding opportunities in trade and become a location of choice for IT and other industries and services so that growth rates, along with employment, are substantially enhanced. It must also keep some safety nets handy by building a diversified and efficient financial system which can aid and protect the development process at all times — good and bad. Can these objectives be met? This is the real question to ponder for the future.

India's Tryst with Destiny?

There has been a fair amount of debate in the country on the implications of the new directions in India's economic policy. As far as I can see, there is no major disagreement with the ends or objectives of new economic policies. Most, though not all, commentators seem to agree that efficiency in the use of resources and growth performance of the economy need to be improved. There is also broad agreement that the Government's fiscal deficits should be reduced, that exports should be increased, and that more should be done for improving the health and education of the poor. There is, however, a substantial difference of views on the instruments that should be used to achieve these objectives, and whether current policies will succeed in raising the growth rate of the economy in the long run. Concern has also been expressed on certain political and social implications of the new policies, particularly whether they will make the country more amenable to external pressures and hurt the development of the country's domestic resources. These issues are important, and deserve to be fully considered in the evolution of India's economic policy in the Twenty-First century.

In considering these issues, it is not possible to escape from the responsibility of paying attention to the nature and character of our State apparatus, and to our previous record. We cannot decry the widespread corruption and 'criminalisation of politics' - a phrase which has figured prominently in Parliament in recent years - on the one hand, and ask for more discretionary powers for the State on the other. To do so is to suffer from a form of 'cognitive dissonance'. It is also important to remember that, as pointed out in the earlier part of this talk, the results of India's old policies in promoting growth or reducing poverty were highly unsatisfactory, and in any case, far worse than those registered by more open and competitive economies. As for external pressures, there is hardly any doubt that an aid-dependent economy with persistent balance of payments crises (as was the case in India from 1956 to 1991) is likely to be much more vulnerable than a country which is not so dependent on aid or emergency assistance from abroad.

In my judgement, keeping in view the actual economic and non-economic results of the old strategy, the phenomenal changes that have taken place in the world economy, and India's present comparative advantage, the present direction of policies to make India more open and more competitive is right and deserves to be accelerated. Without a major transformation of our economic policies and effort to align them with contemporary realities of global trade, investment and technology, it is not feasible for India to occupy the high ground and realise its full potential for growth and development.

A decisive move towards more and deeper economic reforms is the first strategic priority for the future. However, it will be a grave mistake to misconstrue the need for economic reforms with a call for less role for Government or public policy in widening opportunities and creating a positive environment for equitable development. In developing countries, such as India, with massive illiteracy and underdevelopment of infrastructure, Government must continue to have an important and crucial role in creating the necessary conditions for growth through investments in areas, such as, education, health, water supply, irrigation, infrastructure, etc. These tasks cannot be taken over by the market. Successful economic reforms must result in strengthening the ability of Governments to do what they need to do by helping to generate higher growth, higher revenue and higher productivity. As the recent experience of several transitional and emerging market economies shows, economic reforms are necessary but by no means a sufficient condition for growth and development.

In this connection, a core issue, with multiple dimensions, which would need to be resolved in years to come is what can perhaps be described as growing "public-private" dichotomy in our economic life. It is a striking fact of our present situation that economic renewal and positive growth impulses are now occurring largely outside the public sector — at the level of private corporations (e.g. software companies), autonomous institutions (e.g. IIMs or IITs), or individuals at the top of their professions in India and abroad. In the Governmental or public sector, on the other hand, we see a marked deterioration at all levels — not only in terms of output, profits and public savings (to which I made a reference earlier), but also in the provision of vital public services in the fields of education, health, water and transport. These two elements — fiscal deterioration and inability to provide essential services — are, of course, intimately connected. Most of our public resources are now dissipated in payment of salaries or interest on past debt with little or no resources available for expansion of public or publicly supported services in vital sectors.

In considering the reasons for the decay and deterioration that is taking place in our public services, I am reminded of an observation by A.H.Hanson nearly 40 years ago on the reasons for the then prevailing crisis of Indian Planning. He was an admirer of Indian planners, but after seeing the results on the ground, he was compelled to ask:

> "The men are able, the organization is adequate, the procedures are intelligently devised. Why, then, have the Plans, since 1956, so persistently run into crisis?"

Hanson's answer to this question is also revealing:

> "For various reasons, Indian Planners have never treated the 'objective function' with sufficient respect. Their tendency is to give themselves the fullest benefit of every possible doubt ... Too many of their aims are contingent upon the adoption, by various sections of the Indian community, of attitudes they are exceedingly unlikely to adopt ....."[4]

That was 1963! Today, in 2001, and after more than 50 years of experience of independent administration, we still seem to be giving ourselves the benefit of the doubt. Over time, our problems in the management of public resources at different levels have only become more and more intractable. Let us look at some of the problems that now bedevil our public delivery systems:

- We can be justifiably proud of the fact that the "rule of law" prevails in our country, and that even the mightiest are not above the law. The delays in the judicial process may be legendary, but there is a widespread respect for the "rule of law". However, for historical reasons, it is also a fact that our legal system provides full protection to the private interests of the so-called "public servant", often at the expense of the public that he or she is supposed to serve. In addition to complete job security, any group of public servants in any public sector organisation can go on strike — hospitals, universities, schools, banks, buses, post offices, railways, municipalities — in search of higher wages, promotions and bonuses for themselves irrespective of the costs and inconvenience to the public (in whose name they have been appointed in the first place). Problems have only become worse over time and there is little or no accountability of the public servant to perform the public duty.

- The "authority" of Governments at, both Centre and States, to enforce their decisions has eroded over time. Governments can pass orders, for example, for relocation of unauthorised industrial units or other structures, but implementation can be delayed if they run counter to the private interests of some (at the expense of the general public interest). Similarly, Governments may decide to restructure public utilities to cut down waste or output losses, but these decisions do not necessarily have to be implemented if they adversely affect the interests of public servants employed in these organisations.

- Governments at different levels may announce plans and programmes to provide social services (such as, expand literacy), but these initiatives are unlikely to be implemented on the ground because of fiscal stringency. For example, in 1994, the Tenth Finance Commission projected a rate of growth in real terms of 2.5 per cent for expenditure on elementary education upto the end of the century in respect of four States where the incidence of poverty and illiteracy was among the highest in the country. This projected rate of growth in expenditure was lower than the growth of population in the relevant age group, and grossly insufficient to cover new programmes of adult literates. In the five years since the Tenth Finance Commission's report, it is interesting to note that the real expenditure on elementary education, outside of salaries of Government teachers, in these four States has actually been negative!

- The process and procedures for conducting business in Government and public service organisations, over time have become non-functional. There are multiplicity of Departments involved in the simplest of decisions, and administrative rules generally concentrate on the process rather than results. There is very little decentralisation of decision-making powers, particularly financial powers. Thus, while local authorities have been given significant authority in some States for implementing national programmes, their financial authority is limited. Transfers to local authorities for health spending, for example, average less than 15 per cent of State Government budgets.
- The multiplicity of functions and responsibilities placed upon ill-equipped and ill-trained staff in public offices and local institutions make it almost impossible to deliver services with any degree of efficiency, particularly in rural areas. For example, a "multi-purpose" female health worker is required to perform as many as forty-seven tasks to be undertaken on a regular basis!

Let us also ponder, for a moment, who suffers the most from fiscal stringency and the atrophy of the public delivery systems. It is certainly not the affluent classes, or persons elected or appointed by the people to serve them. They can always go to private hospitals, private schools, autonomous universities or institutes of higher education, and have similar alternative means of meeting their other requirements. The worst affected are likely to be the poor, the unemployed, and the illiterate who are dependent on public services, public investment and public programmes. It is useful to keep this perspective in mind as a fair amount of defence of the "status quo" in respect of the public sector is done in the name of the weaker sections of the society.

In addition to economic reforms, which already figure

prominently in the national discourse, it is now important to embark on an urgent programme to revitalise the governance and public delivery systems at all levels of Government — centre, state and districts. Without strengthening the ability of the Government to do what it alone can do, and narrowing the focus of its activities to what matters most for the future development of the country — education, health, clean environment, and a functioning infrastructure — India cannot adequately seize the opportunities that lie ahead.

In my view, this is really the harder part of the so-called second generation reforms. The non-governmental sector now has a dynamism and momentum of its own. While there will be problems, and there will be arguments for and against a particular policy to liberalise, to open up, or to introduce more competition, I am confident that progress in the desired direction is unavoidable and irreversible. At the same time, it is also clear that unless we put our fiscal house in order and improve our public delivery systems, no amount of macro-policy reforms by themselves will be sustainable or yield permanent results. If lakhs of primary schools run by Government agencies, thousands of primary health centres set up by district authorities, and hundreds of Central and State Universities continue to under-perform or decline, two or three hi-tech cities and one or two new business schools and technical institutes cannot make up for the gigantic loss of human resources. It is simply a question of relative proportions, and inextricable linkages between public good and private progress.

In order to overcome some of the problems that I mentioned a little while ago, we need to move on a number of fronts. We need legal reform to focus sharply on the interests of the public, and not those of the public servant, in the functioning of the governmental and public delivery systems. Clear mechanisms for establishing accountability for performance are essential, and all forms of special protection for persons working for Government or public sector agencies (except for armed forces or agencies engaged in maintenance of law and order) deserve to be eliminated. We need institutional reform. All public monopolies should be eliminated, and there should be no purchase preference for public sector enterprises or agencies. Government should be free to engage the services of non-governmental organisations or private service providers at competitive costs to ensure effective delivery of essential services. We need freedom of information and full disclosure of all financial decisions made by Governments and its multifarious agencies on a daily rather than quarterly or annual basis. We need a new "political-bureaucratic" compact based on well-defined division of responsibility and accountability. The public system cannot function without respect for conventions and mutual trust and harmony among different agencies of the state. Above all, we need fiscal empowerment as, without financial resources, it is not feasible to lay a road or build a school. The last is a most difficult task in view of the deadweight of the past, but it can no longer be avoided.

Let me end with two prognostications about India's potential for long-term growth that I came across recently. The first is by a well known Indian economist with a distinguished record of forecasting. He has observed that, "it is possible for India to have a per capita income of US $ 30,000 by the year 2047. If the Indian economy does as well as some of the world's fast-growing economies have done, it could be even higher."[5] The second projection is by a Professor in business management in the United States.7 He estimates that, by the year 2025, India's GDP would exceed that of Japan and India would then be the third largest economy in the world (behind US and China).

Both forecasts, independently arrived at in two different parts of the world, are, of course, contingent on a number of factors. There is, however, no doubt that, if we have the will, and we are able to realise even half our potential in the next 20 or 25 years, India's poverty would have become a distant memory.

Notes

1. Paul Krugman, *The Return of Depression Economics*, The Penguin Press, London, 1999.
2. W.A. Lewis, "Economic Development with Unlimited Supplies of Labour", *Manchester School,* Vol.22, 1954.
3. It may be mentioned that some parts of the public sector, particularly oil and telecommunications have been quite profitable. This partly reflects their erstwhile monopoly position and the administered price regimes. These profitable sectors have been largely self-financing without the need for budget transfers.
4. Hanson A.H., "The Crisis of Indian Planning", Political Quarterly,

October-December 1963, reprinted in Hanson A.H., *Planning and Politicians,* London: Routledge and Kegan Paul, 1969.

5. Kirit Parikh, "Economy" in *India Briefing - A Transformative Fifty Years*, published by M.E.Sharp Inc., New York, 1999, for Asia Society. Parikh's per capita income forecasts assume a dollar-rupee exchange rate based on purchasing power parity.
6. Rosensweig J.A., *Winning the Global Game,* The Free Press, New York, 1998. Rosensweig's forecasts are also on purchasing power parity basis.

C.D. Deshmukh Memorial Lecture, January 2001, India International Centre, New Delhi.

3

Indian Economy 1950–2000–2020

Y. V. REDDY

The post-Independence period, commencing from the inception of planning in 1950 to the onset of Gulf crisis in 1990 was characterised by a massive improvement over pre-Independence performance coupled with some avoidable inadequacies, particularly, in terms of incentives and institutional structures and punctuated with droughts, wars and oil-crisis. The performance of our economy during the 'nineties demonstrates rapid recovery from a deep crisis and a dramatic upward shift in expectations of levels of growth and greater resilience to withstand shocks. The daunting task of tackling poverty and misery remains a significant problem – even half a century after independence.

As we enter the new Millennium, we should frankly assess where we are vis-a-vis other countries in terms of various indicators, such as growth, stability and poverty. The major part of my address will, therefore, be on India in a global context, with reference to four sets of indicators viz., economic, institutional, infrastructural and social. The concluding part would thus be derived from an understanding of what these indicators with all the known limitations signify for us. In a way, I am juxtaposing historical and cross-sectional perspective in the current context and, on this basis I hope to share with you, my perception of the performance and prospects before us as we move towards 2020. I believe that the advantage of this method of presentation

The assistance by Mr. Jeevan Khundrakpam is gratefully acknowled is that, each of you can draw your own inferences and develop your own perceptions. The tabular data are appended to the text of this lecture. My purpose would be served if you are provoked into questioning and thinking about the future, which of course includes preeminently the future of each one of us.

Pre-Independence : 1900-47 It would serve the purpose of today's deliberations if one looks at a few facts brought out by Sivasubramonian (1998) on performance of Indian economy during the pre-Independence era of 20th century.

First, real Gross Domestic Product (GDP) which is broadly the national cake, or the total sum of all the final goods and services produced within the geographical boundary of our country, grew only by an average of 0.9 per cent per annum. But, the individual share of this national cake, i.e., the real per capita GDP grew even lower at an average rate of 0.1 per cent. Real per capita GDP which stood at Rs. 224 in 1900-01 increased, if it can be called an increase, to only Rs. 233 on the eve of Independence.

Second, even this very low growth was associated with considerable fluctuations due to number of years of drought and famine and epidemics. Thus, aggregate GDP declined in 17 out of the 47 years and its per capita in 26 years.

Third, after 1920, epidemics were better controlled and some improvement was perceivable in health services. The infant mortality rate was on an average 205 out of 1000 in 1911 and, this declined to 136 in 1946. Every Indian was expected to live for 23.8 years at the beginning of the century and by 1951 the life expectation increased to 32.1 years.

Fourth, during the second decade of the century, on an average, 535 grams of food was available per Indian per day. The availability actually declined to 408 grams per day by 1950.

Fifth, in 1901, 94 out of every 100 Indians could neither read nor write. By 1941, this had gone down to 85.

Sixth, no doubt the manufacturing sector had grown at 4.0 per cent per annum. Goods carried and passenger miles by Indian railways increased by six times. Communications and government services also maintained moderate growth rates. But as the economy was primarily an agricultural one, the progress in these areas could not make any worthwhile impact on the overall situation in the economy.

Post-Independence : 1950-1990

After Independence, the country embarked on an ambitious task of planned economic growth to move the country out of the critical stagnation in the pre-Independence era. The country had to also reckon with the after effects of the Second World War, and Partition, in addition to consolidating the nation and building an administrative and political apparatus. As these complex tasks were being tackled, the country had to face famines and wars during the 'sixties and the 'seventies – apart from the oil crisis of early 'seventies and early 'eighties. These factors should be kept in view while considering the facts that would be narrated now.

First, the real GDP growth rose from 0.9 per cent in pre-Independence era to an average annual rate of about 4.0 per cent. Significant acceleration of growth rate took place in the 'eighties. In fact, the growth during the 'eighties, at an annual average rate of 5.9 per cent bettered the world output growth of 3.3 per cent, that of developing countries at 4.3 per cent, and even that of Asia excluding China and India at 5.1 per cent.

Second, as compared with the pre-Independence era, the fluctuations were relatively less and the growth in GDP was steady in all the years disregarding four years characterised by crisis.

Third, while the growth was a remarkable improvement as compared to that of pre-Independence days, the surge in population growth to an annual average rate of over 2.0 per cent, could raise the per capita GDP by about 2.0 per cent per annum only, though this is twenty times the growth in pre-Independence era. In fact, the annual growth in per capita GDP in the 'eighties was over 3.5 per cent.

Fourth, in contrast to the decline in per capita food availability, despite the acceleration in population growth, food availability improved from 395 grams per day in 1951 to 510 grams per day in 1991.

Fifth, agriculture also experienced much higher growth of over 2.5 per cent, with post-green revolution showing even higher growth of over 3.0 per cent. Importantly, the sector became less dependent on the vagaries of the monsoon.

Sixth, industry grew at an annual average rate of over 5.5 per cent. Importantly, with the setting up of large-scale and heavy industries, the industrial base expanded rapidly thereby laying the base for sustained industrial growth. Services also grew by about 5.0 per cent and it was close to 6.0 per cent since the second half of the 'seventies. Sectoral composition of GDP gradually changed. Agriculture which contributed to more than half of GDP during the first three five-year plans decreased its share to about one-third around the end of the 'eighties. On the other hand, services improved its share from about one-third to more than two-fifth. Industry's share also improved from about 15.0 per cent to about one-fourth.

Seventh, the post-Independence period witnessed a marked rise in the rate of saving (as proportion of GDP). It rose from an average of about 11.9 per cent during the first one and half decades to a little over 20.0 per cent during the 'eighties. Rate of investment also rose from 13.7 per cent to about 22.5 per cent during the corresponding period.

Eighth, in terms of inflation record, the price rise was low at 1.2 per cent during the first decade after Independence. This rose to 6.3 per cent during the 'sixties and further to 9.0 per cent during the 'seventies. During the 'eighties it was around 8.0 percent.

While all the above indicators of growth are remarkable achievements, particularly over the pre-Independence days, many of our goals that we set out to achieve did not materialise. There are at least five areas where this can be noticed.

First, on the income front, the aim of doubling the average real per capita income by the end of the 'seventies was attained only at the end of the 'eighties.

Second, despite all the economic growth and the attempt to tackle the problem head-on, poverty, broadly defined as people unable to incur expenditure to meet the required minimum calorie intake per day of 2400 in rural areas and 2100 in urban areas, continued to remain unacceptably high.

Third, even by 1990 we could not make little less than half the population (48 per cent) either to read or to write. We had one primary school teacher for every 46 pupils in 1989-90.

Fourth, infant mortality rate declined, to 80 per 1000 in 1990 as compared with 136 per 1000 prior to Independence. On an average, life expectancy in 1990 was about 60 years. In 1989-90, a quarter of our people did not have any access to safe water and as much as 87 per cent did not have any sanitation facility. During the second half of the 'eighties, for every 2,520 Indians, there was only one doctor available, while only one nurse was available to 1,700 Indians.

Fifth, even though we set out to achieve self-reliance in the external sector, we faced considerable pressures on the balance of payments. Exports in US $ terms grew below 5.0 per cent during the first two decades and the first half of the 'eighties while imports grew faster. Only during the 'seventies and the latter part of the 'eighties, particularly during the former period, was the export growth impressive by our own past records. But then, in the 'seventies also, imports outpaced exports. In the international context, we were marginalised as India's exports which were about 2.0 per cent of world exports at the beginning of the 'fifties went below 0.5 per cent by the end of the 'eighties. In brief, although the performance of the economy was remarkable when compared with the earlier period, it was not adequate to meet the challenges, and more importantly, by the late 'eighties it was not conducive to continued accelerated growth.

The growth indicators show that the performance of the Indian economy during the post-Independence period up to 1990 was at its best during the 'eighties, but there were deep structural imbalances. These problems arose in the form of structural rigidities, lack of competition both at home and abroad, poor performance of public sector enterprises, lack of fiscal prudence and an incentive framework inconsistent with productivity gains.

An important factor propelling the growth during this period was the rapid rise in government expenditure, reflecting in the fiscal deficit jumping from 4.0 per cent of GDP in the 'seventies to 8.33 per cent in the crisis year of 1991. The problem was not just the size of fiscal deficit, but the fact that there was also a revenue deficit, since the assets such as public enterprises created out of borrowings did not yield adequate returns. The high fiscal deficit also got reflected in the emergence of a current account deficit during the 'eighties which peaked at 3.2 per cent of GDP in 1991. Recourse was taken to external debt, often on commercial terms, and a large amount with short maturity. In some ways, the high growth of 1980s was facilitated by growth in internal and external debt or borrowed money and borrowed time. Thus, triggered by the Gulf-crisis, a severe balance of payment crisis had to be faced in 1991 that made introduction of comprehensive programme of reforms inevitable.

Gulf-Crisis and Reforms : 1990-2000

In the aftermath of the payment crisis of 1991, a number of measures were undertaken to remove the structural rigidities afflicting various sectors of the economy. For instance, industrial licensing has been done away with to improve the efficiency of markets; extensive reforms have been undertaken in the financial sector and a more effective system of regulation and supervision has been put in place; cautious liberalisation has been undertaken in the external sector; the way in which fiscal transactions have impinged on the financial sector has been altered so as to contain the monetisation of the deficit, thereby giving the Central Bank some elbow room to implement monetary policy. The prime aim of these measures was to bring about increased competition, both domestically and externally, and reduce rent seeking activities. All these measures have brought about some positive changes in the macroeconomic scenario, though several concerns have been expressed.

First, we find that the annual rate of growth of GDP was around 6.1 per cent during the 'nineties. The post-reform growth i.e., excluding the years of crisis and adjustment (1991-92 and 1992-93) with lower rates of growth, was placed at 6.8 per cent as against 5.9 per cent in the 'eighties.

Second, the fluctuations in GDP growth were minimal, and except in the Gulf-crisis year of 1991-92, the rate of growth of GDP was above 5.0 per cent in all the years. The growth performance was maintained in the face of unprecedented domestic political uncertainties and external uncertainties like the sanctions imposed, border tensions, Asian crisis and steep increases in oil prices, though from a low base. Fluctuations in output of agriculture were also moderate.

Third, the per capita GDP increased at an annual average rate of about 4.25 per cent during the 'nineties.

We also find that gross domestic saving as percentage of GDP crossed 22.0 per cent in all the post-reform years as against only twice during the previous 40 years. In fact, the ratio was close to, or even crossed, 25.0 per cent in number of years. The gross domestic investment as a percentage of GDP also rose to 26.0 to 27.0 per cent in number of years as against over 24.0 per cent only twice during the preceding 40 years.

Inflation, on the other hand, rose at an annual average rate of 8.9 per cent during 1990-98 and was higher than the annual average rate of 8.0 per cent during the 'eighties. However, during 1998-99 and 1999-2000, the rate of price rise remained much more subdued.

In the external sector, external debt to GDP ratio came down from 41.0 per cent in 1991-92 to 23.5 per cent in 1998-99. The debt service payments as a ratio to current receipts continued to improve steadily from 30.2 per cent in 1991-92 to 18.0 per cent in 1998-99. The average annual rate of growth of exports of goods and services of 11.3 per cent during 1990-99 has been markedly above the average of 8.1 per cent in the 'eighties. The current account deficit (CAD) remained on an average well below 2.0 per cent of GDP in all the years after the Gulf-crisis and in fact also fell to 1.0 per cent of GDP in 1998-99. It must be noted that this period witnessed liberalisation of imports, including that of gold and steep reduction in tariffs.

Thus, during the 'nineties, we accumulated over US $ 30 billion of foreign currency assets, while reducing external debt and liberalizing trade and maintaining consistently high rate of growth in GDP.

Though we have seen tangible improvement on the economic front, I must at this juncture also emphasise on the social dimension, which is a more important ingredient of economic development.

First, as per NSS surveys, over 1/3rd of the population in 1997 still could not have the required minimum daily calorie intake, same as on the eve of reforms.

Second, during 1990-96, 19 Indians out of every 100 did not

have access to safe drinking water sources and 84 did not have any access to sanitation showing little improvement from that of 1990.

Third, infant mortality rate of 70 per 1000, life expectancy of 63 years and daily per capita supply of calories of 2496 in the late 'nineties have also not improved much from 1990.

Fourth, there is evidence that the acceleration in growth is concentrated among some regions while others continue to maintain relatively low levels of growth.

Finally, the savings of public sector as a whole viz., government and public enterprises combined is close to zero. The size of borrowing as well as cost of borrowings by government is considerable. The fiscal situations, especially of some states are causing concern.

In brief, there was a significant improvement in terms of growth and stability as well as position in regard to external sector in the 'nineties while several concerns especially in regard to poverty and social welfare remained. Indeed, a growth rate of five per cent, which was considered an achievement till a decade ago is considered a sign of failure of policy now, and this reflects the phenomenon of rising expectations.

India in the Global Context

There have been several indices and ranking exercises undertaken by various international ranking or rating agencies. These indices have gained importance in the context of globalization and countries are often ranked for purpose specific reasons on these indices. A cursory look at these indices will help us understand where India stands with respect to peers as well as developed countries. Greater details on the ranking, composition and methodology of index, etc., are given in the Annexures. For this presentation, the indices are broadly classified under four major heads: a) economic indicators; b) institutional indicators; c) infrastructural indicators; and d) social indicators. Selection of indices was governed by the mere accident of availability and its relevance. Thus, they are tentative and illustrative, and certainly not conclusive. Nine countries are assumed to be fairly representative of geographical distribution of countries on the globe, differences in the level of income, sizes of the economy and of our neighbouring countries. Besides India, these countries are Singapore, China, Pakistan, Sri Lanka, South Africa, Mexico, USA and Japan.

Economic Indicators

Economic indicators include factors such as the level of income and its growth over a period, its capacity to grow as evidenced by savings and investment rate, the performance of the external sector, etc.

India is admittedly a large economy, and in terms of size, is ranked 11th or 3rd in the world depending on the measure. In per capita terms, however, we are among the lowest in the world, irrespective of the measure. In 1999, India's Gross National Product (GNP), which is the sum total of all the factor incomes accruing to Indian citizen, stood at US $ 442.2 billion and ranked 11th in the world. What each Indian on an average could get from this total, i.e., the per capita GNP, was only US $ 450 and ranked 162nd in the world which was the lowest among the 9 countries in our group. But this GNP is calculated on the basis of market exchange rate i.e., the rate at which $ exchange for Rupees in the market. Some analysts question this methodology on the count that there are differences in the prices of comparable goods, which are not traded amongst countries. Therefore, market exchange rate cannot value these goods properly. When these differences are adjusted, we get what is called as GNP measured in Purchasing Power Parity (PPP) terms. In this measure, India's GNP rises to US $ 2144.1 billion and is behind only USA, China and Japan. The per capita GNP also rises to US $ 2149. Even then, India was still ranked 153rd in the world, higher than only one country among these 9 countries.

It should be noted that as mentioned already, India's growth performance has been impressive, and in particular, annual average growth rate of GDP during the 'eighties and the 'nineties was rivaled by few like Singapore and China. In other words, despite the higher GDP growth during the last two decades, India continued to remain low in the league of per capita GNP. The culprits, is well known of course, are the size and the rate of growth of population in our country, and the low base of income with which we started.

Savings and investment rates of 20.3 per cent and 23.9 per cent, respectively, during 1997-99, have been comparable or were even better than many developing and developed countries. But these rates were much lower than high growth countries like Singapore (savings rate of 51.4 per cent and investment rate of 34.5 per cent) and China (savings rate of 42.5 per cent and investment rate 38.8 per cent). Almost all the savings in India are from the household and the private corporate sectors. The savings in the public sector, during 1993-94 to 1998-99 averaged just around 1.0 per cent only. It is noteworthy that, the main reason for low savings in India lies in government savings being negative on account of revenue deficits.

It may also be noted that growth of exports of goods and services at an annual average rate of 11.3 per cent during the 'nineties was impressive and only lower than the high performers like China (13.0 per cent) and Mexico (14.3 per cent). The external debt to GDP ratio of 23.0 per cent in 1998 was also much lower than that of Pakistan, Sri Lanka and Mexico.

The flow of foreign direct investment (FDI) in India also increased during the 'nineties and reached US $ 2.26 billion in 1998, which was among the 20 largest FDI recipients among the developing countries. Yet, the level of inflow was still far lower than countries like Singapore (US $ 7.22 billion), China (US $ 45.5 billion) and Mexico (US $ 10.24 billion).

To reflect dynamic elements of the economy, reference may also be made to several indices relating to country-risk, technology, economic creativity, competitiveness, globalization, recessionary expectation, etc.

In the composite International Country Risk Guide (ICRG), risk rating, which is an overall index of investment risk in a country, as of March 2000, India with a rating of 64.3 was placed better than two of the nine countries in the group. The same is more or less true for the institutional investor credit rating, which indicates the probability of a country's default.

In the context of globalization, technology is the propeller of growth. How active is the involvement of India in technological innovation and in the import of technology from abroad? And how conducive is the environment in India for business start-ups?

World Economic Forum (WEF) captures the former by 'Technology Index' and the latter by 'Start-up Index'. When these two indices are combined, an index is derived, which is called 'Economic Creativity Index' that gets reflected in the growth performance of a country. Out of the 59 countries surveyed in 2000, India was ranked 38th in all the three indices and was placed higher than that of China (48th). Though business start-up environment in Mexico is worse than India and that of Japan marginally more favourable than that of India, their involvement in technological innovations is considerable and consequently, their creativity indices are superior to India.

WEF also prepares another index called 'Growth Competitiveness Index' (GCI) to measure the factors that contribute to future growth of per capita income of an economy in order to explain why some countries are improving faster than others. In 2000, out of 59 countries, India was placed low at 49th position. Countries like China, Mexico and South Africa were placed higher but their ranks were at 41st, 43rd and 33rd, respectively.

Besides the macroeconomic factors, the microeconomic foundation i.e., operating practices and strategies of firms and the environment in which these firms compete are important for economic development. The 'Microeconomic Competitiveness Index' (MCI) for 1999 by WEF, which captures the above again places India low at 42nd position out of 58 countries surveyed. However, India is placed higher than China at 49th position. Mexico (34th) and South Africa (26th) are placed much higher.

What factors then underpin high current productivity and current economic performance of India? WEF captures these factors by its 'Current Competitiveness Index' (CCI). For 2000, India was at 37th position out of 58 countries, much higher than the GCI rank of 49th position. Interestingly, unlike GCI rank, our CCI rank was higher than China (44th) and Mexico (42nd), reflecting that factors determining our current growth are better than these countries though not the factors, which contribute to future growth. Nevertheless, we are still at the lower end of the ranking.

'Emerging Market Index' measures the market openness of a country. Our index at 46 in the year 2000 was higher than only

China. With regard to integration with the rest of the world, which is captured by 'Globalization Index', our rate of integration during 1993-97 was at about 2.0 per cent per annum which was at the slower end. But in 'Recessionary Expectations Index' which indicates the extent of confidence that a country will not go into slump, our economy was placed quite high in 2000, higher than China, Mexico and even USA and Japan. The perception is clearly that ours is a stable economy.

Institutional Indicators

All economic transactions and social provisions are made under a set of given institutions. Evaluation of institutional factors is complex and methods are still in their infancy. Since much of the data are from opinion surveys, the views are subjective rather than definitive. In this presentation, reference will be made to an index of perception on corruption and to five selected indicators of governance.

Transparency International and Gottingen University brings out a ranking of countries based on the perception of business people on the transparency of the politicians and public officials of a country. The index is called 'Corruption Perception Index'. In it's 1996 survey, of the 54 countries ranked by transparency, India was placed at the 46th position or as the 9th most corrupt country among these countries.

On governance, the World Bank in its publication India — *Reducing Poverty, Accelerating Development (2000)* has brought out 5 broad indicators. They are: a) government effectiveness and stability, which include institutional and government stability and general public's satisfaction with the government policies; b) role of law and business environment, which include corruption/ kickbacks, law and order, legal rights, etc.; c) general public administration judged by quality of bureaucracy, its strength and exposure to political interference and accountability; d) public finance, which among others, includes quality of budget, efficiency and equity of expenditure and receipts and management of public finances; and e) outcomes, in which most of the social indicators like poverty, mortality, literacy, etc are included. India's ranking on these indicators against 5 groups of countries in 1995 is available. The groups compared are : the developing countries;

some selected large countries comprising - China, Mexico, South Africa, Brazil and Poland; South East Asia comprising- Indonesia and Thailand; South Asia excluding India; and industrial countries represented by the U.K. and the U.S.

In the effectiveness of government and its stability, India fares worse than all groups of countries.

With regard to the role of law and business environment, India is placed better than its neighbouring South Asian countries. But, in comparison to the group of selected large countries and the industrial countries, India is worse-off.

Except for the industrial countries, our general public administration is ranked higher than all other groups of countries.

Both the group of industrial countries and the selected large countries have better public finance than ours, but we are better than the rest of the other groups.

In the outcomes, however, which are primarily reflected in socio-economic indicators, India fares badly as compared to all the groups.

Infrastructural Indicators

Transport, power, telecommunications, water, sanitation, etc., are part of what we know as infrastructure which is essential for sustained economic development. These facilities enable smooth and efficient transaction of economic activities and also help in providing the basic necessities of life. Here, I would be primarily comparing India with our group of countries on the level of individual indicators.

Let me start with power. In 1997, the power consumption per capita in India was a mere 363 kwh. Though this compares favourably with Pakistan and Sri Lanka, it was far behind the other countries. China consumed almost double the level of India. Typical of South Asian countries, we also wasted lot of power on transmission and distribution, which was 18.0 per cent in 1997 while in China the waste was only 8.0 per cent.

The percentage of our roads in good condition or paved roads in 1998 was only 45.7 per cent. Pakistan (57.0 per cent) and Sri Lanka (95.0 per cent) have a much higher percentage of paved roads.

The railway network in India is fairly good. In 1998, for every million $ of GDP (PPP), railway transported 137.1 thousand ton-km. This was larger than Japan (101.7). However, in comparison to China (304.8) and South Africa (283.3) with large land area, who also rely more on railways for transportation of goods, it was far less.

In 1997, 121 out of 1000 Indians had radios, and all barring one in the group are far ahead. The position in Sri Lanka (209) was about double of India. Only 68 Indians out of 1000 had TV sets, by far the lowest in the group.

With 22 telephone mainlines in 1998, we were only marginally better than one country in the group and China (70) was far ahead of us. And, on an average, the waiting time in India for a telephone connection was one year, which was better than only two countries, but stood nowhere in comparison to China where it was just one month.

There were 2.7 Personal Computers available to every 1000 Indians in 1998, behind all the countries in the group. In China it was 8.9, while others were far ahead. Similar was the picture for internet hosts per 10,000 which was 0.23 in India in 2000 compared to China (0.57), Pakistan (0.34) and Sri Lanka (0.63).

India is known for its vast pool of scientific personnel and engineers. There were 149 such people involved in Research and Development (R & D) per every million Indian during 1987-97. Barring one, even in this field, other countries were in a better position. The picture may not vary significantly even if we reckon the Indian engineers and scientists who have migrated. During the same period, 5.0 per cent of manufacturing exports was technology related, which was behind all other countries, except the South Asian neighbouring countries.

Safe water sources and sanitation are also basic infrastructural needs to improve the health condition of the people. As we shall see in the social indicator, India has not done well on this front also.

Going by some of these infrastructural indicators above, it is not surprising to find that in the 1998 Global Competitiveness Report by WEF, India was rated 53rd out of the 53 countries surveyed in the context of infrastructure (World Bank , 2000).

Social Indicators

Social indicators would include not only access to food, shelter and clothing but also the knowledge and health of the people. A comparison of some of these indicators along with two indices viz., 'Human Development Index' and 'Human Poverty Index' among our select group of countries would be revealing.

An important social indicator in any country is the literacy of its people. In 1998, the adult literacy rate in our country was 55.7 per cent only and better than Pakistan (44.0 per cent) but far below Sri Lanka (91.1) and China (82.8). The picture is the same with respect to youth literacy, which was 71.0 per cent as against 96.5 in Sri Lanka and 97.2 per cent in China. But, it is noteworthy that during 1995-97, public expenditure on education as percentage of GDP at 3.2 per cent was comparable to many countries. Also, during 1994-97, despite our higher illiteracy rate, within the education expenditure, we have spent a lower percentage of 66.0 per cent at the level of pre-primary, primary and secondary level. For example, Pakistan and Sri Lanka spent about 3/4th or more on this level of education.

Besides education, health is a basic necessity of life. Though 81.0 per cent of our people during 1990-96 had access to safe water sources we were better off only in comparison to three other countries. And in sanitation, with just 16.0 per cent of the people having access to it, we were worse-off as compared to all these countries in the group.

70 infants out of every 1000 died in India in 1998. Similarly, in 1998, only one country had a lower life expectancy than India (63 years).

Out of every 1 lakh Indians, 118.3 suffered from tuberculosis in 1997, overshadowed by South Africa (242.7) only.

During 1990-97, 33.0 per cent of the infants were born underweight. Our record is worse than Pakistan and Sri Lanka where it was 25.0 per cent.

In 1997, two countries supplied fewer calories daily to each of their people than the supply of 2496 calorie by India. The daily per capita protein consumption of 59 grams in 1997 was also low. We also spent a much lower percentage of GDP (0.60 per cent) on health services in 1990-98 than other countries have spent.

During 1992-95, there were 48 doctors available to every lakh Indians, better than Sri Lanka only.

The World Bank prepares a composite index called 'Human Development Index' (HDI) to measure the average achievement in basic human development. The index comprises 'Per capita GDP (PPP) Index', 'Education Index' and 'Life Expectancy Index' considered to be the three basic essentials of life. As one would expect based on the discussion above, in 1998, only one country in our group was worse than our position in the first two sub-indices, and only one other in 1998 in the third index. Not surprisingly, India's HDI ranking out of 174 countries in 1998 was 128th.

The World Bank also prepares an index called 'Human Poverty Index' (HPI). As against HDI, this index measures the extent of deprivation, rather than development, in the three essential dimensions of human life reflected in HDI. In the ranking of this index as of 1998, for 85 developing countries, we were at the 58th position.

How We Progressed

In terms of rate of growth, according to Y.V. Reddy, we have done better in the latter half of the 20th century than during the first half, and far better in the final two decades. Over the period, fluctuations in growth of output have been reduced. The resilience to withstand shocks has progressively increased. External sector has become comfortable in the sense that there is no foreign currency constraint on growth now. Yet, we have pervading poverty, high illiteracy and poor condition of health and sanitation. There are islands of excellence like information technology experts amidst a sea of deprivation and misery. Clearly, economic policy, especially of 'nineties has removed several constraints on economic growth, which is in itself an achievement and a necessary condition for the rest of the goals of a civil society. But, there are lurking doubts on whether we are systematically building a system that would ensure continued high level of growth and, achievement of minimum social objectives associated with such growth. Perhaps, India's rank in the indicators that have been scanned will give a clue as to what we should do to dispel the doubts about the future.

How Are We Poised?

Economic indicators show that we are one of the fastest growing economies now, with high savings and investment ratios coupled with a respectable level of productivity as evidenced by capital output ratios. External sector is comfortable, though with relatively low level of capital inflows – a reflection as much of lack of interest of overseas investors as of ambivalent attitude domestically. Our position in 'Current Competitiveness Index' shows confidence in our growth performance in the short run. However, our position in 'Growth Competitiveness Index' indicates a less optimistic picture in the future growth of per capita income. The position in regard to other related indicators also gives rise to a feeling that factors contributing to current growth are relatively stronger than those contributing to future growth, unless strong policy actions are initiated soon. At the same time, there is impressive confidence that our economy will not go into a slump, i.e. ours is a very stable economy.

Institutional indicators may provide some answer to this difference in perception between immediate and medium term to long-term prospects. The evidence is subjective and hence not very reliable, but the high rank in corruption is of concern. More disturbing is the perception that effectiveness of government is low. As regards the role of law and business environment, the picture is satisfactory but does not, as per current indications, appear to assure an environment for a high growth path. The government, law, and business environment are only means to an end, the end being socio-economic well-being of the people. The critical part is in the outcomes as reflected in socio economic indicators where India appears to be lagging.

Yet another significant set of indicators relevant for medium term prospects relate to infrastructure. India seems to score rather poorly in regard to energy, say in terms of power-consumption or wastage of power. Inspite of recent improvements, India is lagging in telecommunications, and is virtually the last in penetration of personal computers. Here is an example of islands of excellence in information technology, but the domestic penetration of information technology is very low. This position is confirmed by the fact that we are also low in regard to percentage of technology related exports in manufacturing exports. While assessing the future, we should note that, though we have a large pool of scientific personnel and engineers, in terms of their deployment in Research and Development, we are almost at the bottom. Our rank at 49 in the 'Growth Competitiveness Index' among the 59 countries surveyed in Global Competitiveness Report may be explained significantly by our position in these infrastructural indicators.

Finally, the end product of all economic policy is social well being, and admittedly the long term prospects for economic growth also depend crucially on the social well being. The social indicators in regard to our country do not give us too much of comfort. Literacy levels are low, though public expenditure as a percentage of GDP is comparable to many other countries. The picture in regard to health and sanitation is not encouraging, and it is unfortunate that we spent in this area a much lower proportion of GDP than others.

Overall, we rank rather low in human development and high in human deprivation. Inspite of this, one notices relatively low levels of public expenditures in health, and in primary education though mere expenditures may not reflect actual delivery of services. I believe that there is a very disturbing insensitivity among many of us to human suffering and needs of the poor, relative to say costs of subsidies and welfare of employees in organised sector. The policy makers and more importantly opinion makers including academics perhaps need to consider issue of the mending of mindset in favour of the poor. For now suffice it to say, apart from the issue of social conscience, in assessing long term prospects for growth in cold economic terms, acceptable levels of social development and consequent appropriate role of government appear critical for an assured prosperous future for our country.

What are the Inferences for Future?

The inferences from the above analysis of past performance and current status in the global context are mainly five-fold.

First, performance since our plan-era has been mixed in terms of our needs and capacities, reasonable on a global-scale, and is getting progressively better especially in the recent years. We have lagged behind in the social dimension of growth. The current mood of confidence needs to be tempered with realisation of actions overdue in these areas, to sustain the momentum in the medium term.

Second, the immediate prospects for growth with stability are good and are mainly a result of removing the structural bottlenecks to growth especially in terms of deregulation and liberalisation. Obviously, that is not enough to continue with high growth in the medium term. For the medium term, immediate attention to institutional and infrastructural issues appear to be urgent, and the tasks are complex.

Third, the long term prospects are even more contingent on immediate actions in the areas covered by social indicators. In the context of growing awareness of people and inevitable global competition, mere meeting of minimum health needs and imparting literacy would certainly be inadequate. Healthy population with potential for rapid skill-upgradation is absolutely essential for us to survive as a nation with dignity and respect.

Fourth, both the medium term challenge relating to institutions and infrastructure as well as the longer term one relating to social development demand a more focused government and a government that efficiently delivers the essential services that it is supposed to deliver, as an overarching priority. What we need is not less government and not even more market, but better government and genuine market. I humbly submit that it is on this basis that the debate on state versus market or government versus market should now be resolved in our country. So far, perhaps the reality in our country was often state and market versus poor people but effort should now be to aim for State and market for the people, or better government and genuine market for the people.

Finally, the refocused role of government demands both professional skills and personal integrity among all leading participants. Tomorrow's problems cannot be solved with yesterday's strategies, and cannot even be understood with day before yesterday's knowledge. That is why we need more, much more of Vivek Vardhini and Vivek Vyapthi.

Annexure – 1

Comparison of Economic Performance Among Select Countries

	Indices	India	Singapore	China	Pakistan	Srilanka	South Africa	Mexico	USA	Japan
1.	GNP (World Bank Atlas method)									
	a. per capita 1999 (in $)	450	29610	780	470	820	3160	4400	30600	32230
	b. ranking of countries	162	9	140	160	137	86	71	8	6
2.	GNP (PPP)									
	a. per capita 1999 (in $)	2149	27024	3291	1757	3056	8318	7719	30600	24041
	b. ranking of countries	153	7	128	159	136	69	75	4	14
3.	GDP annual growth rate in %									
	a) 1980-90	5.8	6.7	10.1	6.3	4.0	1.0	1.1	3.0	4.0
	b) 1990-99	6.1	8.0	10.7	4.0	5.3	1.9	2.7	3.4	1.4
4.	Average annual rate of Inflation 1990-98 (in %)	8.9	2.1	9.7	11.1	9.7	10.6	19.5	1.9	0.2
5.	Gross domestic investment (GDI) as % of GDP (1997-1999)	23.9	34.5	38.8	15.7	24.8	15.9	24.8	18.5	29.2
6.	Average annual growth of GDI (1990-99)	7.4	8.5	12.8	2.1	6.2	3.0	3.9	7.0	1.1
7.	Gross domestic savings as % GDP (1997-1999)	20.3	51.4	42.5	11.2	18.3	17.3	23.8	16.7	30.0
8.	Average annual growth of exports of goods & services (1990-99)	11.3	-	13.0	2.7	8.4	5.3	14.3	9.3	5.1
9.	External debt as % of GNP (1998)	23.0	-	16.4	52.8	54.9	18.9	42.0	-	-
10.	Gross reserves in US $ billion									
	a) in 1990	5.64	27.75	34.48	1.05	0.45	2.58	10.22	173.1	87.83
	b) in 1999	32.7	76.84	157.73	1.51	1.64	6.35	31.78	60.5	286.92

11. Net foreign direct investment (in US$ billion)									
a) annual average 1987-1992	0.06	3.67	4.65	0.23	0.06	-0.024	4.31	46.21	0.91
b) 1998	2.26	7.22	45.5	0.5	0.35	0.37	10.24	193.4	3.19
12. Composite ICRG risk rating (March 2000)	64.3	89.0	72.3	54.3	60.3	70.5	70.5	80.0	82.0
13. Institutional investor credit Rating (March 2000)	45.3	80.4	56.6	18.8	35.4	45.2	49.8	92.9	86.9
14. Stock market capitalization (in US$ billion) in 1999	184.6	198.4	330.7	6.97	1.58	262.5	154.0	16635	4547
15. Stock market capitalization as % of GDP in 1997	33.7	110.4	22.9	17.8	13.9	179.8	38.9	144.4	52.9
16. Subsidies & other current transfers as % of total expenditure in 1997	40	8	-	8	20	49	51	60	-
17. Education Profile									
a) Public education expenditure as % of GNP (1995-97)	3.2	3.0	2.3	2.7	3.4	8.0	4.9	5.4	3.6
b) Public education expenditure as% Govt. Expenditure (1995-97)	11.6	23.4	12.2	7.1	8.9	23.9	23.0	14.4	9.9
c) Share of pre-primary, primary and secondary in education expenditure (1994-97)	66.0	60.3	69.6	79.8	74.8	73.1	82.8	74.8	81.2
d) adult literacy rate 1998	55.7	91.8	82.8	44.0	91.1	84.6	90.8	99.0	99.0
e) youth literacy rate 1998	70.9	99.7	97.2	61.4	96.5	90.8	96.6	-	-
18. Health Profile									
a) Public expenditure on health as % of GDP (1990-98)	0.6	1.1	2.0	0.9	1.4	3.2	2.8	6.5	5.9
b) % of population with access to improved water source (1990-96)	81	100	90	60	46	70	83	-	96

(Contd...)

c) % of population with access to sanitation (1990-96)	16	100	21	30	52	46	66	-	100
d) infant mortality rate per 1000 live births (1998)	70	4	31	91	16	51	30	7	4
e) life expectancy at birth	62.9	77.3	70.1	64.4	73.3	53.2	72.3	76.8	80
f) daily per capita supply of calories (1997)	2496	-	2897	2476	2302	2990	3097	3699	2932
g) daily per capita supply of protein in grams (1997)	59	-	78	61	52	77	83	112	96
h) Doctors per 1 lakh of population (1992-95)	48	147	115	52	23	59	85	245	177
i) Tuberculosis per 1 lakh People in 1997	118.3	57.5	33.7	3.1	35.7	242.7	25.0	6.4	33.6
j) per cent of infants with low birth weight (1990-97)	33	7	9	25	25	-	7	7	7
19. Military expenditure as % of GNP in 1997	2.8	5.7	2.2	5.7	5.1	1.8	1.1	3.3	1.0
20. Highest marginal tax rate in % in 1999 a) individual	30.0	28	45	-	35	45	40	40	50
b) corporate	35	26	30	-	35	30	35	35	35
21. Power & Transportation									
a) power consumption per capita KWH (1997)	363	7944	714	333	227	3800	1459	11822	7241
b) T&D losses (1997)	18	4	8	24	17	8	14	6	4
c) paved road as % of total (1998)	45.7	97.3	-	57	95	11.8	29.7	58.8	74.9
d) goods transported by rail thousand ton-km per $ million of GDP (PPP) (1998)	137.1	-	304.8	26.3	2.03	283.3	62.1	213.8	101.7
e) air passenger carried '00000s (1998)	165.2	133.3	532.3	54.1	12.1	64.8	177.2	5881.2	1017

(Contd...)

22. Communications, information & science & technology per 1000 people									
a) radios (1997)	121	822	333	98	209	317	325	2146	955
b) TV sets (1998)	69	348	272	88	92	125	261	847	707
c) Telephone mainlines (1998)	22	562	70	19	28	115	104	661	503
d) PCs (1998)	2.7	458.4	8.9	3.9	4.1	47.4	47	458.6	237.2
e) internet hosts per (January 2000) 10,000	0.23	452.3	0.57	0.34	0.63	39.2	40.9	1940	208
f) scientists & engineers in R&D per million people (1987-97)	149	2318	454	72	191	1031	214	3676	4909
g) high technology exports as % of manufacturing exports	5	59	15	0	-	9	19	33	26
h) waiting time for telephone connection in years (1997)	1.0	0.0	0.1	1.2	6.3	0.4	0.8	0.0	0.0
23. GFD of Central Govt. (% of GDP)									
a) 1990	-7.5	10.8	-1.9	-5.4	-7.8	-4.1	-2.5	-3.9	-1.6
b) 1998	-5.2	11.8	-1.5	-6.3	-8.0	-2.9	-1.1	0.9	-
24. Capital Expenditure of Central Government(% of GDP)									
a) 1990	1.8	5.1	-	2.6	6.1	3.1	2.5	1.8	2.0
b) 1998	1.6	5.1	-	2.5	5.3	1.2	1.9	0.6	-

Note: The data for making country comparisons are primarily culled out from World Development Reports and Human Development Reports, World Bank. For the performances of Indian economy during the post independence period they are mostly drawn from Economic Survey, Government of India, World Development Report, World Bank and RBI Occasional Papers vol. 18 Nos. 2 and 3.

Annexure – 2

Socio-economic Indices and Their Interpretation

	Type of Index	What does the Index Attempt to Gauge and its estimation
1.	Technology Index	Based on observed data and survey results the index measures the level of technology in a country. It takes into account of countries' involvement in innovation and import of technology from abroad.
2.	Startup Index	This index is also based on observed data and survey results. It measures the condition favouring business start-ups.
3.	Economic Creativity Index	This index combines the above two indices in order to gauge a countries' involvement in economically effective innovation or transfer of technology ('technology index') and the condition favouring business start-ups ('startup index'). The most creative countries are also among the fastest-growing over the past decade. America has pace setting innovation and the best start-up environment. Though Singapore is not a great innovator its economic creativity is very high through rapid import of technology.
4.	Growth Competitiveness	It aims to measure the factors that contribute to future growth of an index economy, measured as the rate of change of GDP per person, in order to explain why some countries are improving their prosperity faster than others. Variables that contribute to levels of productivity, high rates of accumulation and innovation and improvements in productivity and statistically significantly are taken into account in constructing the index. The indices are 'economic creativity index', as explained above, 'finance index' and 'international index' all of which are assigned equal weights of one-third. 'Finance index' measures the efficiency of financial system which is conducive to high rates of saving and investment and the 'international index' measures the degree of economic integration with the rest of the world.
5.	Microeconomic competitiveness index	It attempts to measure the microeconomic foundations of economic development, rooted in firm operating practices and strategies as well as in the business inputs, infrastructure, institutions and policies that constitute the environment in which a nation's firms compete. Bivariate relationships between these microeconomic variables and GDP per capita are estimated. And weighting all the variables, common factor analysis

		is employed to provide a single composite picture of relative microeconomic competitiveness. The factor score of the dominant factor which captures the variance among the variables is interpreted as the index.
6.	Current competitiveness	This index is built upon the microeconomic competitiveness index. This index aims to identify the factors that underpin high current productivity and hence current economic performance, measured by the level of GDP per person. The index takes into account of a nation's firms' operating practices and strategies and the quality of the nation's business environment. A variety of measures reflecting the sophistication of company operations and strategies are statistically related to GDP per capita and are combined into a sub-index of the sophistication of company operations. Next a variety of measures reflecting the quality of business environment viz., quality of inputs, availability and sophistication of local suppliers of components, machinery, etc., sophistication of local demand and rules governing vitality of competition and the incentives for productive modes of rivalry are statistically related to GDP per capita and combined into another sub- index of the quality of the business environment. The two sub-indices are then combined to obtain the current competitiveness index.
7.	Human Development Index	It measures average achievement in basic human development in one simple composite index. It is based on 3 indicators: a) longevity, as measured by life expectancy at birth; b) educational attainment, as measured by a combination of the adult literacy rate (two-third weight) and the combined gross primary, secondary and tertiary enrolment ratio (one-third weight) and c) standard of living, as measured by GDP per capita income in PPP US$. The index for each of these indicators are obtained as ratio of the difference of the actual value from the minimum value to the difference of maximum value from the minimum value. HDI is then obtained as the simple average of these three indices.
8.	Human poverty index	For the developing countries (HPI-1), it concentrates on the deprivation in the three essential dimensions of human life already reflected in HDI. First deprivation is represented by % of people not expected to survive age 40 (P1). Second deprivation is represented by % of illiterate adult (P2). The third deprivation is represented by the simple average of % of people without access to safe water and without access to health services

	and % underweight children under five (P3). The index is obtained as cubic root of the simple average of cube of all the three variables. For the industrialized countries (HPI-2), there are four deprivation: a) % of people not expected to survive age 60; b) functionally illiterate; c) % of people below income poverty line, set at 50% of median disposable household income and d) rate of long-term unemployment. The index is obtained as cubic root of the simple average of cube of all the four variables.
9. Transparency or Corruption	It attempts to access the level at which corruption among the politicians Index and public officials is perceived by people working for multinational firms and institutions as impacting on commercial and social life. The index is poll of polls prepared by using 10 different surveys and at least 4 surveys are required to include a country in the list. The score for overall integrity of a country as perceived in the surveys are placed between 0 to 10, with higher score indicating cleaner country. The divergence of views among surveys are recorded by variance.
10. Emerging Market access index	It measures the market openness based on 16 indicators which include average tariff levels, import quotas, rules on intellectual property rights, export subsidies, government procurement policies & investment barriers.
11. Recessionary expectations	It is based on the survey of executive opinion on the likeliness of a country going to slump in the next year. The scores are placed from 0 to 7, with higher score reflecting less likeliness of being in recession.
12. Globalization index	It ranks countries by variables such as openness to trade and investment, creditworthiness and the importance of tourism and transfers from foreign workers.

Annexure – 3

	Indices	India	Sing-apore	China	Pakistan	Srilanka	South Africa	Mexico	USA	Japan	Total No. countries surveyed
1.	Economic creativity Index (2000)	38	3	48	-	-	26	35	1	21	59
	a. Technology Index (2000)	38	3	47	-	-	32	11	1	6	59
	b. Startup Index (2000)	38	7	46	-	-	19	51	1	37	59
2.	Growth competitiveness Index (2000)	49	2	41	-	-	33	43	1	21	59
3.	Current competitiveness Index (2000)	37	9	44	-	-	25	42	2	14	58
4.	Microeconomic competitiveness Index (1999)	42	12	49	-	-	26	34	1	14	58
5.	Environmental regulatory regime index (2000)	43	-	40	-	-	27	30	9	12	53
6.	Financial market sophistication (1999)	39	9	50	-	-	14	35	1	26	59
7.	Corruption perception Index (1996) $	46	7	50	53	-	23	38	15	17	54
8.	Human Development Index (1998)	128	24	99	135	84	103	55	3	9	174
	a. GDP (ppp) index	0.51	0.92	0.57	0.47	0.57	0.74	0.73	0.95	0.91	174
	b. Education index	0.55	0.86	0.79	0.44	0.83	0.88	0.84	0.97	0.94	174
	b. Life expectancy index	0.63	0.87	0.75	0.66	0.81	0.47	0.79	0.86	0.92	174
9.	Human Poverty Index (1998)*	58	-	30	68	35	33	12	18	9	
10.	Recessionary expectations (January 2000) (on score between 0 to 7) #	6	6.2	5.4	-	-	6.3	5.2	5.7	4.6	
11.	Globalisation Index annual average % change, 1993-97	2.0	6.0	7.0	-	-	4.0	-4.5	5.0	0.5	
12.	Emerging market access Index (2000)	46	86	37	-	-	72	68	-	-	

* for 85 developing countries and 18 industrialized countries (in which USA and Japan belong) separately $- higher the rank greater is the degree of perceived corruption or lack of transparency. # - higher the value less is the recessionary expectations.

Annexure – 4

Source of Information of Various Socio-Economic Indices

Source of Information	Type of Index/Ranking
a. Primary Sources **World Economic Forum**	1. Growth Competitiveness Ranking (composite) 2. Current Competitiveness Ranking 3. Microeconomic competitiveness 4. Economic Creativity Index 5. Technology Index 6. Startup Index 7. Environment Regulatory Regime 8. Level of Sophistication of Financial markets
Transparency International & Gottingen University	1. Corruption Perception Index
World Bank	1. Human Development Index 2. Human Poverty Index 3. Purchasing Power Parity Real GDP per capita 4. Data on Infrastructure 5. Data on Information 6. On Macro-economic Variables 7. On Socio-economic Indicators
b. Secondary Sources	
The Economist	1. Recessionary Expectations 2. Change in Globalization Index 3. Emerging Market Access Index 4. Emerging Market Listings
c. Other Sources	
S. Sivasubramonian (1998) "Twentieth Century Economic performance of India"	Information on pre-independence days
World Bank (2000) "India Reducing Poverty, Accelerating Development	1. Governance Ranking 2. National Sample Surveys (NSS) on Poverty
Reserve Bank of India (1997) Occasional Papers Vol.18 Nos. 2 & 3	Information on Indian Economy During 1950 to 1990
Government of India, Economic Survey (1999-2000)	Information on Indian Economy During 1950 to 1990

Golden Jubilee Commemoration lecture delivered on the occasion of Swarna Mahotsavam of Vivek Vardhini College, Hyderabad, October 30, 2000. (RBI Bulletin, December, 2000).

4

India's Emerging Economic Challenges

VIJAY L. KELKAR

Current Economic Challenges

In the last few years, Indian economy has been a sea of tranquility in the turbulent world economy especially in the Asian region. In fact, in the year 1998, India achieved one of the highest growth rates in the world. Equally, in terms of other macro economic indicators, such as, rate of inflation or exchange rate stability, once again the performance of the Indian economy in the recent years has been quite outstanding. Presently the rate of inflation is less than 4% and exchange rates have been relatively stable. There is, in fact, some evidence that during the 90s growth rate in India has shown some acceleration. However, there are a number of weaknesses which we need to overcome to meet the objective of rapidly removing poverty. It has become necessary for us to look at the Indian economy in somewhat longer perspective and identify the necessary policy reforms and initiatives.

In India's economic history, there is little doubt that our Independence will be marked as a major discontinuity. Since Independence, India has achieved remarkable progress in overcoming the long-term Colonial stagnation and economic backwardness. We were indeed fortunate that our destiny was guided by a group of remarkably talented leaders led by India's

First Prime Minister Pandit Jawahar Lal Nehru. They had a well-defined world view and equally well articulated strategy. The strategic objective was to create a self-reliant economy independent of the international capitalist blocks. The aspiration of national leadership was clear: they wanted to create a vibrant national economy and eradicate poverty as rapidly as possible. Given the weakness of the entrepreneurial class and an absence of well-functioning capital markets, the State was assigned the role of accelerating capital accumulation and the State was also required to become an entrepreneur particularly for creating heavy and basic industries. Consequently, the public sector became the leading agent for industrialisation.

This strategy did pay off. It substantially accelerated the growth rate, it created the social and industrial infrastructure and the technological base for defence production as well as in the sophisticated and strategic nuclear and space fields.

In implementing the strategy one of the major problems soon faced was the failure on the agricultural front, which led to our dependence on PL-480 Food imports. This strategic shortcoming was quickly overcome by Smt. Indira Gandhi by launching the Green Revolution to achieve the objective of self-reliance in food security.

These achievements are indeed historic when we recognise that all this was achieved essentially under a democratic form of governance, without any colonial exploitation and while facing the challenges of demographic explosion.

These achievements are outstanding when compared to our own historical standards, but seen in the context of the contemporary experience of other economies of Asia, such as, China, Japan or Korea, our performance is perhaps far short. India, at the time of Independence, had almost similar levels of per-capita income as that of China or that of Korea but since then both these economies have surpassed India in terms of per-capita incomes or even in terms of share in the global economy whether in manufacturing output or in global trade. The per-capita income in Korea is 10,550 US$ while ours is still 390 US$. The Gross Domestic Product of China which in the year 1997 was US$ 825 billion which is more than two times than ours has been achieved through a sustained growth rate of more than 7% per annum over the last two decades. The per capita income growth rate of other miracle economies of South East Asia has been two to three times higher than ours for more than the last few decades. Comparison with these economies is also not very flattering for us in the area of human development index. Although we have made gains in life expectancy and in other indicators, once again we are behind compared to these dynamic economies of Asia in Human Development Index. Similarly, while we see an outstanding performance of these economies in overcoming poverty, we have the dubious distinction of housing the world's largest number of poor.

While talking about such international comparisons there is one interesting and an important point to which I want to invite your attention, namely, although in the levels of living as measured in per-capita income terms or human development index terms, India lags behind, in terms of indicator of equity such as 'Gini Index' which summarises the distribution of income or consumption of an economy, India is in the top ten amongst all developing countries. The latest World Development Report 1998 of the World Bank shows that our consumption distribution is perhaps less inequitable compared to the income distribution obtained in the United States and in some developed economies. There is also a recently published paper by Prof. Hashim who is a Member of the Planning Commission showing that in India the "Gini Index" may have been, in fact, improving over the plan periods, albeit, marginally. Given the quality of data regarding consumption distribution, I would argue that we can at least maintain a weaker version of this finding, i.e., there is no evidence that the distribution has deteriorated. This is an important point because in the opinion of many of our left analysis, India is considered to be one of the worst sufferers from income inequalities and it is said to be getting worse. Obviously, data do not support this. This brings us to the heart of our economic problem, namely, for the curse of our poverty the villain is the low per capita income due to the comparatively lower growth rates. In other words, what India faces is the problem of low productivity across the sectors as well as of the low growth in this productivity. I would submit that this is the crux of India's persistent cruel poverty.

Now an important issue is how did we get in this situation if otherwise, the development process seems to have done the trick, namely, that of transforming a low savings economy into high-savings/ high-investment economy. During 50 years of our planning, the rate of savings and investment which were only 10.4% and 10.2% respectively in 1951-52 have been more than doubled to 23.1% and 24.8% respectively by the end of Eighth Five Year Plan. In other words, the Indian people have made great sacrifices for making large investments but the total rate of return on these resources has not been increasing either to catch up with the dynamic developing economies or making available resources to eradicate poverty.

I think many factors have contributed to this low productivity and low growth impasse. The first strategic error was the relative neglect of international trade. By neglecting international trade we forewent the possibilities of exploiting productivity enhancing exchanges. In the manufacturing sector we opted for an across-the-board import substitution strategy where we sought to produce everything in a production chain whether the product was a commercial vehicle or a steel mill. And by this, the weakest link decided the fate of the strength of the whole production chain. We entered into production of a number of activities in which we just did not possess the competitive edge. It resulted in a loss of efficiency for the entire industry. For instance, forcing the Indian fertilizer industry to use only Indian designed catalyst, the entire fertilizer industry's productivity suffered. Same was the case for electronics sector where our software industry took time to take off because of the insistence on the use of domestic computer hardware. What all these examples show is that we just did not allow international trade to enlarge the possibilities of using our own resources more efficiently and we ended up taxing our own productive sectors. Even in foreign trade we concentrated on socialist economies and neglected the trade linkages with emerging dynamic areas particularly that of East Asia including Japan. Had our external trade been linked to rapidly growing Japan, the whole economic growth trajectory could have been so different.

Yet another strategic limitation was the relative neglect of agriculture. Professor Arther Lewis, a distinguished Noble Prize winner has so clearly shown that it is the productivity of agriculture which decides the gains from economic development. Not only did we neglect investments in agriculture and in related activities such as irrigation, but we also manipulated the terms of trade against agriculture. This was a copy book revisit to the debate between Joseph Stalin and Bukharin. I think the arguments of Shri Sharad Joshi has considerable power when he argues for liberating India's agricultural sector from the present regime of controls. I think we missed the exciting possibilities of employment expansion from value added agriculture. This neglect also had a profound impact on the growth process itself. Prof. Sukhamay Chakravarty has shown that the failure on the food economy front led to stop/go policies regarding public investment and this induced sharper business cycles, thereby reducing the underlying growth rate.

Equally, one of the major sources of the weakness has been due to the working of our public sector. In designing the public sector we did not adequately think of the role of incentives, particularly incentives provided for management or the bureaucracy to ensure that the shareholder value or national wealth is maximised. Even our legal system may have further aggravated the problem by treating public sector as an extension of the state, which only meant that we finally robbed the public sector of any risk taking ability; a key hallmark of an entrepreneur. Consequently, public sector which was supposed to be the primary motive force of capital accumulation became a drain on fiscal resources.

There is yet another major source adversely affecting the long term growth rate. This is what I call the curse of growing subsidisation and cross subsidisation. The growth in subsidies have been very high. In 1971, the total explicit subsidy provided in the budget amounted to 3% of Gross Domestic Product and within two decades or so this share has increased almost four times at 12% of GDP. According to recent research the subsidies now perhaps account some as much as 16% of GDP. Of course, not all subsidies are bad. There are these merit subsidies. There are the subsidies where social benefits are higher than that of the social costs. But these are even less than 1/3rd of the total subsidies of which we are talking about. Subsidies essentially imply under recovery of costs. These are being showered by both Centre and States through direct budgetary outgo or through foregone revenues. Similarly, there are implied subsidies through under-performing of public sector as well as other forms of indirect subsidies through cross subsidisation. Let us take the example of non-performing public sector enterprises. Between 1950-1997 the stock of public sector investments has increased to almost two lakh crores. This is when valued at Book value. In terms of replacement value which is analytically more correct definition these stocks are even higher. What is the rate of return? It is less than 3% or so. If these investments had been achieving comparable returns as efficient enterprises do, then the rates of return would have been two to three times higher. The difference between these is also an implicit subsidy paid by the tax-payers.

Had the subsidies been going to poor it could have been more defensible but that is not the case. Bulk of these subsidies go to people who are not so poor. This is true even in the case of food or fertilizer subsidies. These do not go to rural poor. I would submit that this ubiquitous and growing subsidy culture reflects a distortion of the vision of our founding fathers who aimed at accelerated development and increasing living standards of all our people through higher and higher incomes. What we are getting instead, is a new grammar of Indian politics where subsidies have become a full stop for growth acceleration.

If these direct subsidies are bad enough, the impact of the curse of indirect subsidisation is deleterious. Not only are these subsidies non-transparent, as these are not made out from the Budget, being effected through differential pricing of public sector produced goods and services. Further, they also lead to loss of international competitiveness of many of our major industries. The working of the curse of cross-subsidisation can be seen in all major sectors, such as, electricity, railway transport, petroleum sector, telecommunications and so on and so forth. It is felt that charging prices differently to different class of consumers promote the goal of social justice. Ruefully, what happens is exactly opposite. Giving power free to the agricultural sector not only knocks out any incentive for efficient use of electricity on demand side, but also on supply side, it leads to a deterioration in the quality of electricity supplies. In a market economy, you can either fix price or fix quantity but cannot do both over a long period of time. Consequently, farmers get intermittent power supplies which adversely affects his economics while simultaneously affecting the SEB's financial health. This has further adverse implications for the industrial sector. The electricity charges for industrial sector are many times higher than that paid by agricultural and household sector. This higher than cost price phenomenon is seen only in India and not anywhere else in the world. This adversely affects the competitive strength of our industry and once again weakens the growth of exports and employment. Similar phenomena exist in railways where the rail freight rates are pegged much higher than costs to cross-subsidised passenger travel. This has affected efficient use of resources and international competitiveness. Till recent reforms in telephone tariffs a similar phenomenon existed in the telecom sector.

Finally, one of the biggest drags on India's development has come from the growth of Government consumption which is expenditure on current consumption. This is because of the size of the Government and the compensation given to employees of government and employees of semi-government organisations. With successive Pay Commissions, the compensation of the Government employees has been revised upwards not always consistent with the States' capacity to pay or with the underlying quality of supplies.

With the recent Pay Commission decision, the public consumption will go up by as much as 2% of the Gross Domestic Product and this has become the major source of fiscal stress for both the Centre and State Government finances.

These growing revenue and fiscal deficits lead to enhanced market borrowing by the Government. This leads to squeezing out private sector borrowing as well as to higher interest rates, Currently, almost 80% of private financial savings are being absorbed by public sector borrowing. Consequently, a cruel choice is between higher inflation by printing of money or higher interest rates which choke investment and employment growth. The ultimate outcome is, of course, lowering growth rates. Clearly, the key to India's prosperity lies in reversing these factors.

Next Wave of Reforms

If the analysis presented so far is correct, then the policy initiatives that are required are obvious. I would suggest that what is necessary now is the launching of the next wave of reforms. The first wave of reforms launched in 1991 by Dr. Manmohan Singh and Shri Narasimha Rao were essentially crisis-driven. This time round we can have consensus-driven reforms so that we can act in anticipation of a crisis which would definitely visit on us if the present trend is allowed to continue.

The foremost reform measure that is required is to ensure fiscal health. It is for Parliament to adopt the Fiscal Responsibility Act, which would limit the revenue deficits and budgets deficits and safeguard the economy from a debt trap. Such a strategy has been successfully deployed by a number of countries. Of course, merely passing the Fiscal Responsibility Act will not achieve the fiscal balance. What is required is simultaneous action both at the Centre and the States to increase user charges particularly of electricity, water, transport, etc. so that resources are generated to increase investments and also improve the quality of these services. These measures would encourage private investment in these sectors and would reduce the costs for consumers and improve the quality by promoting competition.

Towards this, the most important reform would be redefining the role of Government and down-sizing the Government while improving the quality of governance. The down-sizing of the Government will also mean privatisation of non-strategic public sector enterprises including banking sector. To my mind, the only strategic public sector enterprises should be those dealing with atomic energy, space and defence production. Of course, in this programme of re-engineering of the Government, the State needs to play a more focussed role in the fields of education, health and environment protection. Government also will have to play a critical role in promoting transparency and good governance.

Equally, the new Parliament will need to review the policies regarding size of the Government and also the principles of compensation to employees of Government and semi-Government agencies. Such new initiatives alone can ensure that the fiscal situation of the States and the Centre becomes sustainable and also ensure that tax-payers get their moneys worth.

One of the major implications of reforming the role of the Government would be to create a new institutional architecture for the management of the Indian economy. By recognising that we are now aiming to become a fullfledged modern market economy, where stability, predictability and transparency of policies are of fundamental importance. Such a new institutional architecture will have to have an independent monetary authority by giving greater independence to Reserve Bank of India on the lines of autonomy enjoyed by the Federal Reserve in USA or The Bank of England in U.K.

The new institutional architecture will also imply strengthening of independent regulatory agencies such as SEBI, TRAI, CERC etc. and start treating their independence at par with the independent judiciary. This will inspire confidence amongst both investors and consumers and promote competition in these sectors. What one also will be achieving is the reduction of distributive politics of cross-substitution.

The most important outcome of the fiscal correction would be reduction of both short-term and long-term real interest rates in the economy. Currently they are at unprecedented levels of between 6-8%. No country in the world has achieved sustained growth rate with such high interest rates. Bringing the real interest rates in the neighbourhood of 3-5% can trigger a spectacular growth boom throughout the economy.

The centre piece of reforms will be to promote competition in product markets and services sector by allowing free entry and freer international trade. This also means giving level playing field to all entities, i.e., private sector and public sector. To achieve this, one of the foremost policy measure would be to reduce our tariff barriers. Today, India has one of the world's highest tariff barriers – where the dynamic Asian economies has average rate of tariff is 5% or so, ours is nearly 25%. We need to accelerate the program of tariff reduction and bring tariffs at par with the Asian level. But, in my view, the removal of non-tariff barriers is even more important which means rapidly removing import controls against consumer goods and agricultural products and the elimination of reservations of small scale sector which is preventing India to make rapid strides in the export of labour-intensive products such as readymade garments, leather, toys etc. Reservation means low levels of output which are unable to achieve quality of international standards. To capture international market, the quality and the timely delivery are of strategic importance. When I was in Tariff Commission, I had requested National Council for Applied Economic Research (NCAER) to do quantitative effects of liberalisation, i.e., effects of promoting external and internal competition. The results show that the returns on internal liberalisation are far more important than the external liberalisation. If you reduce non-tariff barriers by 50%, the gains would be 1.5% of India's Gross Domestic Product, mind you this 1.5% will be accruing every year implying larger employment opportunities. The provision of internal liberalisation if you include privatisation of public sector monopolies which are producing intermediate goods and services, the gains to the economy are even more spectacular. The experience of United States for the last 20 years, where US liberalised power industry, natural gas industry, airlines, road transportation, rail road transportation, etc., the gains have been 10-15% of sectoral GDP. The experience of other countries is also similar. The NCAER study indicate that the additional benefit of the economy can be as high as 3-4% of the GDP. Mind you these are static efficiency gains. If you take in account after dynamic efficiency gains due to new investments and new technologies, the gains will be truly spectacular. These gains are essential because of better incentives through the forces of competition. In other words, this is due to the potential which is already there in the economy and would not require any new physical investment or any new capital.

Finally, the next wave of reforms should encompass factor markets. In the 1991 reforms, the emphasis was on reforms of product markets by abolishing industrial licensing and import barriers. These reforms left the factor markets such as labour markets, land markets, capital markets, natural resources market such as water and institutions somewhat untouched. Notice that I am including "institutions" as a factor of production. The term "Institutions" which includes State and quasi-State institutions as well as judiciary and civil society. The reforms of labour markets are particularly important. The new post-industrial revolution requires flexibility in all operations. This means flexibility in labour markets is of phenomenal importance so that companies can respond with speed to the changing market conditions. Our present laws of bankruptcy and corporate control also require reforms so that the market for corporate control become competitive. Factor market reforms would also need to cover financial markets. The reforms of factor markets would also need to be accompanied by innovative measures for creating a social safety net such as employment guarantee schemes of Maharashtra. In addition to such employment oriented schemes perhaps time also has come to eliminate product-based subsidies including food subsidies and replace it by a negative income tax to improve equity while controlling adverse impact on efficiency. The interesting variation of such policy instruments could be experimenting with food stamps and education vouchers for meeting the needs of socially disadvantaged and weaker sections of the society. These innovations recognise the fact that Government can be a financier but need not be a producer of such services. The heart of these reforms is to promote competition in all economic activities and support the creation of human capital particularly through enlargement of quality primary education facilities to all. Evidence across the various countries at different stages of development show that education or human capital provide a lasting success in promoting equality in a society.

I would like to make one more point regarding the next phase of reforms. In the first phase of reforms, the reforms essentially concentrated on reforms at Central Government. Now these have to be taken to the level of our States. Almost 40% of our revenue and fiscal deficits is because of the State finances. They need to be rectified. Similarly, a number of reforms are required for improving the delivery system as afterall all basic services such as Education, Health, are delivered at State level. Of course, there are a number of States taking a new initiatives for improving the quality of services for instance. There are similar equally interesting things happening in the States of Madhya Pradesh, Rajasthan, Himachal Pradesh, Karnataka etc. in the fields of Education and Health. People are accepting the dictum to "think-global but act local" and consequently there is growing competition amongst State Governments to give better and improved services to industry particularly information technology industry which has the potential of transforming India at a very rapid rate.

I now come to my final point regarding the launching of next wave of reforms. We need to show greater vigour and greater sense of urgency. The reason for emphasizing the urgency is due to the unique state of our demographic transition. In the next couple of decades India will have once in a life time chance of having a population structure where we will have the largest share of working population. Naturally, after these decades, the process of aging will catch and the vigour of the working population would decline. Like a satellite when it is put to the orbit, it requires high velocity to ensure exit from the Earth's gravitational force, if our economy is to exit from the gravitational pull of poverty, it also requires a high exit velocity of double-digit growth rate over the next two decades.

This kind of high growth is feasible, as other miracle economies achieved it precisely when the share of working population was highest, maintaining high savings and investment rates and also increasing labour supply and productivity.

As we enter into the new century, the Indian economy stands at cross roads. Either it can take the "business as usual" road which means continued poverty and a low growth trap or take the high road to prosperity through accelerated reforms. If we take this road, then there is no reason why India, by the year 2020, cannot achieve a per capita income of more than one thousand dollars or more than ½ lakh rupees of per-capita income and wipe out the poverty and illiteracy and also increase life expectancy by ten years or more and become an Economic Super Power. Presently, we are in the bottom twenty amongst all the countries in terms of Human Development Index. In the year 2020 we should be amongst the first twenty. This is surely possible and it is entirely up to us to build the necessary consensus for accelerated reform and implement it.

5

Economic Reforms: A Policy Agenda for the Future

MONTEK S. AHLUWALIA

I

Some Positive Features

A policy agenda for the future should be determined by looking at existing strength and weaknesses and building on the strength while correcting the weaknesses. It is natural that public discussion usually focuses on our weaknesses which therefore always look daunting. But to put matters in perspective, I would like to begin by acknowledging that we enter the new millennium with some important strengths. Let me just mention three :

(i) First, our growth performance is now much better than the frustratingly slow 3.5 per cent to 4 per cent growth which characterised the first three decades after independence. India's GDP grew at an average rate of 5.8 per cent in the 1980s. It accelerated to around 6.5 per cent in the Eighth Plan period (1992-93 to 1996-97) and this is expected to be maintained in the Ninth Plan period. This record suggests that the Indian economy is adjusting well to the new policies. It is not generally realised that if we focus on the 1980s and 1990s, India has been one of the ten fastest growing economies in the world !

(ii) The educational deficiencies of our population have long been a drag on our growth potential. We have always taken pride in the quality of our highly skilled personnel, our scientists, our managers and more recently our software wizards. But the general level of education for the bulk of our population has long been extremely low. Adult literacy was only 18.3 per cent in 1951 and only increased to 28.3 per cent by 1960 and 34.4 per cent by 1971. This was undoubtedly one of the reasons for our persistently low growth in the years. The most recent estimates by the NSS show that literacy had increased to 62 per cent in 1996-97. This is still low, but it is now in the range which is consistent with achieving growth rates of 7 to 8 per cent.

(iii) Population growth, which for long remained stubbornly above 2 per cent, at last appears to be declining. Kerala's justly celebrated achievements in this area have been matched by Tamil Nadu and it appears that Andhra Pradesh and Karnataka are not far behind. Birth rates are much higher in the northern States but even in these States they are declining. India's population in the next decade is expected to slow down to 1.5 per cent.

These positive developments have important implications for our prospects in the next decade. If GDP growth can be pushed up from around 6.5 per cent at present to say 7 per cent at the start of the decade, and then to 8 per cent by the end of the decade, it would give us an average growth of around 7.5 per cent for the decade as a whole. With population growing at 1.5 per cent, this means per capita income would grow at about 6 per cent per year. Growth of this order is much higher than we have experienced in the past and can create many virtuous circles. If it is reasonably well distributed, it would guarantee a sharp reduction in the level of poverty by the end of the next decade. One can go further and say that unless we can achieve growth of this order, we cannot expect to see a significant improvement in the conditions of living of the mass of our people.

What are the policies we need to follow to achieve such growth and especially to make it broad-based? Fortunately, a substantial consensus has now emerged in professional and even in political circles on economic policies. There is general agreement that the process of economic reforms must be strengthened and deepened and this is sometimes described as implementing "the second generation of reforms". I am not entirely comfortable with this description. It implies that we have successfully completed the first generation of reforms, and must now move on to the next hierarchical level. The reality is somewhat different. I would classify the reform agenda ahead of us into three categories.

- The first item on this agenda on which there is a great deal of agreement must be to restore fiscal discipline. This is actually a first generation reform, which we have not been able to carry out as planned.
- The second category consists of first generation reforms which are more or less on track, but are still to be completed because of our deliberate choice of gradualism as a reform strategy.
- The last category consists of what can be called genuine second generation reforms, which take the reform process to new areas not addressed thus far.

II

Fiscal Discipline

Let us begin with fiscal discipline, which is a first generation reform which got lost somewhere on the way. The seriousness of the fiscal problem facing the country is now so widely recognised that it is useful to put it in some perspective.

In 1991, when the economic reforms began, we faced an exceptionally severe crisis and the Central Government's fiscal deficit – which had reached 8.3 per cent of GDP in the preceding year – was seen as a root cause of the crisis. This gave a sense of urgency to the need for fiscal correction and we were able to reduce the deficit to around 6 percent of GDP in the very first year. It was recognised at the time that even this was too high and further reduction was needed to release resources into the economy and reduce interest rates, both very necessary to stimulate private investment. The medium term objective, outlined in a discussion paper circulated by the Finance Ministry in 1993, was to reduce the fiscal deficit to around 3 per cent by 1996-97. Unfortunately this target was never achieved. The actual deficit was 5.2 per cent in 1996-97, it deteriorated to 6 per cent in 1997-98, and has remained at about that level subsequently. The result has been that interest rates remain very high.

Meanwhile, the fiscal position of the States, including the so called better administered States, has deteriorated significantly. Unlike the Centre, the States are not allowed to borrow freely and this puts an automatic limit on their fiscal deficit. However, this only means that their fiscal weaknesses are reflected in an uncontrolled growth in non-Plan expenditure, and mounting losses on the supply of various economic services. The scale of the problem can be judged by the fact that the losses of all the State Electricity Boards amounted to about Rs. 11,000 crores in 1997-98. The losses on account of irrigation are about Rs. 2000 crores even if we count only the maintenance cost of the systems. If interest on capital invested in irrigation is included, the losses would be much higher. Losses in the State Road Transport Corporations are about Rs. 1000 crores.

With such large losses it is not surprising that the States are unable to meet their targets for Plan expenditure. In the Eighth Plan period (1992-93 to 1996-97) Plan expenditure by the States in real terms was 20 percent lower than targeted. The position has worsened in the Ninth Plan because of the impact of the Fifth Pay Commission. Besides, what is shown as Plan expenditure in the States' Budgets exaggerates the actual extent of new development projects. This is because Plan projects which have been almost completed continue to be shown as ongoing projects, which enables the salary and running costs of these projects, which should normally be covered by the non-Plan budget, to be financed from the Plan budget. In effect, therefore, a large portion of Plan expenditure is not financing new development projects but only covering salaries and rising costs of old projects. The situation in some States is such that they find it difficult to meet salary payments.

The consequences of not correcting this situation are self-evident. The high deficit will perpetuate the present high interest rates which hurt investments in the economy and indeed hurt the small producers the most. The low level of Plan expenditure will jeopardise much needed public investment in critical areas and jeopardise our growth objective. I am not saying that growth depends only on Plan expenditure, or that all Plan expenditure is sacrosanct. Most of the investment needed to achieve our targeted 7 to 8 per cent growth can and should come from the private sector, and there are many areas where Plan expenditure can be effectively replaced by private investment. However, the ratio of Plan expenditure of the Centre and States combined was 11.3 per cent of GDP in 1990-91 and has declined to a little over 9 percent today. This has squeezed investment in many areas which are critical for accelerating growth to 7-8 per cent.

This resource squeeze has direct implications for our ability to accelerate growth in agriculture. Faster agricultural growth and broad based rural development is central to our strategy for reducing poverty. To achieve this, we have to expand investment in irrigation, land development, soil and moisture conservation, agricultural research, development of agricultural marketing facilities, and finally, expansion and maintenance of rural and district roads to improve rural connectivity. These basic investments in rural infrastructure can only be undertaken by the public sector but unfortunately the level of these expenditures has probably declined in real terms because of the severe fiscal problems of the States.

Much larger investments are also needed in health and education, especially in rural areas, to bring our social development indicators up to respectable levels comparable with other developing countries. This again has to come from public sector. In other infrastructure areas such as power generation and distribution, ports, airports, telecommunications and national highways, the private sector can play a much larger role than it has in the past, and this must be encouraged. However, even in these areas, public investment will continue to be extremely important in the foreseeable future and we have large gaps to fill.

The fiscal objective for the next decade must therefore have two dimensions. We must reduce the fiscal deficit to release resources for private investment but we must simultaneously increase public investment in critical areas. This suggests that the scale of fiscal effort needed is very large. The combined fiscal deficit of the Centre and the States was around 8.5 per cent of GDP in 1998-99. The Finance Minister has already said that we should try to reduce the Centre's fiscal deficit (as recently redefined) to around 2 per cent over the next three years. This would suggest that the combined fiscal deficit of the Centre and the States should be reduced to say 4.5 per cent over a three year period. Simultaneously, we should aim to increase total Plan expenditure of the Centre and the States taken together by say 1.5 per cent of GDP from the present level. The total fiscal improvement required to achieve these twin objectives is around 5.5 per cent of GDP over a three year period i.e. around 1.8 percentage points per year.

This improvement has to be achieved partly by the Centre and partly by the States. I will not go into the issue of what should be the exact balance between the two. The important point to note is that a fiscal correction of 5.5 percentage points of GDP over the next three years is an extremely difficult task in any situation. It cannot be achieved by acting on one or two instruments. Action will be needed on several fronts. Let me mention some :

i) Improving Tax Administration to Raise Larger Revenues

Anyone who has studied the Indian tax system, both at the Central and the State level, is struck by the fact that the system is archaic with complex and cumbersome procedures, a multiplicity of rates, numerous exemptions and large areas of discretion, all of which lends itself to evasion by tax payers and harassment by tax authorities. The system also lends itself to corruption at all levels, which explains the relatively low levels of tax realisation. Experience of other countries shows that a tax reform which brings about a system change could generate additional revenues of 3 per cent of GDP in a relatively short period without necessarily increasing tax rates. Half the fiscal adjustment needed could therefore come from effective implementation of tax reform. This can be done if we can translate general statements about "improving tax administration" and "widening the tax" into specific proposals for removal of exemptions, simplifying the system by reducing the number of rates and also modernising procedures. Hopefully, the new Tax Reforms Committee, referred to in the President's Address, can quickly come up with specific recommendations in this regard.

ii) Reducing Subsidies

Almost everyone is willing to endorse general statements about reducing subsidies, but agreement vanishes as soon as one focuses on specific proposals. And yet the total volume of direct and indirect subsidies in our system has risen to unsustainable levels. The major direct subsidies in the Central Government are the subsidies on fertilizer, food and sugar and these amount to Rs. 24,000 crores according to the Budget Estimates for 1999-2000 though they may turn out to be higher. In addition, there are large implicit subsidies such as massive undercharging for higher education and for hospital services, undercharging for railway passengers, undercharging for postal services, etc. The subsidy on kerosene is Rs. 8000 crores and on LPG around Rs. 4000 crores. These subsidies are not technically borne by the Budget, but are covered by overcharging for other petroleum products such as petrol and aviation turbine fuel. However, this clearly represents a loss of potential resources since the cross subsidy element built into the high price of some petroleum products could otherwise be mopped up in the form of tax revenue. These subsidies are not specifically targeted at the poor but actually accrue to relatively higher income groups, or at best to the average consumer. However, the subsidy burden effectively prevents the government from spending on programmes which would stimulate broad based growth that would have a large beneficial effect which is probably better distributed.

The State sector too is burdened by massive subsidies which could be reduced. Electric power is supplied to farmers at 10 to 20 percent of the cost of production in most States and free in some. Household consumers of electricity are also undercharged as is water for irrigation, passenger bus services and, of course, higher education.

I must emphasise that what is needed is not complete elimination of all these subsidies, but only a substantial reduction combined with better targeting. This will release resources which will enable us to finance some of the critical expenditures which need to be increased to meet our development objectives.

iii) Downsizing of Government

This is another area where we can save some resources. Government departments, including the Railways and Posts, have long been overmanned. There are also too many government departments. A liberalised economy needs far fewer Ministries and Departments than a controlled and regulated economy and some steps have to be taken in this direction. The Fifth Pay Commission, an expert body, had estimated that a 30 per cent reduction in government staff should be achieved over time. Proposals to downsize government are sometimes resisted because it is perceived that unemployment is a serious problem and government employment helps to meet demands for jobs. However redirecting resources from paying for surplus manpower in order to build much needed economic and social infrastructure will create many more jobs in the rest of the economy. We have to recognise that the purpose of government is to provide essential services efficiently, and not to create employment.

iv) Bolder Privatisation

Many developing countries have been able to bring about a substantial improvement in their fiscal position by undertaking major privatisation of public sector enterprises.This option is also open to us and should be aggressively followed not only by the Centre, which has begun the process, but also by the States. I will say more on this subject later in this lecture.

v) Reprioritize Plan Schemes

Finally, it is necessary to re-prioritize Plan expenditure to eliminate schemes which are of doubtful value. Detailed post evaluation studies show that many of our Plan schemes, though well intentioned, simply do not achieve their stated objectives, or do so only to a limited degree, making the schemes cost-ineffective. This is due to a combination of poor design of the schemes and inadequate administrative capability. Unfortunately, such schemes continue to remain in operation, absorbing resources which could be deployed in other areas. The administrative agencies responsible for these schemes become strong vested interest for their continuation and criticism of the effectiveness of the scheme only leads to demands to "strengthen" the schemes through better administration and monitoring, which usually means more staff and more resources. A thorough re-examination of all Plan schemes, with a drastic elimination of schemes which are demonstrated to be ineffective, would release resources which would enable the more important and more cost-effective schemes to be fully funded. Strict application of such tests of effectiveness in a framework of formal zero based budgeting would automatically ensure better design of schemes and also appropriate mid-course restructuring, to ensure that they remain funded.

Implementing reforms along these lines is obviously not a simple matter. Each of these proposals viewed in isolation is bound to generate controversy. But then, a fiscal correction of 5.5 percent of GDP cannot be achieved without such effort. Unfortunately, our present system, with its tradition of secrecy about the Budget, makes it very difficult to confront these choices. Difficult decisions cannot be taken if they have to be kept secret from everyone except a very small group, and then suddenly unveiled on the last day of February to be subjected to instant analysis by TV experts! It will be necessary to prepare the ground by actively debating the available options, and more importantly, identifying the implications of not pursuing them.

The need for taking these difficult decisions would become much clearer if we were to adopt the practice followed in some countries of presenting budgets with projections for subsequent years also. This would present a comprehensive picture of the scale of effort needed if we want to get to where we want in the next three years. In this framework the effort needed today can be reduced only if we explicitly plan for a much larger effort tomorrow.

Whatever we do, we can be sure of one thing. If we do not make a move on most, if not all, of the issues I have listed, we will not see significant progress on the fiscal front. This in turn will mean a continuing erosion of public investment in critical areas, continuation of high interest rates limiting the flow of funds for private investment, and an international rating which remains below investment grade. It is unlikely that we can achieve 7 to 8 per cent growth in such circumstances.

III

Completing First Generation Reforms

Having emphasised the overwhelming importance of fiscal correction, let me now turn to my second category which consists of reforms which have proceeded more or less in the gradualist manner originally envisaged, but which need to be completed, or in some cases modified to reflect new developments.

i) Industrial Deregulation

Liberalisation of industrial licensing and opening up industry to foreign investment was an important part of first generation reforms. This element has progressed fairly well as far as Central Government controls are concerned. Investors still face many problems in implementing projects, but these are largely at the State level, which is a second generation area. However, there are some areas of industrial deregulation where further action is needed.

The sugar industry is one such area. Sugar is an extremely important agro-based industry and the second largest industrial employer in the country after cotton textiles. If liberalisation is beneficial to industry it should be beneficial to sugar also. Yet this industry remains subject to extensive control associated with the existing dual price system. State advised prices to be paid to farmers are often unconnected with market conditions, a portion of the production has to be surrendered as levy sugar at an unremunerative price, the so called free market sugar is also subject to release control, and the industry complains of a non-level playing field against imports which do not suffer from the levy. There is a strong case for decontrolling sugar and opening up this area to market competition. If it is felt necessary to retain sugar in the PDS, this should be done by purchase of sugar at market prices with a separate subsidy from the budget. However,

I would argue that the sugar subsidy is very poorly targeted and benefits mainly urban middle income consumers. There is a very strong case for removing sugar from the PDS.

Coal is another area where industrial de-regulation should be extended. This is a critical energy source, where private investment is not allowed at present except for captive mining. If we have opened up petroleum to the private sector, there is no reason why coal should not be opened up also. The additional coal production needed to meet the country's energy demands in the next decade is so large that it simply cannot be met by the nationalised coal industry. Failure to increase coal production will only make us more dependent on oil where we are already heavily dependent on imported supplies. The need to allow private investment in this sector is therefore urgent. Private investment will add a competitive spur to the industry, and also bring in new technology which is important in view of the fact that environmental considerations are likely to impose restrictions of various kinds on coal and coal quality. Since coal mining is a difficult area where environmental clearances are bound to take time and the development of a mine also takes several years, we need to act now if we want additional production in six to seven years time!

Another area of industrial policy which needs to be addressed relates to the policy of reservation of certain products for the small scale sector. Many experts have argued that reservation is not the best way of helping small scale industry and their arguments are persuasive. In fact, it is not generally realised that the sectors which are reserved for SSIs have grown more slowly than the unreserved SSI sector. Nevertheless, I recognise that this is a sensitive issue on which it will take time to build a consensus. However, there is a strong case for immediately de-reserving certain areas which have a strong export potential such as garments, toys, and leather footwear. Let me just illustrate the point by looking at two items which in India are reserved for SSI production. In 1997, whereas India's exports of toys and sporting goods were US$ 70 million, China's exports were US$ 8 billion. In other words, China exported 120 times the amount India did! The story in footwear is nearly the same. We exported about US$ 350 million whereas China exported US$ 8 billion, or about twenty two times our level. Continuing with small scale reservation in these areas is preventing us from developing a dynamic export sector which we desperately need, and which would generate high quality employment. We complain about lack of market access for our exports, but the fact is that in critical areas where we have a strong comparative advantage our own policies have prevented us from penetrating world markets.

(ii) Opening the Economy to Trade

Opening up the economy to foreign trade was another important part of the reform agenda and the reforms in this area are now more than half complete. Government has announced that all quantitative restrictions (QRs) will be removed by the year 2003 and this is being done in a phased manner. The time frame of the transition has been made quite clear and has been well accepted by Indian industry. However, we do not have an equally clear time frame for tariff reduction. The government has given a broad indication that tariff rates will be reduced to bring them in line with East Asian countries in about three years time. It would be desirable to give Indian industry a clearer idea of what is intended. Industry is also rightly concerned that tariff reduction should not create tariff anomalies in which tariffs on inputs remain high while tariffs on outputs are reduced.

The time has come for us to quantify our intentions more clearly. We could, for example, indicate that the average tariff level, which is around 30 per cent at present, will be reduced to say 15 per cent over a three year period. This would imply an annual reduction of approximately 5 per cent per year on average, which could be easily absorbed by Indian industry. We should also clearly identify the major tariff anomalies and lay down a phased programme for their elimination. Our anti-dumping mechanisms and procedures should also be strengthened in parallel to reassure industry that they will not be subjected to unfair competition.

There are some who fear that Indian industry will not be able to survive foreign competition if tariffs are reduced further. Personally, I think this is a mistaken view. Indian industry has been able to adjust to large tariff reductions in the past few years and there is no reason to believe that the process cannot be pushed further, especially since the market determined exchange rate will ensure that any excessive pressure of imports will produce an offsetting depreciation which will help domestic industry, while also helping exports. Reduced tariffs on inputs will obviously help domestic industry to become more competitive.

iii) Disinvestment and Privatisation

Disinvestment is another first generation area where the reforms are poised to be carried to the next higher level. The reforms began with "disinvestment" which would still leave the government with a majority stake in PSUs. The United Front Government indicated a willingness to reduce the government's stake to a minority in the non-core and non-strategic area. The present government has gone further still, with a clear declaration that we will go down to 26 per cent in the generality of cases. Disinvestment proposals involving a change in management are currently being processed for Modern Foods and Balco, and for the introduction of a strategic partner in IPCL.

Nevertheless, uncertainties remain in the public mind about the extent to which the government should go. Many people believe that while sale and transfer of management is acceptable for weak PSUs, we should not give up majority control in the so-called "navaratnas". Others believe that the revenues from disinvestment should be used to strengthen other public sector units. As far as the issue of majority ownership is concerned, the fact is that we cannot achieve the desired fiscal correction if we do not off-load a majority stake in the equity of many of the navaratnas. The public must therefore be persuaded that such disinvestment or privatisation is desirable and will help to pay for the creation of socially more useful assets such as schools and hospitals and other forms of rural infrastructure. Nor should we assume that the revenues from disinvestment will necessarily be ploughed back into other PSUs. We have to consider what is the best use for these resources and if hospitals and schools and roads are more important, that is surely what we should build.

The fiscal problem facing us suggests that we should try to achieve disinvestment levels exceeding, if possible, the Rs. 10,000 crores budgeted for 1999-2000, though I recognise that even this level has never been reached in any single year. A business as usual approach to disinvestment will not do. We should move away from annual planning of disinvestment and indicate the scale of effort needed over the next three years. On this basis we should clearly identify the companies and also the extent of disinvestment in those companies which is needed to achieve our target. The Government has indicated that it is considering a new mechanism for implementing disinvestment including the setting up of a separate unit. This is a very welcome development. The key to its success will be our willingness to take the PSUs to be privatised out of the administrative control of the administrative Ministry and transfer it to the new unit. The Ministry's views will of course be taken into account but the critical decisions on the pace and manner of disinvestment and privatisation should be with the new unit.

The manner of the disinvestment, i.e. whether it should involve retail sale to broad based investors or an outright sale to a single buyer, or the induction of a strategic partner will of course vary depending on the enterprise, and the rationale of the specific choice can be made transparent. We should also explain to the public that there is no reason to be alarmed because we are reducing government equity to a minority stake. Our objective should be to ensure that the navaratnas are strengthened as corporate entities, and not that they do not slip out of government control. In fact, a strong case can be made that ending government control over these enterprises is essential if they are to have the commercial autonomy and flexibility they need to survive in competitive markets. No one seriously believes that the presence of the government as an owner adds any value to the company from a commercial point of view. This is as true of Maruti as it is of SAIL or IOC.

iv) Financial Sector Reforms

The financial sector is another area where first generation reforms are well underway but the process needs to be accelerated. The Reserve Bank of India has made commendable progress in upgrading prudential and regulatory standards in our banking system to meet the international standards laid down by the Basle Committee. This is an area where all developing countries will be under much greater international scrutiny in future given the increased concern about financial sector weaknesses in the aftermath of the East Asian crisis. Fortunately, although we still have some way to go, the gaps that remain are easily bridged.

However, the next step is, in some ways, more difficult : how to make sure that our banks, especially the public sector banks, can meet the new prudential standards and compete effectively against foreign banks and private sector banks while doing so. Competition in the banking system will be intensified by technological change, especially the introduction of information technology. The more dynamic banks which take to the new technology will be able to increase their market share without having an extensive branch network. The public sector banks, whose great strength has been their branch network, must be ready to meet this challenge. They will need autonomy and flexibility to restructure in many ways. They will need flexibility in recruiting and promoting personnel, the ability to negotiate wage agreements which reflect productivity and profitability in individual banks and flexibility to redeploy staff and deal with excess staff through voluntary retirement. They will also need flexibility to close loss making branches.

These are difficult issues on which the first reaction of many of the interest groups involved, and even of the general public, may be negative. However we need to develop greater understanding on the part of these groups of the necessity for making these changes in the interest of the banking system itself together with assurances that these changes can be achieved without too much disruption. Some of these problems have to be faced in the near future as the difficult problem of the three weak banks identified by the Verma Committee is addressed.

An important positive development in the financial sector is the opening of the insurance sector to private investment. This will enable new private sector entrants to come into this sector sometime in the year 2000. A strong and competitive insurance industry will strengthen long-term contractual savings, improve service quality to customers, and also serve as a vehicle channeling long term finance, which is relatively scarce at present, to the capital market. This is of course absolutely essential to finance infrastructure. Even so, we have to remember that it will take 5 to 6 years for the new entrants to reach any credible size. Substantial flows of finance from new insurance companies to infrastructure can therefore only be expected in the second half of the decade. This only underscores the urgency of beginning the process as soon as possible.

v) Private Financing of Infrastructure

Private investment in infrastructure is another critical area which was part of first generation reforms but where a major push is needed to carry the reforms forward. Achieving rapid growth in today's more open and competitive environment requires a much higher level of international competitiveness. This in turn requires a very high quality of infrastructure. Unfortunately, our infrastructure, whether we look at roads, power, ports or telecommunications, is clearly inadequate. There are severe shortages in quantity and equally serious deficiencies in quality. Public investment will continue to have an important role in all these areas, but the scale of the need is such that it must be supplemented by private investment. Private investment is especially helpful in the effort to improve quality.

The power sector and telecommunications were opened up to private investment as part of first generation reforms and this was extended to ports, airports and roads. The results so far have been mixed. The good news – and there is some – is that it has been possible to attract investment in all these sectors. About 9000 MW of power capacity has come up, or is under construction, in the private sector. There has also been substantial private investment in cellular phones and other value added segments of telecommunications. Significant private investment has come in ports and the first joint sector airport was recently commissioned in Cochin. Sceptics who say that nothing has happened are clearly misinformed. However, the results achieved thus far are less than was expected and there have been serious implementation problems in all these areas for different reasons.

In the power sector the financial condition of the State Electricity Boards makes it difficult for private power generators to raise the necessary financing as long as the SEBs are seen to be unreliable paymasters because of unviable tariffs and large transmission and distribution losses, much of which is just due to theft and corruption at the distribution end. In retrospect, it would have been better to start the power sector reforms with reforming tariffs and privatising distribution to improve the financial viability of the sector. In telecom there have been other sorts of problems, first because of the inability of new private investors to meet their obligations regarding license fees, and then because of continuing disputes on the jurisdiction and the powers of the regulatory authority.

I do not propose to go into these issues in detail. I would only say that we must recognise that attracting private investment into regulated infrastructure sectors is much more complex than we had realised. Private investors in infrastructure are subject to price regulation and also have to deal with other large public sector organisations in a monopoly situation. Price regulation can cause problems if the tariffs are not sufficiently remunerative, or if they are perceived to be unfair by the public. Dealing with public sector organisations in a monopoly situation poses its own problems. Private telecommunication companies have to deal with the public telecommunication system for interconnection. Private ports have to deal with the Railways to get rail connectivity. It is necessary to provide an environment in which private investors can have reasonable certainty about the rules of the game and which is also seen to be fair to consumers and the public. This calls for strong and credible regulatory agencies which can ensure fairness in fixing regulated tariffs and also provide assurance of fair treatment for private investors.

We need to review our policies and benchmark them against best international practice. This may require changes in many areas to bring our policies in line with best practice. In telecommunications, the government has announced that it will amend the law to strengthen the Telecom Regulatory Authority of India (TRAI). This is a very important decision which should be speedily implemented on the basis of experience elsewhere. We should also look at the other regulatory authorities in the system – the SERC, the TAMP etc. – to see whether similar strengthening is needed.

IV

Second Generation Reforms

Let me now turn briefly to what I would call the real second generation reforms, i.e. reforms that have not formed part of the explicit reform agenda thus far, but now need to be brought to the top of the agenda for the next decade.

i) Extending Reforms to the States

First, there is the issue of extending the reforms process to the State Governments. There has been much discussion and public debate about reforms in the Central Government, but the need for parallel reforms at State government level has not received enough attention. And yet, most of the areas where the common man interfaces with the government agencies lie in the State government area. Health, education, agricultural extension and agriculture related services, irrigation, power distribution, rural, state and district roads, municipal services in urban areas, are all areas where the quality of government output directly affects the lives of the people. All these areas are in the purview of State Governments.

Some State Governments have recognised the need for reforms in particular sectors, e.g. in the power sector, and this is indeed a welcome development. The number of such States is still small, but hopefully it will expand. The key to success in this area, as in many others, is the willingness to introduce reasonable user charges which make the sector financially viable. This is true for power and also for many other services. If States can take significant steps in this area, it would take care of some of the most critical constraints in the next stage of development.

Many of the developmental problems in the State sector are a reflection of the fiscal crisis facing State governments and corrective action in this area, along the lines mentioned earlier, would help resolve these difficulties. However, resources are not the only problem. Additional resources will not improve education if the system tolerates teachers who do not teach, or even attend school. It is a sad fact that efficiency levels in our governmental system have deteriorated greatly in many parts of the country.

This is partly due to the fiscal crisis itself because underfunding leads to loss of elan and morale. However it is also in large part a reflection of a deterioration in governance standards which has led to a decline in accountability and performance. One should of course beware of generalisation. Some States perform much better than others. Individuals can always make a huge difference everywhere. However the system as a whole is becoming dysfunctional. Administrative reforms designed to improve performance and increase accountability are therefore essential if resources are to be translated into effective developmental work. The specific solutions needed will vary from State to State. I share the view of many people that greater involvement by the people at the ground level will on the whole improve the responsiveness and efficiency of the system.

State Governments also need to undertake liberalisation of their controls and procedures. The number of separate permissions needed to set up a small business in most States ranges between thirty and forty, and each one of these becomes an occasion for harassment and corruption. What is worse, these burdens fall especially heavily on small businesses increasing transactions costs for them enormously. A serious effort to reduce the rigours of "inspector raj" at the State level would be a major boon to small business and would encourage investment. States would achieve much more by way of attracting investment if they tried to compete with each other in providing an investor friendly environment and in providing superior infrastructure than in the usual effort to offer sales tax incentives.

ii) Labour Legislation

An area that has not been touched by the reforms thus far, but which must now be addressed urgently, relates to reforms in the labour markets and especially labour laws. Economists have long known that India's labour laws deny firms the flexibility they need to operate successfully in highly competitive markets. Enterprises do not have the flexibility to retrench labour or to close down a particular unit in the company in response to changing market conditions without getting prior government permission. The labour laws also specify the "service rules" which govern employment and which cannot be changed very easily.

This can make it difficult even to redeploy workers to different activities when needed.

The intention behind these laws was to protect employment. However in trying to protect existing employment they actually discourage growth of new employment. This was less of a problem in earlier years, when the economy was closed and even domestic competition was limited, and the additional costs could simply be passed on to consumers in the form of higher prices. This is no longer possible in an open economy, especially one subject to strong competition from imports. Indian industry needs flexibility to deal with the new and much more competitive situation. They need flexibility to downsize when needed and also to restructure and reorganise businesses through sale, acquisition and merger. The present labour laws are a serious impediment to this process. The resulting inflexibility discourages businesses from expanding freely, and also prevents restructuring which would improve efficiency and create a basis for future expansion of employment.

The provisions relating to contract labour also need to be amended. They make it difficult for establishments to contract out services which have to be performed on the premises - e.g. gardening, cleaning, security and cafetaria. Greater flexibility in this area would lead to a profusion of smaller businesses providing services to existing firms which are otherwise unwilling to increase their own labour force. It would contribute to total employment generation and even to enterprise development.

The time has come to amend our labour laws to bring them in line with practices in other countries. It should be kept in mind that the existing laws apply only to the organised sector labour force, which constitutes only 8 per cent of the total labour force. Ninety-two percent of the labour population derive no benefit from these laws. In fact these laws actually discourage the growth of high quality employment in the organised sector and to that extent are against the interest of those who are seeking employment.

iii) The Functioning of the Legal System

My final candidate for second generation reforms is the legal system. If we want to integrate with the world and to benefit from large inflows of foreign investment we need a well functioning legal system in which contractual rights and obligations can be effectively enforced. The legal system must be one in which the laws are clear and transparent, procedures are speedy, the judiciary is independent of politics and outcomes are perceived to be fair. I have no doubt that we score very well on independence of the judiciary and fairness, but not on clarity or the speed of procedures.

I must confess that I am not professionally competent to pronounce on legal infirmities but I would like to mention some commonly perceived problems.

- First, there is no doubt that we have a plethora of outdated laws, many of which need to be scrapped.
- Second, the laws that are not outdated are often drafted in a manner that is open to multiple interpretations and the resulting lack of clarity has been the subject of a surprising amount of unnecessary legislation. Bibek Debroy in a recent study has highlighted some particularly absurd examples arising out of lack of clarity in the excise law. In 1959 the Supreme Court had to pronounce whether charcoal is coal. On Several other occasions it has had to pronounce on whether betel leaf, chillies, lemons and green ginger are vegetables because if they were, they would be free of tax. My favourite example is the one in 1985 when the Supreme Court had to decide on the vegetable status of coconut - it led to a split decision!
- Third, our legal procedures are enormously time consuming. They seem to be designed to help those seeking postponements. If justice delayed is justice denied there is not much justice in our system.
- Finally, the Government itself has a voracious appetite for litigation and routinely appeals all decisions against it, even decisions by its own appellate bodies! An important motivating factor behind such appeals is the perception that failure to appeal may impunge the integrity of the relevant administrative authority.

The end result of all this is that our courts are clogged with cases and litigation takes an enormously long time. Interestingly it is ordinary citizens and small businesses that are hurt most by these problems. Large corporations, with a battery of lawyers, are much less vulnerable. Drastic change in this area is desperately needed.

I am conscious that there are many important issues of policy which I have not touched upon. One cannot be comprehensive and still observe the normal time constraints of a lecture. My objective was only to outline the broad agenda of reform that we must address in the coming years. As you can see the agenda is fairly large and some of it quite difficult. I would only say that if we can make significant progress in most of the areas I have mentioned, we would be well set to achieve 7 to 8 percent growth over the next decade, and what is more, a growth which will be distributionally balanced and will dramatically reduce poverty.

13th Jawaharlal Nehru Memorial Lecture (IFFCO), November, 1999.

6

Achieving Higher Economic Growth

RAKESH MOHAN*

I. The Need for Long Term Economic Growth

We have come a long way since independence (see Table 1). 1947 marked a major departure from almost a thousand years of political, economic and social subjugation. The country was then literally in darkness. Compared with 85,000 MW of installed power generation capacity today the total installed capacity in 1947 was 1362 MW. The life expectancy at birth was 32 and overall literacy was 17 per cent. By 1991 life expectancy had increased to 60 and literacy to 52 per cent. Official poverty estimates hovered around 50 per cent in the first three decades after independence but have declined since to about 35 per cent. The 1960s witnessed a serious bout of food insecurity but measures taken since then have resulted in more than 20 years of relatively comfortable food self sufficiency.

Although most of us feel justifiably disappointed at the progress made by India since independence, we must recognise these positive achievements that have indeed been accomplished. After a century or more of zero economic growth, the first three decades of the post independence period laid the foundation for sustained economic growth of a kind not seen in the recorded history of India. But this growth at less than 1.5 per cent annual growth in

* I am grateful to D.K. Joshi for very able assistance in compiling all the data.

per capita income was undoubtedly inadequate to make any dent in the high poverty levels prevalent in the country. Benefits from this growth were simply not palpable. However, the foundations for modern economic growth were well laid and we saw significant acceleration in the 1980s and 1990s. The higher annual growth of per capita income at about 3.5 per cent achieved in the 1980s become palpable and major poverty ratios fell significantly.

Table – 1

Progress Since Independence: Key Indicators

Year	Poverty (Percent)	Literacy (Percent)	Life Expectancy (Years)	Power Capacity (MW)
1951	45	17	32	1,362
1961	45	31	45	4,653
1971	52	38	50	14,709
1981	43	44	55	30,214
1991	35	52	60	85,000

The progress achieved in the 1980s should have taught us the lesson that higher economic growth must be the key objective of economic policy, and that it is only higher economic growth that can reduce poverty and provide sustainable economic security. No distribution can take place when there is nothing to distribute. The nation cannot be secure without economic strength and economic strength cannot be achieved without substantial economic growth. This can be seen by looking at the long-term decline of both China and India. India began its decline as an economic power from the early part of the eighteenth century, while China's decline perhaps began in the early part of the nineteenth century (see tables 2a and 2b) It would appear that the India accounted for about 16 per cent of world income in the early 1800s whereas China was about double that at 32 per cent. The share of both these countries declined over the next century and a half and fell to about 4 per cent for India and 5 per cent for China by 1950. Correspondingly it was Europe and the United States that gained substantially over this period. It is also notable that Europe's economic peak was at the turn of this century, which also coincides with its zenith in terms of political and military power. India's improved economic performance since the early 1980s has substantially increased its share of world income from about 3.4 per cent in the late 1970s to about 4.6 per cent now. However during this period China's superior economic performance doubled its share of about 5 per cent in the late 1970s to about 11 per cent now. This has been achieved by a major step up in investment and economic efficiency brought in through the active implementation of economic reforms throughout this period. Thus the achievement of long term and sustainable economic welfare requires a major acceleration in Indian economic growth over the next 10 to 20 years. This requires substantial enhancement of overall investment levels and improvement in economic efficiency.

Table – 2a

Shares of World GDP, 1700-1995

(Percent)

	1700	1820	1890	1952	1978	1995
China	23.1	32.4	13.2	5.2	5.0	10.9
India	22.6	15.7	11.0	3.8	3.4	4.6
Japan	4.5	3.0	2.5	3.4	7.7	8.4
Europe	23.3	26.6	40.3	29.7	27.9	23.8
United States	0.0	1.8	13.8	28.4	21.8	20.9
USSR/Russia	3.2	4.8	6.3	8.7	9.2	2.2

Table – 2b

Rates of Growth of World GDP, 1700-1995
(Annual average compound growth rates)

	1700-1820	1820-1952	1952-78	1978-95
China	0.85	0.22	4.40	7.49
India	0.26	0.54	4.02	4.63
Japan	0.21	1.74	7.85	3.21
Europe	0.68	1.71	4.27	1.74
United States	2.57	3.78	3.46	2.47
USSR/Russia	0.86	2.08	4.75	-5.56
World	0.57	1.62	4.52	2.70

Source: Angus Maddison. Chinese Economic Performance in the Long Run. Paris: OECD, 1998.

The countries which have achieved high annual growth in excess of 6 per cent in per capita income in the last three decades have done so through significant increases in their gross investment rates (see table 3). The achievement of per capita income growth of 6 per cent in India over the next 10 years will require a GNP growth rate of over 7.5 per cent per annum. Even if this were achieved Indian per capita income in the year 2010 would not exceed what the per capita income was of countries such as Thailand before 1985. In other words, even if we are able to achieve a significant step up in our economic growth we will still be substantially behind most East Asian countries.

Table – 3

Gross Investment Rates in Current Prices: Selected Countries (1952-94)

Country	Gross Investment/GDP (Percent)		
	1952-57	1958-77	1978-94
India	12.0	16.4	23.3[1]
China	23.2	28.0	34.2
Japan	26.9	34.3	30.3
Korea	NA	23.3[2]	32.5
Taiwan	15.2	24.4	25.9
France	18.8	25.2	21.0
Germany	23.4	25.2	20.6
United Kingdom	15.3	18.7	17.4
United States	19.0	18.5	18.7

Source: Angus Maddison. Chinese Economic Performance in the Long Run. Paris: OECD, 1998.

[1] 1978-91. [2] 1960-77

Most countries which have succeeded in stepping up their growth rates to about 6 per cent were able to do so by substantial increases in gross domestic capital formation in excess of 30 per cent of GDP. The current Indian investment ratio is hovering around 25 per cent to 27 per cent. This needs to be stepped up to more than 30 per cent within the next few years. A primary driver of higher economic growth is investment in infrastructure. The India Infrastructure Report had projected that the achievement of

GDP growth of over 7 per cent will require an increase in investment in infrastructure from the prevalent levels of about 5 to 5.5 of GDP in the mid 1990s to about 8 per cent of GDP by 2005-06. It had concluded that it would not be possible to achieve this unless the public sector kept up its existing rate of investment in infrastructure amounting to about 4.5 per cent to 5 per cent of GDP, while increasing private sector investment in infrastructure substantially to account for the balance. Private investment in infrastructure would have to increase from about 0.5 to 1 per cent of GDP in the mid 1990s to 2.5 per cent to 3 per cent of GDP by about 2005. Thus, the achievement of higher growth requires the maintenance of public investment in infrastructure facilities at a high level while policies are changed to facilitate increasing levels of private investment.

The main impediment to the achievement of this scenario is the deteriorating fiscal situation of both the central and state governments in India. Government's ability to invest has been declining continuously since the late 1980s because of its deteriorating fiscal position (see Table 4). What is encouraging, of course, is the increase in private corporate sector investment levels subsequent to the 1991 reforms. The reforms have therefore succeeded in encouraging higher levels of private investment as envisaged. But furthei increases are constrained by declining public investment levels.

Table – 4

Declining Public Investment

Gross Capital Formation (Percent of GDP)

Period	Total	Private Corporate Sector	Public Sector
1980-85	21.9	4.3	10.2
1985-90	23.7	4.5	10.5
1990-95	23.7	6.0	9.1
1995-98	24.0	8.3	7.0

Source: Government of India: Economic Survey (Various Issues).

I am therefore concentrating today on the rapid deterioration of the fiscal balance at both central and state levels. I believe that the key deterrent to achieving higher economic growth in the country lies in its deteriorating fiscal performance.

II. Finances of the Central Government 1980-2000

In order to understand the current fiscal predicament of the central government it is necessary to examine the pattern of central government expenditure and revenues over at least the last 20 years. As already mentioned above, the key threat to sustainable economic growth and to economic security is the substantial decline in investment expenditures made by the government.

The total expenditure of the central government increased from an average of 16.8 per cent of GDP in 1980-85 to about 20.5 per cent in 1985-90 and has then declined to between 16 to 17.5 per cent in the late 1990s. At the same time non-plan expenditure has increased substantially from about 10 per cent in the early 1980s to about 13 per cent of GDP now. (See table 5). What is most notable is the very significant increase in expenditure that occurred in the second half of the 1980s. These increases took place in almost all categories of non-plan expenditure such as interest payments, defence expenditure, subsidies, pensions, and loans to states. During this period other non-plan expenditures, which consist mostly of salary payments to government servants, remained roughly stationary at about 2.25 per cent of GDP. Plan expenditures were kept high at about 6.5 per cent to 7 per cent of GDP throughout the 1980s. Correspondingly capital expenditures of central government were sustained at levels of 6 per cent to 7 per cent of GDP. Both plan expenditures and capital expenditures of the central government have fallen to levels of about 4 per cent of GDP or less now.

The great improvement in growth in the 1980s(see Table 6) was therefore partially bought by high government expenditures: both plan and non-plan and revenue and capital. That this was not a sustainable pattern of growth was demonstrated dramatically in 1991 by the twin balance of payments and fiscal crises, which led to the economic reform programme begun in 1991. The non-sustainability of such fiscal expansion is demonstrated by the sustained increase in interest payments from 2.2 per cent of GDP in the early 1980s to about 4.7 per cent now. Interest payments now constitute the largest component of expenditure of the central government. The Fifth Pay Commission is currently regarded as

Table – 5a

Profile of Total Expenditure of the Central Government (1980-2000) (Percent of GDP)

	1980-85	1985-90	1990-95	1995-99	1997-98	1998-99 (RE)	1999-00 (BE)
Non-Plan Expenditure	**10.09**	**13.41**	**12.72**	**12.17**	**12.22**	**13.14**	**11.46**
1. Interest Payment	2.20	3.38	4.38	4.63	4.64	4.75	4.87
2. Defence	2.81	3.35	2.63	2.43	2.49	2.53	2.53
3. Total Subsidy	1.41	1.95	1.78	1.34	1.38	1.52	1.32
– Food Subsidy	0.44	0.60	0.51	0.51	0.53	0.54	0.45
– Other Subsidy	0.97	1.34	1.27	0.84	0.85	0.98	0.87
4. Police	0.21	0.28	0.29	0.32	0.35	0.35	0.33
5. Pensions	0.27	0.42	0.40	0.47	0.49	0.62	0.56
6. Loans & Advances to States & UTs	0.51	1.23	0.96	1.09	1.12	1.47	0.01
7. Grants to State and UTs	0.43	0.56	0.46	0.40	0.31	0.28	0.45
8. Other Non-Plan Expenditure	2.25	2.25	1.82	1.48	1.45	1.62	1.39
Plan Expenditure	**6.73**	**7.06**	**5.17**	**4.18**	**4.17**	**4.21**	**4.26**
Total Expenditure (Plan + Non Plan)	**16.82**	**20.47**	**17.89**	**16.35**	**16.39**	**17.34**	**15.73**
Rev Exp	10.69	13.70	13.27	12.78	12.74	13.42	13.13
Cap Exp	6.13	6.78	4.62	3.58	3.65	3.92	2.60
Developmental	10.76	11.38	9.49	7.72	8.02	7.96	NA
Non-Developmental	7.32	8.79	8.89	8.94	9.11	9.04	NA
Total Exp (Developmental + Non-Dev)	18.09	20.16	18.39	16.66	17.13	16.99	NA

Source: Govt. of India, Budget documents various years

Table – 5b

Composition of Total Expenditure of the Central Government (1980-2000) (Percent of Total Expenditure)

	1980-85	1985-90	1990-95	1995-99	1997-98	1998-99 (RE)	1999-00 (BE)
Non-Plan Expenditure	**59.90**	**65.52**	**71.02**	**74.41**	**74.54**	**75.75**	**72.89**
1. Interest Payment	13.07	16.52	24.59	28.34	28.28	27.40	30.99
2. Defence	16.72	16.35	14.70	14.89	15.20	14.61	16.09
3. Total Subsidy	8.35	9.52	9.86	8.20	8.40	8.76	8.39
– Food Subsidy	2.62	2.94	2.85	3.09	3.23	3.09	2.89
– Other Subsidy	5.74	6.58	7.01	5.11	5.17	5.67	5.51
4. Police	1.24	1.35	1.65	1.94	2.11	2.00	2.08
5. Pensions	1.60	2.04	2.25	2.87	2.97	3.57	3.57
6. Loans & Advances to States & UTs	2.86	6.03	5.31	6.62	6.82	8.48	0.04
7. Grants to State and UTs	2.58	2.76	2.52	2.49	1.90	1.61	2.87
8. Other Non-Plan Expenditure	13.48	10.95	10.14	9.07	8.86	9.33	8.86
Plan Expenditure	**40.10**	**34.48**	**28.98**	**25.59**	**25.46**	**24.25**	**27.11**
Total Expenditure (Plan + Non Plan)	**100.00**	**100.00**	**100.00**	**100.00**	**100.00**	**100.00**	**100.00**
Rev Exp	63.55	66.91	74.30	78.15	77.71	77.38	83.49
Cap Exp	36.45	33.10	25.70	21.85	22.29	22.62	16.51
Developmental	59.53	56.41	51.56	46.34	46.81	46.82	NA
Non-Developmental	40.47	43.59	48.44	53.66	53.19	53.18	NA

Source: Govt. of India, Budget documents various years

the villain of the piece in causing the current fiscal problems. Analysis of the data as documented here suggests that this is not the case at the central government level. The total cost of government salaries excluding defence and police (roughly corresponding to the item "other non plan expenditure") when expressed as a proportion of GDP, can be seen to be much lower now then it was right throughout the 1980s. In other words, non-plan expenditure on government salaries and wages has not increased as fast as GDP over this period. Interest payments are now at least three times that of non-plan government expenditure excluding the military and the police. The key area for action in correcting this fiscal imbalance is related to rising debt servicing obligations of the central government.

Table – 6

Growth of the Indian Economy

Year	GNP	Per Capita
1950-1980	3.5	1.3
1980-1990	5.5	3.5
1990-2000	6.0	4.3
2000-2010*	7.5	6.0

* Projected

What becomes clear from the examination of the data is that the 1980s were characterised by a significant increase in public sector investment as well as other government expenditure. It is also noteworthy that defence expenditure increased substantially in the late 1980s, rising from about 2.8 per cent of GDP in the early 1980s to about 3.4 per cent in the late 1980s and then declining to a relatively constant level of about 2.5 per cent of GDP.

The debt service burden of the government would not rise as a proportion of total expenditure if the investments made by the government from borrowings yield it adequate returns either through the generation of non tax revenues or through tax revenues. As the government borrows resources from the public to invest in new assets, tax revenues should rise through additions to public good assets. Improvement in public infrastructure should lead to improvement in efficiency and in aiding new private investment, and hence to buoyancy in tax revenues. Similarly, non-tax revenues should rise through increasing dividends from public enterprise investment in infrastructure and other activities. If, however, resources are borrowed for investment in activities which do not yield adequate returns, debt service payments will rise continuously as a proportion of total revenues. This is what seems to have happened in India over the last 20 years. The return on net worth in central public sector enterprises, excluding the petroleum companies is not significantly different from zero.

Thus investments made in infrastructure or other activities through public sector enterprises have not yielded pecuniary returns to the government. Such returns would occur as increasing dividend payments from the public enterprises to the central government. In the budget they would be shown as "non tax revenues". Wrong pricing policies, inefficient public enterprise operations and other difficulties have all contributed to this situation of low returns. With the government running a revenue deficit since the early 1980s, all government and public sector investment has come from resources borrowed by the central government. In the presence of no returns from such investments, debt service payments are bound to become an increasing burden.

It is now useful to examine the revenue pattern of the central government over the last 20 years to understand how debt service payments have been increasing so continuously. Corresponding to the increase in expenditure in the late 1980s an attempt was clearly made to also increase revenues over that period. The main

Table – 7a

Profile of Total Revenues of the Central Government (1980-2000)
(As Percent of GDP)

	1980-85	1985-90	1990-95	1995-99	1997-98	1998-99 (RE)	1999-00 (BE)
Revenue Receipts (net)[1]	**9.43**	**11.11**	**10.07**	**9.72**	**9.46**	**9.70**	**9.59**
I. Gross Tax Revenue	**9.93**	**11.20**	**10.26**	**9.75**	**9.84**	**9.15**	**9.28**
(i) Direct Taxes	2.06	2.08	2.36	2.84	2.62	2.98	3.03
- Corporate	1.16	1.07	1.24	1.50	1.41	1.66	1.65
- Income	0.90	1.01	1.12	1.34	1.21	1.32	1.38
(ii) Indirect Taxes	7.50	8.82	7.54	6.45	6.23	5.90	5.98
- Customs	2.76	3.92	3.28	3.00	2.84	2.62	2.71
- Excise	4.74	4.89	4.27	3.44	3.39	3.27	3.27
(iii) Other tax revenue	0.37	0.30	0.35	0.47	0.99	0.27	0.27
@ Share of states in tax revenue	2.64	2.84	2.75	2.71	3.08	2.41	2.48
II. Non-Tax Revenue	**2.13**	**2.77**	**2.57**	**2.68**	**2.70**	**2.96**	**2.80**

Source: Govt. of India, Budget documents various years.

Note: 1. Revenue Receipts (net) = Gross Tax Revenue (share of states) + Non Tax Revenue.

Table – 7b

Composition of Total Revenue of Central Government (1980-2000) (Percent of Total Revenue)

	1980-85	1985-90	1990-95	1995-99	1997-98	1998-99 (RE)	1999-00 (BE)
Revenue Receipts (Tax+NonTax Revenue) (net)[1]	**100.00**	**100.00**	**100.00**	**100.00**	**100.00**	**100.00**	**100.00**
I. Gross Tax Revenue	**105.46**	**100.80**	**101.84**	**100.31**	**103.97**	**94.31**	**96.72**
(i) Direct Taxes	21.91	18.76	23.60	29.18	27.72	30.75	31.56
– Corporate	12.27	9.64	12.42	15.44	14.95	17.16	17.18
– Income	9.64	9.12	11.18	13.74	12.77	13.59	14.38
(ii) Indirect Taxes	79.64	79.35	74.79	66.29	65.84	60.79	62.35
– Customs	29.27	35.28	32.43	30.87	30.02	27.05	28.23
– Excise	50.37	44.07	42.36	35.42	35.82	33.74	34.12
(iii) Other tax revenue	3.90	2.69	3.44	4.84	10.42	2.77	2.81
@ Share of states in tax revenue	28.07	25.61	27.39	27.93	32.52	24.84	25.86
II. Non-Tax Revenue	**22.55**	**24.94**	**25.63**	**27.62**	**28.55**	**30.53**	**29.14**

Source: Govt. of India, Budget documents various years.

Note: 1. Revenue Receipts (net) = Gross Tax Revenue (share of states) + Non Tax Revenue

increase in revenues took place in collection from custom duties, rising from about 2.8 per cent of GDP in the early 1980s to about 3.9 per cent in the late 1980s. This happened both as a consequence of increased imports (which led to the balance of payments crisis) and increase in levels of custom duties. The latter of course led to greater inefficiency in resource allocation as well as decline in export competitiveness. By the end of the 1980s, at an average of almost 110 per cent India probably had the highest level of customs duties in the world. Subsequent to the economic reforms in 1991 there has been a consistent increase in the share of direct taxes from about 2 per cent of GDP right through the 1980s to about 3 per cent now. This increase has taken place both in corporate income tax collection and in personal income tax collection (see table 7) despite reduction in rates. The loss in tax revenues has taken place in indirect taxes, both in customs and in excise duties. Whereas customs duties collection were expected to fall as a result of major cuts in customs duties levels the fall in excise duty collection is more difficult to understand. In principle, rising industrial production should give rise to buoyancy in excise duty collection levels as a proportion of GDP. However two factors have inhibited such expected growth. First, apart from the period 1993-96 industrial growth has not been as high as had been expected from the economic reforms. Thus the share of industry in GDP has remained stagnant. It is the share of services that has risen continuously, and services largely remain untaxed at the central level. Second, the progressive extension of MODVAT to the whole industrial sector has also led to a fall in excise duty collection as a proportion of GDP. The share of non-tax revenues has remained stagnant between 2.6 per cent and 3 per cent since the mid 1980s higher investment has not provided higher returns.

Gross tax revenues have remained at a level of about 10 per cent over the last 20 years except for the second half of the 1980s. During this period total expenditure, however, was at much higher levels both for the late 1980s and in the early 1990s. The shortfall in revenues has been made up by the central government through consistently high capital receipts, of between 6 per cent to 7. 5 per cent of GDP right through the last 20 years (see table 8). The notable feature in the pattern of capital receipts over the last 20 years is the increasing share of both public borrowing (internal debt) and small savings: the most expensive sources of capital receipts for the government. Whereas these two sources amounted to about 2.7 per cent of GDP in 1980-85 and about 43 per cent of total capital receipts in 1980-85 they now account for about 6 per cent of GDP and about 75 per cent of total capital receipts. External assistance is no longer an important source of financing for the government. Small saving receipts are extremely expensive forms of borrowing for the government because of the associated tax benefits that are given to small savers. 75 per cent of small savings receipts are passed on to state governments to finance their fiscal deficits. (It is because of this that the system was changed as of the current year 1999-2000 to exclude both the receipts and advances to state governments related to small savings).

Table – 8

Profile of Capital Receipts of Central Government

	1980-85	1985-90	1990-95	1995-99	1997-98	1998-99 (RE)	1999-00 (BE)
Percent of GDP							
1. Internal Debt (Net)	1.93	1.85	1.79	2.70	2.30	3.99	3.72
2. External Assistance	0.86	0.66	0.65	0.10	0.08	0.06	0.05
3. Recovery of Loans	1.32	1.15	0.87	0.62	0.59	0.71	0.61
4. Small Savings (net)	0.76	1.47	1.29	1.46	1.73	1.78	0.44
5. State Provident Funds (net)	0.19	0.24	0.22	0.26	0.31	0.33	0.33
6. Special Deposits (net)	0.49	1.27	1.07	0.46	0.32	0.57	0.58
7. Disinvestment	0.00	0.00	0.26	0.17	0.06	0.55	0.55
8. Other Capital Receipts	0.66	0.66	0.40	0.34	1.55	-0.55	-0.16
Total Capital Receipts	**6.21**	**7.30**	**6.54**	**6.10**	**6.94**	**7.44**	**6.14**
Percent Share							
1. Internal Debt (Net)	31.43	25.37	26.39	43.99	33.11	53.64	60.67
2. External Assistance	14.38	9.03	10.26	1.82	1.11	0.75	0.76
3. Recovery of Loans	21.46	15.79	13.65	10.35	8.47	9.51	10.01
4. Small Savings (net)	11.48	20.38	19.39	23.90	24.95	23.96	7.22
5. State Provident Funds (net)	3.14	3.23	3.41	4.14	4.46	4.42	5.42
6. Special Deposits (net)	7.96	17.54	16.50	7.82	4.56	7.63	9.44
7. Disinvestment	0.00	0.00	4.12	2.40	0.93	7.44	9.03
8. Other Capital Receipts	10.14	8.65	6.28	5.59	22.40	-7.36	-2.54
Total Capital Receipts	**100.00**	**100.00**	**100.00**	**100.00**	**100.00**	**100.00**	**100.00**

Source: Govt. of India, Budget documents various years.

Two changes in the system have made the cost of borrowing much higher for the central government in the 1990s. Earlier, a substantial portion of the fiscal deficits was financed by monetisation (see Table 9). This is no longer resorted to and hence the explicit interest cost of a fiscal deficit has consequently increased. Second, interest rate deregulation has made the cost of government borrowings equivalent to market rates, which was not the case earlier, when banks had to lend to the government at lower than market interest rates.

Table – 9

Composition and Financing of Gross Fiscal Deficit of the Central Government (As Percentage of GDP)

	1980-81	1985-86	1990-95	1995-97	1995-96	1996-97	1997-98
I. Total Expenditure (A+B)	**15.20**	**19.03**	**17.61**	**16.27**	**15.78**	**15.57**	**16.39**
A) Revenue Expenditure	10.59	12.94	13.27	12.99	12.93	12.87	12.74
B) Capital Expenditure	4.60	6.09	4.33	3.28	2.85	2.70	3.65
II. Total Receipts (A+B)	**9.10**	**10.69**	**10.93**	**10.45**	**10.39**	**10.35**	**10.11**
A) Revenue Receipts	9.10	10.69	10.07	9.94	10.27	10.31	9.46
B) Non-Debt Capital Receipts	0.00	0.00	0.86	0.52	0.12	0.04	0.65
III. Gross Fiscal Deficit	**6.10**	**8.33**	**6.68**	**5.82**	**5.38**	**5.23**	**6.28**
Financed by:							
1) Domestic Financing	5.16	7.78	5.95	5.51	4.51	4.99	6.21
a) Market Borrowings	1.97	1.86	1.77	2.70	2.96	1.57	2.30
b) Other Liabilities	1.37	3.89	2.94	2.54	1.52	2.39	3.91
of which:							
i) Small Savings	0.82	1.64	1.20	1.34	0.90	0.95	1.73
ii) State Provident Funds	0.16	0.16	0.22	0.26	0.20	0.18	0.34
c) Conventional Deficit	1.82	2.03	1.23	0.27	0.03	1.03	0.00
2) External Financing	0.94	0.55	0.74	0.31	0.88	0.23	0.08
Conventional Deficit/ Domestic Financing (Percent)	35.29	26.04	20.85	10.66	0.63	20.68	0.00

Source: Govt. of India, Budget documents various years.
Reserve Bank of India : Currency and Financial various years

The consequence of a sustained high fiscal deficit over 20 years can be seen in table 10. Debt service payments of the central government have risen inexorably from about 30 per cent of tax revenues in 1980-85 to about 70 per cent now. The day is not far off when the tax revenues will equal debt service payments. As a proportion of total revenue receipts debt service has increased from about 24 per cent in 1980-85 to about 50 per cent now. As a proportion of GDP, debt service payments have increased from about 2.2 per cent in 1980-85 to about 5 per cent now. Another consequence of rising debt service is that the revenue deficit has increased from about 17 per cent as a proportion of fiscal deficit in 1980-85 to about 50 per cent now. In another words half of current borrowing goes to finance current expenditure. By definition current expenditure yields no economic returns in the future and hence debt service payments will continue to rise in the foreseeable future unless a significant correction is made in this situation.

Table – 10

Burden of Rising Debt Service of Central Government (1980-2000)

	1980-85	1985-90	1990-95	1995-99	1997-98	1998-99 (RE)	1999-00 (BE)
As:							
% of Tax Revenue	30.1	40.5	58.9	65.9	68.6	70.5	71.7
% of Revenue Receipts	23.5	30.4	43.7	47.6	49.0	49.0	50.8
% of Total Revenue	14.3	18.4	26.4	29.3	28.3	27.7	31.0
% of Total Expenditure	13.3	16.5	24.6	28.3	28.3	27.4	31.0
% of GDP	2.2	3.4	4.4	4.6	4.6	4.8	4.9
Revenue Deficit/ Fiscal Deficit	17.0	32.0	48.0	50.0			

Source: Govt. of India, Budget documents various years.

I now summarise the story so far. The central government has resorted to a fiscal system of high fiscal deficits on a consistent basis over the last 20 years. The second half of the 1980s was exceptional in the attainment of much higher fiscal deficits than other periods and this resulted in the crisis of 1990-91. The consequences of such a sustained high fiscal deficit are many. With increasing levels of borrowing financing activities which have zero or low yields, interest payments increase inexorably. Thus non-productive committed current expenditures rise giving rise to higher and higher revenue deficits. This leads to yet higher and higher borrowing levels. Second, because of debt service payments forming a higher proportion of both revenues and expenditures all other activities of the government suffer, since wages and salaries, interest payments, defence expenditures, pensions, food subsidies are all committed expenditures with little or no flexibility. The main sufferer in this process is government capital expenditure in both social and infrastructure facilities. Third, high debt service payments also preclude increase in or even maintenance of current real levels of expenditures in social services. The continued high levels of public borrowings also have an effect on the rest of the economy through prevalence of high interest rates. Because of the necessity to finance government deficits the Reserve Bank of India has to keep the level of both CRR (Current Reserve Ratio) and SLR (Statutory Liquidity Ratio) high on the deposits in commercial banks. This leads to the necessity for banks to have higher margins on their commercial activities thereby subjecting the rest of the economy to high interest rates. Moreover, because of the voracious appetite of the government for garnering resources from the whole financial sector, including small savings, insurance and the like, the continued high fiscal deficit levels also impede financial sector reforms which are necessary for the economy to achieve higher efficiency levels. With this scenario the possibility of achieving a growth rate in excess of 7 per cent would seem to be ruled out. Such a growth rate cannot be achieved without investment levels higher than 30 per cent of GDP and this cannot be achieved without substantial increase in both public savings and public investment levels.

III. Deteriorating Situation of State Finances

Having documented the sorry state of central government finances it is now useful to examine state finances. We can remind ourselves of the function of state governments in order to appreciate the deteriorous effects of deteriorating state finances on the economic security of the country. State governments are responsible for most public expenditures for the provision of social services. Further, they are responsible for most infrastructure services except for telecommunications, civil aviation, railways and major ports. They are also responsible for law and order. Thus a deterioration in the state's ability to invest is very serious for human development and hence for internal security, in addition to the harmful effects on economic growth.

I first examine the overall profile of state government finances before focussing particularly on their plan expenditure. As in the case of the central government, a significant increase took place

Table – 11

Profile of Total Expenditure of State Government (1980-2000)

Category	1980-85	1985-90	1990-95	1995-99	1997-98 (RE)	1998-99 (BE)
Percent of GDP						
(A) Revenue Expenditure (I+II+III)	**11.1**	**13.1**	**13.6**	**13.5**	**13.9**	**14.1**
I Developmental	7.9	9.1	8.9	8.1	8.5	7.8
II Non-Developmental	3.1	3.8	4.6	5.2	5.2	6.0
- Interest Payments and Debt Servicing	0.9	1.5	2.0	2.2	2.3	2.3
- Pensions	0.3	0.5	0.6	0.8	0.8	0.9
- Other Expenditure	1.9	1.7	2.0	2.2	2.1	2.8
III. Other Expenditure	0.1	0.1	0.2	0.2	0.2	0.2
(B) Capital Disbursements (I+II)	**5.0**	**4.3**	**3.4**	**2.8**	**3.0**	**2.8**
I. Total Capital Outlay	2.1	2.0	1.6	1.6	1.7	1.5
I.1 Developmental	2.1	1.9	1.6	1.5	1.6	1.4
I.2 Non Developmental	0.1	0.1	0.0	0.1	0.1	0.1
II Others	2.9	2.3	1.8	1.3	1.3	1.3
Total Expenditure (A+B)	**16.1**	**17.3**	**17.0**	**16.4**	**16.9**	**16.8**

(Contd...)

Table – 11 (Contd...)

Category	1980-85	1985-90	1990-95	1995-99	1997-98 (RE)	1998-99 (BE)
Percent of Total Expenditure						
(A) Revenue Expenditure (I+II+III)	**68.9**	**75.5**	**80.0**	**82.7**	**82.1**	**83.6**
I Developmental	48.9	52.7	52.3	49.6	49.9	46.4
II Non-Developmental	19.1	21.9	26.8	32.0	30.8	35.9
- Interest Payments and Debt Servicing	5.3	8.8	11.5	13.4	13.6	13.9
- Pensions	2.1	3.2	3.7	4.8	5.0	5.2
- Other Expenditure	11.7	10.0	11.5	13.7	12.2	16.8
III. Other Expenditure	0.9	0.8	0.9	1.1	1.3	1.3
(B) Capital Disbursements (I+II)	**31.1**	**24.5**	**20.0**	**17.3**	**17.9**	**16.4**
I. Total Capital Outlay	13.2	11.2	9.7	9.5	10.0	8.9
I.1 Developmental	12.8	10.9	9.4	9.1	9.6	8.5
I.2 Non Developmental	0.3	0.3	0.3	0.4	0.4	0.4
II Others	17.9	13.2	10.3	7.9	7.9	7.5
Total Expenditure (A+B)	**100.0**	**100.0**	**100.0**	**100.0**	**100.0**	**100.0**

Source: RBI Report on Currency and Finance, various years

in total expenditures during the late 1980s, from a level of about 16 per cent of GDP in 1980-85 to 17.3 per cent in 1985-90 (see table 11). This has been falling in the 1990s to about 16.5 per cent in the last 1990s. Similar to the central government, the main adjustment has been made in capital expenditure, falling continuously from a level of about 5 per cent of GDP in the early 1980s to about 3 per cent now. Whereas the ratio of revenue to capital expenditure was about 70: 30 in the early 1980s, it is now about 83:17, which constitutes a significant deterioration in the quality of expenditure. In the case of state governments, unlike the central government, capital expenditure fell during the late 1980s as well. But, just as in the central government, the main problem lies with increasing debt service payments, from only about 0.9 per cent of GDP in the early 1980s to about 2.3 per cent now. Similarly, other committed expenditures such as pensions have also been rising. The net result is that, with falling overall expenditure and rising "non developmental" expenditures, the state governments' ability to invest in productive activities has been compromised very significantly.

It is interesting to observe that, relative to the central government, states have performed better in keeping up their tax effort. Their own tax revenues have increased marginally from about 5.7 per cent of GDP in the late 1980s to about 6 per cent now (see table 12). Their share of central taxes has also remained stable. Hence, unlike the central government, they have not suffered from erosion of tax revenues. But it can be argued that, since service taxes such as sales tax are the responsibility of state governments, their share should have risen. In contrast, non-tax revenues (User charges + return from state public enterprises) have fallen. The net result is some deterioration in revenue receipts. Consequently with a rise in revenue expenditures in the 1990s, on account of rising debt service and other non-development expenditures, states have also recorded increasing revenue deficits in the 1990s. This has had serious consequences for their ability to sustain plan expenditure.

State finances have been undergoing significant deterioration particularly since the early 1980s. This has resulted in slowing growth in their plan expenditures relative to the Centre. This is

Table – 12

Profile of Total Revenue of State Government (1980-2000)

	1980-85	1985-90	1990-95	1995-99	1997-98	1998-99 (RE)
Percent of GDP						
(A) Revenue Receipts (I+II)	**11.5**	**12.8**	**12.8**	**12.3**	**12.5**	**12.3**
I Tax Revenue	7.6	8.5	8.5	8.6	8.8	8.9
– Revenue from State taxes	5.1	5.7	5.7	5.8	6.0	6.0
– Share in Central taxes	2.5	2.8	2.7	2.8	2.8	2.9
II Non-tax Revenue	3.9	4.3	4.4	3.7	3.7	3.4
(B) Capital Receipts	4.1	4.6	4.3	3.9	4.2	4.1
– Loans from Center	2.3	2.7	2.1	2.0	2.2	2.2
– Recovery of Loans	0.4	0.3	0.4	0.3	0.3	0.1
– Other Receipts	1.5	1.6	1.8	1.6	1.7	1.8
Total Revenue (A+B)	**15.6**	**17.4**	**17.1**	**16.2**	**16.7**	**16.5**
Percent of Total Revenue						
(A) Revenue Receipts (I+II)	**73.7**	**73.6**	**75.0**	**75.9**	**74.9**	**74.8**
I Tax Revenue	48.6	48.8	49.5	53.2	52.9	54.1
– Revenue from State taxes	32.5	32.6	33.5	36.1	35.9	36.7
– Share in Central taxes	16.2	16.2	16.0	17.1	16.9	17.4
II Non-tax Revenue	25.1	24.8	25.5	22.7	22.0	20.7
(B) Capital Receipts	**26.3**	**26.4**	**25.0**	**24.1**	**25.1**	**25.2**
– Loans from Center	14.6	15.5	12.1	12.4	13.1	13.4
– Recovery of Loans	2.4	1.7	2.3	1.8	1.6	0.8
– Other Receipts	9.3	9.1	10.6	9.9	10.4	11.0
Total Revenue (A+B)	**100.0**	**100.0**	**100.0**	**100.0**	**100.0**	**100.0**

illustrated in Table 13, which shows the share of states in total plan outlays. Since the Second Five Year Plan the share of states had been relatively stable from the mid 1950s to the late 1970s at around half of total plan expenditures. This has since deteriorated to only about 40 per cent or less in the late 1990s. The consequence is that the ability of state governments to invest in both social and physical infrastructure has declined considerably, since sub national governments such as states are unable to indulge in deficit financing unlike the central government. Hence, whereas the states suffered slowing public investment through plan expenditures in the 1980s the central government was able to accelerate central plan expenditures which were financed by rising fiscal deficits, including deficit financing, right through the late 1980s.

Table – 13

Share of States in Plan Outlays (1951-2002)

Plan	Centre (Percent)	States (Percent)
First (1951-56)	36	64
Second (1956-61)	54	46
Third (1961-66)	49	51
Annual(1966-69)	51	49
Fourth(1969-74)	50	50
Fifth (1974-79)	48	52
Annual (1979-80)	46	54
Sixth (1980-85)	53	47
Seventh (1985-90)	59	41
Eighth (1992-97)	62	38
Ninth (1997-2002)	58	42

Notes: First Plan to Seventh Plan: Actuals Eighth Plan: Estimated Ninth Plan: Projected

Source: First Plan to Seventh Plan: Amaresh Bagchi and others (1992b) Eighth and Ninth Plan: Planning Commission (1998)

The existing planning system has essentially resulted in the central government acting as a giant financial intermediary, borrowing from the public in different ways to finance plan expenditures at both the central and state levels. In this system there is no connection between the viability of projects and their financing costs. Since the introduction of the Gadgil formula for bloc plan assistance to the states, which comprise of loans to the extent of 70 per cent regardless of the end use of expenditures, the nexus between resources for financing and end uses has been completely broken. Different Finance Commissions have remarked on the untenability of this system, which does not distinguish between financing of public goods and private goods by state governments. The consequence has been that returns from these investments have been consistently low.

In the existing system state governments borrow from the central government on the basis of the Planning Commission's Gadgil formula. Further, the volume of their market borrowings is governed by the central government, and the Reserve Bank of India borrows on their behalf at the same interest rate for all states. Thus their borrowings are not related in any way to their credit worthiness. Second their debt service payments, both to the central government and other institutional creditors are built into their budgets and are not at all related to the success or otherwise of the projects in which borrowed resources have been invested in. So far, all states have been able to keep up their debt servicing. But rising debt service payments have eroded their capacity to both maintain adequate levels of current expenditure and to make new investments. Since Finance Commission subventions are essentially formula based as well, there is little that it can do to address these problems. What is needed is some system of conditionalities to be embedded in both the Planning Commission and Finance Commission based fiscal devolution. If Finance Commission transfers to the states were increased, they would only result in higher fiscal deficits for the central government. The lack of connection between their fiscal health and ability to borrow or to receive subventions has encouraged states to be fiscally irresponsible and to subject user charges to populist considerations.

In principle, investments in public goods should result in higher tax revenues, whereas investment in private goods should result in higher revenues through the imposition of user charges for public services. This is true at the state government level also. The majority of public expenditures at the state level have gone into the financing of power generation, transmission and distribution through state electricity boards, the financing of state road transport corporations, the financing of urban development authorities for investing in urban infrastructure services, irrigation, housing and the like. Most of these activities (except irrigation) are carried out through public sector enterprises of different varieties. Irrigation is administered directly by government irrigation departments at the state level. If these enterprises had been able to impose appropriate economic pricing of their services they would have provided returns to state governments as dividends, and would have been able to service their direct debt fully. In fact, neither have they been able to provide appropriate dividends to state government's budgets nor have they been able to meet their own debt service payments to the state governments. They have also not been able to generate net positive internal resources for investment for expansion of their services.

This is illustrated in table 14, which shows the financing pattern of state plans for the Sixth, Seventh, and Eighth five year plans, and the first two years of the Ninth Plan. The contribution of the balance of current revenue (BCR) to the financing of state plans which was as high as 40 per cent of the total in the Sixth Five Year Plan, has now declined to less than zero during the Eighth Five Year Plan. Similarly the contribution of PSEs has been consistently negative through the whole period. Consequently, the share of borrowing by state governments has increased substantially from about 34 percent of total resources for the state plan during the Sixth Plan to more than 50 percent in the Eighth Plan (1992-97). Correspondingly the share of central assistance has also increased from 37 percent in the Sixth Plan to more than 50 percent plan in the Eighth Plan. The situation has taken a significant turn for the worse in the current Ninth Plan period. The Balance of Current Revenue is significantly negative and the states have begun borrowing to finance current expenditures in substantial amounts. Thus the current situation is that almost the entire plan expenditure are now being financed by borrowing of one kind or another. Within the pattern of borrowing itself the share of market borrowing has been increasing consistently and quite dramatically during the last few years.

That the overall worsening fiscal situation of state governments is relevant for the financing of investment expenditures is illustrated in Table 15. Capital outlays as a proportion of gross fiscal deficits have fallen from about 62 per cent in the late 1980s to less than 50 per cent now. Similarly revenue deficit has risen as a proportion of gross fiscal deficit from about 7.7 per cent in the late 1980s to more than 35 per cent now. Consequently borrowing by state governments is now being devoted more and more to the financing of revenue expenditures rather than capital expenditures. This can only lead to further worsening of the fiscal situation in coming years. The resources available for investment will decline continuously in the foreseeable future unless there is a change in the system.

Table – 14

Financing Pattern of State Plans

Source	Sixth Plan[1] (1980-85) (1979-80 prices)		Seventh Plan[1] (1985-90) (1984-85 prices)		Eighth Plan[2] (1992-97) (1991-92 prices)		Ninth Plan[3] (1997-98) (Current prices)		Ninth Plan[3] 1998-99[4] (Current prices)	
	Rs.Crore	Per Cent Of Total	Rs.Crore	Per Cent Of Total	Rs.Crore	Per Cent Of Total	Rs.Crore	Per Cent Of Total	Rs.Crore	Per Cent Of Total
1. Balance from current Revenue	14826	41	17368	23	-2009	-1.4	-8703	-17.7	17360	-25
2. Contribution of PSEs	-4620	-13	-3757	-5	-2723	-1.9		NA		NA
3. Total Borrowings	12679	35	27644	37	75750	52	38350	78	61110	88
a) Net Borrowing	3406	9	9242	12						NA
b) Small savings	5901	16	19070	26		N.A				
c) Term loans from Fis	1887	5	4445	6						
d) Miscellaneous capital receipts	-2012	-6	-5113	-7						
e) Budget Deficit	3497	10	-							
I. Total State Resources	22885	63	41255	55	70335	48	29650	60	43750	63
II. Central Assistance	13690	37	33264	45	75750	52	19520	40	25695	37
III. Total Resources	36575	100	74519	100	146085	100	49172	100	69445	100

Note: 1 Actuals 2 Estimated 3 Anticipated Outlay 4 Approved Outlay

Source: Sixth and Seventh Plans: Amaresh Bagchi and Tapas Sen (1992) Eighth Plan: Planning Commission (1998)

Ninth Plan: N. J. Kurian. "State Government Finance: A Survey of Real Terms"

Table – 15

Selected Fiscal Ratios for State Governments (1985-98)

Year	Capital Outlay/ Gross Fiscal Deficit (Per Cent)	Interest Payments/ Revenue Expenditure (Per Cent)	Revenue Deficit/ Gross Fiscal Deficit (Per Cent)
1985-90	62.4	10.8	7.7
1990-95	55.3	13.6	24.6
1996-98	47.5	15.8	35.8

Source: Reserve Bank of India Bulletin February 1998. Supplement: Finances of State Governments.

The overall state averages exhibited above naturally mark the considerable differences between states. In general, the economically more advanced and better off states also exhibited more responsible fiscal behaviour in the past. This is no longer the case. The fiscal malaise has now spread across all the states. In the Annual Plan for 1998-99, the balance of current revenue (BCR) was negative for all major states except Karnataka. Borrowings of some states such as West Bengal exceed the total plan outlay. As many as 7 major states are now borrowing more than two thirds of plan outlay requirements.

Key Issues

The current system for the financing of investments by state governments in India is clearly unsustainable. The problem has essentially arisen because of the lack of a nexus between borrowing and end use of expenditures in capital investment. This is ironic since the existing system was designed to preserve the fiscal health of the state governments in India through appropriate control being exercised by the Central Government. The State Governments are not allowed to run deficit-financing activities and are therefore constrained from fiscal excess. The result however has been the opposite.

In view of the limits being placed on state government's borrowings and because of pressing demands for expenditures there has been a rising tendency by state governments to resort to public borrowings through public sector enterprises. There has been a rise in the issue of state government guarantees for their public sector entities enabling them to borrow directly from the market. Until recently, the issue of state government guarantees was adequate to enable their public sector entities to borrow successfully in the market. But with the rise in the volume of these guarantees lending institutions are now beginning to question the quality of these guarantees. There is also much greater demand by lenders that state governments subject themselves to credit ratings. Thus there is now a move to collate information on the volume of existing guarantees so that the existing liabilities of state governments can be made more transparent.

The problem that has been outlined above suggests that action have to be taken at both ends of the system. Expenditure on investments for the provision of private goods must be related more directly to the generation of returns through the levy of appropriate user charges. The problem at present is that because of the lack of nexus between borrowing ability and returns to the activity, the levy of user charges is essentially done politically. It may be expected that once the ability to raise resources is dependent on the financial health of the entities this will affect political thinking on the appropriate levy of user charges.

For the raising of resources for investments for the provision of public goods, it may be desirable to subject state governments systematically to credit ratings so that their ability to borrow depends on their fiscal health. It is possible that such a system which provides appropriate signals to policy makers might be more successful to ensure fiscal health of state governments in the future since the existing system has clearly failed in this objective. The possibilities of this alternative system are explored more fully in later section of this paper.

IV Key Issues for Achieving Higher Growth: Where Do We Go from Here?

We have therefore seen that the current fiscal situation of both the central and state governments is unsustainable and poses a grave threat to economic growth. Whereas there is widespread recognition that all is not well with the fisc, the gravity of the situation has not received adequate appreciation. The combined fiscal deficit of the centre and states amounts to almost 10 percent of GDP (See table 16). In other words, the governments of the centre and the states combined are borrowing resources amounting to a tenth of national income every year: about a half of these resources are being borrowed to defray current expenditures on items such as wages and salaries. The current trend is such that before long almost all borrowing will essentially finance current expenditure leaving almost nothing for investment. With declining public investment the current pace of increased private investment will also not be sustained. The consequence will be slowing of economic growth which will itself lead to a further worsening of the fiscal predicament.

Table – 16

Centre and State Deficits (1980-2000)
(Percent of GDP)

	1980-85	1985-90	1990-95	1995-99	1997-98	1998-99 (RE)	1999-00 (BE)
Centre							
- Fiscal Deficit	6.3	8.2	6.7	5.8	6.3	6.5	5.8
- Revenue Deficit	1.1	2.6	3.2	3.1	3.3	3.7	3.0
States					**1997-98 (RE)**	**1998-99(BE)**	
- Fiscal Deficit	2.9	3.1	3.0	3.2	3.6	3.7	NA
- Revenue Deficit	-0.4	0.3	0.7	1.3	1.4	1.6	NA

Note: Not comparable with other years because of change in investment in small savings.

Some clue to the possible consequences of such fiscal irresponsibility was provided by the Brazilian crisis of 1998 when one of the Brazilian states defaulted on its obligations to the Brazilian federal government. The credit rating of Brazil plummeted, its currency had to be devalued and immediate action had to be taken to make appropriate policy corrections. Technically, some Indian states have already defaulted to the Centre, with the Centre having to make adjustments of different kinds to avert an actual default. At the central level, if the fiscal deficit is not brought under control, excessive central borrowing will lead to further hardening of interest rates, which in turn affect private investment rates, leading to slower industrial and overall economic growth. The external balance of the country has been under reasonable control: external debt has been kept under strict watch since 1991; and foreign currency reserves are more than adequate for any feasible contingency for the present. Yet, the international rating agencies downgraded India's rating last year. The reason for this action related to their concerns about the fiscal situation of the Centre and the states. Thus the serious fiscal situation has not escaped the eye of international analysts. As noted at the outset, the key objective of economic policy should be the enhancement of India's growth process. One projection for China's growth prospects suggests that if Chinese per capita income grows by about 4.5 percent annually (as compared with 6 percent over the past 20 years or so) Chinese national income will exceed that of the United States by 2015. If India's per capita income grows at 3.5 percent annually over the same period its national income will then amount to only about 40 percent that of China, a proportion not too different from that of today. Thus policy action must be taken to accelerate Indian economic growth to at least 6 percent per capita annual income growth. This cannot be achieved unless a significant fiscal correction is successfully implemented.

Higher economic growth requires concerted action on all fronts. Major improvements have to be made in the provision of public health services, education, nutrition and the like. In the areas of physical infrastructure, large investments have to be made in areas such as roads (from rural roads to national highways), railways, ports, power, telecommunications, civil aviation, urban infrastructure, irrigation and the like. Whereas in areas such as power, telecommunications, ports, and civil aviation, private investment can form a significant proportion of the needed investment, in other areas it is the state that will continue to play a dominant role. Even in the areas where private investment is relatively easy, public investment has to continue. As the economy grows and industrializes urbanization will also grow apace. A critical area for increased investment is in urban infrastructure: water supply, sewerage, sanitation, roads, and transportation. All of these are difficult areas of investment and large amounts of resources will be required for these purposes. The lack of these basic facilities in our towns and cities gives rise to high degrees of anomie and alienation leading to social unrest. This in turn necessitates higher expenditures on internal security. Thus a renewal of public investment in a wide variety of areas in the social and physical infrastructure field is essential for higher economic growth and sustained national security.

What is to be done? The key objective of fiscal reform has to be a reduction in debt service payments. This has to be achieved by a progressive reduction in public debt and through higher revenues. The possibility of achieving higher revenues through increased rates of taxes is both undesirable and infeasible. Higher tax revenues can be achieved only through buoyancy and expansion of the tax base. Thus the main instruments for achieving a sustained increase in overall revenues are (i) Expansion of the tax base; (ii) widespread and bold imposition of user charges on all non-merit goods and (iii) widespread and bold privatisation.

Expansion of the Tax Base

As has been documented above, the 1990s has witnessed a fall in the collection of indirect taxes when expressed as a proportion of GDP. With the opening up of the economy leading to large reductions in customs tariffs, tax collected from custom duties were expected to decline and it will fall further in the years to come as these tariffs are brought down further. Buoyancy in indirect taxes can therefore only be achieved through increase in excise tax collections at the central level. The structural problem that exists in this regard is the constitutional provision which assigns excise tax to the central government and sales tax to state governments. As the share of agriculture falls with overall development there should be an increase in revenue since agriculture is largely untaxed. In fact the share of agriculture in GDP has fallen from about 40 per cent in 1980-81 to about 26 per cent now. Correspondingly the share of the secondary sector increased from about 24 per cent to about 28 per cent and that of services from 36 per cent to about 45 per cent. The long term scenario is that the share of agriculture will continue to fall and that of services in particular will continue to rise.

Hence for tax revenues to increase as a share of GDP the imposition of indirect taxes on the service sector is imperative. This can essentially be achieved by the imposition of a widespread value added tax on all sectors of the economy. This would mean the levy of tax at every stage of value addition from production to sale of both goods and services. Levying such a tax will require an amendment of the constitution along with the achievement of consensus with the states so that it becomes feasible to do so. Thus long term buoyancy in indirect tax revenues can be achieved only if this major structural change can be brought about.

Importance of User Charges

A good deal of public sector investment is in the provision of public services. The pattern and organisation of the provision of such infrastructure services has been done in such a way that the public has got used to not paying economic charges for these services. This includes key services such as power, water supply, irrigation, and transport, among others. The Finance Ministry has calculated that hidden subsidies on non-merit goods amount to as much as 10.7 per cent of GDP on an annual basis. It is no wonder that the combined fiscal deficit of the centre and the states amounts to almost 10 per cent of GDP. In the case of power alone the losses resulting from lower than economic pricing to the agriculture and domestic sectors amount to almost Rs 25,000 crore a year. It is primarily the absence of appropriate pricing of public services that has caused the large fiscal imbalance that afflicts the country. As the data showed, government wages and salaries are not the key cause of excess government expenditures. Whereas downsizing of government may be desirable for other reasons, the gains in expenditure reduction will be small on a proportionate basis.

Public investments made in the last fifty years have imposed an increasing burden on the budget rather than providing returns in the form of non-tax revenues through dividend payments to the government. The public has got used to not paying adequately for these services for two reasons. It is perceived that the services are provided by the government and therefore do not have to be paid for. Second, with the quality of service being poor, the public is loath to pay higher charges. This is a vicious circle, which needs to be broken. The imposition of higher user charges has to be accompanied by palpable improvements in the quality of service. The attainment of higher efficiency in the provision of service can, progressively, lead to lower charges.

It is only if government receives returns from the investments it makes, which are financed from borrowing, can fiscal health be restored. The argument for not charging appropriate user charges has essentially been based on equity considerations. It is argued that the poor are not able to pay adequately for these essential public services. This argument has little basis in actual practice, since the better off sections of the society essentially consume most such services. For example, at least 60 percent of rural households and about 20 percent of urban households do not have a power connection; only 60 percent of urban households have taps within their homes, even fewer have in-house latrines. Most infrastructure subsidies are therefore not going to the poor. Thus it should be possible to levy appropriate charges without affecting the welfare of the poor: in fact, if the better off are made to pay it would then become possible to provide essential services for the poor.

The fiscal health of both the central and state governments can improve dramatically over, say, a five-year period if this correction is made. It is only then that they would be able to invest adequately for the provision of social and physical infrastructure that is so essential for social justice, economic growth and economic security. But this reform cannot be done by mere announcement. It needs research, public awareness, public education and persuasion. The central government must lead this campaign and forge understanding and consensus with state governments, who must do the same with local bodies. At the same time, acceptability of higher charges for such services will not be feasible unless there is greater efficiency in the delivery of these services. This requires widespread reform in the public sector.

Increase in user charges will only benefit the budget progressively in the future. This will involve great process change and will take some time to yield fruit. The government has to examine each infrastructure sector closely and programme the gradual imposition of economic pricing in each sector. The appointment of autonomous regulatory authorities can help in depoliticising the process. But this process will be successful if the regulatory authorities are made autonomous by statute and the bureaucracy and political authorities learn to respect this autonomy. Some regulatory authorities have already been formed and may be expected to lead this process. They must be strengthened professionally and allowed to function independently. The campaign must be time bound: we cannot afford more than five years to restore fiscal health in the country. In the interim, resources have to be found by retiring debt. These resources must be found from privatisation.

Privatisation

The retirement of public debt requires generation of large volume of capital resources. The main source for such resources can be the proceeds from a programme of bold and widespread privatisation at both the central and state levels. Time is now ripe for shedding old shibboleths and proclaiming a clear position on privatisation of all but strategic public sector enterprises. Such a programme must be distinguished from the disinvestment programme which has been sporadic, half hearted and poorly administered. I believe that this has mostly been due to lack of clarity in the objectives of disinvestment.

Jawaharlal Nehru's idea of the public sector was very different from the way it has evolved through the years. Nehru's conception for the public sector was for attaining the commanding heights of the economy and not its commanding depths. Private sector enterprises were then seen to be inefficient and public sector enterprises were expected to induce a greater degree of efficiency in the economy. The assumption was that the efficient public sector would be instrumental in the generation of large surpluses. The record has been the opposite. However, we must recognise that public sector enterprises do dominate key sectors of the economy in the infrastructure and heavy industry areas. It is all the more necessary for the economy that these enterprises become more efficient.

The achievement of higher investment and consequent higher growth in both public and private sector companies will require a more widespread pattern of share holding. The government does not have the resources to invest in the magnitude required to enable the existing public enterprises to grow faster. With the opening of trade, the de reservation of areas reserved earlier for public enterprises, and the liberal introduction of foreign investment, public sector enterprises are now faced with intense competition of the kind which they have not faced before. The restrictions implied by government ownership are inconsistent with the kind of freedom required for flexible operation in a free and competitive framework. We must now explicitly accept that the kind of freedom envisaged for successful enterprises is practically not feasible within our framework as long as government share holding remains greater than 50 per cent, and the enterprise is classified a public sector enterprise.

A clear position must be articulated to privatise existing public sector enterprise except those that may be regarded as strategic. This action is not only necessary for generating resources for retiring public debt but is also necessary for the long term health of the enterprises generating themselves. We must adopt a new approach to public sector enterprises which recognises that privatising them would be the best way of making sure that the core of Indian industry grows, remains competitive and is enabled to compete internationally. These are the enterprises which may have the potential of becoming Indian multinationals in the future. They are indeed the industrial enterprises in the country which have potentially the highest technological competence and which can indeed hold their own against the new competition but to do this they must be freed from the shackles of government controls.

It is now clear that the procedure adopted for disinvestment has not been successful. The objectives of disinvestment have not been clear; the procedure has been too bureaucratic and time consuming; and the targets for disinvestment have seldom been achieved. Bold privatisation cannot be done in a business as usual manner.

Such a bold approach is clearly not easy. The government must first clarify the objectives of the process of privatisation and seek to forge a consensus. The objectives must be both the strengthening of these enterprises to enable them to compete and grow, and to contribute to the restoration of fiscal health of the country. Once again, this cannot be done by announcement and requires process change at the political and bureaucratic level alike. But there is now no time to lose and the problem has to be attacked headlong.

The returns from privatisation must not be used for current expenditures. They should be explicitly used for retiring public debt so that the interest burden is progressively reduced. Privatisation will bring back to public coffers the fruits from past public investments. How do we ensure that future public investments provide adequate return to the government so that it can retain fiscal health on a sustainable basis? I believe that the whole system of public investment through the plan process needs reexamination. The existing process induces lack of accountability at every level. The decisions to invest are too remote from the point of investment. The central government acts a giant financial intermediary, borrows resources from the public and the allocates them on the basis of certain conventions and formulise to state governments and other entities. State governments in turn pass on these resources to state government organisations. The receipt of such resources is not dependent on performance and their ability to pay back appropriate returns for the funds received. This system is no longer sustainable and needs a new approach.

Ensuring long term economic health of the nation requires acceleration of economic growth on a sustained basis. I have argued that the main impediment constraining India's growth in the future is the continuing fall in public investment in infrastructure which has been caused by the deteriorating fiscal environment at both the central and state government levels. Apart from ensuring higher buoyancy in tax revenues, the key solutions to India's fiscal predicament are bold programmes for improving user charges for all public services amenable to such charges, and the implementation of a crash programme of privatisation. In the absence of such urgent action, the already serious fiscal situation will get worse and will pose a serious threat to economic security in the very near future.

With permission from the author; Economic and Political Weekly, June 10-16, 2000.

7

Economic Reforms: Some Issues and Concerns for the 21st Century

C. RANGARAJAN

It is a decade since economic reforms were introduced in India and this is an appropriate time to look back at the road we have travelled and chart out what the future course of action should be. Let me, therefore, in this light make a few comments on the impact of economic reforms and the emerging areas of concern.

In the post Independent economic history, 1991 is an important landmark year. The country went through a severe economic crisis triggered by a serious balance of payments situation. The crisis was converted into an opportunity to introduce some fundamental changes in the content and approach to economic policy. The response to the crisis was to put in place a set of policies aimed at stabilization and structural reform. While the stabilisation policies were aimed at correcting the weaknesses that had developed on the fiscal and the balance of payments fronts, the structural reforms sought to remove the rigidities that had entered into the various segments of the Indian economy. The structural reforms introduced in the early Nineties broadly covered the areas of fiscal policy, industrial licensing, foreign trade, foreign investment, exchange rate management and the financial sector. Since then it has been extended to other areas.

In the 1950s and 1960s, the dominant view in the literature on development economics was that the Government had an important role to play and that it should undertake activities that would compensate for "market failure". "Market failure" was perceived particularly in the inability of markets to optimally allocate resources over time, that is, for investment because of the "myopic" nature of market participants. The literature also emphasised the benefit of a co-ordinated and consistent set of investment decisions. However, four decades of development experience have shown that there can be both "Government failure" and "market failure" and that the critical issue is not so much the presence or absence of State intervention, as the extent and quality of that intervention. The new economic policy builds on this experience.

There is a common thread running through all the measures introduced since July 1991. The objective is simply to improve the efficiency of the system. This is to be achieved by removing the barriers to entry and the restrictions on growth of firms. While the industrial policy seeks to bring about a greater competitive environment domestically, the trade policy seeks to improve international competitiveness subject to the protection offered by tariffs. The private sector is being given a larger space to operate, as some of the areas earlier reserved exclusively for the public sector are also now allowed to the private sector. There is, however, nothing in the new economic policy which takes away the role of the State or the public sector in the system. The New Economic Policy of India has not necessarily diminished the role of state; it has only redefined it, expanding it in some areas and reducing in some others. As it has been said, somewhat paradoxically 'more market' does not mean 'less Government', but only 'different Government'.

Post Reform Performance

The performance of the Indian economy in the post-reform period has been extensively commented upon. Judged by the standard criteria of growth rates of national income and per capita income, external balance and inflation rate, the Indian economy has done well since liberalisation. The year 1991-92 was an exceptionally bad year for reasons well known. Indeed, there is no justification to include that year as part of the post-reform period, particularly while judging the effectiveness of the reform process. On the contrary, there is a justification to include 1991-92 as part of the pre-reform period. If we leave out 1991-92, between 1992-93 and 1999-2000, the average annual growth rate comes to 6.3 per cent. Even if we include 1991-92 the annual growth rate in the Nineties will be 5.8 per cent. Inflation rate as measured by the Wholesale Price Index though high in the early Nineties started declining from 1995-96 and the average inflation rate has been around five per cent since then. The current account deficit after reaching the high of 3.1 per cent of GDP in 1990-91 has been steadily declining during the Nineties and has been around one per cent of the GDP in the last few years. With the current account deficit remaining low and with continued capital inflows, it has been possible to add to the foreign exchange reserves. These reserves have increased from $ 5.8 billion in 1990-91 to $ 38.0 billion by March, 2000. They have subsequently increased by $ 10 billion. The macro economic indicators do show a distinct improvement in the performance as compared with the previous periods. However, even in relation to the growth rate a disturbing trend is that there has been a distinct slowing since 1997-98. While the growth rate between 1992-93 and 1996-97 was 6.5 per cent, in the subsequent four years the growth rate has been 5.8 per cent. The growth rate in the current year is not likely to be higher than this average.

The liberalisation process has come in for criticism from two opposite ends. First, there are those who feel that the process has been slow and not sufficiently comprehensive. These critics attribute the current slow down in the growth rate to this factor. On the other hand, there are critics who view the reform process as misconceived, ignoring the basic realities of our country. There are four aspects of these criticisms, which deserve attention.

A major criticism made against liberalisation process is that the higher growth rate achieved has made no dent on poverty and unemployment. While some earlier data pointed towards an increase in the poverty ratio since 1993-94, more recent data available on consumer expenditure for 1999-2000 do show a decline in poverty ratio. While there are some criticisms regarding the methodology followed in the latest National Sample Survey on consumer expenditure, it is, nevertheless, true that the poverty ratio has come down which is corroborated by the data available from other surveys. However, the decline in the employment growth rate is very perceptible which has led to the comment that the growth rate that we have achieved in the recent years is job less growth. The Nineties have seen a substantial slowdown in agriculture. This has implications for the strategy of growth to be adopted in the coming decades. The second criticism is that the reduction in the fiscal deficit has been brought about by reducing capital expenditures of the Government. This is very much true. However, there is not the required will to bring down the revenue expenditures. Also part of the answer lies in raising the revenue to GDP ratio which has remained stubbornly at the same level as in the pre-reform period. The third area of concern is that enough attention is not being paid to social infrastructure areas. While admitting that this is the fact, it has to be noted that this fault does not stem from liberalisation. The roots go much deeper. The fourth area of concern has been the growing disparities in income among states. The populous states have grown weakly in the last decade and this has been also one of the reasons for the increase in the people below the poverty line. If the regional disparities have grown, it is at least in part a reflection of the quality of governance.

As one surveys the period since 1991-92, it is clear that the economy has shown distinct improvement in several areas. The broad philosophy of promoting a competitive environment must be pursued. At the same time, if the growth momentum is to be maintained, some areas need focussed attention. First, mention was made earlier of the problems arising from the slowdown in agriculture. A comprehensive agricultural policy encompassing a higher level of public investment, a shift from revenue expenditures to investment, consolidation of holdings, a proactive programme to foster exports, intensified agricultural research to raise yields and evolving a better cropping pattern needs to be thought of. Growth in agriculture has several implications for the economy. It leads to a reduction in poverty, a greater expansion in employment and a more broad based growth.

Second, an important constraint over growth can be infrastructure availability. Future infrastructural investment needs are expected to be large, because of the demand created by economic growth, rising population, rapid urbanisation as well as the need to make up for the backlog.

The financing requirements of infrastructure as a whole are massive. For this massive magnitude of investment to materialise, a definitive, transparent and concrete policy framework should be put in place. Such a framework should focus on increased commercialisation of infrastructure services, appropriate legal, regulatory and administrative frameworks to support both foreign and domestic private sector involvement, and introducing new and innovative financial products for infrastructure funding. In order to achieve the desired levels of investments, both public and private, in the infrastructure sectors, it is essential that the issues of appropriate pricing and cost recovery be tackled at the earliest with transparent and explicit subsidisation where needed. This in turn will require the establishment of statutory and regulatory authorities for ensuring fair competition among public and private operators, and protecting consumer interests, public safety, and environmental concerns.

There has also to be a significant increase in investment in social infrastructure. Education and health must receive priority attention. The universal primary education is a goal which is still to be achieved. In fact, the very purpose of liberalisation is to reduce the role of the state as an entrepreneur and direct investor and expand its role in areas such as social infrastructure, where state alone can play a dominant role. It is also to be noted that better education and health are a function of not only levels of expenditures but also the efficiency with which such expenditures are incurred.

The public sector will continue to dominate the economy in several important sectors. Even as attempts are being made to disinvest wherever feasible, there is no doubt that we must pay adequate attention to improving the functioning of public sector enterprises where their presence is essential. Many Committees and Commissions have studied these problems. It is high time that a policy package is put together and implemented for bringing about a significant improvement in the efficiency of public sector enterprises.

Fiscal consolidation is a necessary prerequisite for sustained growth. The finances of the State Governments are particularly under greater pressure. The appropriate level of fiscal deficit has a relationship to the level of household savings and more particularly to the savings in financial assets. Even as of now, very nearly the whole of the household savings in financial assets is appropriated by the public sector. There is validity in the argument that Government expenditures should shift in favour of capital expenditures. Unfortunately, the trend has been in the opposite direction. Containing the growth rate of revenue expenditures has become essential. In a developing economy like India, where a significant proportion of people remains poor, subsidies are an essential component of Government expenditures. However, they need to be targeted appropriately, so that they accrue only to the deserving. We must make an effort to evolve a consensus on how to deal with subsidies, user charges and reducing revenue expenditures. This is indeed the task of the political managers of the economy. With different parties in power in different States, it should be possible to achieve a degree of consensus on this issue of fiscal prudence.

Clearly the lesson of Indian development experience is that monopolies, whether of state or private sector, do not lead to efficiency. The need to create, promote and sustain a competitive environment is absolutely essential. However, even as we do create conditions for more effective functioning of the enterprises, some of the issues discussed earlier, such as emphasis on agriculture, social and physical infrastructure development, public sector reforms and fiscal consolidation need special attention. Both in the short and medium terms, the key to accelerating India's growth lies in raising the investment rate. Enhanced investments must occur both in the public and private sectors. In the short-term, public investment with high domestic demand component such as housing and roads may spur economic growth.

Future Challenges

Indian economy which was caught in the trap of a low growth rate of 3.5 per cent for nearly four decades broke out of it in the Eighties and moved on to a higher growth path. The economy needs to set before itself a minimum growth rate for the coming decades. One way of addressing this question is to focus on a growth rate which will enable the economy to absorb in productive employment the increase in labour force and also clear the backlog of unemployment. Studies show that the employment elasticity of output has been coming down. The decline in employment elasticity is to some extent offset by a slower increase in the labour force. The growth in employment is not simply related to the growth in output. The composition of output has also a significant effect. However, taking into account a certain pattern of the composition of output, it has been estimated that it will be safe to assume an employment elasticity of 0.22 for the coming decades. On this assumption, it is seen that a growth rate of seven per cent over the next 15 years will ensure that at the terminal year of 2015, unemployment will be eliminated. This is also based on the assumption that the labour force will be increasing at a rate a little lower than 1.5 per cent per annum. This gives us a rough picture of what needs to be achieved in the next 15 years. However, even for achieving a seven per cent growth rate in a sustained way, the investment rate of the economy has to move to 28 per cent of the GDP as against current rate of 23 per cent of GDP. If it is assumed that 2.0 per cent of the GDP is the appropriate level of the current account deficit consistent with the maintenance of external balance, this will require that the domestic savings rate must increase from the current level of 22 per cent to 26 per cent. Thus, achieving even a seven per cent growth rate calls for a determined effort. In fact, we need initially to stabilise the growth rate at six per cent and then move on to raising to higher levels so that at least on an average, over the next 15 year period, we will achieve a growth rate of seven per cent.

As the world moves into *the new century and the new millennium*, a country like India with continental dimensions has to reckon with changes that are occurring in the rest of the world. The new millennium is being looked forward to with great hopes and expectations and also with some trepidation. How will this new millennium be different? What are the challenges and opportunities for which we should be prepared? It is difficult to forecast what the future is going to be. Nevertheless, we can perceive three strongly emerging trends. First, technological changes are going to be even faster. It will be no exaggeration to say that the new millennium will be characterised by some fundamental changes in technology. Second, the new millennium will see greater integration of the economies. The process of globalization will gather further momentum. And third, the wave of rising expectations will surge even further. All countries will become aware of the changes happening all over the world and the developing economies will naturally demand that their aspirations are met. Not only different countries but also different segments within a country will demand that their rights are fully respected.

Associated with rapid changes in technology will be the acceleration of globalization. But globalization, in one sense, is not a new phenomenon. It is as old as history, starting with the great migrations of people across the great landmasses. Only recent developments in computer and communication technologies have accelerated the process of integration, with geographic distance becoming less of a factor. Is this 'end of geography' a boon or a bane? Borders have become porous and the sky is open. With modern technologies which do not recognise geography, it is not possible to hold back ideas either in the political and economic or in the cultural spheres. Each country must prepare itself to meet the new challenges so that it is not bypassed by this huge wave of technological and institutional changes.

What should be India's attitude in this environment of growing globalization? At the outset it must be mentioned that opting out of globalization is not a viable choice. We need to stay and fight. What is needed is to evolve an appropriate framework to wrest maximum benefits out of international trade and investment. This framework should include (a) making explicit the list of demands that India would like to make on the multilateral trade system, (b) measures that rich countries should be required to undertake to enable developing countries to gain more from international trade and (c) steps that India should take to realise the full potential from globalization.

Nothing is an unmixed blessing. Globalization in its present form though spurred by far reaching technological changes is not a pure technological phenomenon. It has many dimensions including ideological. To deal with this phenomenon, we must understand the gains and losses, the benefits as well as dangers. To be forewarned, as the saying goes, is to be forearmed. But we should not throw the baby with bath water. We should also resist the temptation to blame globalization for all our failures. Most often, as the poet said, the fault is in ourselves.

Risks of an open economy are well known. We must not, nevertheless, miss the opportunities that the global system can offer. As an eminent critic put it, the world cannot marginalise India. But India, if it chooses, can marginalise itself. We must guard ourselves against this danger. More than many other developing countries, India is in a position to wrest significant gains from globalization. However, we must voice our concerns and in cooperation with other developing countries modify the international trading arrangements to take care of the special needs of such countries. At the same time, we must identify and strengthen our comparative advantages. It is this two-fold approach which will enable us to meet the challenges of globalization which may be the defining characteristic of the new millennium.

What is the model of economic growth that is appropriate for India? Development has many dimensions. Economic growth is only one aspect. Nevertheless, accelerated economic growth is a necessary condition for achieving many other dimensions of development. Development must ensure equality of opportunities for all. However, equality of opportunities does not necessarily guarantee equalities in incomes. With some people being good at converting opportunities into income and others not being so, different individuals will end up with different levels of income. That is why it is necessary to assure every one a minimum level of living along with equality of opportunities. Every citizen must have his basic needs met. These basic needs include access to services such as education, health care and shelter. Without sacrificing these goals, the economy must remain efficient. It is only an efficient economy that can generate the surplus necessary to meet the socio-economic goals. We need, therefore, to stress simultaneously economic development in the conventional sense of accelerating growth rate and social development in the sense of securing for every one the basic needs. The two have a mutually interacting beneficial impact and the two must be pursued together.

Any strategy of development which ignores any one of the two legs will be unsustainable. Efficiency and equity should not be posed as opposing considerations. They must be weaved together to produce a coherent pattern of growth.

Lecture delivered at the 84th Annual Conference of the Indian Economic Association, Vellore, December 28, 2001.

8

Structural Transformation of the Indian Economy in the Last Decade of the 20th Century and Future Prospects

UMA KAPILA

There has been a marked structural transformation of the Indian economy in the 'nineties' vis-a-vis that of the 'eighties'. The intersectoral composition of GDP underwent a significant change after the initiation of the reform process in 1991. The services sector has come to occupy a place of prominence in terms of relative contribution to GDP. The higher contribution of the services sector to GDP has a number of implications for the economy, the most important being the increased resilience of the economy.

The relative share of the 'agriculture and allied activities' in GDP during the period 1990-91 to 2000-01 declined to 28.6 per cent from 36.4 per cent during the period 1980-81 to 1989-90. On the other hand, the share of industry increased from 25 per cent to 27.1 per cent and that of the services sector (including construction) moved up substantially from 38.6 per cent to 44.3 per cent in the same period.

As per the New Series of National Accounts (base 1993-94), the services sector accounted for as much as 50.1 per cent of GDP during 1993-94 to 1998-99.

The RBI report on Currency and Finance (2000-01) states, the compositional shift in favour of services has been brought about by accelerated expansion in the services sector output at a rate of 7.6 per cent in the period 1990-91 to 2000-01 compared with 6.6 per cent during 1980-81 to 1989-90. While the growing contribution of the services sector to GDP is in line with the development experiences of a number of countries of the world, it is, however, not yet clear whether it is the comparative advantage that is driving up the share of the services sector in GDP or whether the sector also derives strength from the policies that are being pursued since the early 'nineties.

There has been a relative deceleration in the performance of agriculture during the 'nineties despite favourable monsoons, increase in net irrigated area and positive terms of trade. The decline in public investment and the limited infusion of new technologies may have contributed to the poor performance of agriculture.

However, Indian economy attained and maintained a high GDP growth in the 'nineties despite substantial deceleration in agricultural growth. For example in 1995-96 when the economy achieved a record 8.6 per cent growth in GDP, the agricultural sector witnessed a negligible 0.2 per cent growth over the previous year. In fact, as the RBI report on Currency and Finance states, "the recent years' experience shows that the growth of services sector has imparted much of resilience to the economy particularly in times of adverse agricultural shocks."

Thus, economic growth is becoming less vulnerable to agricultural performance and to vagaries of the monsoon. While the improvement in growth has emerged from both the industrial and services sectors, there is a marked difference in the sectoral composition of growth as between these two major sectors. Within the industrial sector, the major impetus to growth has come from manufacturing, while both 'mining and quarrying', and 'electricity, gas and water supply' registered lower rates of growth. The services sector, on the other hand, experienced higher growth in a more uniform and consistent manner with sectors like 'trade, hotels, restaurants, storage and communication', whereas 'financing, insurance, real estate, and business services' are experiencing high trend growth rates. A possible interpretation of this phenomenon could be an upsurge of industry-related services sector in recent years.

The phenomenal expansion of services world-wide led to services being regarded as an engine of the growth and even as a necessary concomitant of economic growth. Development economics suggest that development is a three-stage process. The dominance of the services sector in the growth process is usually associated with the third stage of growth. During the 1980s and 1990s, services accounted for a share of close to or above 70 per cent of GDP in industrialised countries and about 50 per cent in developing countries. In India, services accounted for 38.6 per cent of the GDP in the 1980s and 44.3 per cent in the 1990s.

The Evidence

The weighted contribution of the services sector to GDP growth has been rising since the 1960s except during the 1980s when industry and agriculture recorded substantial acceleration, which led to erosion in their contribution to GDP growth. However, a resurgence of services in the 1990s with a growth of 7.6 per cent enabled services sector to contribute 57.6 per cent to GDP growth.

A notable feature of the structural transformation of the services sector has been the growth of skill intensive and high value added sectors, i.e., software, communication and financial services. The rapid growth of services can be attributed to the advent of information technology (IT) and the knowledge economy. This has enhanced the growth of the high productivity segment of the services sector as well as a variety of service activities involving low productivity activities catering to a large mass of people. The phenomenal growth of low skilled service activities has occurred due to reduced opportunities in the manufacturing sector, particularly in the unorganised sectors.

Trade, hotels, restaurants and transport and communication are the major segments in terms of their share within the services sector; however, their share in the value added in the services sector has remained constant at around 49 per cent during the 1970s and 1980s, before marginally declining in 1990s. The share of finance, insurance, real estate and business services witnessed significant improvement during the 1990s on account of the rapid

Table – 1

Sector-wise Average Shares, Growth Rates and Contribution to GDP Growth

(Per cent)

Period	Services			Industry#			Agriculture		
	Share in GDP	Growth Rate	Contri-bution to GDP Growth	Share in GDP	Growth Rate	Contri-bution to GDP Growth	Share in GDP	Growth Rate	Contri-bution to GDP Growth
1	2	3	4	5	6	7	8	9	10
1950-51 to 1959-60*	28.2	4.1	32.2	16.0	5.7	25.3	56.0	2.3	42.5
1960-61 to 1969-70	31.4	4.9	38.1	21.1	6.5	32.9	47.8	2.5	29.2
1970-71 to 1979-80	34.4	4.5	52.7	22.8	3.7	28.7	42.8	1.3	18.6
1980-81 to 1989-90	38.6	6.6	43.6	25.0	6.8	28.9	36.4	4.4	27.5
1990-91 to 2000-01	44.3	7.6	57.6	27.1	5.9	27.6	28.6	2.9	14.8

\# Inclusive of construction

* 9 year data for growth and weighted contribution since data for 1949-50 are not available. Due to rounding off, sectoral data may not add up to 100.

Source : National Accounts Statistics, CSO.

pace of financial development (Table 2). The buoyancy in the services sector output is concentrated in the new economy sectors such as computer software and financial and business services. In the national income accounts, the contribution of the software industry in the real GDP is estimated at 0.78 per cent in 1999-2000. If raw materials in this sector are accounted for, contribution of the software sector (net of inputs) to GDP stands at about one per cent as per the estimates of the NASSCOM and the CMIE.

Table – 2

Average Share of Sub-sectors in Services Value-added (at constant prices)

(Per cent)

Period	Trade, Hotels, Transport and Communication	Finance, Insurance, Real estate and Business services	Social and Personal services
1	2	3	4
1950-51 to 1959-60	44.3	23.0	32.8
1960-61 to 1969-70	48.2	19.5	32.3
1970-71 to 1979-80	49.1	18.4	32.5
1980-81 to 1989-90	48.7	20.4	30.9
1990-91 to 2000-01	46.3	26.1	27.1

Some of the activities in the services sector are multidimensional, being part of industry as well as services, such as information technology and construction. Service statistics in most countries including India provide information on value-addition of various activities of business services, hotels, trade, financial services, etc. For an empirical analysis, sub-sectors including trade, transport and communication, financing, insurance, real estate and business services can be categorised as producer services with hotels and restaurants and other services as consumer services. Government services comprise public administration and defence services. During 1999-2000, producer services accounted for about 70 per cent of the total services followed by consumer services (17 per cent) and government services (13 per cent). The high share of producer services reflects the strong inter-linkages between services and goods producing sectors of the economy.

Income Elasticity of Demand for Services

A rising share of services in GDP is regarded as an outcome of higher income elasticity of demand for services. The empirical studies have shown that the income elasticity of demand for services could be greater than or equal to unity. Income elasticity of demand for services increases with rising income which favours the fulfillment of more sophisticated desires.

The empirical estimates of price and income elasticity for various categories of services in India are summarised in Table-3. It is important to mention that the actual behaviour of the services sector in real GDP depends on the relative strength of the coefficients of income and price elasticity.

Table – 3

Income and Price Elasticities for the Services Sector

Sector	Income Elasticity	Price Elasticity
1	2	3
Services	1.20*	-0.68*
1. Producer Services	1.22*	-0.78*
2. Consumer Services	1.00*	-0.10
3. Government Services	1.41*	-1.05*

* Statistically significant at 1 per cent.

The income elasticity of demand is greater than unity and price elasticity is negative and significant for the total services, producer services and government services. In other words, demand for overall services rises with increase in per capita GDP and decreases with increase in prices of services. The higher income elasticity of demand in the case of producer services underscores its forward linkages. This is corroborated by the emergence of producer services comprising advertising, publicity, marketing and other IT-related activities in the recent period as important service industries in India. Therefore, producer services can be regarded as a major source of economic growth.

Services, Employment and Productivity

The level of employment in services is strongly correlated with the stage of economic development; while agricultural and manufacturing activities account for a major share of employment in developing countries, services activities account for a major portion of employment in most developed countries.

In India, the services sector accounted for 18.1 per cent of the total employment during 1965-66, going up to 23.5 per cent in 1999-2000. Generally a substantial increase in the share of services in employment in most countries could imply a growth of low productive, low income, informal sector (Bhaduri, 1996). However, the increase in earnings per worker in the services sector compared with the industry could mean that at least part of the increase in employment in the services sector is in the formal, perhaps public sector, or in the new IT-related industries with higher use of capital per worker (Table 4).

Table – 4

Share of Services Sector in Total Employment

Period	Employment in Services Sector (in crore)	Total Employment (in crore)	Share of Services in total Employment (%)
1	2	3	4
1965-66	3.97	21.93	18.1
1970-71	4.82	24.09	20.0
1980-81	5.71	30.24	18.9
1990-91	8.70	35.68	24.4
1999-2000	10.29	43.81	23.5

Source: National Sample Survey Organisation (various rounds) and Visaria,1996.
RBI Report on Currency and Finance 2000-01.

In this context, it needs to be mentioned that the developmental experience of the Indian economy has been different from that of the developed countries, as the share of services sector in GDP surpassed that of the agricultural and the industrial sectors in a relatively short span of time. In other words, the economy leap-frogged from the stage of lower order of value addition, generally associated with the agriculture sector, to the higher level of value addition accounted for by the services sector. This positive experience in India could probably be explained in terms of the great advantage derived by being a late starter in the developmental paradigm. In other words, the economy did not have to pass through the incremental process of improving technology in stages for the advancement of a steady growth process.

The expansion in the services sector has wider implications for production, employment, and trade prospects of the economy:

(a) The growing share of the services sector points to the need for policy initiatives towards introducing greater competition and efficiency in this sector so as to ensure its sustained contribution to exports (especially software) and to higher long-term growth.

(b) The gains in productivity in the agricultural and industrial sectors resulting from technological progress and innovation will have the effect of shifting employment away from the non-services sector to the services sector. This may also indicate a shift in real expenditure from commodities to value added services.

(c) The services sector constitutes a tax-base with vast but unexploited potential, and therefore, its growth has long-term implications for the fiscal policy.

Structural Transformation in Industry

The growth of value added in the industrial sector in India slowed down in the 1990s after recording significant improvement in the 1980s, with similar trends at the sectoral level. The growth of the industrial sector is affected by intersectoral imbalances in the growth process. The significant deceleration in the growth rate of the mining and quarrying and electricity sectors during the 1990s affected the overall growth of industrial output. The mining and quarrying and the manufacturing sectors have also exhibited higher volatility in the growth rate during the 1990s. These fluctuations in the growth rates and imbalances across the sectors have implications for stabilising output growth at higher levels (Table 5, 6).

Table – 5

Trend Growth of Industrial Production in India

(Per cent)

Period	Mining and Quarrying	Manufacturing	Electricity	General
1	2	3	4	5
1970-1980	4.7	4.1	7.4	4.6
1980-1990	7.7	7.3	8.7	7.5
1990-2000	3.8	6.8	6.6	6.5

Note : The trend growth rates are derived from a semi- logarithmic function.

Table – 6

Coefficient of Variation of Industrial Production

(Per cent)

Period	Mining and Quarrying	Manufacturing	Electricity	General
1	2	3	4	5
1970-1980	110.1	85.0	67.4	72.9
1980-1990	53.0	32.3	21.2	23.7
1990-2000	125.1	62.2	21.4	55.7

Changes in the relative contribution of different sectors to the general Index of Industrial Production reflect another dimension of the structural changes. The relative contribution of the manufacturing sector rose from 70.0 per cent during the 'eighties to 81.6 per cent during the 'nineties. However, in case of mining and quarrying, there was a noticeable decline.

During the 'nineties, while the relative contributions of basic and capital goods sectors declined, there was a rise in those of intermediate and consumer goods sectors. In the new series (Base: 1993-94=100), the weights of basic and capital goods sectors were reduced and those of intermediate goods and consumer goods sectors were raised.

Table – 7

Relative Contribution of Sectors to the Industrial Production

(Per cent)

Sector	1981-82 to 1990-91 (Average)	1992-93 to 1998-99* (Average)
1	2	3
i) Manufacturing	70.0	81.6
ii) Electricity	14.4	14.4
iii) Mining and Quarrying	15.6	4.0
General Index	100.0	100.0

* The data relating to 1991-92 were excluded in this period because production was almost stagnant.

Source: RBI Report on Currency and Finance, 1998-99.

The relatively low contributions of the basic and capital goods sectors to overall industrial output in the 'nineties reflect, among others, the impact of trade liberalisation, particularly imports, and of financial liberalisation that enabled the corporate sector to make financial gains through 'other income', as also the lack of competitiveness requiring industrial restructuring and modernisation of technologies in a number of industries.

The restructuring of the Indian corporate sector in the recent period has been prompted mainly by the globalised business environment. The structural reforms initiated in the early 'nineties have compelled the Indian industry to adopt focused strategies like corporate restructuring by shedding non-core activities, and mergers and acquisitions.

In recent years, mergers and acquisitions have been employed as corporate strategies for achieving faster growth. Mergers and amalgamations would enable Indian companies to exploit the *scale economies* to enable increased access to the capital market, increase capacity, induct new technology and develop export markets. In this context, the process of restructuring of firms through consolidation has emerged as an inevitable logical sequence if private and public sector enterprises have to integrate themselves effectively into global competitors and to maintain their relative levels of performance in the domestic market.

No doubt the process of development of the economy gained momentum during the 'nineties with the initiation of major economic reforms in 1991. The economy has since then been successfully launched on to a higher growth trajectory and has registered an improvement in a number of macro-economic indicators in a short span of one decade.

Economic reforms are a continuous process which need to be adjusted as the economic environment changes, both domestically and internationally. The year 2001 has been a difficult year for almost all economies of the world. World economic growth slowed down as did trade growth. The current signals are that recovery is expected in 2002. This should help in the expansion of international trade and in the rejuvenating of Indian export growth. As the world economy picks up, the deflationary trend experienced in the prices of commodities and manufactured products would also begin to be reversed enabling improved profitability in the Indian manufacturing sector as well. The continued implementation of reforms along with this upturn in the economic environment is likely to help in regeneration of economic activity in the months and years to come.

[illegible]

II

Banking & Finance

9

Banking and Finance in India Managing New Challenges

BIMAL JALAN

Introduction

In my inaugural address last year, I had indicated a vision for Indian banking in the new millennium – that of a vibrant, internationally active banking system, drawing upon its innate strengths and comparative advantages to make India a major banking centre of the world. I had pointed out then that, while it may take up to 10 or even 15 years to achieve this vision, the time to begin was now. Recent developments have only served to bring forward the urgency attached to embarking upon this quest. Even as we do so, it is necessary to recognise that, in view of recent global developments and the economic slowdown, the progress towards this goal would call for even greater effort and determination. In this context, the theme chosen for this year's Conference i.e., "Indian Banking: Paradigm Shift" is most timely as it provides an opportunity to deliberate on the new challenges ahead, and the action that we must take to manage them.

As you are aware, global economic prospects turned sharply adverse since September 2001 following the terrorist attacks on the US. The possibilities of a recovery in the global economy have become highly uncertain, belying the initial expectations of a V-shaped recovery as well as the subsequent hopes of a U-shaped recovery. As of now, the consensus of forecasts settles around 2.4 per cent for world GDP growth for 2001. World trade volume growth could slow down to around 1.3 per cent and net capital outflows from developing countries may now be larger than anticipated earlier. Although the sharp spurt in international oil prices has abated, their future behaviour remains unclear. Macroeconomic weaknesses have also been associated with an erosion of business confidence. Insurance, airlines, tourism and hotel industries have been hit hard and the exposure of financial institutions to these industries can be a potential source of vulnerability.

Despite the relatively inward-looking nature of the Indian economy, it cannot remain insulated from these international developments. The direct effects of these external developments on our banking system are expected to be limited. Indirect effects, especially through exports and subdued industrial activity could, however, impact upon the asset quality of our banking system and other segments of the financial system. The need to constantly monitor international developments and take appropriate and often, preemptive action add an entirely new dimension to the progress of our banking system towards its longer-term vision.

We have made considerable progress in implementing banking and financial sector reforms. There is also some improvement in the financial performance of the banking system in terms of various indicators of operating efficiency. Nevertheless, there are several areas regarding the efficiency of our banking system – rather than its stability – that raise concerns, especially during a period of generalised uncertainty. The level of non-performing assets (NPAs) continues be high by international standards, preempting funds for provisioning and eating into the performance and profitability of financial intermediaries. The response to the debt recovery and asset restructuring initiatives undertaken as part of financial sector reforms has also been slow.

In the period ahead, our financial system will also have to prepare for a tightening of the prudential norms as the new Basel Accord becomes effective and a fuller response to the current financial environment emerges. Our financial institutions continue to be susceptible to financial market turbulence, especially in the equity market. Upgrading technical skills, technology, research and human capital, developing effective 'front-office' strategies and fortifying internal rules of governance and responsibility assumes a renewed priority in the fast changing scenario.

The face of banking, as we have known it, is also changing rapidly. India is approaching an era of financial conglomorisation and 'bundling' in the provision of financial services. Besides infusing heightened competition, there are implications for the regulatory and supervisory regime. Banks and financial institutions have to prepare for changes in the regulatory framework towards a more focussed, comprehensive and efficient environment that eschews regulatory forbearance. Legal reforms accordingly will have to ascend the hierarchy of priorities in the reform process.

Against this background, in this talk, I propose to focus on the main challenges facing Indian banking, such as, the role of financial intermediation in different phases of the business cycle, the emerging compulsions of the new prudential norms, and benchmarking the Indian financial system against international standards and best practices. I will also say a few words about the changing context of regulation and supervision of the financial system in India, the need for introducing new technology in the banking and financial system, and the importance of strengthening skills and intellectual capital formation in the banking industry.

Recent Macroeconomic Developments and the Banking System

For a greater part of the twentieth century, the role of the financial system was perceived as mobilising the massive resource requirements for growth. Since the 1970s and 1980s, development economics underwent a paradigm shift. The financial system is no longer viewed as a passive mobiliser of funds. Efficiency in financial intermediation i.e., the ability of financial institutions to intermediate between savers and investors, to set economic prices for capital and to allocate resources among competing demands is now emphasised. Developments in endogenous growth theory since the late 1980s indicate that efficiency in financial intermediation is a source of technical progress to be exploited for generating increasing returns and sustaining high growth. These changes have provided the rationale for many developing countries to undertake wide-ranging reforms of their financial systems so as to prepare them for their true resource allocation function. As important financial intermediaries, banks have a special role to play in this new dispensation.

The sharp downturn in global macroeconomic prospects and the continuing sluggishness in domestic industrial activity have necessitated a revision in the forecast for India's real GDP growth in 2001-02 from 6.0-6.5 per cent expected at the time of the April 2001 Monetary and Credit Policy Statement to 5.0-6.0 per cent in the mid-term review of the policy. The downward revision is primarily predicated on the outlook for the industrial sector which grew by barely 2.2 per cent in April-October 2001 as against 5.9 per cent in the corresponding period of last year, mainly on account of the slowdown in manufacturing and mining and quarrying. Capital goods production declined by as much as 6.6 per cent and several sectors recorded a slow down in growth rate or an absolute decline. On the other hand, agriculture sector, supported by reasonable monsoon, recorded a rebound in growth. The kharif output is expected to cross a new peak of 105.6 million tonnes and prospects for the rabi crop are also good. On the external front, merchandise exports increased marginally by 0.5 per cent in the first eight months of 2001-02. While oil imports fell by 13.4 per cent, the non-oil imports showed an increase of 8.4 per cent. Despite a moderate widening of the trade deficit, continuing buoyancy in net invisible receipts has kept the current account deficit very low. According to available data, net capital flows are also likely to be of a higher order than in the preceding year. Foreign exchange reserves rose to US $ 48.0 billion as on December 28, 2001 recording an accretion of the order of the US $ 5.8 billion over the end-March 2001 level.

In the context of the recent deceleration in the economy the intermediation role assumes even greater relevance. Banks and financial institutions should endeavour to play a 'supply-leading' rather than 'demand-following' role in initiating the upturn by energising the financial intermediation process. By virtue of a bird's eye view of the economy and their superior credit assessment of the investment proposals and the efficiency of capital, banks should endeavour to economise on 'search' costs in identifying and nurturing growth impulses in the commodity and service producing sectors of the economy.

In the recent period, monetary policy in India has also moved into a counter-cyclical stance signalled by cuts in key interest rates and cash reserve requirements. At the same time, market operations have ensured adequate liquidity to support the revival of aggregate demand with a clear preference for softening of interest rates within the overall institutional constraints on the interest rate regime. Inflation has been steadily falling and this has had a positive impact on inflation expectations, along with the underlying resilience of the macroeconomic fundamentals of the Indian economy. The 50 basis point reduction in the Bank Rate and the 200 basis point reduction in the CRR, announced recently, are expected to significantly enhance the lendable resources of the banking system.

The current situation of comfortable liquidity provides an opportunity for banks to transform idle liquidity into investible resources for growth. The easy interest rate environment would make it possible for banks to 'price in' projects which would have earlier remained unfunded due to inherently lower returns to capital or due to lack of access to prime lending rates. This will, however, require reassessment of portfolios and internal liquidity constraints, even adjustments in risk profiles and risk management. The deceleration in the industrial growth scenario, of course, opens up the moral hazard of adverse selection and the possibilities of large-scale contamination of portfolios. In a situation of generalised slowdown, unviable projects can look potentially bankable given the scarcity of investment avenues.

Nevertheless, the possibilities for financial intermediation in the current situation are too varied and challenging to ignore. There is no systematic evidence that financial sector reforms by themselves and without supportive policies in other areas, can contribute to a revival of the economy; yet this is a time when the responsibility on the financial system to contribute to the process of economic revival is greater than before. Periods of downturn in economic activity also provide opportunities for banks to undertake consolidation and strengthening. There is a strong complementarity between financial stability and macroeconomic stability. The interests of both are served by a stable and resilient financial system.

In recent years, various measures have been taken to improve the functioning of different segments of the financial markets and thereby, to improve the operational effectiveness of monetary policy. The Liquidity Adjustment Facility (LAF), which was introduced in June 2000 has emerged as an effective and flexible instrument for managing liquidity on a day-to-day basis. In the second stage of the LAF, which commenced from May 2001, variable rate repo auctions replaced the collateralised lending facility and Level I support to primary dealers. Standing facilities were rationalised and a back-stop facility was introduced at variable market-related rates. Concurrently, LAF operating procedures were recast to improve operational flexibility and complementary measures were undertaken to improve the functioning of money and government securities market segments and to facilitate their orderly integration.

In order to enable the call money market to evolve into a pure inter-bank market, lending by non-banks was reduced to 85 per cent of their average daily call lending in 2000-01 from May 2001. The minimum maturity for wholesale term deposits of Rs.15 lakh and above has been reduced to 7 days from the earlier minimum maturity of 15 days. The maintenance of daily minimum cash reserve requirements has been lowered to 50 per cent from 65 per cent for the first seven days of the reporting fortnight. Interest paid on eligible balances under CRR has been raised to the level of the Bank Rate from November 3, 2001. The market has responded positively with an appreciable rise in turnover and a decline in volatility.

Several measures have also been taken to improve the functioning of the government securities market. 14-day and 182-day Treasury Bills were withdrawn and the notified amounts of 91-day Treasury Bills has been simultaneously increased. A Negotiated Dealing System (NDS) is being introduced to facilitate electronic bidding and to disseminate information on trades on a real-time basis. For this purpose, the Reserve Bank has begun the automation of its public debt offices. An important step is the setting up of the Clearing Corporation of India Ltd. (CCIL) to act as counterparty in all trades involving government securities, Treasury Bills, repos and foreign exchange. The entire system will operate in a networked environment and INdian FInancial

NETwork (INFINET) will provide the backbone for communication.

Prudential Norms

A strong and resilient financial system and the orderly evolution of financial markets are key prerequisites for financial stability and economic progress. In keeping with the vision of an internationally competitive and sound banking system, deepening and broadening of prudential norms to the best internationally recognised standards have been the core of our approach to financial sector reforms. This has been supported concurrently by heightened market discipline, pro-active and comprehensive supervision of the financial system and the orderly development of financial market segments. The calibration of the convergence with international standards is conditioned by the specific realities of our situation; however, the New Capital Accord of the Basel Committee on Banking Supervision which was released in January 2001 adds urgency to the process of convergence. It is against the backdrop of these exigencies that prudential norms are being constantly monitored and refined. In the recent period, banks are being encouraged to build risk-weighted components of their subsidiaries into their own balance sheets and to assign additional capital. Risk weights are being constantly refined to take into recognition additional sources of risk. The concept of 'past due' in the identification of NPAs has been dispensed with. Banks and financial institutions are being urged to prepare to move to the international practice of the '90 day norm' in the classification of assets as non-performing by 2003-04.

The new Basel Accord, as contained in the second Consultative Paper on Capital Adequacy of the Basel Committee on Banking Supervision released in January 2001 is in response to the perceived rigidities in the 1988 Accord's capital requirements, the scope for capital arbitrage and the increased sophistication in the measurement and management of risk. The new Accord rests on three mutually reinforcing pillars i.e., minimum capital requirements, processes of supervisory review and market discipline. Under the first pillar, the current definition of capital and the minimum requirement of 8 per cent of capital to risk weighted assets is retained. Capital requirements would be extended on a consolidated basis to holding companies of banking groups.

The primary emphasis of the new Accord is on improving the measurement of risk. The process of measurement of market risk is maintained. Three alternatives for calculating credit risk capital requirements are proposed to be made available to banks, depending on the complexity of their business and the quality of their risk management operations. The 'standardised approach' which can be employed by less complex banks remains conceptually the same as in the 1988 norms; however, it expands the scale of risk weights and uses external credit ratings to categorise credits. Banks with more advanced risk management capabilities can employ an internal ratings based (IRB) approach – 'foundation' and 'advanced' variants are proposed on a progression scale – in which banks may categorise exposures into multiple credit ratings of their approved internal rating systems. The internally estimated probability of default, the maturity of exposure and the credit type i.e., corporate or retail, will determine risk weights. There is a new explicit capital charge proposed on operational risk.

The processes of supervisory review contained in the second pillar emphasise the need for banks to develop sound internal procedures to assess the adequacy of capital based on a thorough evaluation of its risk profile and control environment, and to set commensurate targets for capital. The internal processes would be subject to supervisory evaluation, review and intervention, when appropriate. The third pillar aims at bolstering market discipline through enhanced disclosure by banks. Disclosure requirements are set out in several areas under the new Accord, including the way in which banks calculate their capital adequacy and their risk assessment methods.

The Basel Committee on Banking Supervision has received more than 250 comments on the January 2001 proposals. The Committee is expected to release a fully specified proposal, based on these comments, in early 2002 and to finalise the Accord during 2002. An implementation date of 2005 is envisaged. The Reserve Bank forwarded its comments to the Basel committee in May 2001. It has supported flexibility, discretion to national supervisors and a phased approach in implementing the Accord. The Accord could initially apply to internationally active – banks with over 15 per cent of their business in cross-border transactions, as proposed by the Reserve Bank – and significant banks whose domestic market share exceeds 1 per cent – with a simplified standardised approach to be evolved for other banks. Material limits on cross-holdings of capital and eschewing of direct responsibility on external credit rating agencies in the assessment of bank assets have also been proposed by the Reserve Bank. It has also expressed its preference for external credit rating agencies that publicly disclose risk scores, rating processes and methodologies.

The new accord, when implemented, is likely to have significant implications for the banking system as a whole. Besides requiring increased capital, it attaches urgency to the development of efficient and comprehensive internal systems for assessment and management of risks, setting up and adhering to adequate internal exposure limits and improving internal control generally. The guidelines for risk management and asset liability management provided by the Reserve Bank serve as a useful foundation for building more sophisticated control systems. The feedback received from few banks indicates the need for substantial upgradation of existing management information systems, risk management practices and technical skills. Capital allocation is also expected to be more risk sensitive and, therefore, banks and financial institutions will have to plan in advance so that there are no disruptions in the capital structure. Further sophistication in risk management and control mechanisms will have to evolve as experience with preferential risk-weighting and sensitivity to external ratings is accumulated.

A key requirement when the new Accord, after further modification, becomes operational is that of high quality human resources to cope with and adapt to the new environment. Enhancing technical skills and abilities to handle new technologies and new risks, exploiting information flows to price them in, and developing foresight in anticipating changing risk-return relationships will become essential.

Market Discipline

Processes of transparency and market disclosure of critical information describing the risk profile, capital structure and capital adequacy are assuming increasing importance in the emerging environment. Besides making banks more accountable and responsive to better-informed investors, these processes enable banks to strike the right balance between risks and rewards and to improve the access to markets. Improvements in market discipline also call for greater coordination between banks and regulators.

India has been a participant in the international initiatives to ensure improved processes of market discipline that are being worked out in several fora, such as, the multilateral organisations, the BIS, the Financial Stability Forum, and the Core Principles Liaison Group. Concurrent efforts are underway to refine and upgrade financial information monitoring and flow, data dissemination and data warehousing. Banks are currently required to disclose in their balance sheets information on maturity profiles of assets and liabilities, lending to sensitive sectors, movements in NPAs, besides providing information on capital, provisions, shareholdings of the government, value of investments in India and abroad, and other operating and profitability indicators. Financial institutions are also required to meet these disclosure norms. Banks also have to disclose their total investments made in equity shares, units of mutual funds, bonds and debentures, and aggregate advances against shares in their notes to balance sheets.

From this year onwards, notes to banks' balance sheets will disclose the movement of provisions against NPAs as well as those held towards depreciation on investments. Guidelines relating to non-SLR investments through the private placement route mandate the disclosure of information on issuer composition and non-performing investments in a similar manner. Efforts have been made to identify and monitor early warning indicators of financial crises. The overall approach is to combine the use of micro-prudential indicators with macro-economic indicators in order to develop a set of aggregate macro-prudential indicators. This brings about a mix between bottom-up and top-down assessment. As the methodology gets refined and the indicators are stress-tested for predictive power, financial stability surveillance will be significantly improved. This process will involve greater transparency and objectivity in the disclosure practices of banks.

Efforts have also been made to set up a Credit Information Bureau to collect and share information on borrowers and improve the credit appraisal of banks and financial institutions within the ambit of the existing legislation. The Bureau has been incorporated by the State Bank of India in collaboration with Housing Development Finance Corporation (HDFC) and foreign technology partners. Collection and sharing of some items of information have already been initiated. Efforts are also going into the collection and sharing of information on private placement of debt under the Bureau so that there is greater transparency in such trades. The possibility of collecting and disseminating information on suit-filed accounts by the Bureau (in place of the Reserve Bank) is being explored by a Working Group constituted for this purpose with representation from across the financial system. The Group will also examine the prospects of on-line supply of information and the processing of queries. A draft legislation covering various aspects of information sharing, including issues relating to rights, responsibilities, and privacy has been prepared, which would considerably strengthen the functioning of the Bureau when it is enacted.

Benchmarking the Indian Banking System by International Standards

The impetus given to the strengthening of domestic financial systems and the international financial architecture by the Asian crisis has gathered momentum in recent years. An important development in this regard has been the move to set up universally acceptable standards and codes for benchmarking domestic financial systems. Moreover, multilateral assessments of country performance are increasingly focusing on observance of standards. The IMF's Article IV consultations, its Financial Sector Stability Assessment and the Reports on Observance of Standards and Codes of the IMF and the World Bank are indicative of the fact that a country's adherence to benchmark standards and codes is being considered integral to the preservation of international monetary and financial stability. While the process has begun with the predominant involvement of governments and regulators, the search for standards and codes is progressively encompassing the private sector with consideration of issues relating to market discipline, corporate governance, insolvency procedures and credit rights.

It is important to recognise that new standards and codes are not being regarded as final goals but as instruments or enabling conditions for enhancing efficiency in financial intermediation while ensuring financial stability. There are three levels at which action is necessary, viz., legal, policy and procedures, and market practices by participants. In several areas, fundamental changes in the legal and institutional infrastructure are pre-requisites. Since these changes can impinge upon the socio-cultural as well as politico-economic ethos, appropriate adoption and some prioritisation in implementation are unavoidable.

We have made some noteworthy progress in generating a constructive debate on the applicability of international standards and codes to the Indian financial system. Participative consultation has been supported by internal self-assessments as well as external assessment. In several areas, the issues are of a technical nature. Accordingly, the Standing Committee on International Standards and Codes, set up in December 1999, constituted ten Advisory Groups comprising eminent experts, generally non-official, to bring objectivity and experience into studying the applicability of relevant international codes and standards to each area of competence.

The Advisory Groups have submitted their reports. They have set out a roadmap for implementation of appropriate standard and codes in the light of existing levels of compliance, the cross-country experience, and the existing legal and institutional infrastructure. The Advisory Group on Banking Supervision has assessed the Indian banking system vis-a-vis the principles of the Basel Committee on Banking Supervision. It has found the level of compliance to be generally of a high order. The Advisory Group on Bankruptcy Laws has, inter alia, recommended a comprehensive bankruptcy code incorporating various aspects including cross-border insolvency and the repeal of the Sick

Industrial Companies Act. The Advisory Group on Corporate Governance has made recommendations relating to rules and responsibilities of boards and has advised amendments to the Companies Act.

The Advisory Group on Data Dissemination has found that India's data dissemination compares favourably with many other countries and has proposed the compilation of forward-looking indicators. The Advisory Group on Fiscal Transparency is of the view that current fiscal practices meet the IMF's Code of Good Practices on Fiscal Transparency. It has recommended amplifying the scope of fiscal responsibility legislation in order to include the essential elements of a budget law. The Advisory Group on Insurance regulation has recommended flexible minimum capital requirements depending on the class of business. With regard to actuarial and solvency issues, the Group has found the Indian standards to be at par with international norms. The Advisory Group on International Accounting and Auditing Standards has set out an agenda for the future for convergence in auditing and accounting practices. It has recommended a single standard setting authority and the need for convergence of corporate and tax laws.

The Advisory Group on Transparency in Monetary and Financial Policies has recommended inflation as the single mandated objective for the central bank and necessary autonomy to fulfill the mandate. It has also made recommendations on the operating procedures of monetary policy. The Advisory Group on Payments and Settlement has recommended legal reforms to empower the Reserve Bank to supervise the payment and settlement system, application of the Lamfalussy standards to deferred net settlement (DNS) and introduction of Real Time Gross Settlement (RTGS). It has also recommended the setting up of the Clearing Corporation and a separate guarantee fund for foreign exchange clearing. The Advisory Group on Securities Market Regulation has compared India against the International Organisation of Securities Commissions (IOSCO) principles and emphasised the need to strengthen inter-regulator cooperation.

Thus, in India, we have made considerable progress in the identification of international standards and codes in relevant areas, expert assessment regarding their applicability, including comparator country evaluation and building up possible course of action for the future. The next step is to sensitise all concerned – policy makers, regulators and market participants – to the issues involved and to seek the widest possible debate on issues as well as expert assessments with a view to generating a broad consensus on implementation of a universally recognised set of codes and standards.

Universal Banking

Since the early 1990s, banking systems worldwide have been going through a rapid transformation. Mergers, amalgamations and acquisitions have been undertaken on a large scale in order to gain size and to focus more sharply on competitive strengths. This consolidation has produced financial conglomerates that are expected to maximise economies of scale and scope by 'bundling' the production of financial services. The general trend has been towards downstream universal banking where banks have undertaken traditionally non-banking activities such as investment banking, insurance, mortgage financing, securitisation, and particularly, insurance. Upstream linkages, where non-banks undertake banking business, are also on the increase. The global experience can be segregated into broadly three models. There is the Swedish or Hong Kong type model in which the banking corporate engages in in-house activities associated with banking. In Germany and the UK, certain types of activities are required to be carried out by separate subsidiaries. In the US type model, there is a holding company structure and separately capitalised subsidiaries.

In India, the first impulses for a more diversified financial intermediation were witnessed in the 1980s and 1990s when banks were allowed to undertake leasing, investment banking, mutual funds, factoring, hire-purchase activities through separate subsidiaries. By the mid-1990s, all restrictions on project financing were removed and banks were allowed to undertake several activities in-house. In the recent period, the focus is on Development Financial Institutions (DFIs), which have been allowed to set up banking subsidiaries and to enter the insurance business along with banks. DFIs were also allowed to undertake working capital financing and to raise short-term funds within limits. It was the Narasimham Committee II Report (1998) which suggested that the DFIs should convert themselves into banks or non-bank financial companies, and this conversion was endorsed by the Khan Working Group (1998). The Reserve Bank's Discussion Paper (1999) and the feedback thereon indicated the desirability of universal banking from the point of view of efficiency of resource use, but it also emphasised the need to take into account factors such as the status of reforms, the state of preparedness of the institutions, and a viable transition path while moving in the desired direction.

Accordingly, the mid-term review of monetary and credit policy, October 1999 and the annual policy statements of April 2000 and April 2001 enunciated the broad approach to universal banking and the Reserve Bank's circular of April 2001 set out the operational and regulatory aspects of conversion of DFIs into universal banks. The need to proceed with planning and foresight is necessary for several reasons. The move towards universal banking would not provide a panacea for the endemic weaknesses of a DFI or its liquidity and solvency problems and/or operational difficulties arising from undercapitalisation, non-performing assets, and asset liability mismatches, etc. The overriding consideration should be the objectives and strategic interests of the financial institution concerned in the context of meeting the varied needs of customers, subject to normal prudential norms applicable to banks. From the point of view of the regulatory framework, the movement towards universal banking should entrench stability of the financial system, preserve the safety of public deposits, improve efficiency in financial intermediation, ensure healthy competition, and impart transparent and equitable regulation.

Issues in Supervision and Regulation

Progressive strengthening, deepening and refinement of the regulatory and supervisory system for the financial sector have been important elements of financial sector reforms. In the long run, it is the supervision and regulation function that is critical in safeguarding financial stability. There is also some evidence that proactive and effective supervision contributes to the efficiency of financial intermediation. Financial sector supervision is expected to become increasingly risk-based and concerned with validating systems rather than setting them. This will entail procedures for sound internal evaluation of risk for banks. As mentioned earlier, bank managements will have to develop internal capital assessment processes in accordance with their risk profile and control environment. These internal processes would then be subjected to review and supervisory intervention if necessary. The emphasis will be on evaluating the quality of risk management and the adequacy of risk containment. In such an environment, credibility assigned by markets to risk disclosures will hold only if they are validated by supervisors. Thus effective and appropriate supervision is critical for the effectiveness of capital requirements and market discipline.

In certain areas, as for instance, in the urban cooperative banking segment, the regulatory requirements leave considerable scope for regulatory arbitrage and even circumvention. The problem is rendered more complex by the existence of regulatory overlap between the Central Government, the State Governments and the Reserve Bank. Regulatory overlap has impeded the speed of regulatory response to emerging problems. The need for removing multiple regulatory jurisdiction over the cooperative banking sector has been reiterated on several occasions. In this regard, the Reserve Bank has proposed the setting up of an apex supervisory body for urban cooperative banks under the control of a high-level supervisory board consisting of representatives of the Central governments, the State governments, the Reserve Bank and experts. The apex body is expected to ensure compliance with prudential requirements and also supervise on-site inspections and off-site surveillance.

Recent developments in certain segments of the financial sector have also brought to the fore issues relating to corporate governance in banks. As part of on-going reforms, boards have been given greater autonomy to prescribe internal control guidelines, risk management and procedures for market discipline and accountability. It is extremely important that greater vigilance over adherence to these norms goes hand-in-hand with greater autonomy. Recent evidence of transgression of prudential guidelines by a few banks has raised the issue of the audit and supervisory functions of boards. As we move towards a more deregulated financial regime, these functions have to be transferred from either the Government or the Reserve Bank to bank boards.

This imposes a greater responsibility and accountability on the bank management. It is in this context that a consultative group of directors of select banks and other experts has been set up to recommend measures to strengthen the internal supervisory role of boards. The objective is to obtain a feedback on how boards function vis-a-vis compliance with prudential norms, transparency and disclosure, functioning of the audit committee, etc., and to devise effective mechanisms for ensuring management discipline.

Several other initiatives in improving the supervisory function have been undertaken, including a prudential supervisory reporting system for financial institutions, improvements in procedures for financial inspection, sensitising the general public for better regulation of the activities of NBFCs and enactment of appropriate legislation to protect depositor interests in some States. Major legal reforms have been initiated in areas such as security laws, the Negotiable Instruments Act, bank frauds and the regulatory framework of banking. The Reserve Bank has also accepted the principle of transfer of ownership to the Government in respect of some financial institutions in view of the conflict of interest that may arise in the conduct of its supervisory function. It is expected that these initiatives will pave the way for an efficient, and risk-based supervisory environment in India.

Technology in Banking

Nobel Laureate Robert Solow had once remarked that computers are seen everywhere excepting in productivity statistics. More recent developments have shown how far this state of affairs has changed. Innovation in technology and worldwide revolution in information and communication technology (ICT) have emerged as dynamic sources of productivity growth. The relationship between IT and banking is fundamentally symbiotic. In the banking sector, IT can reduce costs, increase volumes, and facilitate customised products; similarly, IT requires banking and financial services to facilitate its growth. As far as the banking system is concerned, the payment system is perhaps the most important mechanism through which such interactive dynamics gets manifested.

Recognising the importance of payments and settlement systems in the economy, we have embarked on technology based solutions for the improvement of the payment and settlement system infrastructure, coupled with the introduction of new payment products such as the computerised settlement of clearing transactions, use of Magnetic Ink Character Recognition (MICR) technology for cheque clearing which currently accounts for 65 per cent of the value of cheques processed in the country, the computerisation of Government Accounts and Currency Chest transactions, operationalisation of Delivery versus Payment (DvP) for Government securities transactions. Two-way inter-city cheque collection and imaging have been operationalised at the four metros. The coverage of Electronic Clearing Service (Debit and Credit) has been significantly expanded to encourage non-paper based funds movement and develop the provision of a centralised facility for effecting payments. The scheme for Electronic Funds Transfer operated by the Reserve Bank has been significantly augmented and is now available across thirteen major cities. The scheme, which was originally intended for small value transactions, is processing high value (up to Rs.2 crore) from October 1, 2001. The Centralised Funds Management System (CFMS), which would enable banks to obtain consolidated account-wise and centre-wise positions of their balances with all 17 offices of the Deposits Accounts Departments of the Reserve Bank has begun to be implemented in a phased manner from November 2001.

A holistic approach has been adopted towards designing and development of a modern, robust, efficient, secure and integrated payment and settlement system taking into account certain aspects relating to potential risks, legal framework and the impact on the operational framework of monetary policy. The approach to the modernisation of the payment and settlement system in India has been three-pronged: (a) consolidation, (b) development, and (c) integration. The consolidation of the existing payment systems revolves around strengthening Computerised Cheque clearing, expanding the reach of Electronic Clearing Services and Electronic Funds Transfer by providing for systems with the latest levels of technology. The critical elements in the developmental strategy are the opening of new clearing houses, interconnection of clearing houses through the INFINET; optimising the deployment of resources by banks through Real Time Gross Settlement System, Centralised Funds Management System (CFMS); Negotiated

Dealing System (NDS) and the Structured Financial Messaging Solution (SFMS). While integration of the various payment products with the systems of individual banks is the thrust area, it requires a high degree of standardisation within a bank and seamless interfaces across banks.

The setting up of the apex-level National Payments Council in May 1999 and the operationalisation of the INFINET by the Institute for Development and Research in Banking Technology (IDRBT), Hyderabad have been some important developments in the direction of providing a communication network for the exclusive use of banks and financial institutions. Membership in the INFINET has been opened up to all banks in addition to those in the public sector. At the base of all inter-bank message transfers using the INFINET is the Structured Financial Messaging System (SFMS). It would serve as a secure communication carrier with templates for intra- and inter-bank messages in fixed message formats that will facilitate 'straight through processing'. All inter-bank transactions would be stored and switched at the central hub at Hyderabad while intra-bank messages will be switched and stored by the bank gateway. Security features of the SFMS would match international standards.

In order to maximise the benefits of such efforts, banks have to take pro-active measures to :

- further strengthen their infrastructure in respect of standardisation, high levels of security and communication and networking;
- achieve inter-branch connectivity early;
- popularise the usage of the scheme of electronic funds transfer (EFT); and
- institute arrangements for an RTGS environment online with a view to integrating into a secure and consolidated payment system.

Information technology has immense untapped potential in banking. Strengthening of information technology in banks could improve the effectiveness of asset-liability management in banks. Building up of a related data-base on a real time basis would enhance the forecasting of liquidity greatly even at the branch level. This could contribute to enhancing the risk management capabilities of banks.

Human Resource Development in Banking

A recurring theme in the annual BECON Conference has been the need to focus on developing human resources to cope with the rapidly changing scenario. The core function of HRD in the banking industry is to facilitate performance improvement, measured not only in terms of financial indicators of operational efficiency but also in terms of the quality of financial services provided. Factors such as skills, attitudes and knowledge of personnel play a critical role in determining the competitiveness of the financial sector. The quality of human resources indicates the ability of banks to deliver value to customers. Capital and technology are replicable, but not human capital which needs to be viewed as a valuable resource for the achievement of competitive advantage. The primary emphasis needs to be on integrating human resource management (HRM) strategies with the business strategy. HRM strategies include managing change, creating commitment, achieving flexibility and improving teamwork. These processes underlie the complementary processes that represent the overt aspects of HRM, such as recruitment, placement, performance management, reward management, and employee relations. A forward looking approach would involve moving towards self-assessment of competency and developmental needs as a part of a continuous learning cycle.

The Indian banking industry has been an important driving force behind the nation's economic development. The emerging environment poses both opportunities and threats, in particular, to the public sector banks. How well these are met will mainly depend on the extent to which the banks leverage their primary assets i.e., human resources in the context of the changing economic and business environment. It is obvious that the public sector banks' hierarchical structure, which gives preference to seniority over performance, is not the best environment for attracting the best talent from among the young in a competitive environment. A radical transformation of the existing personnel structure in public sector banks is unlikely to be practical, at least in the foreseeable future. However, certain improvements can be made in the recruitment practices as well as in on-the-job training and redeployment of those who are already employed. There are several institutions in the country which cater exclusively to the needs of human resource development in the banking industry. It is worthwhile to consider broad-basing the courses conducted in these institutions among other higher-level educational institutions so that specialisation in the area of banking and financial services becomes an option in higher education curriculums. In the area of information technology, Indian professionals are world leaders and building synergies between the IT and banking industries will sharpen the competitive edge of our banks.

The changing environment, the forces of globalisation and liberalisation and the advances in information and communication technology have major HR implications for the Reserve Bank as well. Financial products are becoming increasingly complex and diverse, while the markets in which they trade get progressively deregulated. The need to adopt global best practices in financial sector regulation and supervision, and adapt them to the domestic environment, places a premium on the skills and expertise of the Bank's human resources. Again, the functioning and policies of public institutions, such as the Reserve Bank, are increasingly subject to public discussion and debate. This calls for greater transparency, more effective communication, and a high degree of professionalism in the Bank's staff. This warrants continuous upgradation of human resource management strategies with a view to enhancing the level of knowledge, sharpening skills and also to instill the necessary attitudes and work culture. The Reserve Bank is now devoting considerable attention to these areas at the entry level as well as at different levels of career development of its staff.

The Role of Economists

In my inaugural address to BECON, 2000 I had discussed the crucial role of bank economists in transforming the banking system in India. Economists have to be more 'mainstreamed' within the operational structure of commercial banks. Apart from the traditional functioning of macro-scanning, the inter-linkages between treasuries, dealing rooms and trading rooms of banks need to be viewed not only with the day-to-day needs of operational necessity, but also with analytical content and policy foresight.

Today, operational aspects of the functioning of banks are attracting intensive research by professional economists. In particular, measuring and modeling different kinds of risks faced by banks, the behaviour of risk-return relationships associated with different portfolio mixes and the impact of fluctuations in financial markets on the financial performance of banks are areas which lend themselves to analytical and empirical appraisal by economists and econometricians. They, in turn, are discovering the degrees of freedom and room for analytical maneuver in high frequency information generated by the day-to-day functioning of banks. It is vital that we develop an environment where these synergies are nurtured so as to serve the longer-term strategic interests of banks. Even in real time trading and portfolio decisions, the fundamental analysis of economists provides an independent assessment of market behaviour, reinforcing technical analysis.

A serious limitation of the applicability of standard economic analysis to banking relates to the inadequacies of the data-base. Absence of long time series data storage in the banking industry often poses serious problems to the quest for the formal analytical relationships between variables. Even if such data exist, the presence of structural breaks may blur meaningful analysis based on traditional formulation. Economists need to think innovatively to overcome this problem. Use of panel regression, non-parametric methods and multivariate analyses could go a long way in understanding and validating behaviourial relationships in banking.

Another important challenge for the economics profession is to develop proper models for measurement of various risks in Indian conditions. This is a necessity in view of the move towards risk-based supervision. Quantification of operational risks and calibration of Value at Risk (VaR) models pose major computational challenge to bankers and policy makers alike, particularly in India. A major difficulty lies in identifying the right statistical model that determines the underlying distribution suited to the particular category of operational loss, and building the necessary database for deriving operationally meaningful conclusions.

In my inaugural address last year, I had also emphasised the need for bank economists to come out of their narrow specialisation and address operational issues relating to banking and finance. In order to make a meaningful contribution to banking, economists must have the experience of working in operational areas of banks. For this purpose, economists need to 'soil their hands' in dealing rooms, treasuries and investment units, credit authorisation and loan recovery, strategic management groups and management information systems of the banks to understand the ground realities. There are also 'economies' to be gained from field-level credit appraisal, asset recovery, debt restructuring, market and consumer behaviour in which banks are involved. Thus, the profession needs to amalgamate the objectivity and theoretical soundness of economics with the functional dimensions of banking and finance. It is this combination of specialist training with operational experience, which is going to make the economics profession relevant to the changing face of banking in India.

Conclusion

How close are we to the vision of a sound and well-functioning banking system that I outlined a year ago? It is fair to say that despite a turbulent year and many challenges, we have made some progress towards this goal. There has been progressive intensification of financial sector reforms, and the financial sector as a whole is more sensitised than before to the need for internal strength and effective management as well as to the overall concerns for financial stability. At the same time, in view of greater disclosure and tougher prudential norms, the weaknesses in our financial system are more apparent than before.

There is greater awareness now of the need to prepare the banking system for the technical and capital requirements of the emerging prudential regime and a greater focus on core strengths and niche strategies. We have also made some progress in assessing our financial system against international best practices and in benchmarking the future directions of progress. Several contemplated changes in the surrounding legal and institutional environment have been proposed for legislation.

Nevertheless, several sources of vulnerability persist. The NPA levels remain too large by international standards and concerns relating to management and supervision within the ambit of corporate governance are being tested during the period of downturn of economic activity. There is also a sense that we have a lot to acquire and adapt in terms of the technical expertise necessary to measure and manage risks better. The structure of the financial system is changing and supervisory and regulatory regimes are experiencing the strains of accommodating these changes. Certain weak links in the decentralised banking and non-bank financial sectors have also come to notice. In a fundamental sense, regulators and supervisors are under the greatest pressures of change and bear the larger responsibility for the future. For both the regulators and the regulated, eternal vigilance is the price of growth with financial stability.

We should strive to move towards realising our vision of an efficient and sound banking system of international standards with redoubled vigour. Our greatest asset in this endeavour is the fund of technical and scientific human capital formation available in the country. The themes which are being covered in this Conference under structural, operational and governance issues should help in defining the road map for the future.

Inaugural address at the 23rd Conference of Bank Economists, January 14, 2002, Kolkata.

10

Some Critical Issues in Monetary Policy

C. RANGARAJAN

The evolution of monetary management in the 1980s and 1990s in India provides interesting insights into the role of monetary policy, as an instrument of economic policy. These two decades and more, particularly the 1990s, were marked by substantial changes in the overall institutional environment in which monetary policy operated. What are the lessons that can be drawn from this experience as regards objectives and effectiveness of monetary policy? This essay begins with the recommendations of Sukhamoy Chakravarty Report which set the ball of thinking rolling in the mid-1980s. After a brief description of the salient events of the 1980s and 1990s, an attempt is made to raise and answer some of the critical questions in relation to monetary management.

I

CHAKRAVARTY COMMITTEE

Issues relating to stabilisation assumed importance in the context of developments in the 1970s and early 1980s. The Chakravarty Committee was appointed at a time when monetary policy was getting determined increasingly by the fiscal stance.

The author is grateful to S S Tarapore and Y V Reddy for their comments on an earlier draft. The author is thankful to Amaresh Samantaraya for his assistance.

Government's borrowing programme was steadily increasing. The requirements of government could be met only by raising the statutory liquidity ratio to be maintained by banks and by increasing the credit to government from the Reserve Bank. Net Reserve Bank credit to the government was the dominant factor contributing to the increase in reserve money and the consequent expansion in money supply. The cash reserve ratio had to be increased from time to time in order to neutralise, to the extent possible, the expansionary impact of financing the deficits of the government by the Reserve Bank. It was in this context that the Chakravarty Committee was appointed to review the functioning of the monetary system. Chakravarty himself interpreted his responsibility as one of reviewing the monetary system, as he put it "from the point of view of ensuring non-inflationary planned development in the years to come".

The Chakravarty Committee Report contains several major observations and recommendations. First, on the objectives of monetary policy, the committee recognised the existence of a multiplicity of objectives. It set down a long list of eight possible objectives. It, however, came to the conclusion that the objective for which monetary policy could be most properly utilised was price stability. The committee did not see a trade-off between growth and price stability over the medium term. After referring to the importance of price stability as the appropriate objective, Chakravarty writes "That does not mean that other objectives are any less important or that the other instruments will not need to be utilised. But to use monetary policy as a primary instrument for achieving the desired income distribution is not an acceptable proposition to me for an economy such as ours. To use monetary policy for stimulating growth would be a more maintainable objective. But that policy too can be quite counterproductive if you do not give adequate attention to the problem of price stability". Second, the committee recommended monetary targeting as a means to achieve price stability. The concept of monetary targeting that the committee had in mind was somewhat different from what was being advocated in other countries. As Chakravarty put it, "The phrase monetary target is not necessarily to be equated with rigid targets. Only pure monetarists might view monetary targeting as being nothing other than an inflexible rule. What the committee has advocated is 'monetary targeting with feed back'." In practical terms, this implied that target ranges had to be modified in the light of the information available on expected output performance which might itself be a consequence of several factors. There is a great deal of ignorance in our country on what constitutes monetarism. An essential postulate of monetarism is a fixed rate of growth in money supply. The scheme of fixing monetary targets based on expected increase in output and the tolerable level of inflation is far removed from the Friedmanite or any other version of monetarism. Third, recognising the fact that government borrowing from the Reserve Bank has been a major factor contributing to the increase in reserve money and therefore, money supply, the committee wanted an agreement between the central government and the Reserve Bank on the level of monetary expansion and the extent of monetisation of the fiscal deficit. Without such a coordination, Reserve Bank's efforts to contain monetary expansion within the limit set by expected increase in output could become impossible. It is in the light of this recommendation that budgets since then started specifying net RBI credit to government as a memorandum item. Fourth, while the committee did not recommend the scrapping of the administered structure of interest rates, it nevertheless drew attention to the fact that interest rate played an important role in the economy in terms of the mobilisation of savings and the allocation of resources. Therefore, it felt that interest rates cannot be arbitrarily set at any level. It provided a scheme of interest rates as follows:

> Maximum deposit rate to earn a positive real rate of interest of 2 per cent. Long-term government securities should carry 3 per cent real rate of interest. The basic minimum lending rate was to be fixed at 3 per cent above the maximum deposit rate. Banks were free to adopt higher lending rates.

The scheme also recommended for two concessional rates of lending. In effect, without abandoning the administered structure of interest rates, the committee wanted the rates to be fixed in such a way that they satisfied certain criteria. It recognised that positive real rates of interest conferred important benefits on the system.

II

MONETARY POLICY IN THE 1980s

The recommendations of the Chakravarty Committee had a strong impact on monetary policy in the second half of the 1980s. Two other committees set up around this time had also an impact. One was the Working Group on Money Market headed by Vaghul and the other on housing finance which resulted in the formation of the National Housing Bank. During the 1980s, monetary policy had to contend with the growing borrowing programme of the government. This could be met only by increasing the statutory liquidity ratio year after year. By 1990, the SLR had touched 38.5 per cent. Since increasing the SLR was not adequate, the RBI became a residual subscriber. During this period, virtually the entire increase in reserve money was due to Net RBI credit to government. In order to curb the expansionary impact of reserve money, the cash reserve ratio also had to be progressively increased. By 1990, the average CRR had touched 15 per cent. The Reserve Bank's constant appeal to the government was to contain its borrowing programme and more particularly its borrowing from RBI. In the aftermath of the Chakravarty Committee recommendations, the government also realised that it would be prudent to reduce its dependence on RBI. As a first step, net RBI credit to government was indicated as a memorandum item in the budget documents from 1987. The operational significance was, however, diminished as the figure was qualified by the observation 'Not independently estimated'. The RBI had always indicated in its credit policy statements the expected order of increase in money supply. Since 1985, a great deal of thinking went into making such forecasts. Much research effort was spent on estimating the demand function for money and of the relationship between reserve money and money supply. The money supply target was fixed taking into account (a) expected increase in real income, (b) the income elasticity of demand for money, and (c) acceptable increase in price level. It is quite true that there was considerable divergence between the projected increase in money supply and the actual increase. This was because of the weak control RBI had over the fiscal deficit and the more or less automatic monetisation of deficit through the issue of ad hoc treasury bills. Those bills were 'ad hoc' only in name. These treasury bills had to be rolled over indefinitely. At some stage, they had to be funded at the same rate of interest as for ad hocs into long dated securities with no specific date of redemption. In this situation, the only way to control monetary expansion was to raise CRR. While this was repeatedly done, it had its own limitations. While policy aimed at attaining an inflation rate of no more than 5 per cent, the actual inflation rate (as measured by wholesale price index) in the second half of the 1980s was 7.1 per cent.

The second half of the 1980s saw several steps towards expanding and activating the money market. The government securities market could not be activated so long as the interest rate was below the market determined rate. A conscious effort was made to activate the short end of the market with considerable relaxation of money market rates. Treasury bills of 182 days duration were introduced and the Discount and Finance House of India was set up to provide liquidity to these instruments by creating a secondary market. This period also saw the introduction of financial instruments such as Certificates of Deposit, Commercial Paper and Participation Certificates. Thus, within the limits of an administered structure of interest rates, there was a move towards creating an active money market which could serve as a transmission channel for monetary policy.

The interest rate regime underwent some significant changes. First, even where interest rates were determined by the Reserve Bank, an attempt was made to align the rates with market perceptions, by taking into account trends in inflation. The rate on government securities was raised from time to time. The maturity of long-term bonds was reduced to prevent the government getting locked into high rates. Second, the initial effort at freeing the interest rate on deposits turned out to be difficult. In 1985, freedom was given to banks to fix the interest rate subject to a maximum of 8 per cent on deposits up to one year. This had to be withdrawn, as banks were unable to handle even this very limited degree of deregulation and the experiment showed that a lot more preparation would be required by way of counselling banks to handle a gradual deregulation of interest rates. Third, the complex lending rate structure was simplified in 1990. The revised rate structure had only six slabs with the rate of interest linked to size of the loan (export credit, however, was kept outside this rationalisation). In the case of advances over Rs 2 lakh, only a minimum rate was prescribed. Banks could charge higher rates depending on their assessment of risks of the borrowers.

The beginnings of the banking sector reform were also seen in the second half of 1980s. Branch expansion was becoming more selective. A limit was set on the expansion of staff. The Reserve Bank was concerned particularly with the financial conditions of some of the nationalised banks. A health code system was introduced to classify bank loans, a beginning of the separation of the performing from the non-performing loans.

III

MONETARY POLICY IN THE 1990s

Monetary policy in the 1990s had to deal with several issues, some of which were traditional but some totally new in the context of the changed economic policy setting. In the first few years, monetary policy had to contend with the consequences of devaluation and the need to quickly restore price stability to obtain the full benefits of devaluation. While the fiscal deficit was being brought down, the question of monetisation of the deficit continued to remain an issue and a solution had to be found. This eventually led to a new agreement between government and RBI on financing deficit. During 1993 and 1994, for the first time monetary policy had to deal with the monetary impact of capital inflows with the foreign exchange reserves increasing sharply from $ 9.2 billion in March 1992 to $ 25.1 billion in March 1995. In 1995-96, the change in perception with reference to exchange rate after a prolonged period of nominal exchange rate stability vis-a-vis the US dollar brought into play the use of monetary policy to stabilise the rupee - an entirely new experience for the central bank. Similar situations arose later on also. Monetary policy had begun to operate within a changed institutional framework brought about by the financial sector reforms. It is this change in the institutional framework that gave a new dimension to monetary policy. New transmission channels opened up. Indirect monetary controls gradually assumed importance. With the progressive dismantling of the administered interest rate structure and the evolution of a regime of market determined interest rate on government securities, open market operations including 'repo' and 'reverse repo' operations emerged for the first time as an instrument of monetary control. Bank Rate acquired a new role in the changed context. The 1990s paved the way for the emergence of monetary policy as an independent instrument of economic policy.

It may be useful at this point to set out briefly the events as they unfolded in the 1990s and the response of monetary authorities. The decade of 1990s began disastrously for India. Both the fiscal and balance of payments situations went out of control. The year 1990-91 had to contend against a high fiscal deficit and a widening gap in the balance of payments triggered by the steep increase in oil prices. In 1989-90, gross fiscal deficit of the central government had touched 8.05 per cent of GDP and the inflation rate stood at 9.1 per cent. Monetary policy in 1990-91 had to be tight for all these reasons. While monetary growth somewhat moderated to 15.1 per cent in 1990-91 as compared with an expansion of 19.6 per cent in the previous year, inflation rate rose as high as 12.1 per cent. The import compression measures included several monetary policy actions such as imposition of high cash margins on imports of goods under OGL. The year 1990-91 was also noteworthy for the rationalisation of the structure of lending rates which was announced in September 1990.

1991-92 heralded far reaching changes in economic policy. A definitive shift in economic policy occurred in mid-1991. However, structural reforms could be introduced successfully only, if a degree of stabilisation was achieved. A major step to correct the balance of payment situation was the devaluation of the rupee effected in July 1991. However, devaluation could yield results only if it was accompanied by a monetary policy that put a lid on the expansion of aggregate demand. A tightening of the monetary policy had in fact begun even earlier in April/May 1991, with increases in interest rates and reserve requirements together with direct controls on credit and an interest surcharge of 25 per cent on import finance. The Bank Rate was raised by 1 percentage point from 10 per cent to 11 per cent in July 1991. The minimum lending rate on credit limits over Rs 2 lakh was raised by 1.5 percentage point from 17 per cent to 18.5 per cent in July 1991. The Bank Rate was further raised by 1 percentage point from 11 per cent to 12 per cent in October 1991 and the minimum lending rate for large borrowers was raised to 20 per cent. Simultaneously, interest rates on deposits were raised up to a maximum of 13 per cent. As the balance of payments showed improvement and the inflationary pressures showed signs of abatement, the process of reducing the lending rate started from March 1992. Along side, as part of the financial sector reforms and because of the anticipated decline in gross fiscal deficit of the central government, the statutory liquidity ratio on incremental deposit liabilities was reduced to 30 per cent from 38.5 per cent.

Beginning 1992-93, a conscious effort was made to reduce interest rates in the system, as there was a deceleration in inflation and improvement in the economic situation. In 1992-93 the inflation rate as measured by the wholesale price index came down to 7 per cent. The opportunity was also taken to progressively rationalise the lending rate structure. As the macroeconomic situation further improved, the reserve requirements were brought down. The incremental Cash Reserve Ratio was discontinued in April 1992. A part of the impounded cash balances were also released. Apart from the reduction in incremental SLR, the basic level of SLR was reduced. With the restoration of stability, the stage was set for a vigorous introduction of several financial sector reforms outlined in the Narasimham Committee. An effort was also made to develop the Government Securities Market. The reform measures in this area included the introduction of 364-day and 91-day treasury bills on auction basis, auctions of dated securities and Repo auctions. The exchange rate regime underwent a significant change in March 1993, when the dual exchange rate system came to an end and a unified market came into being, with the exchange rate being determined by the forces of supply and demand.

Monetary policy in 1993-94 was formulated with the major consideration of ensuring adequate support to the banking system for the revival of output by reducing the cost of money and increasing the availability of credit. The minimum lending rate was brought down by 2 percentage points to 15 per cent by

September 1993. The minimum lending rate on term loans of 3 years and above was lowered to 14 per cent. A reduction in the deposit rate was also effected. The incremental SLR was brought down from 30 per cent to 25 per cent. The year was marked by a substantial increase in the foreign exchange assets which went up by US $ 9.4 billion. As a consequence, monetary expansion became very large at 18.4 per cent in 1993-94 as against 14.8 per cent in the previous year and the inflation rate crossed 10 per cent. Open market operations were extensively used to neutralise the expansionary impact of capital inflows. This became possible only because the government securities issued in the previous two years had more or less market determined interest rates and the RBI had a stock of such securities. For the first time, external sector became the main cause of expansion in money supply. Real GDP grow by 6.2 per cent.

There was a clear improvement in the overall performance of the economy in 1994-95. The rate of growth of real GDP touched 7.8 per cent. Current account convertibility on the external account was formalised through the acceptance of Article VIII of International Monetary Fund. There was, however, a slippage in the gross fiscal deficit. Macro economic management faced problems of large capital inflow in the first half of the year, a sharp credit expansion in the second half of the year and an uneasy fiscal balance at the end of the year. An important development in the area of fiscal and monetary policy was the agreement between the government and the RBI to phase out the system of ad hoc treasury bills over a period of three years. The system, as it existed then, amounted to an automatic monetisation of the budget deficit. Monetary policy in 1994-95 had to be framed against the backdrop of a high inflation rate caused by large growth in reserve money triggered by large capital inflows. In the second half of 1994-95, the RBI undertook certain measures to moderate the inflow of capital. The foreign currency non-resident deposits were brought under the purview of CRR. In October 1994, the RBI, however, reduced the lending rates of scheduled commercial banks for credit limits over Rs 2 lakh. Further reductions in Statutory Liquidity Ratio were also made. The government long-term borrowing rate came down slightly to 12.35 per cent. In order to sterilise the expansionary impact of the surge in foreign currency assets, the CRR which had been lowered in the previous year was raised by 1 percentage point. Nevertheless, the monetary expansion was high at 22.4 per cent. Even after allowing for the fact that the last reporting Friday coincided with March 31 and that there were 27 fortnights instead of the normal 26, the monetary expansion was high. Non-food credit expanded by 29.8 per cent. The inflation rate touched 10.8 per cent.

Real economic activity continued to remain buoyant in 1995-96. For the second year in succession, the rate of growth of the economy exceeded 7 per cent. Monetary policy had to act against a background of an inflation rate exceeding 10 per cent in the previous two years. Another important factor influencing monetary policy in the year was the turbulence in the foreign exchange market which started in August 1995. The nominal rupee-dollar rate which had remained totally stable since March 1993 came under pressure. Even a small variation in the exchange rate after years of total stability triggered panic reaction and precipitated a sudden drop in the value of the rupee. The exchange market intervention (net sales) by the Reserve Bank in the spot market led to the withdrawal of liquidity from the money market, leading to sharp increase in the call rates which then restored stability in the exchange market. But the stability in the exchange market was shaken again in mid-January 1996. The Reserve Bank took a number of measures in early February 1996 to accelerate receipt of export proceeds and to prevent an acceleration in import payments. These measures enabled the rupee to stage a strong recovery and in fact, the Reserve Bank started purchasing foreign exchange to prevent a sharp strengthening of the rupee. Between October 1995 and March 1996 the cumulative impact of RBI foreign exchange intervention and release of resources through reduction of CRR was an injection of liquidity, though for a period of two or three months, there was a negative impact which had the effect of pushing up money market interest rates. This was also a year when there was a strong demand for funds both from the government and the commercial sector. The raising of funds through the capital market dropped substantially in 1995-96, while investment demand continued to remain high. The mobilisation of resources from the primary market by non-government public limited companies came down from Rs 26,440 crore in 1994-95 to Rs 16,371 crore in 1995-96. As a consequence, there was a pressure on bank credit and interest rates. In fact, non-food credit by the banking sector expanded by 22.5 per cent in 1996-97, on top of a 30 per cent increase in the previous year. Even though money supply in 1995-96 showed a smaller expansion partly for the reason that the base figure was high, the expansion in bank credit was nevertheless high because the lendable resources of the system increased as a result of the reductions in CRR. In the event there was a significant drop in the inflation rate in 1995-96.

The economy continued to grow at a rate exceeding 7 per cent in 1996-97, for the third year in succession. Given the stability in prices, a major effort was made to bring down the CRR. There was a sharp scaling down of the CRR by as much as 4 percentage points to 10 per cent between April 1996 and January 1997. Capital inflows also recovered in the second half of the year. As a consequence, nominal interest rates at the shorter end declined sharply. The treasury bill rate for 91 days which stood at 12.97 per cent in April 1996 came down to 10.17 per cent in October 1996 and declined further to 7.5 per cent in February 1997. Interest rates at the longer end, however, experienced marked stickiness partly because inflationary expectations had not come down. The money supply growth rate during the year 1996-97 was 16.2 per cent and with the economy growing at 7.5 per cent, the inflation rate remained low at 5.4 per cent.

Signs of the slackening of growth of the economy were visible from early 1997. The Bank Rate was reactivated in April 1997 by linking several interest rates to it. It was also the rate at which refinance was to be provided by RBI. An attempt was thus made to make the Bank Rate as the 'signal' rate. The Bank Rate was reduced from 12 per cent to 11 per cent in April 1997 and further to 10 per cent in June 1997. In October 1997 the Bank Rate was further reduced by 1 percentage point to 9 per cent. A programme to reduce the CRR from 10 to 8 per cent which was announced in October 1997 could not be fully implemented because of the east Asian crisis. Because of the series of measures introduced in relation to CRR and Bank Rate, the government borrowing rate started to decline. In August 1997 the yield on Eight-Year Bond came down to 11.19 per cent. The trend of decline in the interest rate got interrupted in the wake of the measures to stabilise the exchange market. In January 1998 the Bank Rate was raised to 11 per cent and the CRR to 10.5 per cent. While the rupee did depreciate, the depreciation was much less than what the east Asian currencies experienced.

During 1998-99 and 1999-2000 inflation rate continued to remain low. The money supply growth rate in the two years were 19.4 per cent and 13.9 per cent, respectively. The economy grew at 6.8 per cent and 6.4 per cent, respectively. With inflation rates remaining low, there was a softening of interest rates. The long-term borrowing rate of the government started declining. By April 2000, the Bank Rate was brought down to 7 per cent and the CRR to 9 per cent. During 2000-01, Bank Rate was raised and then levelled back to 7 per cent and CRR to 8 per cent.

IV

SOME ISSUES

Monetary economics like many other branches of economics is not a settled science. There are continuing debates on several issues connected with monetary policy. Questions have been raised on the objectives, instrumentalities and impact of monetary policy. In fact, many issues relating to monetary economics can be answered only in the context of the understanding of the functioning of the entire economic system. Monetary economics is thus part and parcel of Macroeconomics. Perhaps to some extent the answers to various questions also change with changing times and the environment in which economies operate. Answers given in the context of a closed economy are not relevant in the open economy. In this article a few of the issues that have been raised in the conduct of monetary policy are answered, keeping in the background the Indian experience.

Objectives of Monetary Policy

The first set of questions that needs to be addressed relate to the objective/objectives of monetary policy. A recurring question is whether monetary policy should be concerned with all the goals of economic policy. The issue of 'objective' has become important because of the need to provide a clear guidance to monetary policy-makers. Indeed, this aspect has assumed added significance in the context of the increasing stress on the autonomy of Central Banks. Autonomy goes with accountability and accountability in turn requires a clear enunciation of the goals.

Since the inception of development planning, the broad objectives of India's economic policy have been to achieve a faster rate of growth, ensure reasonable degree of price stability and promote distributive justice. Working of monetary policy in India over the past several decades would reveal that monetary policy has emphasised these broad objectives of our economic policy. In one of his earlier articles, the present author had said "In a broad sense the objectives of monetary policy can be no different from the over all objectives of economic policy. The broad objectives of monetary policy in India have been: (1) to maintain a reasonable degree of price stability and (2) to help accelerate the rate of economic growth. The emphasis as between the two objectives has changed from year to year, depending upon the conditions prevailing in that year and in the previous year."

The question of a dominant objective arises essentially because of the multiplicity of objectives and the inherent conflict among such objectives. Jan Tinbergen had argued decades ago that there should be as many instruments as there are objectives, if all objectives are to be fulfilled. Faced with multiple objectives that are equally relevant and desirable, there is always the problem of assigning to each instrument the most appropriate objective. This 'assignment rule' favours monetary policy as the most appropriate instrument to achieve the objective of price stability. It is this line of reasoning which has led to the single objective approach.

Trade-Off between Inflation and Growth

The crucial question that is being debated in India as elsewhere is whether the pursuit of the objective of price stability by monetary authorities undermines the ability of the economy to attain and sustain high growth. A considerable part of the relevant research effort has been devoted to the trade-off between economic growth and price stability.

The well known Phillips curve had suggested the possibility of a trade-off between inflation and unemployment. The original article of A W Phillips was published in 1958. Subsequent analyses have, however, clearly shown that the Phillips curve provides at best a temporary trade-off between inflation and unemployment, when the economy is adjusting to shocks to aggregate demand and as long as the expected inflation is lower than the actual inflation. There is essentially no long-run 'trade-off' between inflation and unemployment as the anticipated inflation adjusts fully to the actual inflation. The long-run Phillips curve becomes almost vertical at the 'natural' rate of unemployment. Even the possibilities of 'trade-off' between inflation and unemployment in the short run is being disputed by the adherents of 'rational expectations' theory.

The case of price stability as the objective of monetary policy rests on the assumption that volatility in prices creates uncertainty in decision-making. Rising prices adversely affect savings while they make speculative investments more attractive. The most important contribution of the financial system to an economy is its ability to augment savings and allocate resources more efficiently. A regime of rising prices vitiates the atmosphere for promotion of savings and allocation of investment. Apart from all these, there is a social dimension. Inflation adversely affects those who have no hedges against it and that includes all the poorer sections of the community. The fiscal consolidation also becomes easier in an environment of reasonable degree of price stability. In a period of rising prices, the gap between revenues and expenditures widens. Expenditures tend to grow at a faster rate than revenues because many components of expenditures such as employees' compensation are closely linked to variations in prices.

Commitment to price stability does not mean a blind faith in maintaining a certain level of inflation, without concern for the need to maintain and accelerate growth. Far from it. What this commitment implies is that monetary policy can help the growth process by regulating money supply towards the direction of maintaining price stability in the economy and helping the economy to recover from independent shocks. The objective of price stability needs to be interpreted carefully. In some ways it is not an end in itself. It is a means to achieving sustained growth. In most industrially advanced countries, Central Banks have accepted price stability as the single objective of policy. In fact this is built into the Mastricht Treaty. Even though the enactments setting up the Central Banks in these countries refer to multiple objectives, in recent years Central Banks in these countries have focused primarily on price stability. The evolutionary process has been from multiple objectives to a single or dominant objective. This was the direct consequence of stagflation in the 1970s and high inflation in the early 1980s. Only when risks of inflation are considered to be low, are they willing to accommodate other objectives. This has been explicitly stated by the Federal Reserve in the course of the recent changes in interest rate.[1] In fact, the Federal Reserve prepares a balance of risk statement before deciding the course of action. Unfortunately in India in most of the years we had to act when the risk of inflation was high. Low inflation rates have become a common phenomenon in all the industrial countries now. However, Central Banks do not hesitate on occasions to intervene to fulfil other specific objectives such as reducing the volatility in the foreign exchange market. While most industrially advanced countries are willing to let the markets determine the foreign exchange rate of their currencies, they do intervene and sometimes in a concerted way, when exchange markets become volatile. This holds good even more for developing economies like India. In the long run, a monetary policy geared to domestic price stability can help to avoid disruptive adjustments in exchange rate. This dictum applies strongly to developing countries. Short-term volatility, however, has to be dealt with through appropriate and strong actions. However, focusing on occasions to contain exchange market volatility does not compromise with the basic objective of price stability. Exception proves the rule.

Threshold Level of Inflation

The question that recurs very often in the minds of the policy-makers is whether in the short run, there is a trade-off between inflation and growth which can be exploited. In the industrial countries, a solution is sought through the adoption of Taylor's rule which prescribes that the signal interest rate be fixed taking into account the deviations of inflation rate from the target and actual output from its potential. In this rule, the coefficient of inflation deviation term is fixed at a level higher than unity. While the rule is intuitively appealing, there are serious problems in determining the value of the coefficients. In this context, the critical question to answer is: At what level of inflation, do adverse consequences begin to set in? It is this inflation threshold which will provide some guidance to the policy-makers. Below and around this threshold level of inflation, there is greater manoeuvrability for the policy makers to take into account other considerations. Interestingly, the Chakravarty Committee regarded the acceptable rise in prices as 4 per cent. This according to the committee will reflect changes in relative prices necessary to attract resources to growth sectors. The present author has indicated that in the Indian context, inflation rate in the range of 5 to 6 per cent may be acceptable. There is a lot of judgment involved in this. Econometric models are not in a position to capture all the costs of inflation. An inflation rate of 5 to 6 per cent is higher than what is considered as acceptable in the industrially advanced countries. In a globalised economic system, Indian prices cannot remain too much out of alignment with prices in other countries because this has implications for the exchange rate.

Price stability as an objective is also subject to many interpretations and qualifications. More often, it is interpreted as stabilising the inflation rate rather than the level of prices per se. The latter would imply that there could be years in which there will have to be deflation in order to compensate for slippages in the earlier years. Then there is the issue of the choice of appropriate index of prices. Some attempts have also been made to decompose index into permanent and temporary components and to focus on the behaviour of the permanent component. This is admissible only if the temporary component, as the term implies, is assumed to cancel out over a period of years. Increasingly the services sector has come to dominate the national income. All the price indices that we have in India do not take into account changes in the prices of services. Besides there is the question of accounting for asset prices which may not yet have acquired the same significance in India as in the west.

Money, Output and Prices

The role of monetary authorities in relation to maintaining price stability centres around the inter-relationship that exists among money, interest rate, output and prices. As Chakravarty had mentioned, in the absence of a stable demand function for money, the role of monetary policy itself will be negligible in inflation management. Empirical evidence, as far as India is concerned, shows that the demand for real money is a reasonably stable function of a select set of variables. Perhaps some of the factors that have contributed to the instability of the demand function from money in the industrially advanced countries such as financial innovations and large movements of funds across the border are yet to have the same impact in India. Several countries in the industrial world have moved away from intermediate targets such as money supply to the final inflation targeting.[2] While this has the advantage of specifying the ultimate objective in clear and precise terms, there is uncertainty regarding the route through which this is achieved. In the demand function for money in India, income emerges as the most dominant variable. Such a function enables the authorities to estimate the appropriate growth in money supply, given the expected increase in real output and the acceptable level of price increase. The concept of monetary targeting that flows from such a formulation is a flexible one which takes into account the various feedbacks including changes in expected income. Income growth plays the most crucial role in this formulation. The money supply target is relatively well understood by the public and provides unambiguously the stance of monetary policy. This approach to monetary targeting implicitly takes into account the transmission mechanism through the credit channel as well. Since the target is broad money, monetary expansion means expansion in credit both for the government and commercial sectors. Implicit in the monetary growth target is also a credit growth target.

Many studies on India have shown that the relationship between the prices on the one hand and income and money supply on the other is found to hold reasonably well over a period of time. Averages of price changes over a period of three to five years are predicted with reasonable accuracy by these equations and these predictions fall within a range which should be a sufficient guide to policy. Seeking to find a direct year to year correspondence between changes in money supply and real income and the price level is a simplistic approach to the problem which overlooks the inherent lags in the functioning of an economy. Also administered prices which are changed at unpredictable intervals cause distortions which may, however, work themselves out over a period of time. Our performance in relation to the control of inflation over the last five years has been satisfactory. Since 1995-96 when the first break occurred, the average inflation rate over the five-year period has been 5.2 per cent. The average growth of money supply during this period has been 16.2 per cent and the real growth rate 6.6 per cent. This gives us an implicit income elasticity of demand for money at 1.6 which is what one gets from various estimates of price equations. Though there are lags in the impact of money supply on the price, they are not that long. In the western countries where interest rate changes are used to moderate prices, the lags have been estimated between 18 and 24 months.

Interest Rate and Money Supply

The literature on monetary economics talks of four distinct monetary transmission channels. They are (1) Quantum Channel, especially relating to money supply and credit, (2) Interest Rate Channel, (3) The Exchange Rate Channel and (4) The Asset Prices Channel. While the emphasis in India so far has been on the quantum channel, with the development of financial markets and closer integration of such markets, the interest rate channel is assuming importance. It must be noted at the equilibrium both quantity and price are determined. Changes in interest rates cannot be ordained. The appropriate quantitative changes in money will have to be brought about even though the signal for change may be given by the price variable like interest rate. That is why in the Indian context a downward adjustment in signal rate like Bank Rate becomes more effective, when accompanied by reduction in cash reserve ratio or actions through open market operations.

The impact of interest rate on output will depend upon a variety of environmental factors. The history of industrial growth even in the decade of 1990s shows that high interest rates did not deter higher growth in industrial production, when investment demand was high due to other factors. A lowering of interest rate need not necessarily stimulate output. As the saying goes, 'we can take the horse to the pond but cannot compel it to drink'.

The nominal interest rate comprises of three important elements: (i) the real rate of interest, (ii) inflation expectations and (iii) a discount factor for uncertainties. The real interest rate is not an observed variable. The real interest rate is influenced by several long-term factors such as saving and investment balance in the economy and the rate of return on capital. All that theory tells us is on an economywide basis, this rate should not exceed the real rate of growth. In fast growing economies the real rate of interest will be higher.[3] In South Korea during the years of very rapid economic growth the real rate of interest was around 6 to 7 per cent in several years. The real rate of interest is thus related to the rate of growth of the economy. The effectiveness of monetary policy to bring down the nominal interest rate will depend on the impact that this policy will have on inflation expectations and on the perception of uncertainty in the economy. Our record on inflation control in the recent period has been good. Thus, there is force in the argument that interest rate adjustments should move in sympathy with changes in inflation rate. However, to effect a change in interest rate, what is relevant is not the past trend but the future behaviour. Past behaviour only lends credibility to the decision. What is needed is to assure that the inflation rate in future will remain under control. This is particularly relevant when we are talking of fixed interest rate on long- term obligations. The only enduring way of bringing down the nominal interest rate is by keeping the inflation rate low so that inflationary expectations are broken and the uncertainty element is reduced.

Fiscal and Monetary Coordination

Effectiveness of monetary policy depends among other factors on the stance of fiscal policy. The concerns of fiscal policy and monetary policy are at once same and different. Fiscal policy has a much broader spectrum of objectives to achieve. Nevertheless, the two policies cannot run at cross-purposes. In fact, monetary policy fine tuning has assumed greater importance in the west and particularly in the US because of the changed fiscal situation. The US Federal government is today running a fiscal surplus and is in a position to retire debt and bring down the debt burden. This is in stark contrast with the early 1980s in that country. A lax fiscal policy was accompanied by a tight monetary policy leading to a sharp increase in interest rate which had international ramifications. On the other hand, an accommodative monetary policy in a period of lax fiscal policy can lead to explosive increase in prices. World over there is a recognition of the need to maintain fiscal balance at some reasonable level of fiscal deficit so that monetary policy can play its role. This general proposition is also true of India. If the fiscal deficit remains high and if monetary policy accommodates it, it will make monetary policy ineffective in terms of achieving the objective of price stability. While monetary and fiscal coordination is desirable, it is important at the same time that the monetary authority which has its own specific agenda must have the institutional autonomy and should not be burdened with functions which may come in conflict with its own special objective. It is in this context that the issue of public debt management by the central bank is being debated. It is understandable why initially the Reserve Bank of India was chosen as the institutional agency for the floating or government debt. However, as we move towards greater use of open market operations as an instrument of monetary policy to influence money supply and interest rate, a gradual delinking of the function of the floating of public debt from the Reserve Bank will become a natural corollary.

Financial Stability

Increasingly macroeconomic stability including price stability as an objective of central banking is closely linked to financial stability. It is easy to see how the two are inter linked. Financial stability broadly implies the stability of the important institutions and markets forming part of the financial system. Financial stability requires that the key institutions in the financial system are stable, in that, there is a high degree of confidence about meeting contractual obligations without interruption or outside assistance. While the complementarity between the objectives of macro stability and financial stability is easily recognised, the one question that needs to be addressed is whether there can be a conflict between the two objectives. It is not inconceivable to have situations in which the price stability objective might call for a restrictive policy, while the financial market conditions may demand a somewhat liberal policy to provide relief. Even separation of the powers of supervision from the central bank will not resolve such a dilemma, if it arises. Delinking supervision of banks from the central bank arises out of other considerations which are mainly administrative in character. A common supervisory authority for all financial market participants has been advocated on the grounds of increasing integration among markets. Viewed as part of overall economic stability, financial stability need not run at cross purpose with other dimensions of macroeconomic stability. Interest rate has a key role to play both in relation to price stability and financial stability. Normally, price stability should provide an environment favourable to financial stability. If on occasions dealing directly with financial stability becomes necessary, it must be done as in the case of intervention in the foreign exchange markets. Actions to maintain financial stability in those circumstances may be in the long run interest of economic stability.

In the first several decades after the setting up of the Reserve Bank, a major responsibility of the central bank was to widen and deepen the financial system. The Reserve Bank took the initiative to set up new institutions. This leadership role continued through 1980s and 1990s. New markets, instruments and institutions were routinely introduced. This developmental role in no way conflicts with the other responsibilities. The effectiveness of monetary policy depends on the institutional framework available for transmitting impulses released by the central bank. The efforts aimed at strengthening the institutional structure are a necessary part of the functions of a central bank.

Autonomy of Central Banks

Autonomy of central banks has become an article of faith in the industrial countries. It has been written into the constitution setting up the European Central Bank. The literature on this subject is growing. There is a general consensus to give instrument independence to central banks among countries that have decided that the single objective of monetary policy is inflation control. Autonomy implies discretion to central banks to decide on the timing and nature of monetary policy intervention. It also calls for transparency in relation to both objectives and strategies. The increased use of explicit targets by central banks is part of the broader move to build credibility through transparency. It is quite true that in India, monetary policy has been very much conditioned by the stance of fiscal policy. The system of the scheme of ad hoc treasury bills facilitated monetisation of the fiscal deficit without limit and without prior approval. The 1990s saw the phasing out of the system and the introduction of the scheme of Ways and Means advance. This was a major step towards the achievement of greater discretion. The Fiscal Responsibility Bill takes this to its logical conclusion. When enacted this would be a great step forward not only in fiscal but monetary management. Two associated comments may be made in this context. First, an autonomous central bank does not mean lack of coordination with the government. Nor does it imply lack of harmony. In fact, harmony in the sense in which it is used in classical symphonic music will be achieved. In a symphony, different artistes play different notes simultaneously but in effect produce a blend that catches the height of music. Second, the emergence of an autonomous central bank does not mean that the 'state of bliss' has arrived. It only enables the central bank to pursue a consistent monetary policy over a long time. Then the onus of responsibility for the conduct of monetary policy will rest on the shoulders of the Reserve Bank, where it should logically rest.

There was a time when it was said that central banking was neither a science nor an art but a craft. This is at best a half-truth. Central banking has never been a case of applying well known remedies to well known problems. 'Rules versus discretion' has been a subject of long standing debate in monetary policy. Rigid rules such as those implicit in gold standard will give to central banks no room for manoeuvrability. On the other hand, total discretion with respect to objectives and instruments will make monetary policy indeterminate. That is why the new phrase 'constrained discretion'. This will require the central banks to be transparent and explicit with respect to objectives and strategies, while leaving the freedom to them to choose the timing and nature of their actions. This is the true essence of autonomy.

Notes

[This is a slightly modified version of the Sukhamoy Chakravarty Memorial Lecture delivered by the author in March 2001. Without doubt Chakravarty is one of the most outstanding economists that this country has produced. He was both a scholar and an original thinker. His knowledge of the history of economic ideas was indeed encyclopedic. But this scholarship did not weigh down on his creative thinking. His writings on capital accumulation and optimal savings will remain as lasting contributions to economic theory. Chakravarty, like most Indian economists, was interested primarily in the 'real' sector problems. His ideas on money and finance crystallised largely when he was appointed as chairman of the Committee to Review the Working of Monetary System in 1982. The ideas contained in the report considerably influenced the thinking on monetary policy in the second half of the 1980s.]

1 In his testimony, chairman of the Federal Reserve Board, Alan Greenspan, after the two reductions in the federal funds rate in January, 2001 said, "An essential precondition for this type of response was that underlying cost and price pressures remained subdued, so that our front-loaded actions were unlikely to jeopardise the stable, low inflation environment necessary to foster investment and advances in productivity".

2 The literature on inflation targeting is growing with more and more countries adopting explicitly or implicitly such a procedure. The important advantages claimed in favour of inflation targeting are: (a) It helps to focus on domestic considerations unlike exchange rate targeting, and (b) Monetary policy strategy does not rely on a stable money-inflation relationship. The inflation targeting allows the monetary authorities to use all available information. It is also claimed that inflation targeting reduces political pressures on the central bank to pursue inflationary monetary policy and reduce the likelihood of time inconsistence policy-making. In most countries which have adopted inflation targeting, the inflation target itself is set to be determined by the political authorities while allowing the central bank the freedom of action to achieve the target.

3 The relationship between real interest rate and growth rate is not straightforward. Many writers have examined this relationship within the framework of different types of growth models. Koyck and Hooft-Welvaars (1966) write, "An optimum rate of investment can be found which maximises per capita consumption at every point of time on the equilibrium path. The optimum rate of interest corresponding with this optimum rate of investment appears to be equal to the rate of growth of gross output." Robin Matthews (1960) using the typical Harrod-Domar growth model says, "It may seem paradoxical that a high r is associated with high g. But this is as it should be: a high r means a low K/Y, and a low K/Y means a given rate of saving is able to support a high rate of growth of output". Sen (1970) has argued that in the framework of neoclassical growth theories, a rise in the real interest rate seems to induce a higher rate of growth because in such models there is no investment function and investment is assumed simply to be determined by savings behaviour. Khan and Villanueva (1991) support the positive

association between high interest rate and high growth rate based on the argument that real interest rate is a good proxy for the efficiency (productivity) of capital accumulation. However, if high real interest rate does not reflect the efficiency of investment and is caused by market imperfections, there may not be a positive association with growth rate. Thus a situation of high real rate of interest accompanied by high growth rate must be distinguished from other situations.

References

Arif, R R (1996): 'Money Demand Stability: Myth or Reality - An Econometric Analysis', *Development Research Group Study No 13*, Reserve Bank of India.

Baro, Robert (1995): 'Inflation and Economic Growth', *Bank of England Quarterly Bulletin*, Vol 35, No 2.

Chakravarty, Sukhamoy (1986): 'Report of the Committee to Review the Working of the Monetary System - A Re-examination', Sir Purushotamdas Thakurdas Memorial Lecture, The Indian Institute of Bankers, Mumbai.

Chakravarty, Sukhamoy (1986): 'Analytical Base' *in Monetary Policy: Review of the Sukhamoy Chakravarty Report,* IIC Monograph series No 10, India International Centre, New Delhi.

Fischer, Stanley (1994): 'Modern Central Banking' in Forrest Capie, Charles Goodhart, Stanley Fischer and Nobert Schnadt (eds), *The Future of Central Banking, The Tercentenary Symposium of the Bank of England,* Cambridge University Press, Cambridge.

Friedman, Milton (1975): 'Unemployment versus Inflation? An Evaluation of the Phillips Curve', *Occasional Paper 44*, The Institute of Economic Affairs, London.

Goodhart, Charles A E (2001): 'Whither Central banking?', *Reserve Bank of India Bulletin*, January.

Khan, Mohsin S and Daleno Villanueva (1991): 'Macroeconomic Policies and Long-term Growth: A Conceptual and Empirical Review', *IMF Working Paper,* WP/91/28, IMF, Washington, DC.

Koyck, L M and Maria J 't Hooft-Welvaars (1966): 'Economic Growth, Marginal Productivity of Capital, and the Rate of Interest' in F H Hahn and F P R Brechling (eds), *The Theory of Interest Rates*, MacMillan, New York.

Krugman, Paul (1996): 'Stable Prices and Fast Growth: Just Say No', *Economist*, Vol 31.

Matthews, R C O (1960): 'The Rate of Interest in Growth Models', *Oxford Economic Papers*, Vol 12.

McCallum, Bennett T (2000): 'Alternative Monetary Policy Rules: A Comparison with Historical settings for the United States, the United Kingdom and Japan', *Economic Quarterly* of the Federal Reserve Bank of Richmond.

Mishkin, Frederic S (1999): 'International Experience with Different Monetary Policy Regimes', *Journal of Monetary Economics,* Vol 43.

Phelps, Edmund S (1967): 'Phillips Curves, Expectation of Inflation and Optimal Unemployment Over Time', *Economica*, Vol 34.

Poole, William (1999): 'Monetary Policy Rules?', *Review*, Federal Reserve Bank of St Louis, March/April.

Rangarajan, C (1989): 'Issues in Monetary Management', *Indian Economic Journal*, Vol 36, No 3.

—— (1997): 'Role of Monetary Policy', *Economic and Political Weekly*, December 27.

Rangarajan, C and R R Arif (1990): 'Money, Output and Prices: A Macro Econometric Model', *Economic and Political Weekly,* April 21.

Rangarajan, C and M S Mohanty (1997): 'Fiscal Deficit and External Balance and Monetary Growth – A Study of Indian Economy', *RBI Occasional papers*, Vol 18, No 4.

Reserve Bank of India (1985): 'Report of the Committee to Review the Working of the Monetary System', (Chakravarty Committee).

Sarel, Michael (1996): 'Nonlinear Effects of Inflation on Economic Growth', *IMF Staff Papers*, Vol 43, No 1.

Sen, A K (1970): 'Interest, Investment and Growth' in A K Sen (ed), *Growth Economics,* Penguin Modern Economic Readings.

Steme, Gabriel (1999): 'The Use of Explicit Targets for Monetary Policy: Practical Experiences of 91 Economies in the 1990s', *Bank of England Quarterly Bulletin*, August.

11

Agenda for Financial Sector Reforms

N. A. MUJUMDAR

A sound financial sector is a pre-requisite for efficient macroeconomic management. The process of liberalisation of the Indian economy, initiated in 1991, has meant corresponding changes in the financial sector which has witnessed a significant transformation during the 1990s. This paper seeks to critically review such transformation in selected segments of the financial sector. One general conclusion which seems to emerge from the review is that our strength lies in carrying out what one might call mimetic reforms in the sense of replicating the paradigm of developed countries. Not being able to tailor the reforms to suit the specific socio-economic Indian milieu is our weakness. Furthermore, in the process of implementation of reforms, a number of distortions have also crept in. Correcting such distortions and attending to neglected segments should therefore claim a pre-eminent position on the agenda of future reforms.

Banking Sector

The focus of financial sector reforms has been on the banking sector. Primarily we have successfully implemented the Basle norms, or prudential norms in conformity with the second Narasimham Committee recommendations. These measures aim at increasing the minimum capital adequacy ratio from 8 per cent to 9 per cent by end March 2000; recognising the market risks and prescribing a risk weight of 2.5 per cent in Government approved securities by end-March 2000; moving towards tighter asset classification, income recognition and provisioning norms; putting in place a formal Asset-Liability Management (ALM) system with effect from April 1, 1999; and further enhancing transparency in accounting and disclosure practices.

While we seem to have done well in mechanistically implementing the "borrowed norms", we have failed to grasp the basic issues confronting public sector banks (PSBs). It has become fashionable to deride PSBs as being inefficient and unprofessional and it is this drubbing by even Indian experts which has resulted in the morale of PSBs touching a low level. For instance, the Report of the Working Group on Restructuring Weak Public Sector Banks (Chairman, M.S. Verma) seeks to judge the strength of PSBs on the basis of even criteria covering solvency, earning capacity and profitability; and on the basis of these criteria concludes that only two banks, namely Oriental Bank of Commerce and State Bank of Patiala are strong banks, all others being in a state of semi-sickness from the incipient to the advanced stage! While three banks - Indian Bank, UCO Bank and United Bank - are clearly identified as very weak and therefore needing immediate treatment, six other banks - Allahabad Bank, Central Bank, Indian Overseas Bank, Punjab and Sind Bank and Vijaya Bank are diagnosed as *potentially weak banks*. Again, take the India Development Report 1999-2000 prepared by the Indira Gandhi Institute of Development Research. To quote: "India's banks and financial institutions are a remarkable combination of high leverage, poor knowledge of risk measurement and management, inadequate ability to control the conflicts of interest between employees and share-holders.... However, the severity of the problems suggest that a complete rescue of the banking sector is probably unlikely in the next few years. In years to come bankruptcies and crisis in India's banking system could take place, despite our best efforts at improving prudential regulations" (page 21). So how do we go about rescuing PSBs? Pilgrimages to Korea and Thailand?

Unfortunately, none of these Indian experts has tried to trace the genesis of the Non-performing Assets (NPAs) of PSBs in the Indian context. These NPAs have *not* been a result of PSBs borrowing heavily short-term funds from abroad and investing such funds in real estate or stock markets, as had happened in most East Asian Countries. In India a large proportion of the backlog of NPAs could be attributed to political meddling, what with the loan melas, or the Indian version of the "Crony Capitalism" in terms of some business borrowers enjoying the most-favoured treatment and so on. In terms of professional competence, Indian bankers are second to none in the world and it is therefore unfair to lay the blame for all the ills of PSBs at the doors of bankers. They may not be able to handle the econometric models for measurement of risk but they do know how to practically manage risks. What is to be blamed is the macro environment in which they are made to function and it is this, which needs to be changes. It ill behoves the Government of India or RBI now to adopt a self-righteous attitude to PSBs, because both of them have been a dominant element in the governance of banks. A more pragmatic solution seems to be to grant autonomy to PSBs. The present Boards of Directors could be dismantled and eminent men of unimpeachable integrity could be installed on the Board, retired High Court Judges, eminent economists, chartered accountants and business management experts could be brought in. The best agency to tackle the NPAs is the concerned bank itself and not the Assets Management Companies or Assets Reconstruction Fund.

Intellectual servitude has perhaps been a by-product of the liberalisation era, based on an amateurish understanding of the concept of globalisation. When the State Bank of India wants to appoint its Economic Adviser, it chooses to advertise the post in the London – based "Economist"! Thank God, no Indian expert has so far recommended that weak banks should be handed over, as in the case of Poland, to foreign banks for management on a long-term basis! Indigenous problems are better solved by indigenous approaches, taking into account the specific socio-economic milieu. Self-flagellation neither helps solve the problem nor is it good for the image of the financial sector.

The core issue facing PSBs today, an issue, which none of the experts mentioned above has discussed, is the lending paralysis. The sub-optimal use of banking sector's resources is reflected in the credit-deposit ratio which is hovering around 50 per cent for the last couple of years. A surfeit of liquidity co-exists with large unsatisfied demand for credit by productive sectors of the economy. The excess liquidity – in the sense of investment in Government securities far in excess of the statutory liquidity ratio (SLR) – adds upto a staggering figure of Rs. 95,000 crore. This mountain of liquidity stands as a monument of our ineptitude in management of banking sector's resources. A more meaningful utilisation of these resources holds a key to the improvement of the profitability of PSBs and also to the promotion of faster rate of growth of the economy.

Development Banks

There has been a lot of discussion recently on the question of universal banking. It may be recalled that the Narasimham Committee on Banking Sector Reforms has suggested that Development Finance Institutions (DFIs) should ultimately convert themselves into either commercial banks or non-bank finance companies. Subsequently, the Khan Working Group expressed the view that DFIs should be allowed to become banks. The RBI released a discussion paper on the subject. On the basis of the feedback, RBI has come to the following conclusion: ".... While universal banking is desirable from the point of view of efficiency of resource use, both banks and DFIs should be cautious in moving towards such a system. Corporates continue to depend on DFIs for project finance. On the other hand, the necessary expertise and infrastructural facilities for extending short term finance lie with commercial banks." (Annual Report, 1998-99, page 149). This is an eminently sensible conclusion. Traditionally, banks and DFIs have specialised in extending short and long term credit respectively, and there is merit in continuing to build on this specialisation. The East Asian experience appears to buttress this conclusion.

Capital Market

The Capital market has come of age: significant institutional changes have taken place in the securities markets with the emergence of electronic trading, a clearing corporation, and a depository. The Bombay market has become a truly national market. Derivative trading is in the offing.

In this context, two problems, which have not attracted much attention, need to be raised: private placement market and *exemption of dividends and income from mutual funds* from income tax.

During the last couple of years, private placement market has emerged as the major route for raising resources by corporate entities. In 1998-99, banks, financial institutions, and public and private sector companies mobilised nearly Rs. 50,000 crore through this route, in sharp contrast to an amount of less than Rs. 10,000 crore through prospectus and rights issues. The question, which needs to be posed, is whether the growth of private placement route at the cost of market growth is healthy. This is important because, at present, private placement does not come under the usual disclosure and protection of investors' interest norms, as prescribed by SEBI. For the new entrepreneurs private placement route is also not easily accessible.

The Budget for 1998-99 exempted from income-tax incomes from dividends and from mutual funds. Ostensibly, this was done to encourage investment in equities directly or through mutual funds. Unfortunately, this measure discriminates against banks, because interest income from bank deposits is taxable. This measure, therefore, is non-egalitarian and pro-rich. In fact it may be remembered that commercial banks were responsible for raising India's saving rate from some 12 per cent to more than 25 per cent of GDP. By discriminating against bank deposits, this measure may erode the national savings rate itself. In our over-enthusiasm to develop the capital market we should not harm the other instruments of saving. The earlier this discrimination is removed, the better it would be for the economy.

Rural Credit System

A conspicuous example of our financial sector reforms being imitative is the nearly total neglect of the rural credit delivery system which comprises rural branches of commercial banks, cooperative credit institutions, and regional rural banks (RRBs). This whole system today is in a moribund state. Agriculture and small-scale industries contribute significantly to GDP and exports. Rural credit thus forms an integral part of the Indian financial sector and should be treated as such. Since I have discussed this subject in depth elsewhere I would be content here with merely mentioning that revival of the rural credit system should find a prominent place on the agenda of future reforms of the financial sector. (Reviving Rural Credit, Economic and Political Weekly, June 19, 1999). In this case, it is not a question of merely tinkering with the system – like restructuring some RRBs or entering into memorandum of understanding (MOUs) with some cooperatives, but a question of evolving a new architecture of the system designed to make it both viable and vibrant.

Concluding Comment

It may be *au courant* to talk of second generation financial sector reforms. What this brief paper has sought to emphasise is that correcting some distortions which have crept in the process of implementing reforms, and attending to segments which have been practically ignored in the reform process – are equally important tasks, which the agenda for future reforms can ill afford to ignore.

III

Agriculture

12

Economic Reforms and Indian Agriculture

Recent Experience and the Long Term Issues

V. S. VYAS • V. RATNA REDDY

I

INTRODUCTION

Liberalization has brought about a change in the basic orientation of development policies in the country by placing greater reliance on the markets for allocations of resources, emphasizing private initiative and encouraging domestic and global competition. Since the early nineties a package of economic reforms were introduced to set the stage for gradual liberalization and globalization, to reinvigorate the economy and to reap the benefits of world wide moves in these directions. These reforms were introduced, first as a part of stabilization policy and later to bring in structural adjustment. Stabilization of the economy was important to correct the distortions in key economic areas, but more far reaching results could come only from structural reforms in the economy. These reforms were directed more or less in a sequential order: first to industrial, then foreign trade and financial sectors.

Advisedly, the reforms in the agricultural sector have been slow and cautious for several reasons. Majority of the agricultural producers cultivate marginal and sub marginal holdings. Their dependence on the market for procurement of inputs and the sale of output is insubstantial. The strategic objectives related to these sections of rural population are the expansion of their meager production base, raising productivity of their existing resources, providing them with alternative sources of livelihood and protecting them from risks and uncertainties. Markets have a limited role to play in meeting these objectives. For the medium and the large farmers non-price factors, particularly technological and organizational factors, are more important to augment their production and fetch higher values for their produce. In any event, because of the economic and political power enjoyed by the medium and the large agricultural producers on the one hand, and the competitive, multi-party nature of our polity on the other, it is not easy to introduce reforms which may hurt the interests of this section.

For a large and poor country such as India food security considerations weigh heavily in determining agricultural policies. Comprehensive reforms which may jeopardize the prospects of food security for the rural and urban poor even in the short-run will not be accepted very easily. Besides, some of the major policy induced handicaps faced by agricultural producers were attended to even before the beginning of the reforms. For example, Indian agriculture was much less severely 'taxed' compared to several other developing countries. Agriculture's terms of trade vis-a-vis non-agricultural sector, though still adverse, were progressively improving (Nadkarni, 1993). Apart from these reasons, there was no urgency felt by the policy makers to institute reforms in the agricultural sector due to the complacency about agricultural growth prospects with ten successive good monsoons.

With the beginning of the current phase of reforms, changes in agricultural policies related mainly to agricultural trade and these too reflected rather short sighted and ad hoc considerations. For example, the 1995-96 Economic survey reported, "Rice and wheat are emerging as major export products. Quantitative ceiling and minimum export price in respect of rice have been abolished. To further enhance exports Food Corporation of India has been permitted to export/ sell for export 3 million tonnes of fine/ superfine varieties of rice. Export of wheat up to 2.5 million tonnes in case of non-durum wheat and 0.5 million tonnes in case of durum wheat has also been permitted." (Govt. of India, 1996, p. 41) . But the volatility of Indian agriculture was aptly reflected when the country instead of exporting food grains had to import 2 million tonnes of wheat by the end of 1996 itself. The story of over optimism and subsequent frustration is repeated, year after year, in the case of cotton, sugar and other agricultural commodities.

Due to the complacent attitude of the policy makers reinforced by the objective of reducing fiscal deficit as a part of the reform package, there has been a continuous decline in the public investment for capital formation in agriculture, as well as in the share of the priority sector lending by the public sector banks during the 90s (Mujumdar, 1999). These trends coupled with the ad hoc measures aimed at cutting down input subsidies, raising procurement prices and reducing the food subsidies, had serious, intended or unintended, consequences for agriculture sector in terms of changes in cropping pattern, input usage and commercialization of agriculture. It is necessary to understand the direction of these changes and their long term impact on the economy, especially in the light of the recent east and south east Asian experience (or the Asian crisis) which reemphasized the importance of food security and consequently of the agricultural sector.

This paper is an attempt to address some of the above questions. Firstly, we examine the impact of liberalization policies on agriculture. Next, an attempt is made to understand the likely impact of Asian Crisis on Indian agriculture. Finally, we try to draw lessons to reach the avowed goals of agricultural development.

II

ECONOMIC REFORMS AND AGRICULTURE

Exclusion of agriculture in any serious discussion on structural reforms in the developing countries is indefensible. It is the largest private sector in the developing economies; it produces tradable goods; as it is now well established, agricultural producers respond positively to economic signals. Yet, there is very little discussion on the implications of Structural Adjustment Policies (SAP) on agriculture in specific country context. Focus of reforms in the countries undergoing structural adjustment, as noted earlier, is mainly on industry and financial sectors. In this section we examine direction of macro as well as sectoral reforms in agriculture.

The Macro Scene

Economic reforms in India began in the early 1980s with progressive relaxation of controls on investment and capacity utilization in industry, liberalization of imports and, support to capital markets. It also comprised fiscal reforms, reforms in the public financial institutions and, realignment of external value of the rupee by gradual devaluation. However, the premises on which earlier policies were based, i.e., emphasis on self sufficiency, "commanding heights" for the parastatals, controls on the allocation and use of resources, regulations of markets, and the like, were not challenged. The reforms which were introduced from July 1991 and continuing since then, are qualitatively different. The underlying principles informing the current policies are: greater reliance on the markets for allocation of resources, emphasis on private initiative and, encouragement to domestic and global competition.

The economic reforms introduced in the country as a part of the stabilization policy and those to achieve structural adjustment are more or less on the expected lines. These measures have proved to be reasonably successful. India could tide over its balance of payments crisis swiftly and smoothly. The fiscal deficit in the central budget has come down from about 8 percent (of GDP) during 1990-91 to about 5 percent by the year 1995-96,but has become rigid thereafter. This resulted in high inflation rates in the initial years of reforms, though inflation seems to be under control in recent years. However, the cost of living index of the agricultural and rural workers increased much faster during the these years indicating a disproportionately high burden of adjustment on the poor.

The reforms introduced in industrial, foreign trade and financial sectors have made a good beginning. Industrial licensing, quotas, and permits are gradually being abandoned. A liberalized foreign trade regime is being introduced, with closer links established between exports and imports; import duties are progressively lowered; rupee has been made partially convertible. Major changes have been effected in the financial sector by encouraging inflow of foreign capital, restructuring interest rates, greater autonomy to the financial institutions and strengthening their capital base. It goes to the credit of the reform policies in India that initial destabilization effects of the reforms such as a steep decline in GNP, upsurge in unemployment, major shifts in commodity prices, etc., could be largely contained. Process of deepening of the reforms in these sectors is continuing. Although it should be noted that the real and tougher issues like privatization of loss making public sector enterprises, or reforms in growth inhibiting labor policies, are yet to be tackled

Agricultural Policies

As in other developing countries – in fact, more so in developed countries – in India also, Government interventions in agricultural sector are quite extensive. The principal agricultural crops are subjected to a variety of administered price regimes (minimum prices, support prices, levy prices, issue prices, etc.). There are formal or informal restrictions on the movement of crops. Government agencies play an important role in marketing of agricultural inputs. Credit delivery is regulated as a part of overall financial controls. External trade in agricultural commodities is restricted or canalized through the parastatal organizations. At the same time, huge subsidies are expended to bring down the real prices of inputs for the agricultural producers.

In these and certain other areas, need for policy reforms has been felt since long. It has become more insistent with the adoption of the New Economic Policy in 1991. The types of policy changes advocated, and implemented to an extent, include removing restrictions on the movement of agricultural commodities (i.e., dezoning), reforms in domestic trade and stocking policies, reforms in the policies of administered prices, liberalization of trade in agricultural commodities – abolition of the quantitative restrictions and substitution, wherever necessary, by export and import tariffs

– revamping public distribution system and, gradual removal of input subsidies. However, in practice several measures reflect political compulsions rather than a part of well thought out, long term, growth strategy. The "stop-go" policies on cotton and rice exports and sugar imports are typical examples of the short term, ad hoc, approach.

Even though most of the policies are formulated at the central level their countrywide adoption depends on the cooperation from the state governments. As a result, although there is consensus on reducing input subsidies at the central level, so far the government could tinker with only fertilizer subsidies as most of the other major subsidies, such as subsidies on irrigation, power, etc., are in the purview of the state governments. Most of the state governments are not prepared to reduce these subsidies for political reasons. For example, Government of India has recommended that agricultural power tariff should be raised to Rs. 0.50 per unit, but very few states have implemented this recommendation. Similarly, irrigation subsidies are vertually untouched in most of the states, despite repeated suggestions for cost recovery through increase in water charges. True, privatization of some of the services in agricultural sector has been carried out in recent years. The areas of privatization include seed production, veterinary services, de-licensing of retail input supply, demonstrations and survey work. The focus of the reforms at the states level is to enlarge the scope of privatization. There is very little evidence to ensure cost recovery for inputs and services provided by the state.

Impact of Policy Changes

The policy changes at the macro level and those instituted at the sectoral level seem to have made some impact on agricultural growth, but more importantly on the dynamics of production relations. The impact may be discussed at two levels. Firstly, the impact of macro policy reforms especially the attempts to curtail budgetary deficits and realign the value of domestic currencies on agricultural sector could be looked into. Secondly, we may examine the impact of sectoral policies addressed to agriculture. Latter would include agricultural price policies, subsidy policies, trade policies, credit policies, etc. These two sets of impacts are overlapping. Our main attention however, is on second aspect of economic policies, i.e. the sectoral policies in Agriculture. As a backdrop we review the overall growth of agriculture sector, its contribution to GDP and plan allocation and capital formation in agriculture.

Sectoral Performance

Indian agriculture was characterized by low and stagnant growth performance till the mid sixties. The performance improved from then on till the end of eighties (Table–1).

Table – 1

Average Compound Growth Rates of GDP and by Sectors During 1980s and 90s.

Year	GDP	Agriculture	Industry	Manufacturing	Services	Per capita GNP
1980-90	5.8	3.1	7.1	7.4	6.7	3.4*
1990-96	5.8	3.1	6.8	7.5	7.0	4.9#

Note : GDP= Gross domestic Product.

* Per capita Gross National Product (GNP) is the average of Sixth (1980-85) and Seventh (1985-90).

\# Per Capita GNP pertains to Eighth Plan (1992-97).

Source : CMIE, Agriculture, 1996; Economic Survey, 1996-97.

The nineties have seen a deceleration of the rate of growth in agricultural output. Agriculture maintained a rate of growth of 3.1 percent during the 80s as well as in the 90s. Though the other sectors have recorded high growth rates in the 80s as well as the 90s, in their case also there was no significant difference in performance over two decades. A distinguishing feature in the case of agricultural output is sharp year to year fluctuations. These high variations imply unpredictable nature of agriculture in India and the precariousness of our food security position.

The share of agriculture in GDP is declining steadily, still it continues to contribute nearly thirty percent of the GDP (Table–2). It is interesting to note that agriculture's share in work force is not declining despite its declining importance in GDP (Table–3). This indicates that more and more people are depending on agricultural activities. It also suggests low absorption capacity of the secondary and tertiary sectors. Figures of employment in the rural areas in general, and agriculture in particular, should be interpreted with caution, due to the short interval between two estimates cited in the above table. However, the fact remains that agriculture still employs nearly two thirds of the country's work force. This coupled with declining share of agriculture in GDP

Table – 2

Macro Economic Indicators Relating to Indian Agriculture

Year	GDP Value (in Rs. crores)*	GDP growth rate	Agricultural GDP*	Agricultural GDP growth rate	Share of agriculture in GDP	Capital formation in agriculture (% of GDP)	% of agriculture in Total outlay
1989-90	201453	6.89	67064	1.99	33.29	25.0	5.6
1990-91	212253	5.36	69860	4.17	32.91	27.7	5.5
1991-92	213983	0.82	68480	–1.98	32.00	23.4	6.2
1992-93	225240	5.26	72421	5.75	32.15	23.9	5.8
1993-94	799077	—	262140	—	32.80	22.4	4.8
1994-95	861064	7.76	277033	5.68	32.17	25.4	5.5
1995-96	926412	7.59	279204	0.78	30.14	25.8	4.7
1996-97	998978	7.83	303572	8.72	30.39	25.7	4.9
1997-98	1049191	5.03	301436	-0.70	28.73	24.8	4.5
1998-99	—	—	—	—	—	—	3.7

Note: * GDP figures till 1992-93 are based on old series with 1980-81 base and from 1993-94 are based on new series with 1993-94 base.

Source: Economic Survey of Various years, Government of India.

Table – 3

Shares of Workforce by Agriculture and Non-agriculture.

Sector	Rural		Urban		Total	
	1989-90	1992	1989-90	1992	1989-90	1992
1. Agriculture	75.1	79.4	13.0	13.2	62.1	65.5
2. Non-agriculture	24.9	20.7	87.0	86.8	37.9	34.5
of Which						
Secondary	12.2	9.5	31.5	33.7	16.2	14.6
Tertiary	12.7	11.1	55.4	53.1	21.7	19.6

Source: Natarajan and Patnaik (1999).

indicates low labour productivity and or adverse terms of trade faced by the sector. The sector's adverse position is also reflected in the rise in the percentage of rural population below poverty line between 1990-91 and 1993-94. The rural population below poverty line was at 34.4 percent in 1988- 89, which went up to 44 percent in 1991-92 and came down to 37.5 percent during 1993-94 (Natarajan and Patnaik, 1999).

The plan outlays for agriculture are also showing a downward slide in the recent years. Although capital formation in agriculture as a percentage of GDP has remained stable, at about 25 percent, over the years, the share of public capital formation is on the decline. It has come down from 38.1 percent in 1980-81 to 25.1 percent in 1990-91 and to 21 percent in 1997-98 (Table–4). The decline in public investment in agriculture is causing serious concern as reflected in the recent discussions on the subject. (Dhawan, 1998).This is because, as a recent study has shown, state level growth rates in agriculture are positively and significantly correlated to the level of Government expenditure in that sector (Rao, Shand and Kalirajan, 1999).

Table – 4

Gross Capital Formation in Agriculture and the Shares of Public and Private Capital Formation.

Year	Gross Capital Formation (Rs. '000' Crores)	Share of Public Capital formation	Share of Private Capital formation
1980-81	4636	38.1	61.3
1990-91	4594	25.1	74.9
1991-92	4729	21.2	78.8
1992-93	5372	19.7	80.3
1993-94	5031	22.9	77.1
1994-95	6256	21.0	79.0
1995-96	6961	18.2	81.8
1996-97	6999	16.2	83.8
1997-98	—	21.0	79.0

Source: Economic Survey, 1998-99.

During the last decade two significant changes have taken place in Indian agriculture. These are, (i) significant growth in irrigated farming and, (ii) shifts in the cropping pattern. Net area under irrigation has gone up from 28 percent in 1980 to 35 percent during 1993 (Table–5). Cropping intensity has gone up by 5 percent, from 125 to 130, during the same period. More importantly, distribution of area by source of irrigation (canals and wells) has undergone significant changes between 1981-82 and 1992-93 (Table–6). During the 90s the share of well irrigation has increased while the share of canal and tank irrigation has declined. This has had important distributional repercussions.

Table – 5

Changes in Cropping Pattern

Cropping Pattern		1980-81	1992-93
Gross Cropped Area		172630	185487
Net Cropped Area		140002	142509
Food Crops as Percentage of GCA	Total	73.37	66.39
	Rice	23.27	22.52
	Wheat	12.90	13.25
	Coarse Cereals	24.20	18.55
	Pulses	13.01	12.59
Non-food Crops as Percentage of GCA	Total	26.63	33.61
	Oilseeds	10.19	13.60
	Cotton	16.43	20.01

Source: CMIE, Agriculture, September1999.

Table – 6

Percentage Area Irrigated by Different Sources

Sources	1980-81	1985-86	1990-91	1992-93	1995-96
Total Irrigated Area (Percentage share of canals, tanks, wells, and other sources)	38720	41865	48023	50296	53510
Canal (Government Canals, Private Canals)	15292	16180	17453	16986	17142
Tank	3182	2765	2944	3179	3111
Well (Tube Wells, Other Wells)	17695	20418	24694	26920	29797
Other Sources	2551	2502	2932	3211	3460
Percentage of Net Area Irrigated	27.66	29.71	33.61	35.29	37.63
Irrigation Cropping Intensity	128	130	131	132	133

Source: CMIE, Agriculture, September1999.

It was generally accepted that irrigation distribution in India favours small holdings, i.e., smaller holdings have higher proportion of area under irrigation. Of late, this assumption has been questioned and it is argued that irrigation development in India is, in fact, iniquitous (Sampath, 1992). However, this argument does not appear to be true with regard to public irrigation though it is true in case of private irrigation (Sagar and Reddy, 1995). The shift in favor of well irrigation clearly reflects the increase in private investment, presumably by the large farmers, in irrigation development. In other words, the growth of private investment in irrigation development is resulting in a bias in favour of large farmers (This is not to argue that private investment in ground water development, would lead to inequitous distribution of water per se). In fact, it was observed by Shah (1994) that water markets would help in equitable distribution of ground water. However, the possibility for water markets to emerge in extreme scarcity conditions is remote. This is mainly due to the decline in public investment in agriculture. While this looks like the fallout of the macro policies which aim at compressing public outlay, at the root of the problem lies the sectoral policies reflecting a bias in favor of major projects and high subsidies for canal irrigation. A large chunk of public investment in agriculture has gone for major irrigation projects which are, generally, located in better endowed regions.

Despite the fact that farmers in the canal-irrigated regions have been reaping large benefits due to irrigation, they are not contributing even to the operational and maintenance costs through user charges. The reforms have, so far, failed to address this issue. On the other hand the backward regions, i.e. the arid and semi-arid tracts, have to rely more on private investment (i.e. on well irrigation). This has not only aggravated inter-regional inequalities but also widened intra regional inequalities. The high capital intensive nature of well irrigation has made access to water privy to well-to-do farmers. The poorer farmers in the disadvantaged region are the real losers as their savings are meager and access to credit is limited. On the top of it, the cost of energy to lift water is sought to be raised.

As far as cropping pattern is concerned, the 1980s have seen a significant shift in cropped area towards non-food crops. The major gainers were the oilseed crops which have gained in area at the cost of coarse grains. Superior cereals like wheat and rice have also showed slight improvement in area. Oilseeds have recorded highest growth rate in area as well as output between 1990-91 and 1997-98. All other crops have recorded lower growth rates in output during the post-reforms period, compared to their performance in the 1980s (Table–7).

Table – 7

Compound Growth Rates of output for Selected Agricultural Products (Triennium ending)

Crop	1980-81 to 1989-90	1990-91 to 1997-98
1. Rice	4.29	1.53
2. Wheat	4.24	3.67
3. Pulses	−0.54	0.76
4. Coarse Grains	0.74	−0.49
5. Total Cereals	3.63	1.84
6. All Food Grains	3.54	1.66
7. Oil seeds	—	4.93

Source: Economic Survey 1998-99.

The export thrust of the new economic policies has also accelerated the cropping pattern shifts. (The decline in area under foodgrain crops in favour of exportable or import substitute crops during the post reform period in our country is similar to the pattern observed in China). As a result, the growth in foodgrain production has fallen short of population growth for the first time since 1975 (Natarajan and Patnaik, 1999). The benefits from the export-oriented policies do not seem to have reached all sections of the farming community. While the large farmers are reaping the benefits of the policies, small and marginal farmers are languishing for want of resources such as water, and limited access to capital. A case in point is the distressed cotton growers in Andhra Pradesh, Karnataka and Maharashtra; or for that matter the case of oilseeds growers in the states like Rajasthan (Reddy, 1996).

In dry regions, unless access to water is made equitable through some institutional mechanisms there is no way the small and marginal farmers can reap the benefits of market oriented agriculture. Though small and marginal farmers are very adaptive to crop technologies, lack of resources (especially credit) makes them non- participants. Ignoring this fact, it is sometimes argued that the non-viable farmers should be allowed to leave cultivation and join the labour force. This would only lead to their pauperization. This argument fails to recognize the legitimate right of these farmers to share the available water resources . Besides, it also fails to reckon the impact on real wages if these farmers also join the already surplus labour force in agriculture. From what sources they be able to get even the subsistence level income? Can the industrial sector absorb the additional labour force? The recent evidence, as shown earlier, does not support such optimism.

The preceding discussion brings out some interesting aspects of recent policy changes. The main macro policy impact on agriculture is the shift in terms of trade in favour of agriculture. It has also resulted in the enhanced market sensitiveness of the producers. However, absence of continuity in policies (especially pertaining to agricultural trade) has increased the market induced risk and uncertainty. The recent suicides of the cotton growers in some of the states is attributed to sharp price fluctuations. Government keeps lifting and imposing the ban on cotton exports to appease certain sections. The small and marginal farmers are lured by market signals, but they do not have the strength to deal with the market risks. Their problems are aggravated with declining public investment in agriculture.

The small and marginal farmers, who do not possess the wherewithal i.e. access to capital and hence other resources including water, to face the market, have to fend for themselves. The plight of the small and marginal farmers is becoming increasingly serious in the arid and semi arid regions, which had been even previously neglected by the state. Agricultural producers in these neglected regions are now faced with degraded environment, poor resource base and unfriendly institutional environment. Under these conditions market penetration in the recent yeas has increased the concentration of scarce resources in fewer hands leading not only to increasing inequalities but also pushing the poor farmers to the edge.

While the shrinking state involvement in agricultural sector may have some justification in the light of increasing financial constraints, the failure of the state in mobilizing the resources from within the sector (through user charges) reflects the myopic nature of the politicians and policy makers. However, of late there appears to be some change in the attitude of some state government in this regard. States like Andhra Pradesh and Madhya Pradesh are pushing institutional reforms, which are prerequisites for market reforms, at the grass roots level. These include strengthening local institutions like water user associations and the panchayati raj institution. These institutional reforms are crucial not only for creating unbiased, market-friendly environment but also for sustaining the growth impetus. The institutional reforms have assumed greater prominence in the recent years with the Asian crisis, which is attributed mainly to institutional failure, though at a different level, i.e. financial and macro. This aspect is taken up in the next section.

The changes discussed in the context of sectoral policies, i.e. expansion of ground water irrigation and shift in cropping patterns towards non-foodgrains, are not the direct fall-out of the recent policy changes but the policy changes have certainly accentuated these tendencies. These processes are likely to perpetuate, if not accelerate in the coming years. In rural environment water is the main source of change and agent for growth. The viability of farming depends to a large measure on the access to irrigation. Equitable distribution of water resources ensures equity in the distribution of gains from it. But the recent trend in expansion of irrigation facilities indicates that access to irrigation is moving in favour of the large farmers due to large scale private investment in this area. Some of the important indicators point towards the likely aggravation of 'large farmer' bias in this regard. While at the macro level investment in irrigation is vital for sustaining agricultural growth (Rao and Gulati, 1995: Parikh, et al, 1995), public investment in irrigation is necessary to address the equity issue. In fact, in fragile eco systems public investments is necessary not only in irrigation and water conservation but also in dry farming technologies like watershed development.

While the recent policy changes repeatedly point to resource constraints for public investments, they are conspicuously silent on resource generation. One neglected area in this regard is user charges, especially for irrigation. Unless future developmental programs are funded internally through user charges, feasibility of these programs will be at stake. Provided there is political will and administrative acumen cost recovery is not a difficult proposition. It has been shown that farmers willingness to pay for improved irrigation facilities is significantly above the present rate structure (Reddy, 1998). This is also demonstrated in the case of reduction in fertilizer subsidy. When the subsidy was removed, in 1991, fertilizer use did not decline, in majority of regions, especially in high fertilizer intensive regions; in fact, it increased in few cases (Reddy and Deshpande, 1992).

III

ASIAN CRISIS AND ITS IMPACT ON INDIAN AGRICULTURE

The structural adjustment, with liberalization and globalization policies was seen as panacea for development till the east and south-east Asian economies faced their recent crisis. These economies were viewed as miracle economies before the onset of the crisis in 1997. Since then serious questions have been posed on the efficacy of liberalization policies and their institutional underpinning. These economies witnessed export-led high growth rates for over a decade. They had low budget deficit, sufficient forex reserves, and other positive features. More importantly, these countries could effectively solve the problem of poverty. They were set as examples for other developing countries to follow. Till the crisis occurred in July 1997 neither economists nor policy makers had any inkling of the danger lurking around the corner.

Genesis of the Crisis

Six countries of south east Asia and east Asia have been affected by the crisis, of which four (Thailand, South Korea, Indonesia and Malaysia) are severely and two (Philippines and Hong Kong) are moderately affected (Rao, 1998a and 1998b) . There are number of explanations for the crisis, (CJE, 1998, JDS,1998, IDS Bulletin, 1999). The factors leading to crisis which might have acted singly or in conjunction can be grouped under three principal categories. These are: a) structural aspects, b) macro-economic imbalances, and c) financial failures. However, financial factors are often identified as the main cause of the crisis. In these countries financial systems were poorly regulated, which allowed speculative and unproductive investment on large scale. After reviewing various explanations Bhalla and Nachane concluded that, "volatility of capital inflows and launching of financial liberalization without adequate preparation were the main causes of the financial panic" (p. 2362). The situation was identified as 'crony capitalism' by perceptive commentators (Wade, 1998). An additional factor contributing to the crisis was the artificially fixed exchange rates; which were pegged to dollar. This led to the appreciation of the real effective exchange rates of the local currencies especially, during 1994 to 1997 (Cliff, 1999).

The main impact of this crisis has fallen on the urban poor through loss of jobs and rising food prices. The crisis has reversed the impressive record of poverty alleviation achieved during the previous 20 years. For instance, in Indonesia percentage of population living below poverty line almost doubled (from 13 to 25 percent) after the crisis (Cliff, 1999). This is attributed to the fact that the poverty alleviation achieved in these economies was a result of " trickle down" effect of growth, and not an outcome of redistribution. It is argued that the south east Asian economies had achieved substantial reduction in absolute poverty because of high rate of economic growth, but their strategy was not effective in reducing income inequalities (Rao, 1999). While traditional social security systems were eroded, no modern systems were put in place during the high growth period (Cliff, 1999). This proved to be a costly mistake and resulted in social unrest and political instability in countries, more particularly in Indonesia. The policy of providing social services through private sector proved undependable. The erosion of livelihoods rendered the private systems unaffordable and hence increased the pressure on public services. In the process the private services remained under-utilized and became non-viable. People had to resort to illegal means of survival such as smuggling, prostitution, etc.

India's Economic Relations With South-East Asia

The recent discussions on Asian crisis have, by and large, sidelined the impact on agriculture in the countries which faced the crisis. This may be due to the (wrong) notion, that agriculture sectors in these countries are neither responsible nor affected by the crisis. In the same way, impact of the crisis on Indian agriculture has gone largely unnoticed. This was because of the fact that the immediate impact of the crisis on Indian agriculture was not as conspicuous as in the case of activities, such as stock market operations or foreign capital flows.

The impact of Asian crisis on Indian economy could be assessed at three levels. One, the direct and indirect trade impact due to the downturn in the Asian markets; two, decline in the foreign capital inflow; and, three, slow down in the domestic reforms as a reaction to the crisis. These impacts were blurred due to Pokhran nuclear tests and the consequent economic sanctions by USA, other developed countries and multilateral aid agencies. The vulnerability indicators analyzed by Bhalla and Nachane (1998) do not bring out any possibility of contagion effect (Table–8). According to their assessment "reasonable grounds do exist for supposing that India will wheather the crisis". India's high fiscal deficit seems to have had a far greater impact on the net foreign capital inflows as the foreign direct investment (FDI) declined between 1995-96 and 1996-97 i.e. before the onset of Asian crisis. However, foreign portfolio investors turned net sellers of Indian stocks to make up for their losses in Asian markets (The Banker, March, 1998, as quoted in Bhalla and Nachane, 1998).

Table – 8

India's Ranking on Crisis Indicators vis-a-vis Asian Economies

Indicator	India	Thailand	Korea	Philippines	Malaysia	Indonesia
1. Govt. budget Balance (percent of GDP)	6	1	5	4	3	2
2. External debt/GDP ratio	1	2	na	5	3	4
3. External debt service (percent of Exports)	2	3	na	na	1	4
4. External debt service (percent of GDP)	1	2	na	na	3	4
5. Current account/ GDP ratio	1	5	2	na	4	3
6. External liabilities of Banks (percent of GDP)	1	4	5	3	1	6
	2	4	5	3	1	6

Note: The ratings represent an ascending order of vulnerability, viz, rank 1 corresponds to the least vulnerable country on that criterion and so on.

Source: Bhalla and Nachane (1998).

Another area where the impact of the Asian crisis was likely to be felt strongly is the external trade. The direct outcome was due to depreciation of Asian currencies. The effect was compounded due to slow down in world economy, growth declining from 4 percent to 3.5 percent. This had, naturally, a negative impact on India's exports and consequently on Indian Economy. For our current discussion the trade linkages with the four most severely affected south- east Asian countries, Indonesia, Malaysia, South Korea and Thailand, are more important. Malaysia accounts for 28.9 percent of our exports to these countries, followed by Indonesia (26.1 percent), South Korea (24.7 percent) and, Thailand (20.3 Percent). Thus, structure of India's exports to these countries is not biased in favor of any one country. Growth of India's trade with these countries slowed down during the post- crisis period, i.e., after 1996-97 (Table–9). South- East Asian countries' share in India's exports was 6.2 percent during 1996-97, It came down to 5.4 percent in the following year. Though the magnitude of our exports to these countries is small, given

Table – 9

India's Exports to South-East Asian Economies

(percentage of total exports)

Country	1991-92	1992-93	1993-94	1994-95	1995-96	1996-97	1997-98	Share of Selected Countries (1997-98)
1. Indonesia	0.8	0.7 (9.6)	1.1 (83.7)	1.1 (18.3)	2.1 (154.1)	1.8 (-6.3)	1.8 (-23.0)	26.1
2. Malaysia	1.1	1.0 (10.2)	1.1 (41.1)	1.1 (16.0)	1.2 (46.2)	1.6 (41.6)	1.4 (-5.1)	28.9
3. South Korea	1.4	0.9 (-17.4)	0.9 (27.8)	1.3 (61.2)	1.4 (43.6)	1.5 (18.4)	1.2 (-16.9)	24.7
4. Thailand	1.1	1.4 (50.1)	1.6 (52.2)	1.5 (14.2)	1.5 (23.9)	1.3 (-0.3)	1.0 (-20.9)	20.3
5. Total	4.4	4.0 ((11.4)	4.7 (49.6)	5.0 (24.8)	6.2 (61.6)	6.2 (10.2)	5.4 (-16.5)	100
6. World	100	100 (21.9)	100 (29.9)	100 (18.5)	100 (28.6)	100 (10.5)	100 (6.3)	100

Note: Figures in brackets are rate of growth over previous year. Source: CMIE, Foreign Trade, 1998.

our precarious balance of payments position even the small changes will have serious consequences. Indian exports to these countries had recorded high growth rates during the pre-crisis period, indicating that India had benefited from these booming economies. Since the onset of 'crisis' exports have recorded negative growth in case of all the four countries, and this trend is likely to continue till these economies recover. Thus, the "crisis" has adversely affected Indian economy with a decline in exports to these countries.

Imports from these countries were consistently increasing in recent years. This trend was not much affected by the crisis, which may be due to the cheapening of imports from these countries consequent to the depreciation of their currencies (Table–10). The rate of growth in imports from these countries was higher than India's imports from 'world' as a whole, indicating the strengthening of trade linkages and economic integration between India and the countries of the south-east Asia. But,

Table – 10

India's Imports from South-East Asian Economies

(percentage of total exports)

Country	1991-92	1992-93	1993-94	1994-95	1995-96	1996-97	1997-98	Share of Imports from the Selected Countries
1. Indonesia	0.3	0.3 (5.3)	0.5 (116.1)	1.1 (169.6)	1.3 (52.5)	1.6 (38.2)	1.8 (27.6)	23.2
2. Malaysia	2.0	1.9 (22.5)	1.1 (-33.4)	1.7 (96.7)	2.5 (96.2)	2.6 (19.5)	2.9 (19.2)	37.7
3. South Korea	1.6	1.6 (30.7)	2.4 (72.1)	2.2 (11.6)	2.2 (39.7)	2.2 (7.8)	2.2 (6.2)	31.9
4. Thailand	0.2	0.3 (41.3)	0.2 (6.2)	0.6 (200.3)	0.5 (5.3)	0.5 (23.0)	0.6 (22.3)	7.2
5. Total	4.1	4.1 (25.4)	4.2 (22.0)	5.6 (63.0)	6.5 (55.8)	6.9 (19.3)	7.5 (17.0)	100
6. World	100	100 (32.4)	100 (15.3)	100 (23.1)	100 (36.4)	100 (11.5)	100 (9.1)	100

Note: Figures in brackets are rate of growth over previous year.

Source: CMIE, Foreign Trade, 1998.

crisis seems to have had an adverse impact on growth in imports which slowed down during the year 1997-98. Among the four countries, India's share of Imports is the highest from Malaysia (37.7 percent), followed by south Korea (31.9 percent), Indonesia (23.2 percent) and, Thailand (7.2 percent). Unlike the case of exports, the share of imports is not evenly balanced among these countries.

Impact on Agriculture

The likely impact of the Asian crisis on Indian agriculture becomes clear if we look at the composition of India's exports and imports to these countries (Tables–10 and 11). More than a third of India's exports to these countries consist of agriculture and allied products, while India imports agricultural commodities to the tune of about fifteen percent in it's total imports from these countries (in 1997-98). These countries were net importers of agricultural goods from India. In the trade with these countries agriculture exports are the second largest category after manufactured goods (Table–11). It is clear, therefore, the trade-related impact of the Asian crisis on Indian agriculture could not

Table – 11

Composition of India's Exports to South-East Asian Economies in 1997-98

(percentages)

Commodity	Indonesia	Malaysia	S. Korea	Thailand	Total
All Commodities	100	100	100	100	100
1. Agriculture and Allied products	46.21	33.16	28.59	27.1	33.8
2. Ores and Minerals	5.99	1.92	5.62	1.7	3.8
3. Manufactured goods	45.12	63.12	64.54	68.5	60.3
3.1. Leather & Leather Manufactures	0.45	1.03	0.99	0.6	0.8
3.2. Chemicals & Related Products	11.79	8.98	19.41	14.1	13.6
3.3. Engineering Goods	26.57	39.15	11.93	18.4	24.0
3.4. Textiles (Excluding RMG)	4.66	8.38	29.2	5.1	11.8
3.5. Readymade Garments	0.17	2.05	0.93	0.5	0.9
3.6. Other Manufactured goods	1.49	3.53	2.09	29.7	9.2
4. Other commodities	2.68	1.81	1.26	2.7	2.1

Source: CMIE, Foreign Trade, August, 1998.

be insubstantial and one can not remain complacent about the likely impact of Asian crisis on Indian agriculture. Apart from this direct trade impact, Indian agriculture may loose in terms of competition for its products in the international markets due to the depreciation of the currencies of the crisis hit countries.

If we look at the important countries we are competing with for various commodities, it would appear that about 40 percent of our exports are vulnerable to the crisis (Sathe, 1998). Of this, about 10 percent of the commodities are agricultural commodities (e.g. rice, cashew, spices, floriculture, tea, etc.) while another 45 percent of the commodities (textiles and ready-made garments) are agro-based and would be indirectly affected by competition from these countries (Table–12). Though it is too early to understand the clear impact of the Asian crisis on Indian agriculture, some of the adverse effects could be noticed at the regional level, as they may not figured out at the national level . For instance, recent reports in newspapers suggest growing problems of rubber and coconut growers in Kerala due to the crash in the international prices with cheapening of these products from 'crisis' countries. Similarly, the cotton crisis in Andhra and Maharashtra could also be attributed to price fluctuations initiated by the Asian crisis. However, the clear picture will emerge only after a few years, assuming that the crisis will continue.

Table – 12

Areas Where Indian Exports Compete with South-East Asian Exports

Product		Competitor Economies
1. Jewellery, Gems (14%)	:	Thailand, Indonesia, UAE, Malaysia.
2. Marine products (3%)	:	China, Japan, US, Thailand, Indonesia, Malaysia
3. Spices (1%)	:	China, Iran, Pakistan, Indonesia.
4. Ready made garments (9%)	:	China, Indonesia, Bangladesh, South Korea.
5. Textiles (9%)	:	South Korea, Indonesia, Thailand
6. Foot wear (<1%)	:	US, Denmark, Italy, Colombia, Kenya, Thailand.
7. Floriculture (<1%)	:	Indonesia
8. Rice (1%)	:	Pakistan, US, Thailand.
9. Cashew (1%)	:	Indonesia, Vietnam, Mozambique
10. Tea, Coffee	:	Indonesia
11. Leather, Handicrafts	:	No competitors from South-East Asia.

Note: Figures in brackets indicate share in total exports.

Source: Sathe (1998).

Lessons of Asian Crisis

The East Asian crisis drives the point clear that growth oriented development is not the panacea for all economic and social ills. Equity or distributional aspects need to be given equal weight in the process of economic development. The neglect of distributional aspects in the East-Asian countries made the poor bear disproportionately high incidence of recession. The issue of income inequalities in these countries came to the centre stage once the recession set in (Rao, 1999). In the Indian context also it is clear that distributional aspects are taking back seat as the reward systems dictated by the market tend to dominate the thinking.

Failure to create an effective social security system is another reason for aggravation of Asian crisis. The export oriented growth failed to ensure food security in these countries for the bottom 20 percent of their populations (FAO, 1998). The main victims of the crisis are the urban poor in these countries. In India too the new economic policies do not lay out any specific agenda for creating appropriate social security system. On the contrary, the existing social security systems are being weakened for want of resources. This may prove disastrous in the event of any crisis situation similar to that of east- Asian one. More importantly, in India distress will not be limited to urban areas as agriculture, the main occupation of the rural work force, has continued to remain vulnerable. Though the key economic indicators do not warrant any such situation in the near future, some necessary steps are to be taken in order to protect the economy from a crisis triggered either by internal developments or due to contagious effect of neighbouring countries. The most important among them are the curtailing of the fiscal deficit, injecting efficiency into financial institutions, exercising regulatory measures with regard to foreign investment as well as capital inflows through financial institutions, above all, strengthening the food security of the vulnerable sections.

Given the magnitude of the agricultural sector and its share in the national economy, some hard policy measures, and institutional innovations and strengthening are necessary in this sector also. A number of authors have commented on the macro policy measures. Similar attention is not given to the reforms in agricultural sector. Some of the important issues include: price policies, policies on subsidies, and trade policies. Besides, the issue of Food Security deserves special attention in our context. These issues are briefly discussed in the following paragraphs.

IV

POLICY REFORMS IN AGRICULTURAL SECTOR

Long term goals of economic development as much as the short term considerations suggest the need for clarity of the policy objectives. In our context agricultural policies have to address three principal objectives. As the primary sector, agriculture has to generate surpluses for financing economic growth. Secondly, it has to ensure productive employment and adequate incomes to the large number of households directly dependent on this sector. Finally, in a poor country where a substantial number of people spend significant proportion of their income on food, agriculture has the pivotal role in ensuring Food Security. Non- price, non-market, measures such as institutional arrangements, voluntary cooperation and good governance have important role to play in meeting these objectives. However, economic policies can materially affect the outcome of public efforts as well as private initiatives. We will briefly comment on some of the major policy interventions in agriculture in our country.

Price Policies

By now India has accumulated vast experience in agricultural price formulation and implementation. However, contribution of such interventions in enhancing productivity or ensuring equity is questionable. This is mainly due to the following reasons: a) there is no link between price policies and other policies like subsidy policies and trade policies; b) there is no consistency in the policies and hence they fail to give any clear signals to the producers. (For example, subsidies are being reduced with the objective of restoring economic efficiency, but farmers are not allowed to reap the benefit of market determined prices as government intervention continues in the output market) ; c) as a reaction to the situation obtaining at a point of time, ad hoc decisions are taken in terms of export restrictions, imposition of import quotas, restrictions on the movement of produce, etc.; d) price policies do not take into consideration the equity aspects i.e., which section of producers benefits from these policies. e) with policy interventions in terms of the minimum support price, price induced uncertainty is reduced to some extent. But with the progressive globalization of agriculture the trade induced price fluctuations are becoming a norm. Policy measures to correct violent fluctuations in widely traded commodities are not in place.

In order to fulfill the basic objectives of enhancing productivity and equity in agricultural sector, serious consideration may be given to the following: i) the objectives of the price policy need to be carefully defined and its scope delimited, ii) large measure of flexibility should be imparted in the formulation and administration of price policy, iii) measures such as open market operations should be resorted to in cooperation with the producers and consumers organizations, iv) restrictive practices such as movement on regulation, and compulsory levy or procurement should be abolished, iv) there should be much closer coordination among different types of policy interventions, particularly between the trade policy and the price policy, and v) price policy should not be dictated by the border prices, but use of border prices as one of the important considerations in the formulation of price policy should be recognized (VS Vyas 1994).

Policies on Subsidies

The burden of subsidies is one of the important factors contributing to the large fiscal deficit. Though the growing fiscal deficit calls for a drastic cut in subsidies, there is need for prioritizing the subsidies rather than imposing an 'across the board' cut. The subsidy regime was introduced mainly to implement a policy of 'low input low output' (Acharya 1996). However, the justification of the input subsidies even in this context would be their contribution to increase productivity. As far as input subsidies are concerned, studies have shown that a majority of the implicit or explicit subsidies are unproductive or redundant. In the case of explicit subsidies while the more productive subsidy on fertilizers is sought to be pruned, the major (in terms of outlay) and less productive subsidies on water and power are more or less untouched. Cutting down these subsidies would not only lighten the financial burden but would also lead to efficient allocation of scarce resources. It is important to aim at an orderly withdrawal of subsidies. There is need for a flexible and non-doctrinaire approach. While considering progressive elimination of input subsidies, repercussion on agricultural production, regional imbalances and incentive structure of the 'late users' should be taken into account. The economic reforms, if properly implemented, may create an environment in which the case for the removal of input subsidies would be further strengthened.

On the other hand, there is a strong case for continuing food subsidies for quite some time to come, especially after the recent experience of south-east and east Asian countries. These subsidies should be used as a social security net. In the present context where a sizable number of people are suffering from malnutrition – and periodically from hunger – and when opportunities for gainful employment are inadequate, it is difficult to justify any drastic cut in the food subsidy for the poor. Eliminating this (only) safety device for the poor may prove a recipe for disaster in the event of any economic upheaval. In this context, the recent price hike in the commodities covered by the public distribution is difficult to justify. In fact, an efficient Public Distribution System (PDS) should be a precondition for globalization agriculture. Though, India has a well designed PDS, it has many detractors. True, efficiency of PDS can be improved through reducing cost of storage and handling, and better targeting of the poor. But it should be recognized that no viable alternative to PDS is available for a country like ours.

Trade Policy

Traditionally, a two pronged approach was followed in agricultural trade policy. Keeping food security a primary goal, import substitution policies were favoured in the case of foodgrains, while non-food 'commercial crops' were identified for export promotion. This approach seems to be justifiable given the volatile nature of agriculture in India and primary concern of food security. The Asian crisis has amply demonstrated that it is not wise to abandon the goal of food self-sufficiency for large to medium size developing countries. For, any large- scale imports of foodgrains will have serious repercussions on income and employment prospects of agricultural producers and workers. The existing favorable price ratios may disappear once a large country like India enters the market. This could easily create food shortages. At the same time, the scope for exports of the major foodgrains commodities, especially cereals, is limited. An aggressive policy on food exports initiated in the recent years has so far proved unsuccessful (Mujumdar, 1999). A desirable policy would be to divert resources from foodgrains to non-food crops or even non-agricultural enterprises once the prospects of genuine surplus in foodgrains emerge.

The criteria by which we should judge the export potential of an agricultural commodity should be: a) the place of the commodity in the consumption basket of the people, especially the poorer sections; b) supply and price elasticities; c) the ratio of the import price and the domestic price; and d) future demand/ supply prospects in the international markets. What it implies in terms of trade strategy is an order of priority in export promotion, with high priority accorded to processed agricultural goods, to be followed by non-food agricultural commodities, and some special varieties of foodgrains, e.g., basmati or superfine rice, duram wheat, etc.

Summing Up

Our long term goals as well as contemporary developments, more specifically the experience of the Asian Crisis, suggest a cautious approach to reforms in agriculture without loosing sight of distributional aspects within the sector and vis-a-vis other sectors of the economy. Agricultural will continue to be a primary sector in the true sense of the term. Sequencing of policy reforms should be in such a way that the adverse impact on poor, both urban and rural, could be avoided. In order to achieve the objective of a dynamic surplus generating agriculture, ensure equitable distribution and, provide safety nets for the vulnerable sections, the role of the non-price factors, especially the institutional factors, is important. There is need for building and strengthening delivery systems and local initiatives. Institutions such as water user's associations or joint forest committees, not only help in sustainable resource management but also ensure equitable distribution of the gains. Panchayati Raj institutions provide valuable opportunity for participatory growth and more transparent distribution of the benefits of the state subsidies, including the benefits of PDS. This is not to deny the importance of macro economic policies. India has an opportunity to take a lead in agricultural reforms and avoid pitfalls which the fast growing countries of Asia could not avoid.

References

Acharya S.S. (1996) Marketing Environment for Farm Products: Emerging Issues and Challenges, Visions in Agricultural Marketing. (1987-1996). Vol.1.pp 147-148, IndianSociety of Agricultural Marketing

Bagchi Amiyakumar(1998), "Growth Miracle and its Unravelling in East and South-East Asia: Unregulated Competitiveness and Denouement of Manipulation by International Financial Community", Economic and Political Weekly, Vol. 33, No. 18, May 2-8.

Bhalla Ajit. S and Dilip M. Nachane, " Asian Eclipse: India and China in the Penumbra", Economic and Political Weekly, Vol. 33, Nos. 36 & 37, September 5-7.

CJE (1998), "Special Issue on The Asian Crisis", Cambridge Journal of Economics, Vol. 22, No. 6, November. Clift, Charles (1999), "East Asia Crisis Seminar: Summary of Discussion", IDS Bulletin, Vol. 30, No.1, January.

Dhawan B. D (1998), Studies in Agricultural Investments and Rural Savings, Commonwealth Publishers, New Delhi.

FAO (1998), Poverty Alleviation and Food Security in Asia: Lessons and Challenges, Food and Agricultural Organisation of the United Nations Regional Office for Asia and the Pacific, Bangkok, December. Institute of Development Studies, Jaipur, IDS Bulletin, 1999.

JDS (1998), " Special Issue on East Asian Development: New Perspective" The Journal of Development Studies, Vol. 34, No. 6, August.

Mujumdar, N.A. (1999), Investment in Agriculture and the Globalization Syndrome", Economic and Political Weekly, Vol. 34, No. 14, April 3.

Natarajan Sriram and Utsa Patnaik (1999), "Post Reform Trends in Crop Area, Output and Employment in China and India", Paper presented at the International Seminar on Economic Reforms in India and China, Department of Economics, University of Hyderabad, Hyderabad, March 10-12.

Nadkarni M.V. (1998) " Crisis of Increasing Costs in Agriculture, is there a Way Out?" Economic and Political Weekly, Vol.23, No.39, September 24.

Parikh, Kirit, S., N.S.S. Narayana, Manoj Panda, A. Ganesh Kumar (1995) "Strategies for Agricultural Liberalisation – Consequences for Growth, Welfare and Distribution", Economic and Political Weekly, Vol. XXIX, No. 39, September 30.

Rao M. Govinda; R. T. Shand and K. P. Kalirajan (1999), "Convergence of Incomes Across Indian States: A Divergent View" Economic and Political Weekly, Vol. 34, No. 13, March 27.

Rao V. V. Bhanoji (1998a), "East Asian Economies: Growth Within an International Context", Economic and Political Weekly, Vol. 33, No. 6, February 7.

Rao V. V. Bhanoji (1998b), "East Asian Economies: The Crisis of 1997-98", Economic and Political Weekly, Vol. 33, No. 23, June 6.

Rao V. V. Bhanoji (1999), "East Asian Economies: Trends in Poverty and Income Inequality", Economic and Political Weekly, Vol. 34, No. 18, May 1.

Reddy, V. Ratna (1995) Willingness and Ability to Pay for Water: A Study of Rajasthan, Project Report, Institute of Development Studies, Jaipur.

Reddy V. Ratna (1996), "Liberalisation and the Poor: A Study of Rajasthan", Paper presented at the International Seminar on Liberalization and the Poor: Impact, Barriers and Opportunities, Indo-Dutch Program on Alternatives of Development (IDPAD), March 7-9.

Reddy V. Ratna (1998), "Institutional Imperatives and Coproduction Strategies for Large Irrigation Systems in India", Indian Journal of Agricultural Economics, Vol. 53, No. 3, July-September.

Reddy, V. Ratna and R.S. Deshpande (1992) "Input Subsidies: Whither the Direction of Policy Changes", Indian Journal of Agricultural Economics, Vol. XLVII, No. 3, July-September.

Sagar, Vidya and V. Ratna Reddy (1995) "Irrigation Development in India", Working Paper, Institute of Development Studies, Jaipur.

Sampath, R.K. [1992] "Farm Size-wise Analysis of Irrigation in Indian Agriculture", Journal of Development Studies, Vol. 29, No. 1, October.

Sathe Dhanmanjari (1998), "Asian Currency Crisis and the Indian Economy", Economic and Political Weekly, Vol. 33, No. 18, May 2.

Vyas V. S (1994), "Agricultural Price Policy: Need for Reformulation" in G. S. Bhalla (ed.), Economic Liberalisation and Indian Agriculture, Institute for Studies in Industrial Development, New Delhi.

Vyas V.S. (1996) " Agricultural Trade Policy for the Nineties: Issues and Approaches", Economic and Political Weekly, Vol.29, No.26, pp. A-54-64.

Vyas V.S. (1990) "Food Policy and Food Security in Asia with Particular Reference to South Asia", Increasing Access to Food: An Asian Experience (ed. D.S. Tyagi and V.S.Vyas), Sage Publication India Pvt. Ltd, New Delhi.

Vyas V.S. and kruse-Rodenacker, A.(1974) Cooperative of Agricultural Products, Food and Agriculture Organization of the United Nations, Rome.

13

Planning for Agriculture

Challenges and Opportunities in the 21st Century

K. C. PANT

Our country has still to overcome the problem of poverty. Today an estimated 350 million out of one billion people fall below the poverty line. More than 60 per cent of the population is still dependent on agriculture for its livelihood and employment. The major issue of concern is that although the share of agriculture in the national income has come down rapidly, the proportion of the population dependent on the agricultural sector has changed only marginally. Providing gainful employment opportunities for the rural population in the agricultural sector will be an uphill task in a scenario where land holdings are small and continuously shrinking, and the pressure on land keeps increasing. This calls for vigorous efforts to create sustainable employment avenues for the rural population, especially the rural poor.

Due to innovative planning, well-focused agricultural research and growth oriented policies, we have become a self-sufficient and food secure nation. Foodgrain production went up from 82 million tonnes in 1960/61 to a record level of 203 million tonnes last year, with an annual buffer stock ranging from 20 to 30 million tonnes during the nineties. Our agricultural performance has been globally acclaimed for ensuring that growth in foodgrain production remained consistently higher than growth in population.

The performance of the oilseeds, commercial crops and livestock sectors was also remarkable. Oilseeds production increased from 7 million tonnes in 1960/61 to 25 million tonnes in 1999. Sugarcane production has gone up to nearly 300 million tonnes from 110 million tonnes in 1960/61. There has been a quantum jump in potato production from less than 3 million tonnes to 23 million tonnes. Likewise, milk production has gone up sharply from 20 million tonnes to 75 million tonnes.

Thus, despite rising population, per capita foodgrain availability has increased from less than 400 gms per day in 1950/51 to 510 gms in 1997. Per capita milk availability has also increased from 125 gms per day to 204 gms. These are no mean achievements, and we can take justifiable pride in them.

These successes provide reasonable grounds for hope and confidence that our agricultural experts will measure up to the challenges that lie ahead.

However, we should recognize that the task our agricultural scientists have to tackle may be even more complex and difficult than what they faced in the past. The most important challenge before us is to ensure adequate and sustained increase in food production to meet the nutritional needs of a growing, healthier population. Our population has just crossed the one billion mark, and experts have projected that we would be overtaking China by 2035 as the world's most populous country. To feed this growing population, an additional 5-6 million tonnes of foodgrains will need to be produced annually. In addition, we have to recognise that balanced nutrition, which is essential for the health of our people, demands the consumption of a wide array of food-stuffs. These too must be provided without compromising on the provision of the basic caloric requirements. All this will have to be done in a context which is less favourable than it used to be.

To begin with, we need to recognise that the scope for expansion of area available for cultivation is limited. In fact, there is a possibility that cultivable area may shrink somewhat. Environmental considerations, which are just as important for the well-being of our people, demand that area under forest cover be increased from the dangerously low levels that it has reached. Demands of urbanisation and industry too will eat into our cultivable land, though we should keep this to the minimum. These are imperatives that we cannot ignore. To complicate matters, the past sources of agricultural growth have also been almost saturated. For example, high yielding varieties have already spread to more than three-fourth of the area under rice and to more than 90 percent of the area under wheat. In such a scenario, the question of how to increase our agricultural production takes on an added urgency.

A larger share of growth in the agricultural sector can come from rainfed regions if region-specific innovative planning is done and appropriate policies are pursued. Rainfed agriculture today supports about 40% of the population and 75% of the poor in the country. Currently, it contributes nearly 45% of the foodgrain production in the national food basket. Rainfed regions need protected irrigation for increasing agricultural production and crop intensification. This can be achieved through improved rainwater harvesting management techniques. Promotion of improved water management practices, use of sprinkler and drip irrigation, and farmers' participation in irrigation management need due recognition in the planning process. Government is already giving considerable attention to rainfed agriculture, and resources have been allocated for watershed development through various approaches, ranging from the traditional to the modern. Increasing agricultural production in rainfed regions will not only increase total agricultural production but also generate employment opportunities for the rural poor and also check degradation of soil and water resources. To achieve these goals, region-specific planning would be required due to the wide range of agro-ecological variability that exists in our country.

While our past efforts have undoubtedly contributed to the overall growth process, region-specific planning would also be necessary to tackle regional disparities in agricultural productivity and income which have increased perceptibly, and the gulf between developed and underdeveloped regions which has widened. Whereas the northern and western regions have performed remarkably well, the eastern and northeastern regions have lagged behind in agricultural development. For example, the yield of rice in eastern states is still only half of what has already been achieved in the northern regions. In some of the eastern states, the current yield levels of rice are as low as what Punjab achieved in the early 1970s. It may well be that in the past, higher priority was given to the better-endowed regions with the expectation that the spillover effect would carry the benefits to the other regions. However, we need to recognise that this has not happened.

As a result of this unbalanced regional development and widening disparities, a large number of rural poor have been forced to migrate to developed regions and urban areas in search of jobs. Mitigating, and eventually bridging, regional imbalances through increased agricultural productivity and creation of more productive job opportunities must be high on the priority list of agricultural planners during the twenty first century.

Fortunately, the eastern and northeastern regions have large untapped ground water reservoirs. These regions are endowed with enough natural resources, but the production levels are low. Systematic efforts to harness the potential of these regions for agricultural development and growth should form an important component of our strategy for this sector. However, these regions are lagging behind in infrastructure development. Investment in ground water development, electrification, markets and roads would yield high private as well as social dividends. Many of the improved science-based agricultural technologies have not reached these regions due to poor infrastructure facilities, and this would need to be remedied expeditiously.

There is a need to improve the information stock of the farmers in such regions. In fact, the extension service network needs to be strengthened in all regions. It should be fully supported by a strong service sector, which would ensure timely supply of required inputs to increase agricultural productivity. The planning process in the 21st century should take full advantage of the reach and enormous potential of information technology for rapid information dissemination in the rural areas.

In the past, diversification of agriculture was not given due attention. There are ample opportunities for diversification of agriculture through development of livestock, horticulture and fisheries. The livestock sector has immense potential for complementing and accelerating the growth of the agriculture sector. The productivity of our livestock sector, in terms of milk, meat, wool, and eggs, is the lowest in the world. Though we are the largest producer of milk, we are far behind many developed countries in terms of productivity and per capita availability of milk. The fishery sector has remained underdeveloped. There is ample scope to increase inland fish production. We have about 14 lakh hectares of brackish water area suitable for production of shrimps. Hardly 10% of this area has been utilized for production purposes. These sectors would have to grow in the 21st century and contribute significantly to the economic growth of the nation. These sectors can also provide considerable employment opportunities, especially to small and marginal farmers and landless labourers. Our planning process should take greater cognizance of these sectors for achieving value-addition, and thereby raising incomes and generating employment opportunities in the rural areas.

There is also the issue of environmentally sustainable agricultural development. In the past, excessive focus on intensive agricultural growth has resulted in degradation of natural resources. The Green Revolution of the mid-1960s could have also contributed to the over-exploitation of natural resources. To an extent, this exploitation and mismanagement of natural resources was induced by an under-estimation of the capacity of our farmers, and made worse by over-enthusiastic populism. For example, high subsidy on canal waters, electricity, nitrogenous fertilizer, among others, induced farmers to overexploit soil and water resources without recognising the dangers inherent in such behaviour. Problems of soil salinity, waterlogging, declining water table, deteriorating water quality, nutrient mining and acidification of soils are often reported in those regions which witnessed the green revolution. On the other hand, the regions, which are still operating at subsistence levels, are experiencing large scale degradation in the form of soil erosion, nutrient mining, deforestation and desertification due to the low investment capacity of the farming community and inadequate focus by the government.

The cumulative effect of degradation of natural resources has led to deceleration of agricultural growth. Conserving natural resources to meet the current and future requirements of the growing population would be the biggest challenge in the 21st century. Sustainable agricultural production calls for effective planning and environment-friendly technologies and policies.

Declining public investment in agriculture is another area of concern. During the early-1980s, about 9 per cent of the net domestic product was ploughed back for capital formation in agriculture, which has come down to only 5 per cent during the 1990s. This trend needs to be reversed to avoid the potential adverse effect on agricultural growth and regional performance. Inadequate public investment in the rural infrastructure is also a major challenge. The planning process has been laying emphasis on development of irrigation, roads and transport facilities, credit institutions, markets, warehousing and cold storage facilities, electrification, etc., but considering the vast geographical dimensions of the country and the order of investment required, the existing allocations are relatively scanty and inadequate. The resolution of this problem calls for considerably greater private sector involvement and partnership in infrastructure development and the processing industry. Any policy and procedural hurdles in encouraging greater private sector participation will have to be identified and removed with a sense of urgency.

The domestic and international economic environment is changing rapidly since the early 1990s. Agricultural and food subsidies have been very sensitive issues, but they have been very much in public debate in the context of the rising fiscal deficit. Considering the social objectives of subsidies in agriculture and their high political sensitivity, any reforms in the input sectors, involving withdrawal of these subsidies, have to handled with care by policy makers, who have also to take into account the opening up of international markets for agricultural commodities in the wake of implementation of WTO agreements. As a member of the WTO, we have to remove quantitative restrictions and reduce tariff rates. The import regime will also not be the same. We may trade freely in international markets, but the real issue we have to analyse and assess is as to how it would affect our producers and consumers in terms of efficiency gains and equity aspects. The new trade regime may also affect our natural resource base. These issues need careful and objective assessment. The emerging trade environment calls for appropriate planning for those regions and groups which we expect will be adversely affected. The growth and development of our agricultural sector will depend on our clear-sighted pursuit of national interests and our ability to respond swiftly to a rapidly changing international economic environment.

Globalisation, however, is not just a threat; it also throws up a number of opportunities. We are richly endowed with natural resources and climatic variety. We have one of the largest reservoirs and potential for bio-diversity in the world. There is hardly any crop that cannot be grown in our country. Implementation of WTO agreements is expected to increase our access to the world market. Currently, our share in world export is less than one percent. We need to identify commodities where we have a comparative advantage in the global market. We need to improve our quality standards if we have to compete in the world market. We have the advantage of availability of a relatively cheap and extremely hard-working labour force. We need to assess how this important resource can be utilized more productively to promote labour-intensive activities for competing in the global market.

We also have among us some of the best agricultural brains in the world, who have always risen to the occasion in the past. I have no doubt that these scientists will again take up the challenge and come up with innovative solutions. The nation expects no less of them.

In the agricultural sector, it is high time that India takes stock of all available technologies and devises ways of using them for food grain and other crop production. This not only calls for extensive exploration of alternative possibilities but also requires an immediate long term technology plan for Indian agriculture. In this direction, the frontier technologies, including biotechnology, should be included in the overall work programme so as to get viable solutions to the productivity related problems. Some of these technologies are capital intensive. In their case, one may consider co-operation between industry and Government to exploit economies of scale and overcome capital and infrastructure deficiencies. Finally, I would like to reiterate that our country has great expectations from its agricultural scientists and the system which is responsible for transferring agricultural technologies to the farmers. Our hopes rest on them, and I am certain that we will not be disappointed.

Fifth Foundation Day Lecture of the National Academy of Agricultural Sciences, June 5, 2000.

14

A Viable Agriculture in the New International Trade Regime

C. H. HANUMANTHA RAO

The very first question that comes to my mind is: What is the rationale behind the new or liberalized international trade regime represented by the Uruguay Round agreements, and overseen by the World Trade Organization ? Parties would not engage themselves in trade unless it is mutually beneficial. If each country could produce all the needed goods and services with the same efficiency or cost-effectiveness as the other country, then there is no need for trade or exchange. It is only when there are significant differences between parties regarding the relative or comparative advantage with which different goods and services can be produced that there would be gains for both the parties in entering into exchange by each one specializing in the production of those goods and services in which it has a comparative advantage. Some such specialization and exchange has been going on from times immemorial. The theory of comparative advantage, propounded by David Ricardo nearly two hundred years ago, helps us to understand why trade between countries is found mutually advantageous.

If transactions between parties could be spontaneous because they are mutually beneficial to the parties concerned, then where is the need for a multilateral institutional framework like the W.T.O. with mutually agreed and enforceable rules? The simple answer is that countries differ not only in regard to the comparative advantage in producing various goods and services but also in respect of the *level playing field.* The principle of comparative advantage is built on the basis of the inter-country differences in costs and returns between different commodities, abstracting from taxes and subsidies influencing these costs and returns. In the chapter dealing with international trade in agricultural commodities in Ricardo's *The Principles of Political Economy and Taxation*, one does not find any mention of taxes or subsidies determining the relative costs of production or prices of commodities. In his examples, one finds only production factors like land, labour and capital constituting the cost of production (Ricardo, David, 1817). Now, if some rich countries because of their ability to subsidize agriculture can sell their produce at artificially lower prices and thus undercut the market for the genuinely efficient or low-cost producers, then the playing field is highly uneven as the principle of comparative advantage is not followed or even thrown overboard. Similarly, if some countries are taxing or discriminating against agriculture by heavily protecting their industry and through overvalued exchange rates, as most developing countries have been doing till recently, then their competitiveness is eroded *vis-a-vis* countries which do not tax agriculture. In this case too, the principle of comparative advantage is denied a free play. Moreover, the world – despite increasing interdependence and integration among countries – is highly heterogenous with regard to the levels of development. There are countries at an advanced stage of development in regard to the levels of infrastructure and technology achieved over a period of a few centuries. On the other hand, there are several countries which have only recently emerged from long periods of colonial rule. They have a long way to go before they can achieve a level playing field *vis-a-vis* developed countries in regard to infrastructure, technology and skills. Such countries may need protection for some time in certain specific areas before they can tap and realise their potential so as to be in a position to compete with the advanced countries as trading partners on an equal footing. This is akin to what is usually referred to in the literature approvingly as 'infant industry' argument. Therefore, institutional arrangements such as the W.T.O. are essential for ensuring level playing field so that considerations of comparative advantage can have a free and fair play.

A major issue of contention during the Uruguay Round negotiations was the high domestic support being provided to agriculture in the developed countries, especially the European Union in the West and Japan in the East. Apart from restrictions on the imports of farm products through various tariff and non-tariff barriers, this support consisted of measures such as high support prices for farm produce and export subsidies, which are now shifted to direct measures for income support under the so-called Blue Box, such as deficiency payments in the U.S.A., and compensations to farmers in the European Union *via* acreage and headage premiums which are exempt from reduction commitments. The developed countries did agree to a modest reduction in the domestic support, but the experience in the last 6 years indicates that the implementation of such reduction commitments has been tardy, as evidenced by a significant rise in the share of advanced countries in global exports (Rakshit, 2000; W.T.O., 2001). However, the question that I would like to probe into at the moment is: Why do the developed countries have a tendency to subsidize agriculture? The question assumes significance as this pattern has been in evidence with almost unfailing regularity in the process of development. It was the United States of America first in the 1950s and the 1960s, then came Japan and the European Union, and more recently, the Republic of Korea. It is indeed ironical that the European Union – the continent where David Ricardo was born and worked and propounded his theory of comparative advantage with extensive illustrations from agriculture - should now be at the top in the list in regard to the degree of farm support and thus in undermining the operation of the principle of comparative advantage in trade. This is a classic illustration of how domestic lobbies representing sectional interests can be at logger-heads with the universally acclaimed text-book propositions. The fears of Thomas Malthus – a contemporary of David Ricardo – in regard to population growth outpacing the growth in food output were first proved wrong in Europe on account of technological changes and the rise in agricultural productivity. It appears that the very processes which helped to overcome the Malthusian pessimism led to the growth of interest groups which are coming in the way of the operation of Ricardo's principle of comparative advantage.

The demand for farm products at higher levels of income responds little to changes in incomes and prices. This explains why a small increase in farm output results in a more than proportionate fall in its price. Thus farm incomes declined very often in the developed countries like the U.S.A. despite, and indeed owing to, the rise in farm output. This was the genesis of support prices to the farmers. The problem was mitigated to some extent by finding markets for the export of foodgrains. However, the rising support prices perpetuated high-cost agriculture primarily because there was little incentive to shift resources away from agriculture, especially labour, whose opportunity cost rose on account of overall development and rise in wages. In the U.S.A., for example, during the period 1992-97, agriculture accounted for a mere 2 per cent of G.D.P., but employed 4 per cent of total labour force. On the other hand, the services sector which accounted for 72 per cent of G.D.P., employed 63 per cent of labour force. The productivity of labour in agriculture is thus comparatively much lower. The position is similar in countries constituting European Union: Over the corresponding period, agriculture contributed 2 per cent of G.D.P. in France with 6 per cent share in labour force; In Germany, agriculture's contribution to G.D.P. was 1 per cent with 3 per cent share in labour force; The corresponding figures for U.K. were 2 per cent and 3 per cent (The World Bank, 2000). There is thus a deterioration in the relative productivity of labour in agriculture in U.S.A. and countries of E.U. on account of high farm support. The food surpluses of the farmers produced at high cost could not become competitive in the export market without heavy subsidies on exports.

I often wonder how governments in countries where a mere 3 per cent to 5 per cent of total labour force is employed in agriculture have to succumb to pressures from farm lobbies. Part of the explanation, of course, lies in the sheer ability of these rich countries to foot the bill. Another reason is that since agriculture in these countries is highly input-intensive, a large complex of agro-industries having backward linkage with agriculture as input suppliers constitute the highly organized and vocal sections of these farm lobbies. Moreover, these countries are, in any case, incurring huge expenditures on social security for the unemployed in the rest of the economy. The difference is that in the case of the farm sector, these payments take the form of compensation for lower farm prices, thus providing incentive for committing resources beyond what would otherwise have been allocated if farm prices were allowed to be determined by the market forces.

But the situation can change over time thanks to the pressures from the members of the W.T.O. Already, there is a marked shift away from support prices and export subsidies, which are considered highly trade distorting, towards direct payments in the form of deficiency payments and compensations related to acreage and livestock numbers, which are considered 'minimally trade distorting' and hence placed under the 'Blue' and 'Green' boxes which are exempt from reduction commitments (Aart De Zeeuw, 1997). However, it would be a misnomer to call these payments as 'minimally trade distorting'. This is because, such payments, in so far as they are not fully delinked or decoupled from the use of inputs, do influence the allocation of resources, in the sense that in the absence of such payments, fewer resources would be committed to agriculture, leading to lower output, higher prices, and smaller export surpluses (W.T.O., 2001).

However, there are indications that in E.U. agriculture, where the distortion in the allocation of resources appears to be highest, there is a significant scope for reducing unit costs through the wider application of known technologies. Already there are moves to retire farm labour over the age of 55 through payment of compensations which are fully decoupled. There is considerable scope for reducing labour costs by enlarging average farm size and thus reaping economies of scale. There is also a large potential for reducing unit costs through vertical integration of agro-processing industry - the growth of which has been surprisingly slow - with farming operations (Keyzer and Merbis, 1999). The ongoing biotechnological revolution promises to work in the same direction. If some of these cost-reducing technologies have not already been adopted extensively, it is primarily because of heavy farm subsidies which dampen the incentives for cost reduction. It is very likely, therefore, that the observed trend of a secular decline in the real prices of farm products would be reinforced due to such reforms in the West, which has the requisite technological know-how, as well as to the unilateral pursuit of reforms in certain developing countries towards trade liberalization by doing away with discrimination against agriculture (Valdes and Zietz, 1995). A country like India needs, therefore, to prepare itself for competing with low-cost farm products rather than expecting a significant rise in their prices *via* reform-induced reduction in the export surpluses from the developed countries. Incidentally, this scenario should serve to dispel fears that those of the least developed countries which are net importers of food stand to lose heavily on account of the rise in the prices of food following the reduction of farm support in the developed countries.

While the advanced countries have been heavily protecting agriculture, leading to overproduction, rise in costs and distortion in world trade, several developing countries have been disprotecting agriculture by discriminating against it basically through the heavy protection of domestic industry and overvalued exchange rates (Bautista and Valdes, 1989). This is a consequence of the pursuit of an inward-looking and import substituting development strategy which had an in-built bias against agriculture. The terms of trade were thus deliberately kept unfavourable to agriculture in keeping with the prevailing wisdom to 'extract' surpluses from this sector for promoting industrialization. Such discrimination has led to less than optimal allocation of resources to agriculture as well as denial of avenues for its technological upgradation in a liberalized trading environment, resulting in its slower growth (ESCAP, 1996; Rao, 1996).

This has proceeded independently of the protectionist policies pursued for agriculture in the developed countries. Already, the unshackling of agriculture through market reforms in developing countries like China and Vietnam have led to high agricultural growth and rise in their trade in agricultural commodities. A number of exercises on the post-Uruguay Round scenario have concluded that the expected rise in the prices of farm products on account of reduction commitments by the developed countries would be mitigated and even neutralized by the surge in output and trade due to market reforms and unilateral liberalization in certain developing countries (ESCAP, 1995; Valdes and Zietz, 1995). A major component of this growth in farm output is the expected rise in total factor productivity (TFP) in agriculture on account of technological changes induced by the liberalization of trade following the Uruguay Round commitments (ESCAP, 1995). The recent price trends are consistent with the above prognoses.

It is clear from the above that liberalization of agriculture in developing economies has to proceed basically through macroeconomic reforms which do away with high protection accorded to industry and liberalize trade and exchange rate regime. Viability of Indian agriculture in the new international trade regime scenario has, therefore, to be seen not in isolation in terms of the prospects for each agricultural commodity under the provisions of the W.T.O., but in the wider context of the liberalization of the Indian economy. The fortunes of Indian agriculture, which now accounts for around 30 per cent of G.D.P., depends crucially on its relationship with the rest of the economy which contributes as much as 70 per cent to G.D.P. As such, the impact of macroeconomic reforms on the terms of trade for agriculture, private investment, and its ability to access modern technology and inputs deserve attention, in addition to the consequences of these reforms for public investment in agriculture.

The product-specific support for Indian agriculture in the year 1995-96 – the year for which latest official information from W.T.O. is available – was negative to the extent of 38.5 per cent (Gulati, 2001). However, because of the recent fall in the international prices of farm products and the steep rise in the minimum support or procurement prices for wheat and rice in the country, it is possible that the rate of disprotection would now be much lower. Since the non-product specific support amounts to 7.5 per cent of the value of agricultural production, the aggregate measure of support (AMS) to Indian agriculture could still be well below the *deminimis* of 10 per cent in terms of the Uruguay Round stipulations. In its proposals on the Negotiations on W.T.O. Agreements on Agriculture, India has suggested that the Aggregate Measure of Support (AMS), as the term suggests, be calculated as a sum of the product-specific and non-product specific support (W.T.O., 2001). If the product-specific support is still negative in the case of India, then the aggregate measure of support would be below 7.5 per cent of the value of agricultural production. As it is, input subsidies to resource poor farmers which come under non-product specific support are exempt from reduction commitments under the W.T.O. provisions. If India avails of this, the non-product specific support may come down to less than half of what is being shown today (Gulati, 2001). In view of this, it may not be in India's interest to fight within the W.T.O. for greater domestic support to agriculture, especially if it can blunt our opposition to slow reduction in farm support and inadequate access to markets in the advanced countries. For its further growth, Indian agriculture is in need of substantial public investments in irrigation, power, roads, and agricultural research and extension, rather than subsidies on inputs. Indeed, there is a consensus now among planners and policy makers that the declining investment in agriculture is basically attributable to the mounting subsidies on irrigation, power and fertilizers (Government of India, Planning Commission, 2001).

Besides, our stand on agriculture in the W.T.O. has to be an integral part of the overall position we take on trade liberalization, through the process of bargaining, which necessarily involves some trade-offs. For example, the consequences of the Uruguay Round agreements for the rural poor depend not merely on their possible impact on agricultural growth and employment but on wages and employment in the economy in general following complete Uruguay Round trade liberalization including the phasing out of the Multifibre Agreement (MFA). It has been estimated that the additional welfare gains for the countries of the ESCAP region from complete liberalization of trade, including the phasing out of the MFA, could be two and half times as high as the welfare gains arising from global agricultural liberalization only (ESCAP, 1995).

As for the protection through tariffs, India has already negotiated tariff bindings at the level of 100 per cent for raw commodities, 150 per cent for processed agro-commodities and 300 per cent for most edible oils. These may be considered sufficient to protect the relevant commodities against cheaper imports sustained by high domestic support in countries of their origin. For example, according to a study, the nominal rates of assistance to agriculture *via* trade policies in the post Uruguay Round for agriculture and processed food amounts to 33 per cent in advanced industrial economies as well as newly industrialized economies (Hoekman and Anderson, 1999). According to the estimates given by Ashok Gulati, the average Producer Support Estimate (PSEs) for 1997-99 was 61 per cent for Japan, 65 per cent for Korea, 66 per cent for Norway, 70 per cent for Switzerland, and 44 per cent for countries within the European Union (Gulati, 2001). Producer support in several South and South-East Asian countries is either negligible or even negative. It is from these countries that India has been importing much of edible oils and to some extent other agro-commodities. It is clear, therefore, that tariff barriers in such cases, beyond a point, amount to blocking the import of efficiently produced or low cost-products. If prices of edible oils have fallen steeply in the country recently, despite high tariff bindings at 300 per cent, it is due to the failure of our market intelligence, lack of alertness and inability to act promptly to raise import duties (Chand, 2000; Gulati, 2001).

The major challenge to the viability of agriculture of most developing countries, including India, is posed by the high domestic support, export subsidies and denial of market access through various tariff and non-tariff barriers, in the developed countries. India has been fighting in league with other developing countries in the W.T.O. for the removal of such barriers. In the process of bargaining and in our own interest, the rate of protection to our industry which used to be among the highest in the world has been brought down to less than half of its earlier level. Our agriculture is a major beneficiary from this reduced protection to industry.

As expected, the liberalization of Indian economy which had commenced from around the mid-1980s and accelerated with the launching of fullfledged macroeconomic reforms since the early 1990s has improved the incentive framework for agriculture. With the liberalization of exchange rate and opening up of the economy, the terms of trade for agriculture have shown a significant improvement. As a result, private investment in agriculture registered a steep rise in the post-reform period (Government of India, Planning Commission, 2000). At 1993-94 prices, private investment in agriculture was over 50 per cent higher in 1999-2000 when compared to 1993-94 (Government of India, 2001). The exports of agricultural commodities, particularly foodgrains, accelerated in this period. For example, for the first time since independence, India has been a net exporter of foodgrains consecutively for the last six years, net exports amounting, on an average, to around 1.8 million tonnes per annum (Government of India, 2001).

In the light of this evidence, the fears being expressed in certain quarters that import of foodgrains under the new liberalized trade regime is having a dampening effect on the foodgrain prices in the country is totally misplaced. It is true that, recently, the post-harvest prices of wheat and rice have been ruling below the minimum support prices in certain markets, but this is due to the inability of the Food Corporation of India to lift the grain at the officially announced procurement prices and not due to import of foodgrains. Indeed, we need to understand why there is a glut in foodgrains market and mounting stocks with the F.C.I., despite the deceleration in the growth of foodgrains output in the last decade and the net export of foodgrains consecutively for the last six years.

The obvious explanation is that there has been a steep rise in procurement prices in the recent period, when there has in fact been a downward trend in international prices. Further, the issue prices for the people above the poverty line have been pegged to the economic cost incurred by the F.C.I., leading to reduced offtake of foodgrains. Moreover, whereas the per capita availability of foodgrains was rising at the rate of 1.2 per cent per annum during the 1980s, it has declined at the rate of 0.28 per cent per annum during the 1990s (Government of India, Planning Commission, 2000). This suggests that the trend of a decline in per capita consumption of foodgrains and the diversification of consumption basket in the richer states and among the upper consumption groups, already in evidence in the 1970s and the 1980s according to the National Sample Survey data (Rao, 2000), seems to have been reinforced in the post-reform period of 1990s owing to the availability of a wide variety of non-agricultural goods and services as well as to the rise in the relative prices of foodgrains. Whereas the consumption of foodgrains among the bottom 30 per cent of population was still rising in the 1980s, though slowly, the steep rise in foodgrain prices in the 1990s may have dampened consumption among these poorer sections. It almost appears that we are caught in the 'advanced country syndrome' of support prices feeding on themselves leading to reduced consumption, embarrassing surpluses, reduced incentives for diversification of agriculture and for the adoption of cost-reducing technologies.

This evidence does not lend credence to the view that trade liberalization would endanger India's food security. Achievement of effective food security when we can accumulate enough stocks of foodgrains, thanks to our comparative advantage in respect of major cereals, hinges basically on raising the purchasing power of the poor through the generation of employment opportunities. If the prices of foodgrains at the moment are out of the reach of the poor, it is not due to the rise in exports but to the steep rise in procurement and issue prices.

On the trade front, there is a need for extreme vigilance on our part so as to be able to take timely measures, within the existing tariff bindings, to arrest heavy import of certain commodities. Also, since the philosophy behind trade liberalization is the maximization of global welfare through efficiency gains, mapping out comparative advantages across countries for different commodities in a dynamic setting is necessary as a basis for meaningful negotiations in the W.T.O. The developed countries are very well equipped with technical and legal expertise, even though these capabilities are used for advancing their case towards perpetuation of domestic support to agriculture and restriction of market access, that are quite untenable. On the other hand, the capabilities of developing countries, including India, are poor in this respect despite their approach and line of action on matters relating to agricultural trade being justifiable on theoretical as well as practical grounds. Therefore, we need to give a high priority to the development of these skills in the country.

But our major effort on the domestic front for ensuring the viability of Indian agriculture has to be focused on raising productivity by stepping up public investment, by accelerating the evolution and adoption of cost-reducing technologies, and by removing restrictions on agricultural trade, marketing and processing within the country. All this requires to be achieved through appropriate policy framework and institutional arrangements.

Although private investment in agriculture was stepped up in the post-reform period of the 1990s in response to the liberalization of the economy and favourable terms of trade, real public investment continued to decline on account of fiscal compression and the failure to reduce input subsidies. As a result, the development of infrastructure like irrigation, rural electrification, roads and markets has been a major casualty. as the Mid-Term Appraisal of the Ninth Five Year Plan points out, "there is a strong complementarity between public and private investments, and inadequate public investment could lead to a 25 per cent lower private investment than desired" (P.5). Further, the combined expenditure by the Centre and the state governments on agricultural research and education, which is the most important determinant of total factor productivity (TFP) in agriculture, stagnated around 0.5 per cent of agricultural GDP over this period (Pal, Jha and Singh, 1997), as against the requirement of 1 per cent of agricultural GDP projected by the Indian Council of Agricultural Research for the Ninth Five Year Plan. The Mid-Term Appraisal for the Ninth Plan brings out the glaring deficiencies in the provision of extension services in the recent period. It also points out that the credit extended to agriculture from the commercial banks constituted around 12 per cent to 13 per cent of total net bank credit in recent years as against the target of 18 per cent (P. 65).

These shortfalls in public investment and in the provision of agricultural services account for the failure of agricultural supplies to respond to the favourable incentive framework created by macroeconomic reforms, including trade liberalization, in the 1990s: Agricultural growth has slowed down during the 1990s with the growth in crop output, especially foodgrains output, decelerating sharply to below the population growth rate. The experience of the 1990s clearly demonstrates that far from trade liberalization dampening the performance of agriculture, the failure of public investment and effort is responsible for our inability to benefit from trade liberalization by stepping up and diversifying agricultural output in a cost-effective way.

Reversing this trend would require major reforms in governance and institutions, particularly at the state level. The investible resources with the government have to be raised, among other things, by increasing the tax-GDP ratio as well as through better cost-recovery for the input services provided. Institutional reforms for augmenting and managing the infrastructure and other services through participatory processes such as Water Users' Associations, Watershed Development Committees, and Self-Help Groups, already underway in some states, need to be stepped up.

Such reforms at the grass roots level alone hold the key for improving the viability of Indian agriculture in the wake of trade liberalization.

References

Bautista, Romeo M., and Alberto Valdes, *The Bias against Agriculture: Trade and Macroeconomic Policies in Developing Countries*, (California, ICS Press, 1989).

Chand, Ramesh, *Trade Liberalization, Agricultural Prices, and Net Social Welfare in India*, Submitted at the Third Asian Conference of Agricultural Economists, Jaipur, October 18-20, 2000.

Economic and Social Commission for Asia and the Pacific, *Benefits and Challenges Facing Asia-Pacific Agricultural Trading Countries in the Post-Uruguay Round Period,* Studies in Trade and Investment, 11, United Nations, New York, 1995.

Economic and Social Commission for Asia and the Pacific, *Rural Poverty Alleviation and Sustainable Development in Asia and the Pacific*, United Nations, 1996.

Government of India, Planning Commission, *Mid-Term Appraisal of Ninth Five Year Plan (1997-2002)*, New Delhi, October 2000.

Government of India, Ministry of Finance, *Economic Survey 2000-2001*, New Delhi, 2001.

Gulati, Ashok, *Trade Liberalization and Food Security: Challenges to Indian Policy Makers,* Mimeo, International Food Policy Research Institute (IFPRI), Washington D.C., January 2001.

Hoekman, Bernard and Kym Anderson, *Developing Country Agriculture and the New Trade Agenda*, The World Bank, Development Research Group, May 1999.

Keyzer, M.A. and M.D. Merbis, "CAP-Reform in Agenda 2000: Logic and Contradictions" in, *The External Economic Dimensions of the European Union,* G. Faber and P. van Dijek (eds.), Kluwer, 1999.

Pal, S., D. Jha, and A. Singh, *Agricultural Research and Education in India: Institutional Structure and Investment*, National Centre for Agricultural Economics and Policy Research, New Delhi, 1997.

Rakshit, Mihir, "Post-Uruguay Round Negotiations: A Developing Country Perspective", *Artha Vijnana*, March 2000.

Rao, C.H.H., "Economic Reforms, Agricultural Growth and Rural Poverty",

The Indian Economic Journal, Vol. 43, No. 4, April-June 1995-1996.

------ "Declining Demand for Foodgrains in Rural India: Causes and Implications", *Economic and Political Weekly*, January 22, 2000.

Ricardo, David, "On the Principles of Political Economy and Taxation, London, 1817", in, *The Works and Correspondence of David Ricardo*, edited by Piero Sraffa with the collaboration of M.H. Dobb, Cambridge University Press, for the Royal Economic Society, 1966.

Valdes, Alberto, and Joachim Zietz, "Distortions in World Food Markets in the Wake of GATT: Evidence and Policy Implications", *World Development*, Vol. 23, No. 6, 1995.

World Development Indicators 2000, The World Bank, March 2000.

World Trade Organization, *Negotiations on WTO agreement on Agriculture: Proposals by India in the areas of : (i) Food Security, (ii) Market access, (iii) Domestic Support, and (iv) Export Competition* 15 January 2001.

Zeeuw, De Aart, "International agricultural trade negotiations under GATT/WTO: Experiences, future challenges and possible outcomes" *European Review of Agricultural Economics*, 24 (1997).

IV

Industry & Infrastructure

15

Indian Industry:

Structural Transformation, Performance and Recent Policy Initiatives

The industry in India has undergone a significant transformation in the 'nineties. The process of organisational restructuring and the concomitant supportive changes in industrial policy aimed at creating a more competitive and challenging industrial environment are under way. The structural changes have impacted on the industrial performance. In the 'nineties, the overall industrial growth, based on the Index of Industrial Production (IIP) recorded a much wider variation (ranging between 0.6 per cent to 12.7 per cent) as compared with the relatively low order of variation (ranging between 3.2 per cent to 9.3 per cent) observed in the 'eighties. The need for industrial restructuring has raised several issues associated with mergers and acquisitions in the private corporate sector, reforms in the public sector enterprises and policy initiatives for competitiveness and effective working of the corporate sector. These form the major themes of this chapter. First, an overview is given of the structural transformation of the industrial sector.

Structural Transformation in Industry

Over the past three decades, the industrial sector has not shown any definitive trend either in its growth rate or in its contribution to GDP. During the 'seventies, the average annual growth rate of industrial production was 4.4 per cent. The growth rate ranged from an absolute decline of 2.6 per cent in 1979-80 to a positive growth of 11.6 per cent in 1978-79. In the 'eighties, the average annual growth rate was 7.2 per cent. The growth rate ranged between a low of 1.4 per cent in 1980-81 and a high of 11.2 per cent in 1989-90. During the 'nineties, industrial growth has been volatile, moving down from double digits of 11.2 per cent and 12.9 per cent in the first two years, to an absolute fall of 1.9 per cent in 1991-92 and has been above 6 per cent in the ensuing years. The annual average growth rate during the 'nineties (up to 1998-99) has been lower at 6.6 per cent. The share of industry in GDP rose from 18.6 per cent in 1970 to 27.0 per cent in 1995-96. However, it fell to 22.0 per cent in 1996-97 where it has remained in the subsequent two years.

In terms of the Index of Industrial Production, a slowdown in the rate of growth of production had set in from 1991-92 to 1998-99, which is generally identified as a period of wide-ranging reforms in the industrial sector. The decline in the rate of growth of production during the 'nineties is clearly visible in different sectors of industry, especially in case of mining and quarrying (Table 1).

Table – 1

Annual Average Growth Rate of Industrial Production

(Per cent)

Sector	1981-82 to 1998-99	1981-82 to 1990-91	1991-92 to 1998-99
1	2	3	4
General Index	**6.9**	**7.8**	**5.8**
a) Manufacturing	6.9	7.6	5.9
b) Electricity	8.0	9.0	6.8
c) Mining and Quarrying	6.0	8.3	3.0

Table 2 shows that while the basic and capital goods sectors grew at a faster rate during the 'eighties, it was the intermediate goods sector which recorded faster growth in the 'nineties. The relative decline in the rate of growth of basic, capital and consumer goods sectors in the 'nineties is mainly due to restructuring taking place in the industrial sector.

Table – 2

Annual Average Growth Rate of Industrial Production – Use-based Classification

(Per cent)

Sector	1981-82 to 1998-99	1981-82 to 1990-91	1991-92 to 1998-99
1	2	3	4
a) Basic Goods	7.1	7.9	6.2
b) Capital Goods	7.7	11.5	3.0
c) Intermediate Goods	6.7	5.9	7.7
d) Consumer Goods	6.2	6.7	5.5
i) *Durables*	11.2	13.9	7.9
ii) *Non-Durables*	5.3	5.5	5.0
General Index	**6.9**	**7.8**	**5.8**

Relative Contribution of Sectors to Total Production

Changes in the relative contribution of different sectors to the general Index of Industrial Production reflect another dimension of the structural changes in industrial production. Data presented in Table 3 reveal that the relative contribution of the manufacturing sector rose from 70.0 per cent during the 'eighties to 81.6 per cent during the 'nineties. However, in case of mining and

Table – 3

Relative Contribution of Sectors to the Industrial Production

(Per Cent)

Sector	1981-82 to 1990-91 (Average)	1992-93 to 1998-99* (Average)
1	2	3
i) Manufacturing	70.0	81.6
ii) Electricity	14.4	14.4
iii) Mining and Quarrying	15.6	4.0
General Index	100.0	100.0

* The data relating to 1991-92 were excluded in this period because production was almost stagnant.

quarrying, there was a noticeable decline. This was reflected in the changes in the weights assigned to different sector in the construction of IIP series. The weight for the manufacturing sector rose from 77.1 per cent in the earlier series of IIP with base 1980-81=100, to 79.36 per cent in the current series with base 1993-94=100. Correspondingly, the relative weights of mining and quarrying and electricity sectors declined from 11.46 per cent and 11.43 per cent in the old series to 10.47 per cent and 10.17 per cent, respectively, in the new series (Table 4).

Table – 4

Sector-wise Weighting Pattern

NIC Division	Sector	Base: 1970=100	Base: 1980-81=100	Base: 1993-94=100
1	2	3	4	5
Division 1	Mining & Quarrying	9.69	11.46	10.47
Division 2&3	Manufacturing	81.08	77.11	79.36
Division 4	Electricity	9.23	11.43	10.17
Total	General Index	100.0	100.0	100.0

During the 'nineties, while the relative contributions of basic and capital goods sectors declined, there was a rise in those of intermediate and consumer goods sectors (Table 5). In the new series (Base: 1993-94=100), the weights of basic and capital goods sectors were reduced and those of intermediate goods and consumer goods sectors were raised.

Table – 5

Relative Contribution of Sectors to Industrial Production (Use-based Classification)

(Per cent)

Sector	1981-82 to 1990-91 (Average)	1992-93 to 1998-99* (Average)
1	2	3
i) Basic Goods	43.6	35.8
ii) Capital Goods	25.0	7.1
iii) Intermediate Goods	14.6	35.2
iv) Consumer Goods	16.8	21.9
General Index	**100.0**	**100.0**

* The data relating to 1991-92 were excluded in this period because production was almost stagnant.

The relatively low contributions of the basic and capital goods sectors to overall industrial output in the 'nineties reflect, among others, the impact of trade liberalisation, particularly imports, and of financial liberalisation that enabled the corporate sector to make financial gains through 'other income', as also the lack of competitiveness requiring industrial restructuring and modernisation of technologies in a number of industries.

Recent Organisational Restructuring : Mergers and Acquisitions (M&A)

The restructuring of the Indian corporate sector in the recent period has been prompted mainly by the globalised business environment. The structural reforms initiated in the early 'nineties have compelled the Indian industry to adopt focused strategies like corporate restructuring by shedding non-core activities and mergers and acquisitions.

The restructuring process in the Indian corporate sector involves a) focus on core competency, b) overseas expansion, c) resource mobilization, and d) rationalization of product portfolio. In recent years, mergers and acquisitions have been employed as corporate strategies for achieving faster growth. M&A would enable Indian companies to exploit *the scale and scope economies* to enable increased access to the capital market, increase capacity, induct new technology and develop export markets (Box 1). In this context, the process of restructuring of firms through consolidation has emerged as an inevitable logical sequence of private and public sector enterprises have to integrate themselves effectively into global competitors and to maintain their relative levels of performance in the domestic market.

Box – 1

Principles of Mergers & Acquisitions

Mergers and acquisitions take place because of a variety of reasons. For an acquiring company, the reasons may be for obtaining profitable operations, for tax benefits, benefiting from managerial or technical expertise, product diversification, etc. For a selling company, the rationale may be the need for additional finance, the prospects of marketing or technological changes, the desire for the majority of stockholders to dispose of their holdings, existence of an attractive purchase offer or simply as a means of survival. Another major consideration could be strategic stance of a business unit in moving from the existing product line to an altogether new product line which is perceived to be more advantageous against the backdrop of the changing comparative and competitive global environment. However, M&A have raised important issues both for business decisions and for public policy formulation. M&A may be critical to the healthy expansion of business firms as they evolve through successive stages of growth and development. Thus, entry into new product markets and into new geographical markets by a firm may require mergers and acquisitions at some stage in the firm's development.

Sceptics of the efficiency argument hold that companies acquired are already efficient and that their performance after acquisition does not improve. Moreover, the gains to shareholders merely represent a redistribution of stake among stakeholders. Another view is that M&A activities represent the machinations of speculators who reflect the frenzy of a "Casino Society". Such speculative activities increase debt and erode equity, resulting in an economy slipping into a highly leveraged and vulnerable state of economic instability.

Mergers are intended to benefit both companies- the acquirer and the acquired. If the products and markets are complementary, the M&A strengthen each other. They can be suppliers or end-users which can provide backward or forward integration. Mergers can also lead to elimination or reduction of competition if both companies are in the same line of production. Mergers can save taxes and depreciation or writing off the losses, if the loss-making company is acquired by the profit-making companies.

Takeovers can be friendly or hostile. *Friendly takeovers* are arranged between the companies through bargaining. *Hostile takeovers* are unfriendly acquisitions of shares in a way as to hold a controlling interest in the company.

Mergers and acquisitions are expected to result in *synergy*. *Operating synergy* is mostly in the form of cost reductions which are the result of economies of scale or economies of scope. *Economies of scale* decrease the average cost through technological economies, which affect the minimum size of the plant in an industry, or managerial economies, which result in lower production and distribution costs. *Economies of scope* result from increase in the number of products offered. A company will be able to utilize one set of inputs to provide a broader range of products and services. Operating synergy is most likely to accrue from horizontal merger between two companies in the same line of business. In vertical merger (either backward with integration towards raw materials or forward with integration towards finished products), synergistic gains result when the merging firms are technologically or spatially proximate. Merging of group companies or acquiring those that were engaged in related businesses would enhance product scope/brands/geographical reach.

Financial Synergy, on the other hand, is the impact of the merger on the cost of capital for the merging entities. One of the financial benefits of diversification is termed as the "coinsurance effect". The acquisition of a company which is less responsive to fluctuations in the economy would give the acquiring company a steady stream of earnings. Another reason could be the acquiring company's management belief that it can manage the target company's resources better. Furthermore, a target company having transferable tax losses would be of interest to an acquiring company which could offset its income.

M&A activities help to reduce the gestation period for launching new production facilities and promoting new brands, strengthen products portfolios, minimize duplication in basic research and development expenditure and expand marketing shareholder value. Thus, M&A are perceived as prudent corporate strategy. It is necessary to recognise the importance of human resources too. Unless human resources are properly blended in the merged entity and organisational cross- cultures are properly acclimatized, many of the intended merger benefits will not accrue. Generally, mergers represent a resource allocation and reallocation process in the economy with firms responding to new investment and profit opportunities arising out of changes in economic conditions and technological innovations. Mergers rather than internal growth may sometimes be more efficient in terms of resource utilisation. One reason why merger activity is concentrated in periods of high business activity seems to be that firms are not motivated to make large investment outlays when business prospects are not favourable. Only when future benefits accruing to a business endeavour exceed its costs is the action warranted. M&A activities will be stimulated when such favourable business prospects are combined with changes in competitive conditions directly motivating a new business strategy.

There are certain pitfalls associated with M&A deals, such as insufficient investigation of the acquired company, over-bidding to

acquire control, too broad a diversification, acquisition of companies in unrelated fields, etc. These would pose a potential threat to effective implementation of such activities.
Source: RBI Report on Currency and Finance 1998-99.

Progress of M&A Activity in India

The process of restructuring of Indian industry did not commence immediately after liberalisation. It was the industrial slowdown since 1996 which squeezed the profit margins of Indian corporate entities and forced them to restructure their operations in order to achieve greater competitiveness. This took the form of downsizing, shedding non-core activities and expansion through M&A. Downsizing involved heavy costs for business in the form of voluntary retirement packages for the excess manpower. Focussing on core competencies resulted in reduction of size of enterprises. It was, however, realized that only larger-sized companies could effectively meet the challenges posed by multinationals and one way to achieve this was through M&A.

An enabling policy improvement has come about through the formulation of a takeover code in 1994, and the issue of simplified takeover regulations by the SEBI in 1997 on the basis of the recommendations of the Bhagwati Committee. The major thrusts of the Bhagwati Committee report are greater transparency, fairness, and equity of treatment to all investors, timeliness and accuracy of disclosure of information, prevention of frivolous offers and enforcement against violations. The takeover codes are currently undergoing further revision to make them more investor-friendly.

In India, financial institutions (FIs) have proposed to formulate a comprehensive policy for funding and encouraging mergers and acquisitions in the Indian industry.Since FIs have large exposures, both in terms of loans and equity holding in many companies, a uniform policy would facilitate smooth mergers and takeovers.

The Union Budget 1999-2000 proposed changes to facilitate M&A activities by defining the tax treatment in respect of amalgamations, demergers and slump sales. In the case of amalgamations, the bill proposes to relax the conditions required to be fulfilled by an amalgamated company to avail of the benefits of set-off and carry forward of accumulated losses and unabsorbed depreciation. Demerger is defined as the transfer, pursuant to a scheme of arrangement, by a company of one or more of its undertakings to any resulting company. The company whose undertaking is transferred is the demerged company and the company to which the undertaking is transferred to has been defined as the resulting company. In case of a slump sale, one or more undertakings are transferred for a lump sum consideration without values being assigned to the individual assets and liabilities. The Budget sought to ensure that the gains arising out of such sales would be treated as capital gains and taxed accordingly.

These changes are likely to benefit major business groups which are undergoing restructuring activity. The restructuring dynamics of the Indian corporate sector have been boosted by conducive industrial policies. However, the exit policy needs to be reviewed in the light of the liberalisation of the industrial sector. Restructuring of the corporate sector would be much more growth-friendly with the help of proper corporate governance and a conducive exit policy.

During the financial year 1998-99, M&A deals worth Rs.151 billion were reported with nearly half of these deals reported in the last quarter. There were 66 open offer documents filed with the SEBI as against 37 open offers in the previous year. M&S activity was prominent in sectors like cement, steel, computer software, finance, pharmaceuticals, consumer durables, food products, agro-chemicals and textiles. During the first half of 1999-2000, M&A deals worth Rs.103.68 billion were transacted. Mergers have generally taken place among group companies for consolidation of the business activity. Holding companies have acquired their losing subsidiaries to protect their investments. Losing companies were merged with profitable companies for enjoying the benefit of efficient management. The common directors of the companies played key roles in effecting mergers among group companies. Multinational corporations have been involved in acquiring existing companies or existing capacities, instead of setting up new companies.

Restructuring of Public Sector Enterprises

a) General Policy

The Government's strategy towards Public Sector Enterprises (PSEs) comprises a judicious mix of strengthening strategic units, privatising non-strategic ones through gradual disinvestment or strategic sale and devising viable rehabilitation strategies for weak units. The strategies for restructuring PSEs for improving their performance on a long term basis, *inter alia,* include : (i) revival through the process of the Board for Industrial and Financial Reconstruction (BIFR), (ii) financial restructuring wherever appropriate, (iii) formation of joint ventures, (iv) manpower rationalisation and (v) proper governance through strengthening of boards/management.

b) Memorandum of Understanding

In order to give greater autonomy to the PSEs and at the same time to make them accountable for achievement of their objectives, the concept of Memorandum of Understanding (MoU) has been accepted and implemented by the Government since 1988. The MoU exercise has brought about positive achievements, as revealed by the results of their performance evaluation. The year-wise distribution of MoUs signed by PSEs is given in Table 6.

Table – 6

Year-wise Distribution of MoUs by the PSEs

(Number)

Year	PSEs Signed MoUs	PSEs Evaluated	Excellent	Very Good	Good	Fair	Poor
1	2	3	4	5	6	7	8
1991-92	71	59	21	25	10	3	-
1992-93	98	67	28	22	10	7	-
1993-94	101	97	46	29	12	10	-
1994-95	106	67	39	26	-	-	2
1995-96	104	103	51	31	7	12	2
1996-97	110	110	46	27	19	11	7
1997-98	108	108	45	25	13	21	4
1998-99	109	-	-	-	-	-	-
2000-01	107	107	49	26	12	12	7

c) Disinvestment

The disinvestment of equity of the PSEs was started primarily to subject them to the discipline of market forces and make their managements more professional and result-oriented.

There is a consensus that the government should not be operating commercial enterprises. The reasons for this include scarcity of public resources, inefficient and loss making operations of existing public sector enterprises. Accordingly, as part of the liberalisation process, government has started reforms in public sector enterprises. The main elements of Government policy towards Public Sector Undertakings (PSUs) are:

- Bring down Government equity in all non-strategic PSUs to 26 per cent or lower, if necessary;
- Restructure and revive potentially viable PSUs;
- Close down PSUs which cannot be revived; and
- Fully protect the interest of workers.

A target of realising an amount of Rs. 12,000 crore through disinvestment in Public Sector Undertakings has been set in the Budget for the year 2001-2002. Out of this, an amount of Rs. 7,000 crore will be used for providing restructuring assistance to PSUs, safety net to workers and reduction of debt burden, and a sum of Rs. 5,000 crore will be used to provide additional budgetary support for the Plan primarily in the social and infrastructure sectors. The details of the disinvestment target and receipts since 1991-92 are given in the table 7. The amount realised through disinvestment and expected to be realised during the current year on the basis of decisions already taken is given in table 8.

Table – 7

Profitability of Central Public Sector Undertakings

(Rs. crore)

	1991-92	1992-93	1993-94	1994-95	1995-96	1996-97	1997-98	1998-99	1999-00
1. Number of units	237	239	240	241	239	236	236	235	232
2. Paid-up capital	53,000	59,300	63,500	65,300	67,100	69,800	72,000	76,900	82,400
3. Net Worth	60,300	70,500	79,500	90,000	99,200	1,13,900	1,35,100	1,48,100	1,61,100
4. Capital employed	1,18,000	1,40,100	1,59,800	1,62,500	1,74,000	2,31,200	2,49,900	2,65,100	3,03,400
5. Gross profits	13,700	16,000	18,600	22,600	27,600	30,900	37,200	39,700	42,400
6. Profit before tax	4,000	5,100	6,700	9,800	13,600	15,400	19,200	19,700	22,300
7. Profit after tax (PAT)	2,400	3,300	4,600	7,200	9,600	10,200	13,700	13,200	14,600
8. Gross margin to Capital employed (per cent)	19	18	17	21	23	19	21	21	21
9. Gross profit to Capital employed (per cent)	12	11	12	14	16	13	15	15	14
10. Pre-tax profit to Capital employed (per cent)	3	4	4	6	8	7	8	7	7
11. PAT (Net profit) to Net Worth (per cent)	4	5	6	8	10	9	10	9	9

Source: Economic Survey 2001-02.

Table – 8

Disinvestment Proceeds during 2001-02

	Name of PSUs	Percentage of equity disinvested	Proceeds realised/ to be realised
		(per cent)	(Rs. crore)
1.	HTL Limited.	74	55
2.	CMC Limited.	51	152
3.	India Tourism Development Corporation. – 9 Hotels	100 in 8 hotels Long- term lease – cum management contract in 1 hotel.	181
4.	Hotel Corporation of India Limited. - 3 Hotels **	100	** 243
5.	IBP Limited.	34	1,154
6.	Videsh Sanchar Nigam Limited. (Transfer of Cash Reserves) ***	25	*** 3,689
7.	State Trading Corporation of India Limited. (Transfer of cash reserves)	-	* 40
8.	Minerals and Metals Trading Corporation of India Limited. (Transfer of cash reserves)	-	* 60
	Total #		**5,573**

Notes:

* Decision on withdrawal of reserves taken. Action being taken to implement the decision.

** Proceeds to go to Air India.

*** Includes Rs. 2,250 crore as dividend/ special dividend and dividend tax.

Total may not tally because of rounding off.

Source: Economic Survey 2001-02.

The PSU's in which disinvestment is to be completed by March 31, 2002 are given in Box 2. Other PSUs, which are on the anvil for disinvestment are given in Box 3. The CPSUs returned to the Department of Heavy Industry/Administrative Ministry as no bidders responded are given in Box 4.

Box – 2

PSUs in which disinvestment is to be completed by March 31,2002

1. Maruti Udyog Limited.
2. Hindustan Zinc Limited. (HZL)
3. Indian Petrochemicals Corporation Limited. (IPCL)
4. Paradeep Phosphates Limited. (PPL)
5. Bharat Heavy Plates and Vessels Limited. (BHPV) @
6. NEPA Limited. @
7. Instrumentation Control Valves Limited. (ICVL) @
8. Jessop and Company Limited.
9. India Tourism Development Corporation. (ITDC)
10. Hotel Corporation of India Limited. (HCI)

@ Would be implemented after State Governments take decisions on land issues.

Box – 3

Other PSUs which are on the anvil for disinvestment

1. Air India Limited. (AI)
2. Engineering Project (India) Limited. (EPIL)
3. Hindustan Cables Limited. (HCL)
4. Hindustan Copper Limited. (HCL)
5. Hindustan Organic Chemicals Limited. (HOCL)
6. Hindustan Salts Limited.
7. Indian Airlines Limited. (IA)
8. Madras Fertilisers Limited. (MFL)
9. Minerals and Metals Trading Corporation of India Limited. (MMTC)
10. National Fertilisers Limited. (NFL)
11. Shipping Corporation of India Limited. (SCI)
12. Sponge Iron India Limited. (SIIL)
13. State Trading Corporation of India Limited. (STC)
14. MECON Limited.
15. National Aluminium Company Limited. (NALCO)
16. Tungabahadra Steel Products Limited. (TSPL)
17. Burn Standard Company Limited.
18. Braithwaite & Company Limited.

Box – 4

CPSUs returned to the Department of Heavy Industry/ Administrative Ministry as no bidders responded

1. Reyrolle Burn Limited.
2. Bharat Brakes and Valves Limited.
3. Scooters India Limited.
4. Bharat Pumps and Compressors Limited.
5. Praga Tools.
6. Bharat Leather Corporation.

Performance of Selected Public Sector Undertakings

During the period from 1991-92 to 2001-02, disinvestment of Government equity of Rs. 27596 crore has been realised (Table 9). In the Union Budget for 2001-2002, disinvestment of PSE shares to the tune of Rs.12,000 crore has been proposed

Table – 9

Year-wise Distribution of Disinvestment Receipts

(Rupees Crore)

Year	Disinvestment Receipts	
	Budget Estimates	Actual
1	2	3
1991-92	2,500	3,038
1992-93	2,500	1,961
1993-94	3,500	-48
1994-95	4,000	5,607 @
1995-96	7,000	1,397 @
1996-97	5,001	455 @
1997-98	4,800	912
1998-99	9,006	5,376 @(P)
1999-00	10,000	1829 @@
2000-01	10,000	1869
2001-02	12,000	5000
2002-03	12,000	-

@ Includes bonus shares of Rs. 530 crore, Rs.1.035 crore, Rs.75 crore and Rs.6 crore in 1994-95, 1995-96, 1996-97 and 1998-99, respectively.

@@ Upto September, 1999

P Provisional

Sources : Economic Survey 2001-02 and Budget 2002-03.

d) Autonomy

To make PSEs more efficient and competitive, the Government has granted autonomy, of varying degrees, to select profit making PSEs. Depending upon the degree of autonomy granted, the select industries are called as *Navratnas* and *Mini-Ratnas.*

Navratnas

The Government has selected 11 PSEs for the Navratnas category up to 1998-99 (Box 5). These enterprises, subject to certain guidelines, have full freedom to make capital expenditure, decision regarding joint ventures and setting up of subsidiary offices abroad for technological and strategic alliance.

Box – 5

List of Navratnas

1. Indian Oil Corporation (IOC).
2. Indian Petrochemicals Corporation Limited (IPCL)
3. Oil and Natural Gas Corporation (ONGC)
4. Bharat Petroleum Corporation Limited (BPCL)
5. Hindustan Petroleum Corporation Limited (HPCL)
6. National Thermal Power Corporation (NTPC)
7. Steel Authority of India Limited (SAIL)
8. Videsh Sanchar Nigam Limited (VSNL)
9. Bharat Heavy Electrical Limited (BHEL)
10. Gas Authority of India Limited (GIAL)
11. Mahanagar Telephone Nigam Limited (MTNL)

Mini-Ratnas

The Government has also granted enhanced financial, managerial and operational autonomy to other profit - making enterprises, called *Mini-Ratnas.* These enterprises should have earned profits continuously for the last three years, have positive net worth, do not seek budgetary support or guarantees from the

Government and have not defaulted in the repayment of loans/ interests to the Government. These enterprises can incur capital expenditure, enter into joint ventures, set up technological and strategic alliances, formulate schemes of human resources management, etc., subject to certain stipulations and guidelines.

e) National Renewal Fund

The Government had constituted the National Renewal Fund (NRF) in 1992 as a special safety net for workers to impart a human face to industrial restructuring, technology upgradation and modernisation. Assistance from NRF has so far been made available mainly for implementing the Voluntary Retirement Scheme (VRS) in the Central PSEs. The scope and coverage of the scheme has been widened to include counselling, retraining and redeployment assistance to employees. A dozen nodal agencies have set up Employee Assistance Centres (EACs) in various locations spread over 16 States. As on October 31,1998, a sum of Rs.2,029.84 crore has been released for implementing VRS which has benefited 1,25,184 workers in the Central PSEs. The NRF is being maintained in the Public Account, in which funds, one placed, do not lapse at the end of the financial year. A year-wise financial allocation of funds is given in Table 10.

Table – 10

Year-Wise distribution of National Renewal Fund

(Rs. crore)

Year	Amount allocated to NRF	Amount Transferred to Public Account
1	2	3
1991-92	200.00	..
1992-93	829.66	829.66
1993-94	1020.00	700.00
1994-95	500.00	100.00
1995-96	..	140.00
1996-97	250.00	150.00
1997-98	306.91	306.91
1998-99	300.00	278.00

f) State Public Sector Enterprises

The restructuring process is almost absent in many of the State Public Sector Enterprises (SPSEs), barring a few cases where some activities of restructuring of road transport corporations and electricity boards are visible. Most of the SPSEs have turned either sick or are on the verge of sickness. The inefficiency of these enterprises has caused a drain on the States financial resources. There is, therefore, a need for comprehensive reforms and restructuring of SPSEs. Some States have already initiated steps in this respect. Orissa was the first State to bring reforms in the electricity sector through the enactment of the Orissa Electricity Reforms Act, 1995, which came into effect from April 1, 1996. Reforms in this sector have also been started in Haryana, Andhra Pradesh, Tamil Nadu, Maharashtra, Madhya Pradesh, Uttar Pradesh, Rajasthan, Karnataka and Gujarat. In the port sector, the Maritime States Development Council (MSDC) has been formed to have an integrated approach towards the development of major and minor ports. The State Governments of Gujarat, Maharashtra and Andhra Pradesh have embarked upon ambitious port development programmes through private participation.

A national consensus is needed to gradually privatise the state public sector enterprises without causing large disruption.

Recent Policy Initiatives

The basic framework for the overall industrial policy of the Government of India is contained in the Statement on Industrial Policy, 1991. The Government has been constantly reviewing the policy framework to bring about improvements to suit the emerging situation. Some of the major policy developments which have taken place in recent years are outlined below:

Industrial Licensing

During the year 1998-99, three industries, viz., i) coal and lignite, ii) petroleum (other than crude) and its distillation products and iii) sugar were delicensed. Accordingly, there are only six industries now under compulsory licensing (Box 6). Two industries, viz., coal and lignite and mineral oils were taken out from the list of industries reserved for the public sector. At present there are only three industries reserved for the public sector (Box 7). Nine items (six from 'farm implements and tools' and three from 'leather') were removed from the list of industries reserved for exclusive manufacture by the Small Scale Industry (SSI). Entries on toys now excludes electronic toys from the purview of reservation. During the year 1998-99, the number of items reserved for the SSI sector stood at 812.

Thus all industrial undertakings are exempt from obtaining an industrial licence to manufacture, except for (i) industries reserved for the Public Sector (Annex I), (ii) industries retained under compulsory licensing (Annex II), (iii) items of manufacture reserved for the small scale sector and (iv) if the proposal attracts locational restriction.

Box – 6

List of Industries Requiring Compulsory Industrial Licensing.

1. Distillation and brewing of alcoholic drinks
2. Cigars and cigarettes of tobacco and manufactured tobacco substitute
3. Electronic aerospace and defense equipment; all types
4. Industrial explosives including detonating fuses, safety fuses, gun powder, nitrocellulose and matches
5. Hazardous chemicals
6. Drugs* and pharmaceuticals (according to the modified Drug Policy issued in September, 1994 and subsequently amended in February, 1999).

* Bulk drugs industry has been delicensed.

Notes: The compulsory licensing provisions would not apply in respect of the small scale units taking up the manufacture of any of the above items reserved for exclusive manufacture in small-scale sector.

Box – 7

List of Industries Reserved for the Public Sector

1. Arms and ammunition and allied items of defence equipment, defence aircraft and warships. (Process has been initiated to dereserve this entry)
2. Atomic Energy
3. Railway transport

Location Policy

At present, there is no requirement of obtaining industrial approvals from the Central Government (except for the industries under compulsory licensing) for locations not falling within 25 kms. of cities having population of more than one million. However, industries of non-polluting nature such as electronics, computer software and printing can be located within 25 kms. of the periphery of cities with more than 1 million population. Other industries are permitted only if they are located in Industrial Areas designated prior to July 25,1991. Further, zoning and land use regulations as well as environmental legislation continue to regulate industrial locations.

Special Policy Package for North East Region

The Government had formulated a new Industrial Policy for the North-East region during 1997-98 to address effectively the continuing industrial under-development of the Region. The policy is being actively pursued so as to industrialise the North-East Region and bring it up to the national average.

Foreign Direct Investment Policy

The Government is committed to promoting increased flow of Foreign Direct Investment (FDI) for better technology, modernisation, exports and for providing products and services of international standards. Therefore, the policy of the Government has been aimed at encouraging foreign investment, particularly in core infrastructure sectors so as to supplement national efforts. Towards this, the Government has been striving not only to provide greater transparency in the policy and procedures but also to enable a more dynamic and investor-friendly policy framework. At the same time, to provide a level playing field to the domestic industry and also to protect national interests, on the basis of sectoral sensitivities, simultaneous measures have been introduced in the form of dividend balancing, foreign exchange neutrality, foreign equity capital, etc. The salient features of the FDI policy are :

- There are two modalities for FDI approval: a) automatic approval by the Reserve Bank and b) approval by Foreign Investment Promotion Board (FIBP)/Government.
- 34 categories/groups of high priority industries, identified on the basis of National Industrial Classification, qualify for automatic approval up to 50/51/74/100 per cent FDI, depending on the nature of activity.
- Projects for electricity generation, transmission and distribution and construction and maintenance of roads, highways, vehicular tunnels, vehicular bridges, ports and harbours have been permitted foreign equity participation up to 100 per cent under the automatic route.
- FIPB is required to dispose of applications for FDI within a time frame of six weeks.
- FDI is not permissible in agriculture, real estate and insurance activities.
- Full repatriation of original investment and returns, except for dividend balancing and foreign exchange neutrality conditions in certain sectors.
- Liberal access to foreign technology. Automatic approval to lump sum payment of up to US $ 2 million and royalty at the rate of 5 per cent for domestic sales and 8 per cent for exports subject to a total payment of 8 per cent on sales for a period not exceeding 7 years from the date of commercial production.
- Easy access to domestic debt: Foreign companies that invest in India can leverage in India by way of domestic debt from domestic financial institutions.

- Liberal external commercial borrowings and debt servicing norms; and
- No ceiling on raising Global Depository Receipts (GDRs), American Depository Receipts (ADRs), and Foreign Currency Convertible Bonds (FCCBs).

Infrastructure

The Government has accorded high priority for the development of infrastructure. The role of the Government has been redefined from that of an owner of assets and the sole provider of services to that of ensuring the delivery of infrastructure services in a desirable manner with the involvement of the private sector. Over the last few years, the Government has taken up a number of initiatives for the development of efficient infrastructure and towards creating an enabling environment for private participation and enhancing competition in the infrastructure sector. All major infrastructure sectors have already been opened to private investment and a number of private sector projects are being implemented in power generation, telecommunication services, ports, roads, and airports.

Government Incentives for Infrastructure Development

- Foreign Direct Investment (FDI) upto 100 per cent on automatic basis in most of the infrastructure sectors.
- FDI upto 100 per cent under automatic approval route in respect of projects relating to electricity generation, transmission and distribution, other than atomic reactor power plants. No limit on the project cost and quantum of FDI.
- A Foreign Investment Implementation Authority (FIIA) has been set up for providing a single point interface between foreign investors and the Government machinery, including state authorities.
- Opening of domestic long distance telephone service without any restriction on the number of operators.
- 100 per cent deduction of profits & gains to undertaking providing telecommunication services on or before

31.03.2003 for the first five assessment years and thereafter 30 per cent deduction of such profits and gains for further five assessment years.

- Full repatriability of dividend income and capital invested in the telecom sector.
- Reduction of customs duty for boosting infotech, telecom and other knowledge based industries.
- Corporatisation of Department of Telecom Services (DTS) and Department of Telecom Operations (DTO) by creating Bharat Sanchar Nigam Ltd. (BSNL) w.e.f 01.01.2000.
- Decision to upgrade to international standards the airports at Hyderabad, Ahmedabad, Goa, Kochi and Amritsar.
- Income Tax concessions w.e.f. 01.04.2002 in the form of a uniform 10 years tax holiday u/s 801A of the IT Act to an undertaking, operating infrastructure facilities. Similar tax concessions available w.e.f. 01.04.2002 for undertakings commencing generation of power or laying a network of new transmission and distribution lines during the period beginning 01.04.1993 and ending on 31.03.2006.
- Extension of tax benefits for urban infrastructure viz Water treatment and solid waste management.

Small Scale Industries

The small scale sector has played a very important role in the socio-economic development of the country during the past 50 years. It has significantly contributed to the overall growth in terms of the Gross Domestic Product (GDP), employment generation and exports. The performance of the small scale sector, therefore, has a direct impact on the growth of the overall economy. The performance of the small scale sector in terms of parameters like number of units (both registered and unregistered), production, employment and exports is given in Table 11.

According to projections made by the Ministry of Small Scale Industries during 2000-01, the SSI sector recorded growth in production of 8.09 per cent over the previous year. The small scale industries sector has recorded higher growth rate than the industrial sector as a whole (4.9 per cent during 2000-01). It contributed about 40 per cent towards the industrial production as a whole and 35 per cent of direct exports from the country.

Table – 11

Overall Performance of Small Scale Industry

Year	No. of units (in million)	Production (at current prices)	Production (at constant prices) (1993-94)	Employment	Exports (at current prices)
		(Rs.crore)	(Rs.crore)	(in millions)	(US $ in billion)
1993-94	2.39 (6.2)	2,41,648 (15.5)	2,41,648 (7.1)	13.94 (4.0)	8.07
1994-95	2.57 (7.5)	2,98,886 (23.7)	2,66,054 (10.1)	14.66 (5.2)	9.26 (14.8)
1995-96	2.66 (3.5)	3,62,656 (21.3)	2,96,385 (11.4)	15.26 (4.1)	10.90 (17.7)
1996-97	2.80 (5.3)	4,11,858 (13.6)	3,29,935 (11.3)	16.00 (4.8)	11.06 (1.5)
1997-98	2.94 (5.0)	4,62,641 (12.3)	3,57,749 (8.4)	16.72 (4.5)	11.96 (8.1)
1998-99	3.08 (4.8)	5,20,650 (12.5)	3,85,296 (7.7)	17.16 (2.6)	11.64 (-2.7)
1999-00	3.21 (4.2)	5,72,887 (10.0)	4,16,736 (8.2)	17.85 (4.0)	12.51 (7.5)
2000-01(E)	3.37 (5.0)	6,45,496 (12.7)	4,50,450 (8.1)	18.56 (4.0)	13.13 (5.0)

Notes : Figures in the brackets give percentage growth over previous year.
E : Estimates

Source: Economic Survey: 2001-02.

The Government has been taking various measures from time to time in order to enhance the productivity, efficiency and competitiveness of the SSI sector. In pursuance of the comprehensive policy package announced last year, the major developments that have taken place in the SSI sector during 2001-02 are briefly outlined in the box 8.

Box – 8

Developments that have taken place during the year 2001-02 for the SSI Sector

1. The investment limit for units in hosiery and hand tool sub sectors was enhanced from Rs. 1 crore to Rs. 5 crore.
2. The corpus fund set up under the Credit Guarantee Fund Scheme has been raised to Rs. 200 crore from Rs. 125 crore.
3. Credit Guarantee cover against an aggregate credit of Rs. 22.88 crore was provided till the end of December, 2001.
4. 14 items were dereserved on June 29, 2001 related to leather goods, shoes and toys.
5. A new scheme named Market Development Assistance Scheme was launched exclusively for the SSI sector.
6. Under the Cluster Development Programme, 4 UNIDO assisted projects have been commissioned during the year.

Source: Economic Survey 2001-02

Sickness in the SSI Sector

As on March 31, 2001, there were 2,49,630 sick SSI units which had obtained loans from banks. An amount of Rs. 4,506 crore of bank credit was blocked in these units. Of these only 13,076 units were considered potentially viable by the banks with outstanding credit of Rs. 399 crore. Further, banks had identified 2,25,488 units with outstanding bank credit amounting to Rs. 3,943 crore as unviable. Rehabilitation of sick units is a costly proposition as it involves rescheduling of past overdues with concessions on interest amount due, additional credit for modernisation and technology upgradation and provision for fresh working capital. Presently, the State Level Inter-Institutional Committee (SLIIC) of banks and financial institutions is the only forum looking into rehabilitation of potentially viable sick SSI units. However, in the absence of statutory backing, SLIICs has no power to enforce its decisions.

To tackle the problem of rehabilitation of potentially viable sick SSI units, the RBI constituted a working group on November

25, 2000. The Working Group submitted its report in May, 2001. All the major recommendations of the working group have been accepted by the RBI, including a change in the definition of Sick SSI units, norms for deciding on the viability of sick units, etc. The revised definition would enable banks to take action at an early stage for revival of the units. Based on the accepted recommendations of the Working Group, the RBI has drawn up the revised guidelines for Rehabilitation of Sick SSI units, which have been circulated on January 16, 2002 to all the Banks for implementation.

Industrial Sickness

Continuous efforts are being made by the Government of India and the Reserve Bank to bring down the incidence of sickness in Indian industries. Following the Tiwari Committee recommendations (1981), the Sick Industrial Companies (Special Provisions) Act, 1985 (SICA) was passed and a Board for Industrial and Financial Reconstruction (BIFR) was established (1987) for determining the preventive, ameliorative, remedial and other measures which need to be taken in respect of sick industrial companies and the expeditious enforcement of the measures so determined. Detailed guidelines have been issued by the Reserve Bank covering all areas of industrial rehabilitation, viz., detection of industrial sickness at incipient stage, identification of sick/weak units, carrying out viability study of the unit, then extending relief and concessions to only viable units, coordination among banks and financial institutions and among banks themselves, norms for promoters' contribution, extended period for repayment/rescheduling of loans, conversion of debt into equity, single window concept of lending, interest rate concessions and waiver of penal rate/compound interest, liquidated damages and right of recompense for sacrifices made. Banks and financial institutions have been given full delegation of powers/discretion to extend relief/concessions even beyond the Reserve Bank's parameters wherever considered necessary by them. No prior approval for either normal relives or those beyond parameters are required from the Reserve Bank.

The Reserve Bank guidelines do not envisage any write-off or compromise of the dues of the banks, i.e., either principal amount or interest. The banks in the consortium are not normally expected to continue after reaching One Time Settlement (OTS) of their dues with the units. However, there is no bar in extending credit facilities to a unit even after OTS has been reached, provided it is a part of the overall lending policy of the bank duly approved by its Board of Directors.

According to information compiled by RBI from scheduled commercial banks, as on March 31, 2001, there were 2,52,947 sick/ weak units consisting of 2,49,630 units in the SSI sector and 3,317 units in the non-SSI sector. Among the 3,317 units, the private sector, public sector and joint/ co-operative sector accounted for 2,942 units, 255 units, and 106/14 units, respectively. The total number of sick SSI units has decreased from 3,04,235 units to 2,49,630 units but the number of sick/ weak units in the non-SSI sector has increased from 3,164 to 3,317. The total bank credit blocked in sick units has increased from Rs 23,656 crore (as on March 31, 2000) to Rs 25,775 crore (as on March 31, 2001). The small scale sector has Rs 4,506 crore (17.5 per cent) blocked in its units while the non-SSI sector has Rs. 21,270 crore (82.5 per cent). Bank credit blocked in the non-SSI sector in private, public and joint/ co-operative units was Rs 17,705 crore, Rs 2,986 crore, and Rs 537 crore / Rs. 42 crore, respectively.

Since its inception in May 1987 till the end of December, 2001, BIFR has received 5,192 references under the Sick Industrial Companies (Special Provisions) Act, 1985, (SICA). These references include 262 references from Central and State Public Sector Undertakings (CPSUs and SPSUs). Out of the references received, 3,759 were registered under Section 15 of SICA. While 804 references were dismissed as non-maintainable under the Act, 550 rehabilitation schemes, including 22 by AAIFR (Appellate Authority of Industrial and Financial Reconstruction)/ Supreme Court, were sanctioned and 953 companies were recommended to be wound up. 296 companies have been declared "No Longer Sick" and have been discharged from the purview of SICA, on their net worth turning positive, after the implementation of the schemes.

Among the 262 references for public sector undertakings 178 (76 CPSUs and 102 SPSUs) were registered up to December,

2001. Rehabilitation schemes were sanctioned for 16 CPSUs and 22 SPSUs. It was recommended that 20 CPSUs and 27 SPSUs be wound up. 4 CPSUs and 7 SPSUs were declared no longer sick. The gross disposal of cases by BIFR declined from 188 in 1997 to 141 in 1998, however, subsequently, it rose to 179 in 1999 to 385 in 2000. In the current year, however, the gross disposal of cases was 293 up to December 31, 2001. The status of cases referred to BIFR as at the end of December, 2001 is given in the Table 12.

Table – 12

Status of references received by BIFR (Board for Industrial and Financial Reconstruction)

(As on December 31, 2001)

		Total (a)	Pvt. (b)	Central (c)	State (d)	Total (c+d)
1.	References received	5,192	4,930	95	167	262
2.	Registration declined	1,305	1,226	17	62	79
3.	Under scrutiny	129	124	2	3	5
A.4	**References registered**	**3,759**	**3,581**	**76**	**102**	**178**
	Disposals					
5.	Dismissed as non-maintainable	804	771	5	28	33
6.	Rehabilitation Schemes approved /sanctioned*					
	(i) by BIFR	528	490	16	22	38
	(ii) by AAIFR/SC	22	22	0	0	0
7.	Declared "no longer sick" out of (6) above.	296	285	4	7	11
8.	Winding up recommended to the concerned H.C.	953	906	20	27	47
9.	Dropped because Net Worth became positive during enquiry.	40	37	2	1	3
B.	**Total (5+6+8+9)**	**2,347**	**2,226**	**43**	**78**	**121**
	Pending					
10.	Draft schemes circulated	91	76	13	2	15
11.	Winding up Notice issued	118	105	6	7	13
12.	Under Inquiry	1,049	1,032	9	8	17
13.	Schemes Failed and Reopened.	67	59	5	3	8
14.	Pending cases remanded by AAIFR	36	34	0	2	2
15.	Stay ordered by Courts	51	49	0	2	2
	C = (A - B)	**1,412**	**1,355**	**33**	**24**	**57**

Notes :-*91 Merger cases (87 private sector +3 Central PSUs +1 State PSU)

Conclusion

In the background of recent trends which suggest an all round industrial slowdown, the endeavour should be that the Indian industry must continue to strive to be an efficient and competitive one and able to stand on its own in the face of rising domestic and foreign competition. In order to ensure this, Government on its part must resist any attempts to delay the process of liberalisation and deregulation and continue to deepen the reforms and remove all obstacles and bottlenecks for unleashing competitive forces in the industrial sector. This would entail removal of the remaining infrastructural constraints especially in power, transport and telecommunications; reducing bureaucratic controls in all spheres liberalising the labour and land market and removing other barriers to growth.

Appendix Tables... next pages → → →

Appendix Table – 1

Annual Growth Rates of Industrial Production in Major Sectors of Industry

(Base: 1993-94 = 100)

(per cent)

Period (Weight)	Mining (10.4) (11.5)*	Manufacturing (79.4) (77.1)*	Electricity (10.2) (11.4)*	General (100.0) (100.0)*
1992-93	0.5	2.2	5.0	2.3
1993-94	3.5	6.1	7.4	6.0
1994-95	9.8	9.1	8.5	9.1
1995-96	9.7	14.1	8.1	13.0
1996-97	-1.9	7.3	4.0	6.1
1997-98	6.9	6.7	6.6	6.7
1998-99	-0.8	4.4	6.5	4.1
1999-00	1.0	7.1	7.3	6.7
2000-01	3.7	5.3	4.0	5.0
Apr-Dec.				
1992-93	0.2	4.9	4.7	4.3
1993-94	3.6	5.2	7.4	5.3
1994-95	5.3	5.0	6.3	5.2
1995-96	10.5	13.8	8.9	12.9
1996-97	-1.3	9.1	3.8	7.5
1997-98	6.4	6.9	6.0	6.8
1998-99	0.5	4.1	6.8	4.0
1999-00	0.5	7.0	7.7	6.4
2000-01	4.4	6.0	4.8	5.8
2001-02	1.1	2.4	2.7	2.3

Notes : Growth rates from 1994-95 onwards are based on IIP Base: 1993-94=100 and those for earlier years are based on IIP Base: 1980-81=100.

* Relates to weights for IIP Base:1980-81=100

Source: Economic Survey, 2001-02.

Appendix Table – 2

Growth rates of industrial production by use-based classification
(Base : 1993-94=100)

(per cent)

Sectors	(Weight)	1994-95	1995-96	1996-97	1997-98	1998-99	1999-00	2000-01	April-December	
									2000-01	2001-02
Basic Goods	35.5	9.6	10.8	3.0	6.9	1.6	5.5	3.9	5.1	2.2
Capital Goods	9.3	9.2	5.3	11.5	5.8	12.6	6.9	1.8	3.0	-4.8
Intermediate Goods	26.5	5.3	19.4	8.1	8.0	6.1	8.8	4.7	4.8	2.0
Consumer Goods	28.7	12.1	12.8	6.2	5.5	2.2	5.7	8.0	8.2	5.0
of which										
(Consumer Durables)	(5.4)	(16.2)	(25.8)	(4.6)	(7.8)	(5.6)	(14.1)	(14.5)	(17.8)	(12.5)
(Consumer Non-Durables)	(23.3)	(11.2)	(9.8)	(6.6)	(4.8)	(1.2)	(3.2)	(5.8)	(5.3)	(2.3)
IIP (Index of Industrial Production)	100.0	9.1	13.0	6.1	6.7	4.1	6.7	5.0	5.8	2.3

Note : The indices are based on revised itemwise weights.

Source: Economic Survey, 2001-02.

Appendix Table – 3

Performance of Small Scale Sector

Item	April-March		
	1996-97	1997-98	1998-99(P)
1	2	3	4
1. Number of units (lakh nos.)	28.57 (4.9)	30.14 (5.5)	31.21* (3.6)
2. Production (Rupees crore at 1990 - 91 prices)			
a) Target	231,020	253,705	278,619
b) Achievement	247,311 (11.3)	268,159 (8.4)	294,734* (9.9)
3. Production (Rupees crore at current prices)			
a) Target	385,454	440,098	508,906
b) Achievement	412,636 (15.8)	465,171 (12.7)	538,357 (15.7)
4. Employment (lakh persons)			
a) Target	158.91	166.86	175.20
b) Achievement	160.00 (4.8)	167.00 (4.4)	171.58* (2.7)
5. Exports (Rupees crore at current prices)			
a) Target	20,207	47,905	57,488
b) Achievement	39,249 (7.6)	44,437 (13.2)	49,481* (11.4)

* Projected

P : Provisional

Notes: 1) Figures in brackets represent percentage variations over the previous year.

2) Data pertain to modern SSI Sector inclusive of powerloom and traditional industries.

Source: 1) Office of the Development Commissioner, Small Scale Industries, Ministry of Industry, Government of India.

2) Annual Report, 1998-99, Ministry of Industry, Government of India.

Appendix Table – 4

Employment in Organised Sector

(In lakhs)

At the end of	Public Sector					Private Sector	Total	Women Employed out of Total	Percentage of Women Employed to Total
	Central Govt.	State Govt.	Quasi Govt.	Local Bodies	Total (2 to 5)		(6 + 7)		
1	2	3	4	5	6	7	8	9	10
March 1995	33.95 (+0.1)	73.55 (+0.2)	65.20 (+0.1)	21.97 (-0.3)	194.66 (+0.1)	80.58 (+1.6)	275.25 (+0.5)	43.04 (+3.6)	15.6
March 1996	33.66 (-0.9)	74.14 (+0.8)	64.58 (-1.0)	21.92 (-0.2)	194.29 (-0.2)	85.12 (+5.6)	279.41 (+1.5)	44.26 (+2.8)	15.8
March 1997(P)	32.95 (-2.1)	74.85 (+1.0)	65.35 (+1.2)	22.44 (+2.4)	195.59 (+0.7)	86.85 (+2.0)	282.45 (+1.1)	46.37 (+4.8)	16.4
March 1998(P)	..	..	..	..	195.40 (-0.1)	88.35 (+1.7)	283.75 (+0.5)	48.15 (+3.8)	17.0

P : Provisional

Note : Figures in brackets represent percentage variations over the previous year.

Source : Ministry of Labour, Government of India.

16

Infrastructure and Economic Development

The Need for a New Approach

The availability of adequate infrastructure facilities is vital for the acceleration of the economic development of a country. Governments have traditionally been well aware of this and have accorded high priority to investment in sectors such as railways, roads, power, telecommunications, ports, water supply, sanitation and sewerage and airports.

Infrastructure services are often monopolistic in nature: they usually involve high upfront costs and long payback periods: and investments are typically bulky and lumpy. They are also characterised by the existence of externalities which make it difficult for infrastructure entities to recoup investment costs and operational expenses through the levy of user charges.

Consequently, infrastructure services have been predominantly provided by the public sector in almost all countries for most of the 20th century.

Commercialisation: A New Wave, A New Necessity[1]

A wave of privatisation and deregulation has been sweeping infrastructure sectors around the globe over the last decade or so. These bold new approaches promote improvement in efficiency and service quality. Whereas the specific motivations and circumstances vary by countries, and in countries by sectors, there

1. National Council of Applied Economic Research, The "*India Infrastructure Report*", Volume I, New Delhi, 1996.

are five basic pragmatic and non-ideology-related factors that are leading economies all over the world to consider enhanced commercialisation of infrastructure provision:

- The massive investment requirements arising from sharply rising economic growth rates are pushing countries to look for additional sources of financing against the backdrop of fiscal stringency in most countries.
- The rising awareness of the importance of efficiency in investment and delivery, in the context of tight fiscal conditions, is leading to rethinking on the ability of government-owned entities to supply infrastructure services in a business like manner.
- Changes in technology now make it easier to charge for marginal use of infrastructure services. Such technological changes are making possible the introduction of competition horizontally and unbundling of services vertically.
- The increasing need for countries to compete in the global marketplace is putting additional pressure on countries to provide efficient infrastructure services to their businesses in a cost-effective and competitive manner. Higher infrastructure costs in terms of both price and time delays can make the difference between firms being globally competitive or otherwise.
- The new dynamism and integration of world capital markets have vastly increased the possibility of raising large funds for infrastructure investment on a commercial basis whereas, earlier, it was governments which had better access to resources. In many cases, it is now the private sector which has the capability of sourcing large funds internationally.

While these forces are pushing most countries towards the commercialisation of infrastructure investment services, there is also increasing understanding of the social dimension of infrastructure. In poor countries, in particular, the state bears a responsibility to provide the impoverished adequate access to basic services such as health, education, water supply, sanitation and sewerage. Moreover, despite the new possibilities of competition mentioned above, most infrastructure services retain very strong monopolistic elements. As such, the state continues to be responsible for providing appropriate regulatory framework which assist investors and infrastructure entities on the one hand and protect consumers from monopolistic exploitation on the other. The commercialisation of infrastructure and unbundling also lead to a considerable increase in transaction costs which have to be mitigated through transparent and appropriate regulation.

The general conclusion is that whereas the possibility of commercialisation of infrastructure investment and services has increased tremendously over the last decades, the role of the public sector in investment, delivery of services and in regulation will continue to be vital. The future therefore suggests the introduction of a new framework for public-private partnerships in different forms so that appropriate infrastructure investment can fructify.

The Necessary Regulatory Frameworks

The fact that there is now a market for providing infrastructure services has two implications. One, that such services can be provided by the private sector and second, that private capital would have to be accessed on competitive terms. To meet the twin objectives, regulation must primarily be viewed as a mechanism which brings about risk allocation between the service providers and various other entities in the process, making it easy to access capital. When risk allocation becomes easier, it results in reducing the cost of capital. Hence it is necessary to have an articulate regulatory framework, which is radically different from the existing legal framework in terms of transparency, clarity of obligations, duties, and responsibilities between the participants in the infrastructure projects. The new framework must reduce the layering of approvals or bring about a greater degree of certainty in obtaining them within a definite time frame. Such a regulatory framework is very critical if private sector participation is to be encouraged.

There must be certainty that the 'rules of the game', once set; would not be changed too frequently and without notice, so that providers of infrastructure services may be afforded reasonable planning horizons. However, these changes, to occur, will need a demonstrable political and bureaucratic will for the process and this may not be easily achievable.

Rakesh Mohan Committee Report on Indian Infrastructure recommends a Simple Regulatory Framework

- Existing sector-specific enactments be unified into a single statute.
- An autonomous regulatory body be set for each infrastructure sector, on the lines of SEBI.
- The roles of the regulator and the operator must be separated in every sector.
- Mechanisms to settle disputes quickly must be set up.
- An overarching legislation be made for project formats such as BOT, BOO and the like governing projects across all sectors, on the lines of the BOT Law of the Philippines.
- An Infrastructure Coordination Committee be constituted on the same lines as the Foreign Investment Promotion Board which will clear projects on a national level based on broad principles.
- The present restrictions in FII guidelines be removed for investment in infrastructure projects, or separate guidelines similar to FII guidelines without investment limits be issued. Similar guidelines and tax regime should govern any offshore fund set up by a domestic asset management company registered with SEBI, or by a domestic institution.
- Special Purpose Vehicles (SPVs) be used for funding infrastructure projects. Such SPVs should be able to vary their capital with ease; they should be easy to wind up; they should be tax-transparent.

The Government has recognized that private sector participation including foreign investment is required to supplement the public sector efforts. Various reforms have been made in infrastructure sectors, and rules and procedures for investment have been liberalized in order to provide an enabling environment conducive for private participation. The role of the Government has changed from 'owner' and 'sole provider' to that of a 'facilitator', and of safeguarding the interests of the vulnerable sections of the community by legal and institutional framework.

Box – 1

*Infrastructure Sector in the Report of the PM's Economic Advisory Council**

The council's report on economy laid emphasis on investments in economic infrastructure if India is to achieve a growth target of 8 per cent during the Tenth Five Year Plan. Private sector investments were muted because the pre-conditions for successful large scale entry of the private sector were not yet met. Two main reasons provided in the report were inadequate user charges and regulatory uncertainty.

While infrastructure remains an exclusive public sector monopoly, the rationalization of user charges in infrastructure is absolutely vital. A regulatory regime that is seen to be fair to consumers and also sensitive to the legitimate needs of investors, is absolutely essential.

Power

'The flaw in the policy with regard to electricity was the failure to recognize that the root of the problem lies in the financial unviability of the state electricity boards. This has made independent power projects (IPPs) look for temporary solutions such as escrow arrangements and central government guarantees which simply do not address the core problem.'

It suggested that the huge transmission and distribution losses could be brought down through privatization of distribution as the privatized areas would help achieve better efficiency from the distribution system.

The central government should play a pivotal role in the reform of SEBs (State Electricity Boards) as large parts of these dues are to the central government organizations, such as NTPC, Coal India, Railways, and NHPC.

In view of the rapid convergence of telecom, IT and media, a new comprehensive statute, which creates the framework of single license for multiple services, needs to replace the Indian Telegraph Act of 1885.

The government must levy fees to meet administration and regulatory costs, along with universal service obligation charges, through revenue sharing, and not as an avenue to raise resources for the government. Increasing competition within the sector will ensure

* India Infrastructure Report 2002, 3i Network.

benefits of reduction in license fees is passed on to consumers. The only area where government should collect rent is in the allocation of spectrum, which is a scarce resource.

Roads

The council suggested that the private sector be encouraged to participate in road projects through the BOT (build, operate, transfer)/ Annuity system as 'EPC (engineering, procurement and construction), and O&M (operations and maintenance) contracts be merged and given to the same contractor who would be responsible for construction and maintenance of the road during the concession period.

According to the committee, private sector made little progress for so long because the government found it more attractive to raise money cheaply through riskless gilt-edged debt, rather than paying the private sector's capital costs with their risk-premium.

Ports

The existing port trusts should be corporatized and turned into landlord ports that would then invite different operators, both public and private, to invest in cargo handling and port infrastructure services. The ports as such should concentrate on the development of common user general cargo facilities. Rather than fresh ports it suggested existing ports be optimally utilized through efficiency enhancing investments. Tariff fixing is no longer necessary as intra-port and inter-port competition will ensure competitive pricing of services.

Railways

The council strongly recommended depoliticization of Railways, rationalization of user charges and corporatization of production units. Railways have a key role in initiating development of the key inter- and trans-modal facilities.

Civil Aviation

The council recommended leasing the major airports (Delhi, Mumbai, Chennai and Calcutta), and inviting private sector management of airports. An independent regulatory framework for ensuring economic regulation in the sector was suggested as there are many operators.

The inland air travel tax and foreign travel tax should be converted into a common 'civil aviation cess' to ensure sufficient flow of funds to develop civil aviation facilities in other parts of the country.

Performance of the Infrastructure

Average Annual Growth Rates 1980-81 to 1999-2000

Trends in the average growth rates of infrastructure sectors for the period 1992-93 to 1999-2000 reflect a slowing down in some of the sectors as compared with the period 1980-81 to 1991-92. (Details in Box 2).

Box – 2

Performance of the Infrastructure in 1980-81 to 1999-2000
Average Annual Growth Rates

(per cent)

Sectors	1980-1981 To 1991-92	1992-1993 To 1999-2000
1. Power		
Electricity Generation	8.8	6.7
2. Railways		
a. Railway revenue-earning goods traffic	4.8	3.9
b. Passenger kilometers	3.9	4.1
3. Ports		
Cargo handled at major ports	6.1	7.1
4. Civil Aviation		
a. Cargo handled at AAI Airports	6.5	15.1
b. passengers handled at AAI Airports	6.0	10.2
5. Roads		
a. Length of roads	3.6	0.7
b. Length of National Highways	0.5	0.6
6. Telecommunications		
New telephone connections provided (Direct Exchange Lines)	19.0	27.1

- Power sector performance during the period 1992-93 to 1999-2000 has been disappointing despite significant reforms in the sector, such as setting up of a regulatory authority and opening power generation to private investment, both domestic and foreign.
- Operation of Indian Railways in terms of passenger kilometers as well as rate of growth of revenue earnings goods traffic has slowed down during the period 1992-93 to 1992-2000. Since railways are less energy intensive and more environment friendly there is need for appropriate policies aimed at capacity augmentation and

rationalisation of rail tariffs to reduce cross subsidisation.

- Performance of major ports has improved, in terms of the indicator 'cargo handled at ports' during the period 1992-93 to 1999-2000 compared with the growth in 1980-81 to 1991-92.
- Performance of civil aviation sector, has improved both in terms of cargo and passengers handled at AAI airports during the period 1992-1993 to 1999-2000 compared with the performance during the period 1980-81 to 1991-92.
- There has been a rapid growth in the telecommunications sector in terms of new telephone connections over the last decades.

Performance of Infrastructure during 2001-2002

The performance of infrastructure is largely a reflection of the performance of the economy. Infrastructure industries measured by six key infrastructure and core industries (i.e. electricity, crude oil, the petroleum refinery products, coal, steel and cement) having a weight of 26.7 per cent in the overall Index of Industrial Production (IIP) (base: 1993-94 = 100), recorded growth of 2 per cent during 2001-02 (April- December) as compared with 6.8 per cent during the corresponding period of last year. Among the six core infrastructure industries, performance of the cement industry has improved exhibiting a growth of 6.4 per cent during 2001-02 (April-December) compared to 2.1 per cent in the corresponding period of the last year. There has been a deceleration in the growth rates of power, steel, and refinery throughput. Crude petroleum has shown a negative growth during April-December 2001-02. This is attributable to socio- environmental problems, and technical reasons. Power generation in the country is a combination of thermal, nuclear and hydro-generation. Due to poor monsoons during the last two years in the catchment areas of hydroelectric projects, the overall growth of electricity generation declined during 2001-02.

Cargo handled at major ports, revenue earning goods traffic on the railways, and tele-communications registered positive growth during April-November 2001, but lower than the growth in the corresponding period last year. There is a slowing down in the civil aviation sector (Table 9.1).

There are 194 central projects costing above Rs.100 crore that were in various stages of implementation as on December 31,

2001. Of these there were 36 mega projects costing more than Rs.1000 crore. The average cost overrun for mega projects and major projects is 9 per cent and 26 per cent of revised estimates respectively. The Cost overrun witnessed in these projects is largely attributed to delays in commissioning and technical factors. A degree of cost overrun stems from the extent of time overruns. The average time overrun of all these projects was 12 months for the month of December 2001.

New Initiatives for Infrastructure Development

Given below is a summary list of the measure/initiatives that have been undertaken for infrastructure Development.

Box – 3

Major Initiatives for Infrastructure Development

Fiscal Incentives

- Ten-Year tax holiday for the core sector of infrastructure, namely, roads, highways, water-ways, water supply, sanitation and solid waste management systems, which may be availed of during the initial twenty years.
- In the case of airports, ports, inland ports, industrial parks and generation and distribution of power, which also become commercially viable only in the long run, a tax holiday of ten years has been allowed to be availed of during the initial fifteen years.
- The five-year tax holiday and 30 per cent deduction for next five years available to the telecommunication sector till March 31, 2000 was reintroduced for the units commencing their operations on or before March 31, 2003. These concessions will also be extended to Internet service providers and broadband networks.
- Tax incentives have also been provided for the investors providing long-term finance or investing in the equity capital of the enterprises engaged in infrastructure facility. Any income by way of interest, dividends or long-term capital gains from such investments in fully exempt.

Power

- Electricity Bill 2001 has been introduced in Parliament.
- Central Government to accelerate the program of reforms for State

Electricity Boards (SEBs) anchored in Centre-State partnership on the following:

- A time bound program for installation of 100 percent metering.
- Energy audit at all levels.
- Commercialization of distribution.
- SEB restructuring.

- Allocation to the Accelerated Power Development Program (APDP) stepped up to Rs 1,500 crore from a level of Rs 1,000 crore in 2000-01.
- Enactment of Energy Conservation Act, 2001.

Telecom

- The Communication Convergence Bill 2001 has been introduced in the Lok Sabha.
- Competition introduced in all service segments.

Roads

- The total outlay for this sector enhanced.
- Phase I of the National Highway program to be completed by December 2003.
- Rs 962 crore assistance to States from the cess fund for state roads.

Rural Infrastructure

- Rs 2,500 crore assistance out of Pradhan Mantri Gram Sadak Yojana (PMGSY) to provide connectivity of every village with a population of over 1000 persons through good all weather roads by year 2003 and those with a population of upto 500 persons by the year 2007.
- Pradhan Mantri Gramin Yojna (PMGY) extended to cover rural electrification.
- Total rural electrification by 2007.

Railways

- A sum of Rs.898 crore allotted over and above the normal Budgetary Support, to accelerate the completion of selected projects.
- Joint-ventures with State Governments in accelerating the process

of building up rail infrastructure.

- RailTel Corporation becomes functional to harness the optical fibre network alongside the Railway track.
- Plans drawn for commercial utilization of land and airspace of the Railways – identification of 80 sites; works on many of them in the first phase.
- Indian Railway Catering and Tourism Corporation Limited (IRCTC Ltd.) goes functional for harnessing the tourism and catering potential existing on the Indian Railways estimated at Rs.500 crore.
- Production taken up in Chittaranjan Locomotive Works (CLW) of the state of the art 30 phase 6000 HP electric locomotives; development of new design of 2300 HP Metre Gauge/Cape Gauge diesel locomotive for export market; induction of 4000 HP state of the art fuel efficient diesel locomotives – facilities for production of such locomotives in progress at Diesel Locomotive Works (DLW), Varanasi.
- More powers delegated to General Managers of Zonal Railways to finalize contracts as also the freight rate reducing power to quote station-to-station rates to attract and retain traffic on commercial consideration.

Source: Economic Survey 2001-02.

Power

Power generation at 499.6 billion kWh in 2000-01 recorded a growth of 3.9 per cent. Power generation in April-December, 2001 at 383.2 billion KWh recorded a growth of 2.8 per cent over the generation during the corresponding period in 2000. Thermal and Nuclear generation grew by 3.5 per cent and 17.1 per cent respectively, while hydro generation decreased by 3.6 per cent (Table 1). Owing to heavy transmission and distribution (T&D) losses suffered by State Electricity Boards (SEBs), low user charges and operational and technical efficiencies, the power system in the country is experiencing great difficulty.

Table – 1

Trends in the Power Sector (utilities only)

			April-December*		Change over previous year	
	1999-00	2000-01*	2000	2001	2000-01	2001-02@
	(Billion KWH)				(Per cent)	
1 Power generation**	480.7	499.6	372.7	383.2	3.9	2.8
(i) Hydro-electric	80.6	74.5	59.8	57.6	-7.9	-3.6
(ii) Thermal	386.8	408.1	300.7	311.2	5.5	3.5
(iii) Nuclear	13.3	16.9	12.2	14.3	27.1	17.1
2 Plant load factor of thermal plants (per cent)	67.3	69.0	67.7	68.4	-	-

* Provisional. @ April-December.

** Excludes generation from captive & non-conventional power plants.

The installed capacity of power generation in the country as on March 31, 2001 was 101,630 MW of which 72 per cent was thermal power generation, 25 per cent was hydro (including wind), and 3 per cent was nuclear. Installed capacity crossed 102,907 MW as on October 31, 2001. The capacity addition in 2000-01 was 3776 MW against a target of 4000 MW. A capacity of 1375 MW has been added against a target of 3053 MW during April-October, 2001. Thermal plants at present account for 80 per cent of the total power generation, hydro electricity plants contribute 16 per cent and the nuclear plants account for the rest.

The Working Group on Power constituted by Planning Commission to formulate the 10 th Five Year Plan has estimated a feasible capacity addition of 47,000 MW during the 10 th plan. This is made up of 24,405 MW in Central Sector, 12,033 MW in the State Sector and 10,501 MW in the Private Sector. The funds requirement for these investments would be of the order of Rs.5,66,000 crore.

The Plant Load Factor (PLF) is an important indicator of operational efficiency in thermal power plants. The average PLF in the Central Public Sector Undertakings (CPSUs) in the 2000-01 and during April-October, 2001 was appreciably higher than that achieved by the SEBs as a whole. Wide inter-state variations are noticed in the average PLF of thermal power plants. Plants in the southern and western regions have shown better performance. The average PLF for Eastern and Northeastern regions continues to be much lower than the All-India level. If the PLF for North East and Eastern states is excluded the PLF of SEBs is not very different from the central utilities.

An Expert Group was set up under the Chairmanship of Shri Montek Singh Ahluwalia then member Planning Commission, to recommend one-time settlement of all power sector past dues to Central Power Sector Utilities (CPSUs) and dues from CPSUs to State Power Utilities. The recommendations of the Expert Group have been accepted with minor modification by High-Level group of Chief Ministers for implementation. (Box 4).

Box – 4

Scheme for one-time settlement of SEB dues

A Conference of Chief Ministers/Power Ministers was held in March 2001 under the chairmanship of the Prime Minister. The Conference noted that the large amount of dues owed by the State Electricity Boards to the Central Power Sector undertakings (CPSUs) was a major impediment to power sector reforms and resolved that an Expert Group would be set up to recommend a one time settlement of power sector past dues to the CPSUs and the dues of the CPSUs to State Power Utilities. The Expert Group was set up under the Chairmanship of Shri Montek Singh Ahluwalia, then Member (Energy), Planning Commission. The Group submitted its report in May 2001. The Group proposed a scheme of settlement of outstanding dues linked to a mechanism that would ensure payment of current dues in the future. The recommendations of the Group, interalia, included securitisation of the outstanding dues through bonds issued by the respective State Governments. These bonds would be tax-free bonds and would have a tenure of 15 years. The Group also proposed a 50 per cent waiver of the surcharge on outstanding surcharge as an incentive for the States to take up the scheme of securitisation. In addition, during the first 4 years from the commencement of the scheme, bi-annual cash incentives would be paid by the CPSUs equal to 2 per cent of the value of bonds. This would be linked to the States complying with the provisions of the scheme and reforms to be undertaken by the concerned State Government. The Empowered Group of Chief

Ministers in its meeting held on July 6, 2001 accepted the recommendations of the Expert Group with minor modifications. These modifications included increase in waiver of surcharge from 50 to 60 per cent and incentives for a period of 4 years @ 4 per cent of the face value of the bonds for achievement of performance and milestones by the SEBs shall be increased from 6 per cent in the first year and 5 per cent in the second year. States have been requested to implement the scheme at the earliest by giving their consent for tripartite agreement. So far Andhra Pradesh and Jammu & Kashmir have conveyed their consent.

Source: Economic Survey 2001-02.

The restoration of the financial health of SEBs, and improvement in their operational performance continue to remain a critical issue in the power sector. Under Section 59 of the Electricity Supply Act, 1948, SEBs are required to achieve a rate of return (ROR) of not less than 3 per cent on their fixed assets in service, at the beginning of the year, after providing for interest and depreciation charges less consumers contribution. This provision has become operative from the accounting year 1985. Despite this in the following years there has been a continuing deterioration in the financial performance of SEBs. Managerial and financial inefficiencies in State sector utilities have adversely affected capacity addition and systems improvement. While the SEBs do not have enough resources to finance future programs, they are also unable to raise investible funds from alternative sources due to their poor financial and commercial performance. Also, the inability of SEBs to pay their dues, in full, to Central Power Utilities adversely affects the finances and investment plans of these CPSUs.

Financial health of SEBs has been deteriorating over the years. In 1999-2000 only 7 SEBs had a positive ROR. The number of SEBs with a positive ROR of more than 3 per cent (without subsidy) has also fallen, in 1999- 2000 only 2 SEBs (MSEB & TNEB) had a positive ROR of more than 3 per cent (without subsidy). In order to improve the profitability and financial viability of SEBs we need to tackle the key issues such as curbing of T&D loses, tariff rationalization, reducing gap between cost of supply and revenue/ unit of electricity generated. All this will make electricity revenue generating, and it will then be possible to generate investment etc.

The SEBs, have continued to suffer from high T&D losses which were at 24.8 per cent in 1997-98, have increased to 25.6 per cent in 1998-99 (provisional). The T&D losses are due to a variety of reasons, viz., substantial energy sold at low voltage, sparsely distributed loads over large rural areas, inadequate investment in distribution system, improper billing, and high pilferage. The hidden gross subsidy for agriculture and domestic sectors has increased from Rs. 7,449 crore in 1991-92 to Rs. 34,428 crore in 2000-01 and is projected to go up further to Rs. 38,836 crore in 2002-03 (Table 2).

In 2000-01, the Government has initiated a new Plan Scheme namely the Accelerated Power Development Program (APDP) to provide financial assistance to the States for undertaking Renovation & Modernization Programs of Thermal and Hydro power stations and also for strengthening and improvement of Sub- transmission and Distribution network. Under this scheme, a focused investment program has been initiated in 63 identified distribution circles that would be developed as Centre of Excellence in the first phase of the APDP program. An amount of Rs.978 crore was provided to SEBs/ ED during 2000-01. An amount of Rs.1,500 crore has been budgeted for release to States during 2001-02 under APDP, and proposals are under consideration for the sanction of funds.

The Government of India realized the need for a focused approach to address the issues afflicting states with special reference to their circumstances. The State Governments are thus being encouraged to sign Memoranda of Understanding (MOU) with the Government of India. So far 19 States (Karnataka, Uttar Pradesh, Madhya Pradesh, Gujarat, Haryana, Andhra Pradesh, Maharashtra, Rajasthan, Assam, Punjab, Uttaranchal, Himachal Pradesh, Jharkhand, West Bengal, Orissa, Chhattisgarh, Bihar, Kerala and Goa) have signed MOUs with the Government of India. The MOUs are broadly joint commitments of the State Government and the Government of India to undertake reforms in a time bound manner.

Table – 2

Financial Performance of the State Power Sector

(Rs. Crore)

	1991-92	2000-01*	2001-02 (RE)	2002-03 (AP)
A. Gross Subsidy involved				
(i) On account of sale of Electricity to:				
(a) Agriculture	5,938	24,074	25,571	26,959
(b) Domestic	1,310	9,968	10,894	11,651
(c) Inter-State Sales	201	386	247	226
Total	7,449	34,428	36,713	38,836
(ii) Subventions Received from State Govts.	2,045	8,820	10,099	7,981
(iii) Net Subsidy	5,404	25,607	26,613	30,855
(iv) Surplus Generated by sale to other sectors	2,173	3,435	3,615	7,499
(v) Uncovered Subsidy	3,231	22,172	22,999	23,356
B. Commercial Losses @				
(i) Commercial Losses (excluding subsidy)	4,117	25,395	27,306	24,321
(ii) Commercial Losses (including subsidy)	N.A	16,575	17,207	16,340
C. Revenue Mobilisation				
(i) Rate of Return (ROR) #	(-) 12.7	(-) 41.8	(-) 39.5	(-) 32.1
(ii) Additional Revenue Mobilisation from achieving				
(a) 3 per cent ROR	4,959	27,217	29,404	26,226
(b) from introducing 50 paise/unit from Agriculture/Irrigation	2,176	1,638	1,350	1,330

RE: Revised Estimates. AP: Annual Plan Projection. # In per cent. *Provisional.

@ Commercial losses are different from uncovered subsidy because they include financial results of other activities undertaken by the SEBs.

Note: (i) The information relating to the subsidy for Agriculture, Domestic and Inter-State Sales for the years 2000-01, 2001-02 and 2002-03 in respect of Orissa is not available, as the distribution is entrusted to the Private Companies. The information regarding commercial losses pertains to GRIDCO only.

(ii) Information in case of Andhra Pradesh, Haryana, Rajasthan, Uttar Pradesh and Karnataka states is relating to transmission and distribution companies set up after the reforms. In case of other states, the information pertains to SEBs.

(iii) The estimates do not include information relating to Uttaranchal as these have not been furnished by the State.

Box – 5

Status of Power Sector Reforms in India

Creation of Electricity Regulatory Commissions

The Central Electricity Regulatory Commission formed under the provisions of Electricity Regulatory Commissions Act, 1998 has been made fully functional. The Commission has passed orders on Availability Based Tariff and has also brought out terms and conditions for determination of tariff. Eighteen states including, Orissa, Haryana, Andhra Pradesh, Uttar Pradesh, Karnataka, West Bengal, Tamil Nadu, Punjab, Delhi, Gujarat, Madhya Pradesh, Arunachal Pradesh, Maharashtra, Rajasthan, Himachal Pradesh, Assam and Chhattisgarh have either constituted or notified the constitution of SERC. SERCs of Orissa, Andhra Pradesh, Uttar Pradesh, Maharashtra, Gujarat, Haryana, Karnataka, Rajasthan, Delhi and MP have issued tariff orders.

State Reforms Acts

Orissa, Haryana, Andhra Pradesh, Uttar Pradesh, Karnataka, Rajasthan, Madhya Pradesh and Delhi have enacted their State Electricity Reforms Acts which provide, inter-alia, for unbundling/ corpratisation of SEBs, setting up of SERCs, etc. The SEBs of Orissa, Haryana, Andhra Pradesh, Karnataka, Uttar Pradesh and Rajasthan have been unbundled/corporatised.

Source: Economic Survey 2001-02.

Fifty-five hydro schemes with an aggregate capacity of 9,653 MW were identified for renovation, modernization and uprating works at an estimated cost of Rs.1,493 crore to give a benefit of 2,531 MW/7,181 MUs. Out of these 55 schemes, RM&U work on 27 hydro schemes with an aggregate installed capacity of 6,511 MW have been completed and expected benefits to be accrued are 1498 MW/3586 MUs respec- tively. A National Perspective Plan has been formulated to cover 80 hydro R&M schemes having an aggregate installed capacity of 12,328 MW for execution under Phase II programme. The total capital requirement during 9th, 10th and 11th Plan for RM&U and LE of hydro power stations is Rs.4,660 crore, which could accrue a benefit of 7,751 MW. There are 38 ongoing schemes, which are under different stages of implementation.

A draft Captive Power Policy had been prepared which broadly outlines the guidelines for approval, conditions for usage of captive power, wheeling charges, pricing of power sold to grid and billing methods etc.

The Government has set an objective of providing 'Power for All by 2012' and has launched a "Mission 2012 – Power for All" in this direction. A comprehensive Blueprint for Power Sector Development has been prepared outlining the problems and suggesting integrated solution and strategies for achieving the objective of Power for All.

The primary resources for electrical power generation being unevenly disposed in the country, bulk transmission of electrical power over long distance becomes necessary for supplying the loads. The country's power system has been organized into 5 Regional Grids, each of which is well integrated, and now with a view to deriving further economies, and increasing reliability, strong interconnections between the Regional grids are planned thus creating a strong National grid. It is anticipated that this would be accomplished in a phased manner and by the end of the 11th Five Year Plan (2011-12) a strong National grid will exist in the country.

The Electricity Bill 2001 has been introduced in Parliament in August 2001. The Bill seeks to replace the three existing Acts, viz., the Indian Electricity Act, 1910, the Electricity (Supply) Act, 1948 and the Electricity Regulatory Commissions Act, 1998 (Box 6).

Box – 6

The Electricity Bill 2001

- The Central Government to prepare a National Electricity Policy in consultation with State Governments.
- A Thrust to complete rural electrification and provide for management of rural distribution by Panchayats, Cooperative Societies, non-Government organizations, franchisees etc.
- Generation to be delicensed and captive generation to be freely permitted. Hydro projects would, however, need approval of the

state governments and clearance from the Central Electricity Authority.

- Transmission Utility at the Central as well as State level, to be a Government company – with responsibility for planned and coordinated development of transmission network. Provision for private transmission licensees.
- Open access in transmission from the outset with provision for surcharge for taking care of current level of cross subsidy with the surcharge being gradually phased out.
- Distribution licensees would be free to undertake generation and generating companies would be free to take up distribution licensees.
- The State Electricity Regulatory Commission is a mandatory requirement.
- Provision for license free generation and distribution in the rural areas.
- The SERCs may permit open access in distribution in phased with surcharge for current level of cross subsidy to be gradually phased out along with cross subsidies and obligation to supply.
- Provision for payment of subsidy through budget.
- For rural and remote areas stand alone systems for generation and distribution would be permitted.
- Trading as a distinct activity is being recognized with the safeguard of the Regulatory Commissions being authorized to fix ceilings on trading margins, if necessary.
- The State Governments have flexibility to unbundle the SEBs or continue with them as distribution licensees and State Transmission Utility.
- The Bill does not prescribe any model reform, instead provides flexibility to the State Government to choose the model suiting to their conditions.
- Metering of all electricity supplied made mandatory.
- An Appellate Tribunal to hear appeals against the decision of CERC and SERCs.
- Provisions relating to theft of electricity made more stringent.

Source: Economic Survey 2001-02.

Telecommunications

Telecommunications is now universally acknowledged as one of the prime movers of the modern day economy, hence its vital importance for a developing economy like India. There is already a large unmet and unsatisfied telecom demand which needs to be addressed at the earliest. By adopting the National Telecom Policy, declared in 1994, the Government has placed the required emphasis on the rapid growth of the sector, and has embarked on major sector reforms.

The telecom network in India today is not small in absolute terms. With over 12 million lines, it is the 14th largest in the world. Yet it suffers from an abysmally low penetration of 1.3 per 100 population when the world average is over 10. More than 2.1 million consumers are in the queue waiting for a telephone line.

Paradoxically, India may be fortunate to have such low teledensity. Unlike many advanced countries, it does not suffer from large sunk investments in technologies which today are fast becoming obsolete: It has the opportunity to leapfrog technologies and provide its people the benefits that are increasingly feasible from the incredible and continuing change that the telecommunications industry is going through worldwide. India's vast size, the large number of spread-out settlements and its large unserved population provide a huge potential for the expansion of telecommunication services. This opportunity must be seized.

According to the New Telecom Policy (NTP) 1999, the Government has opened the National Long Distance Service to private operators without any restriction on the number of operators with effect from August 13, 2000. The Government has also issued guidelines for license to Infrastructure Provider-II (IP-II) for leasing/renting out/selling end-to-end bandwidth. For Infrastructure Provider-I (IP-I) providing assets such as Dark fibres, Right of Way, Duct Space and Tower, no formal, license is required. They are only required to be registered as IP-I.

Box – 7

New Initiatives in Telecom Regulation

In 2001-02, regulatory initiatives were taken relating to increased competition, tariff policies, Quality of Service (QOS), Consumer protection, and Universal Service Obligations (USO). Important amongst these are :

- Increasing competition in the market: TRAI provided recommendations to open up the market to competition and to introduce new services in the telecom sector. Recommendations were provided for opening the international long distance sector allowing the use of Voice Over Internet Protocol. The licensing terms and conditions for Cellular Mobile were simplified in order to encourage entry for operators in areas without effective competition. TRAI also addressed the issues relating to implementation of the National Long Distance (NLD) License regime, and provided its recommendations on the Carrier Access Code required for consumers to choose among NLD operators.
- Universal Service Obligation: TRAI produced recommendations in respect of policy on Universal Service Obligations, which provide inter-alia for increase in access to telecommunications within rural areas as well as for increasing tele- density. A detailed scheme including arrangements regarding fulfillment of USO, its funding and administration has been provided. The regime is to be implemented by April 1st, 2002.
- Tariff Policy: TRAI has been following a program of tariff re-balancing for the last three years. The last tranche of the current re-balancing exercise is likely to be implemented by the first week of April 2002. The tariff in respect of cellular phones has been monitored closely with a view to making it more consumer friendly and ensuring a level playing field for all operators.
- Quality of Service and Consumer protection: Following upon the previously notified QOS Regulation for Basic Service and cellular Mobile Service, the TRAI initiated a widespread customer survey to ascertain the extent to which QOS is met in these sectors. The TRAI also issued a regulation on QOS for Dial up Internet Access Network.

Source: Economic Survey 2001-02.

The ongoing reforms in the sector have been completed ahead of the schedule. These included corporatisation of the two service providing Departments of the Central Government on October 1, 2001 and a public sector company "Bharat Sanchar Nigam Ltd." is now fully functional. The telecommunications network of the public sector (BSNL and MTNL) is one of the largest telecom networks in Asia. It has a capacity of 42.2 million lines and 34.1 million working connections comprising 32,509 telephone exchanges in the country as on October 31, 2001. During 2000-01, switching capacity witnessed an increase of 21.8 per cent over the preceding year. Similarly, capacities in Trunk Automatic Exchange (TAX), microwave and optical fibre network were considerably enhanced. The total capacity of TAX is 2.5 million lines. The status of microwave and optical fibre are 1,94,430 and 241,841 Route Kms respectively. The value of equipment production is estimated at Rs.12, 271 crore in 2000-01, which is 14 per cent higher than 1999-2000. Countrywide introduction of cellular mobile services has been planned by BSNL as one of its thrust areas. This service will be provided all over the country covering 850 cities in Phase I and 171 cities in Phase-II.

As on September 30, 2001, there were 934,726 PCOs working all over the country. The PCO population ratio as on September 30, 2001, in urban areas is 311, much better than the National Telecom Policy 1994 target of one PCO for 500 persons. Further, according to the New Telecom Policy, every village was to be provided with one public telephone by December 2002. This target was rescheduled and is expected to be completed by the end of the Ninth Five Year Plan. Accomplishment of this task is the responsibility of both the BSNL as well as the licensed private operating companies. According to the terms of the license agreement, private operators were to provide 97,806 as Village Public Telephone (VPTs) during the first three years. Out of a total 607,491 (1990-91 census) villages in the country 428,214 (including 618 VPTs by private operators) villages were provided with public telephones by the end of December 2001. During the current year 2001-02, it is proposed to provide VPTs in 144,771 villages out of which 18,799(including 225 by private operators) villages have been covered by December 31, 2001.

With a view to encouraging competition in the International Long Distance (ILD) traffic, the government had announced the termination of monopoly of VSNL in ILD services from March

31, 2002 instead of the originally planned date of March 31, 2004. Accordingly, the recommendations received from TRAI for opening up of ILD for the private operators covering terms and conditions of license have been accepted by the Government. In this regard, basic telephone services in the country. Presently, these services are being provided in the states of Andhra Pradesh, Gujarat, Maharashtra, Madhya Pradesh, Rajasthan and Punjab. All the six licensees have started functioning in their respective circles. During 2000-01 and 2001-02 (April- September) 25 new basic service license agreements have been signed by private operators.

In response to these policy changes, in the Indian telecom sector the tariff structure has been substantially altered and tariff rates have been reduced. Though this put revenue streams under stress, the operators are expected to improve efficiency to reduce the adverse impact of rebalancing on revenue generation. These steps are also expected to generate greater demand for the services, apart from benefiting users.

Roads & Road Transport

India has more than 3 million km of road network, making it one of the largest in the world. However, the quality of the roads is inadequate and cannot meet the needs of efficient and fast moving transportation. National Highways which are the prime arterial routes span about 58,112 km throughout the country and cater to about 45 per cent of the total road transport demand.

Roads in India, for the purpose of their management and administration, are divided into National Highways, State Highways, district roads and village roads. Under the Constitution, responsibility for the development and maintenance of National Highways rests with the Central Government, while all other roads are the responsibility of the state governments concerned.

While the National Highways are intended to facilitate medium- and long-haul intercity passenger and freight traffic across the country, State Highways are supposed to carry the traffic within the state. Together, they provide the main mobility function in the transportation system. District roads and village roads serve to connect villages to provide accessibility and market linkages. Major district roads provide the secondary function of linkages between the main roads and the rural roads.

Presently, the National Highways are being developed, maintained and managed under an agency system. The overall responsibility including planning, budgeting, standardisation is handled by the Ministry of Surface Transport (MOST). The Government of India has, however, under the Act of Parliament in 1988, established the National Highways Authority of India (NHAI) for developing, maintaining and managing the National Highways as a single agency. Presently, the functions relating to externally-aided projects, implementation of the policy of private sector participation and development of wayside amenities along the National Highways have been assigned to NHAI.

However, the main road network comprising of National and State Highways has not matched this traffic growth. Much of the expansion of the road network has been through building the rural roads constructed to provide connectivity to rural masses, although 50 per cent of the villages are still to be connected with all-weather roads.

Inadequate road networks have led to higher transportation costs which have also severely eroded international competitiveness of the Indian economy. Commercial vehicles are able to run only 200-250 km on an average per day, as compared to 500-600 km per day in developed countries. The problem is further compounded by congested sections, existence of railway level crossings, octroi posts and other tax barriers, all of which lead to abnormal delays in travel and higher fuel cost. The economic losses due to the bad condition of the main roads are estimated to be of the order of Rs. 200 to Rs. 300 billion per annum. Add to that security, safety and pollution problems.

The main roads comprising National and State Highways need strengthening and capacity augmentation. Supernational Highways are also necessary for safe, fast and economic travel. This trunk route system should be properly planned to meet the road traffic needs at optimum cost to the economy. A 20-year master plan for development of these roads should be prepared.

Sources of Financing

All over the world, four sources, as given below, are used to build and maintain quality road infrastructure.

- Allocations from the existing user taxes collected as part of general revenue
- Creation of an earmarked fund through levy of specific user tariffs
- Development and maintenance of highways on "user pays" basis by raising commercial and multilateral loans
- Private sector participation

India's spending on roads is only about one-third of the revenue raised through road taxes and related levies. The balance is diverted to other sectors. The trend in developed countries in this regard is quite different. Road user taxes and other levies are almost totally set aside for roads in countries like the US, Switzerland, Norway, Germany, Japan and Australia.

Highway Development Fund: Keeping in view the huge fund requirements, and given the massive backlog of the previous years, all sources of financing will have to be tapped — public and private, domestic and foreign. Rakesh Mohan Committee Report recommended that a Highway Development Fund be created as an assured extra-budgetary source for funding Indian highways. Some highway improvements will have to be carried out on 'user pays' basis through NHAI or any other agency which can borrow money from the market and repay the loans through tolls. In addition, it is necessary to involve the private sector to supplement the Government's efforts which, in addition to bringing in additional funds, may also bring in the benefit of private sector management and entrepreneurial skills.

The development and maintenance of financing viable Supernational Highways, bypasses to congested towns/cities and spot improvements on existing highways, such as bridges, interchanges and road overbridges should be taken up through the private sector or in collaboration with it.

Private Sector Participation: Roads Sector

- Pursuing the policy of private sector participation, the Ministry of Surface Transport has awarded 20 projects at an estimated cost of over Rs. 1,000 crore. Of these 20 projects, 6 pertain to construction of bypass and remaining 14 are construction of bridges ROB/tunnels.

- Several State Governments have also taken steps to associate private sector in the development of roads.
  - The State of Gujarat has a long-term plan for development of roads, which envisage a major role for private sector.
  - Maharashtra State has also identified four expressways to be taken up for development under private sector.
  - In Madhya Pradesh, 12 bridge projects and one bypass have been completed by the private sector.

The Central Road Fund Ordinance, 2000 was promulgated on November 1, 2000 to give statutory effect to the creation of Central Road Fund. The bill to replace the said ordinance has been passed by the two houses of the Parliament. Assured user charges in terms of additional cess is being levied on petrol and High Speed Diesel. An additional cess of Re. 1 per litre was levied on petrol with effect from June 2, 1998 and similar additional duty of Re. 1 per litre on imported and domestic High Speed Diesel Oil was levied with effect from March 1, 1999. The revenues from these levies are to accrue to a dedicated Central Road Fund. 50 per cent of the cess on High Speed Diesel Oil will be allocated for the development of Rural Roads. The balance of amount of 50 per cent on High Speed Diesel Oil and entire cess collected on petrol will be allocated for the development and maintenance of National Highways (57.5 per cent), for construction of road over/under bridges and other safety works at unmanned rail road crossing (12.5 Per cent) and development and maintenance of State Roads including roads of economic importance (30 per cent). The fund will be non-lapsable and will be used to fund the development of the total hierarchy of roads, right from National Highways through State Highways to Rural Roads. It has been assessed that an amount of about Rs. 6,000 crore would have been generated from the cess on petrol for the period from June 3, 1998 to March 31, 2000 and cess from diesel for the period from March 1, 1999 to March 31, 2000. During 2000-2001, an amount of Rs. 2,010 crore has been allocated for development of National Highways. Out of this Rs. 1,800 crore has been given to NHAI for NHDP. Further an amount of Rs. 990 crore has been earmarked for development of State Roads through the Central Road Fund.

To encourage private sector participation, a Model Concession Agreement for major projects costing more than Rs. 100 crore has been finalized to be undertaken under BOT Scheme. Another Model Concession Agreement for projects less than Rs. 100 crore has also been finalized by MOST. A Model Concession Agreement based on annuity approach has also been finalized. To date, 20 projects involving an investment of around Rs. 1,020 crore have already been taken under BOT Scheme.

Ports

The Indian coastline is serviced by 11 major and 148 minor ports. A new major port at Ennore, 25 km. North of Chennai is being constructed with ADB assistance. Whereas the responsibility for development and management of major ports rests with respective Port Trusts under the Central Government, the state governments administer the minor ports.

As against the total capacity of 258 million tonnes on March 31, 2000, major ports handled 272 million tonnes cargo during 1999-2000 implying that there is a need to augment port capacity. Capacity addition is being planned according to projected traffic requirements. A long-term perspective plan for the Ports Sector spanning up to the year 2020 is under finalisation.

Problems Faced by Indian Ports: The key problem is low productivity. The major factors contributing to this have been identified:

- Operational constraints such as frequent breakdown of cargohandling equipment due to obsolescence and wrong specification;
- Inadequate dredging and container-handling facilities;
- Inefficient and nonoptimal deployment of port equipment;
- Lack of proper coordination in the entire logistics chain.

Indian ports are costlier than other ports in the region for handling containers. The additional cost burden due to use of second- and third-generation vessels has been estimated at US $

250 million a year. Container delays at Indian ports cost US $ 70 million a year.

The India Infrastructure Report made the following recommendations for the development of Ports:

Recommendations

- Port authorities be permitted to raise resources from the primary market by way of debt and equity and from financial institutions.
- Major Port Trust Boards be delegated powers to incur capital expenditure up to Rs 500 million to facilitate speedy creation and operation of assets.
- The Major Port Trust Act, 1963 be amended to permit expansion projects to be taken up on a BOT basis.
- Options of leasing out berths or other assets, wherever it is cost-effective, be considered.
- A moving away from a monolithic pay structure for workers to a piece-based wage structure.
- At least two ports, one each on the east and west coasts, be developed as megaports – the warehouse for the Indian sub-continent.
- While commercial operation of ports be entrusted to existing port authorities with adequate autonomy, a separate regulatory authority be set up to consider issues relating to pricing and conditions which would govern private sector participation.
- Ports with private participation be continued to be exempted from corporate taxes to augment internal resource base and increase eligibility for raising resources from the market.

A scheme for joint venture formations between Major Port and minor foreign ports has been finalised, between Major Port and Minor Ports, without tender, as well as between major port and company following tender route. The measure is aimed at facilitating Port Trusts to: (i) attract new technology; (ii) introduce better managerial practices; (iii) expedite implementation of schemes; (iv) foster strategic alliances with Minor Ports for creation of optimal port infrastructure; and (v) enhance confidence of private sector in funding ports. The guidelines for joint venture formations have been issued. An amendment to the Major Port Trusts Act for this purpose has also been carried out during the year 2000. Sixteen private sector projects involving an additional capacity of 58 million tonnes and an investment of Rs. 4,427 crore have been approved and are under different stages of construction. Four projects have been completed.

The process of phased corporatisation has been initiated for the major ports. A beginning has been made by registering Ennore Port Company Ltd., for managing Ennore Port. It has also been decided to corporatise existing major ports starting with Jawaharlal Nehru Port at Navi Mumbai.

Railways

The Indian Railways is among one of largest railway systems in the world. Indian Railways have an extensive network, which is spread over 63,028 Route Kilometre, comprising Broad Gauge (44,776 RKm), Metre Gauge (14,987 RKm) and Narrow Gauge (3,265 RKm). Approximately, 24 per cent of the network is electrified.

The Indian Railways have played an integrating role in the social and economic development of the country. Railways also have an advantage of being less energy intensive and more environment friendly. However, Indian Railways have experienced a continuous decline in market share in the transport sector. The economic recovery experienced in 1999-2000 continued until the first half of 2000-01, before a slowdown again set in. Mainly as a result of the same, against the target of 475 million tonnes of revenue earning goods traffic (originating), the Railways' freight traffic aggregated to 473.5 million tonnes during 2000-01. This was 3.7 per cent higher than the performance in 1999-2000. Several parts of the country faced natural calamities, such as, the earthquake in Gujarat and drought in parts of Rajasthan, Gujarat, Maharashtra, Madhya Pradesh, Bihar, etc. The Railways organized massive movement of relief materials including fodder and water to the affected areas, free of charge. lower in respect of Fertilizers, and Petroleum Products. In terms of Net Tonne Kilometre

(NTKM), the increase in revenue earning goods traffic was 4.4 per cent during April-December 2001.

With over 15,50,000 employees, Railways are the largest employer among public sector undertakings in the country and a substantial portion of their Gross Expenditure is spent in staff costs including pension liabilities. This has risen appreciably recently due to the V central pay commission recommendations. With a view to reducing the impact of rising staff costs, Railways have developed a two-pronged strategy. A 10-year perspective plan for manpower planning has been drawn. Simultaneously, a large number of initiatives have been taken to improve staff productivity with a view to providing cost-effective services to customers. Measures towards modernisation of infrastructure and rolling stock, induction of computerisation and information technology at an accelerated pace, enhanced manpower productivity and a significant improvement in work culture at all levels, are being adopted progressively for meeting the challenges posed by economic liberalisation and stiff competition from other modes of transport.

The Railways have been performing a unique and challenging role of functioning both as a commercial undertaking as well as provider of public utility service. The latter involves a measure of cross-subsidisation of passenger service by freight revenues as well as operating certain uneconomic services like those in certain suburban sections and branch lines in order to provide cheap and affordable transport to the public at large.

The Railways have launched a number of schemes to mobilise extra-budgetary resources to meet the needs of growth and development. To supplement investment, partnerships with private sector and State Governments for specific projects are being forged. In addition to Build-Own-Lease-Transfer (BOLT) and Own Your Wagon Scheme (OYWS), other initiatives to attract private participation include setting up a private terminal and public-private partnership to provide railway connectivity to new upcoming ports.

Safety is an inherent element underlying all modernisation and technological up-gradation that have been planned in the Indian Railways.

The Ministry of Railways, Railway Board, had constituted an Expert Group on December 31, 1998, to study the railway sector in order to estimate the financing requirements of an expansion and upgrading programme for Indian Railways, to identify sources of funding of estimated investments over 15-year period, to study models of structure and ownership of rail transport facilities in developed countries and to recommend on their relevance to Indian Railways, and to recommend suitable regulatory arrangements that would facilitate orderly expansion of the system, promote the desired degree of competition and protect the users right to quality service. The Report of the Study Group is under examination. Key recommendations of the Expert Group are given in the Box 9.

Box – 8

Measures to strengthen safety and upgrade Railway infrastructure

- Special Railway Safety Fund – a non-lapsable fund – with Rs.17, 000 crore set up to wipe out the arrears in the renewal of vital safety equipment within a fixed time-frame of 5-7 years, for replacing old assets including tracks, bridges, rolling stock, signaling equipment and other safety enhancement items, as per recommendation of the Railway Safety Review Committee.
- Provision of 25 Watt VHF sets at roadside stations for communication between drivers, guards and station staff.
- Funds allocated from the diesel cess being used for safety-related works pertaining to level crossings and for Road over and under bridges. Sanction of manning 165 unmanned level crossings given during 2001 as against 53 during 1999- 2000.
- Track circuiting of run-through lines on all stations with permitted speed of more than 75 kmph completed.
- Bogie mounted brake system being introduced on wagons in place of the conventional pull/push road type air brake system. Development and indigenous manufacture of Centre Buffer Couplers.
- A cohesive strategy for enhanced security of rail users under formulation as per recommendations of the High-level Committee on Enhanced Security on Railways.

Source: Economic Survey 2001-02.

Box – 9

Major Recommendations of Expert Group on Indian Railways

- The root cause of financial problem confronting the Indian Railways is found in lack of adequate productivity increases that are commensurate with real wages over time.
- Indian Railways has to modernize and expand its capacity to serve the emerging needs of the growing economy.
- Indian Railways has to adopt a "strategic perspective" to achieve high growth in both the passenger and freight segments
- Along with achievement of higher growth the Indian Railway will have to explore every avenue of reduction in costs.
- The Expert Group has made detailed projections for the potential of passenger traffic and revenue growth Among the possible investment strategies the panel has favored a "High Growth Strategy "which will require focused remunerative investment and corresponding organizational restructuring of Indian Railway internally and in relationship with government, including corporatisation.
- Higher profitability in freight segment through a long term strategy of improved speed of freight trains, up-gradation of rolling stock, specific commodity related investment, improved signaling and communication, setting up additional container depots, rationalization of the freight rates structure to remove distortions.
- Unremunerative investments must be stopped.
- The key challenge for Indian Railway in the passenger traffic segments is to maintain its obligations on low price services while at the same time increasing both capacity and utilization in upper classes, through a strategy for higher growth in traffic as well as appropriate tariff rebalancing.
- The Government of India should be in charge of setting policy direction. Indian Rail Regulatory Authority (IRRA) should be set up to regulate tariffs. Indian Railways must eventually be corporatised into "Indian Railways Corporation" (IRC).
- Indian Railways Corporation (IRC), would be governed by a reconstituted Indian Railways Executive Board (IREB).
- The restructuring of Indian Railways will require massive investment.

Source: Economic Survey 2001-02.

Civil Aviation

The activities of the civil aviation sector can be categorised as regulatory-cum-developmental in the area of operations and infrastructure. Air services within the country are provided by Indian Airlines Ltd. and private airlines (scheduled and non-scheduled). The international air services are handled by Air India Ltd., Indian Airlines Ltd., and other international airlines operating to India. Pawan Hans Helicopters Ltd. basically provides helicopters support services to the petroleum sector including ONGC and Oil India Limited and connects remote and inaccessible areas of the northeastern region of the country.

After incurring losses continuously for a period of 8 years from 1989-90 to 1996-97, this is the third consecutive year when Indian Airlines has made a profit. It has retained its position as the major player in domestic air transport services. During the year 1999-2000, Indian Airlines Ltd., has made a net profit (before tax) of Rs. 51 crore. To cope with the sluggish market conditions during the year, innovative and aggressive marketing strategies were initiated by the company to maintain and improve its revenues and market share.

It is proposed to disinvest Government of India's shareholding in Indian Airlines within the framework of 'Domestic Air Transport Policy'. Fifty one per cent of equity of Indian Airlines is proposed to be disinvested, of which 26 per cent equity is to be given to a group, company or individual that may be called joint venture (JV)/strategic partner. The remaining 25 per cent is proposed to be offered to employees, financial institutions and the public.

Airports Authority of India has earned a profit after tax of Rs.214 crore in 2000-01 as compared to Rs.211 crore in 1999-2000. The higher profit is mainly attributed to increase in airport charges and cargo income.

A proposal for restructuring the existing airports at Delhi, Mumbai, Chennai and Kolkata through long-term lease to make them world class is under consideration. This will help in attracting investments in improving the infrastructure and services at these airports. Setting up of new international airports at Bangalore, Hyderabad and Goa with private sector participation is also envisaged.

Urban Infrastructure

The likely increase in urban productivity and population due to the new economic policies of the Government of India will place a heavy demand on all kinds of urban infrastructure and services. The infrastructure bottlenecks in urban centres are likely to pose serious impediments in enhancing productivity.

The situation is grim. As per Census of India estimates, approximately 20 per cent of urban households do not have access to safe drinking water. Only 23.35 per cent had toilet facilities and up to March 1992, National Family Health Survey-II (NFHS II) also provides data on access to toilet facilities. As per the Survey, 64 per cent of households in the country had no access to toilet facilities in 1998-99 in comparison to 76 per cent in 1991 reported by the Census.

According to National Human Development Report (April 2002) the problem of sanitation for the majority, at household level, is essentially of awareness and education and not really of resources. The resources, technology and management aspects of the problem are important, more in the context of urban sanitation and solid waste management. Many cities and small towns generate more solid wastes than they can possibly collect or dispose under present institutional arrangements. A major problem in urban solid waste management relates to sewage disposal. With a large number of towns without sewage systems and inadequate and often malfunctioning systems in some others, the threat to the availability of safe drinking water is quite serious in most urban areas in the country.

Apart from deficiencies in terms of access to facilities, the operation and maintenance (O&M) of infrastructure leaves a lot to be desired. And the investment requirements are colossal. It is estimated that the total funds required for the above purposes for the period 1996-2001 would fall in the range of Rs. 800 billion to Rs. 940 billion. The requirement for water supply and toilet facilities alone has been estimated at Rs 210 billion for the period 2001-2011 and Rs. 228 billion for 2011-2021.

The fact that infrastructure services do not pay for themselves and the Government does not have the financial capacity to continue to subsidise the beneficiaries has resulted in low availability of funds. With increasing requirements, this has meant deficiency in volumes as well as quality of service. Consequently, a parallel unorganised sector for provision of many of these services has developed, resulting in high prices and qualitatively deficient services. From a societal point of view, these are expensive solutions. It is high time that a commercial approach is adopted.

Recommendations

The following recommendations have been made by Rakesh Mohan Committee Report on urban Infrastructure:

- Public-Private Partnerships (P-P-P) be adopted for the present. In water supply projects, it is possible to privatise sourcing, treatment and bulk supply. The retail distribution and pricing may remain with the public sector. Solid waste disposal can be privatised fully. Low-cost sanitation may be privatised fully on the model of Sulabh Shauchalaya. Maintenance of roads can be entrusted to the private sector subject to quality control.
- Differential treatment of water for different uses. Micro-level systems need to be designed to recycle water at the household level. The supply should be metered to plug leakages.
- The cost of collection, treatment and disposal of the solid waste be reduced. Greater attention to segregation of different kinds of waste at the collection point itself will reduce cost of disposal. Wherever environmentally acceptable, disposal can be decentralised to save on transportation cost.
- Proper packaging for instance, clubbing water supply and drainage projects together – be used to reduce project cost and improve viability.
- In solid waste management, the "polluter pays" principle be applied.
- In the roads sector, apart from taxation/user charges and impact fees, costs may be recovered by giving advertisement rights, limited development or license rights

(like running kiosks), long lease for trees and the right to use their product.

- The property tax base be freed from the Rent Control Act.
- The ULB be responsible for providing all urban infrastructure in the city area. The multiple agencies in charge of providing various services should be merged under the ULB.

Rural Infrastructure

Rural infrastructure comprises rural roads, rural housing and rural electrification. Rural road connectivity is an extremely important aspect of rural development. A centrally sponsored scheme has been launched called the Pradhan Mantri Gram Sadak Yojana (PMGSY) which seeks to provide connectivity all unconnected habitations in rural areas with a population of more than 500 persons through good all-weather roads by the end of the Tenth Plan period. In respect of hill states and desert areas, the objective would be to connect habitations with population of 250 persons and above. In order to achieve the objective of the Programme, a requirement of Rs.60,000 crore has been estimated. The available source of funds, for the present, is the 50 per cent share of the cess on High Speed Diesel (HSD), amounting to approximately Rs.2500 crore per annum. For the year 2001-02, a sum of Rs.2500 crore has been earmarked for the PMGSY. Project proposal for Rs.4273crore pertaining to 26 States and two Union Territories have been cleared. While projects worth twice the amount of allocation have been cleared during the current year, actual release in 2001-02 would be limited to this year's allocation and next year's releases will be made from April 2002 onwards depending on the progress of the works.

According to the 1991 Census around 3.1 million households are without shelter and another 10.31 million households reside in unserviceable kutcha houses. Considering the magnitude of the problem, a National Housing Habitat Policy was announced in 1998 which aims at providing 'Housing for All' and facilitates construction of 20 lakh additional housing units (13 lakh in rural areas and 7 lakh in urban areas) annually with an emphasis on extending benefits to the poor and deprived. Government is committed to the goal of ensuring shelter for all by the end of Tenth Plan period. For achieving these objectives a comprehensive action plan for rural housing has been prepared (Box 9.11). The objective of the Indira Gandhi Awas Yojna (IAY) is to provide assistance to the below poverty line households (BPL) belonging to Scheduled caste, Scheduled tribe, and free bonded labor categories. The central assistance under the IAY for 2001- 02 is Rs 1618 crore for construction/up gradation of 1.3 million houses. So far an amount of Rs 1098 crore has been released during 2001-02. The Pradhan Mantri Gramodya Yojana is part of the comphrensive Pradhan Mantri Gramodya Yojana introduced during 2000-01 to achieve the objective of sustainable human development at the village level. During 2001-02, Rs 280 crore has been made available for implementing the "Rural Shelter" component of PMGY.

Conclusion

An important conclusions of the above review of infrastructure development is that the demand for infrastructure services continues to outpace supply. Unless these shortfalls are met by creating new capacities in power, telecom, rail, roads and ports, there would be serious constraints on faster industrial and overall economic growth. Social welfare considerations also make it imperative that a minimum supply of water, housing, power and transport services are made available to every citizen. In fact, one of the biggest challenges facing the Indian economy today is to step up infrastructure investment and to upgrade the technology for better services.

Another important lesson is that greater private sector participation in infrastructure development is essential not only due to constraint of government resources but also to improve the quality of services and the delivery system. Although considerable progress has been made in attracting private investment much more needs to be done for sectoral reforms, rationalization of user charges and strengthening of institutional, legal and regulatory framework for ensuring fair competition among private and public operators and protecting consumer interests.

Private sector investments have taken place in independent

power projects, telecom, new port sites, roads, and airports. The pace of private investment in infrastructure depends on the availability of long term debt finance for such projects at reasonable rates. Appropriate reforms in insurance, pension and provident funds will help channelize investments for infrastructure projects.

Independent regulatory bodies have been set up in power, telecom, ports, and insurance sectors, with a mandate to address the evolving trends in various sectors or attracting private investment. However, the regulators need to be allowed greater autonomy in decision making and financial matters. Concerned ministries of the regulatory bodies have adopted different approaches towards the regulatory process. There is a need to look at the existing regulatory legislation and to bring a comprehensive and uniform approach to regulation in infrastructure.

The Power network is critical infrastructure for overall economic development. Despite significant reforms in the power sector such as, setting up of a regulatory authority and opening power generation to private investment, the performance of the power sector have been disapproving. The private investors in the sector are deterred by high risks of non-payment by financially weak SEBs which are sole buyers. The large investment flows may not materialize unless the important issue of commercial viability of SEBs is properly addressed and re-structuring of SEBs, unbundling of risks initiated by several States, are expedited. There is an urgent need to rationalize the present system of tariff setting, and develop a scientific method for long-term demand forecasting. the captive power generation also needs to be encouraged to reduce the large gap between demand and supply. With appropriate policies and institutional arrangements, power generated by such captive plants could be optimally utilized.

Private sector participation in the telecom services, especially basic services, did not take off as initially expected because of various impediments. The Government has announced several policy measures in order to remove these constraints. There is a need to improve competition into all services. Some major policy issues that still need to be addressed in the telecom sector include tariff re-balancing with the objectives of cost based prices, transparency of subsidies and better targeting improvement in operational efficiency. Opening of Internet telephony and convergence of services and single license regime.

There is a considerable progress in the roads sector as assured user charges in terms of additional cess is being levied on Petrol and High Speed Diesel and creation of Central Road Fund. This will help in the process of strengthening and expanding the road system to meet passenger and freight traffic requirements is underway. However so far, private investments in the roads have been primarily in small projects. Inadequacy of policy and regulatory framework necessary for addressing complexities of private-public partnerships has refrained larger investors from entering the sector.

The present level of productivity in the port sector is very low. Though the productivity of terminals has improved, there is a long-way to go to reach a situation when berths should await for cargo. Major Ports are being corporatized. A definite time frame and milestone standard have to be worked out. The mega ports that are being developed on the east and west coast could be for general cargo handling as well as specialized cargo depending on their hinterland.

The existing modal mix of traffic between railways and roads with the predominant share of roads is non-optimal. As railways are less energy intensive and more environment friendly there is need for railways to regain its share in traffic through capacity augmentation aided by corrective pricing policies and organizational charges. The Indian railways need to reinvent to meet the changing needs that have been generated in the process of economic development. There is a need for re-balancing the tariffs of Indian Railways to reduce the rate of cross subsidization. Rail Tariff Authority on the lines of Telecommunication Regulatory Authority needs to be set up with the mandate to fix tariff on rational basis. There is a need to refocus the investment strategy with high priority to augmentation of capacity on high-density corridors, and ensuring the safety and reliability of services.

Indian Railways have long been the backbone of the Indian

transport infrastructure. The country has been fortunate in the existence of a widespread rail network across the country. However,. the railways have experienced significant financial deterioration over the last decade. This has hampered their ability to modernise and to achieve higher efficiency levels for the benefit of their customers, both passengers and freight. Consequently the share of the railways in the transport sector has been declining for quite some time. The time is now ripe for the railways to launch a bold new programme for directed investments for modernisation and expansion of the key remunerative routes. This will be difficult to do without significant organisational reforms. The railways will need to phase out subsidies in passenger fares while re-balancing freight tariffs to economically competitive levels. They will also need to reorient themselves to a much more customer focussed approach in the provision of both freight and passenger services.

The launch of the National Highway Development Programme and the Prime Minister's Gram Sadak Yojana has provided a new radical thrust to the modernisation and expansion of roads in the country. The availability of adequate finances from the petrol and diesel cess has helped greatly in making these programmes financially viable. The participation of the private sector in the NHDP is also helping to leverage the cess resources available. These resources can be further leveraged through the levy of affordable tolls on the NHDP network. A number of innovative approaches are being tried out in this context. With the progress in implementation of these programmes that has accelerated in the past year the country can look forward to a modern road network within the next 5-6 years.

17

Corporate Governance

C. RANGARAJAN

The subject of corporate governance has assumed great importance in the last few years. In the late 1980s, in the UK the corporate sector was beset with a number of problems. These involved creative accounting, spectacular business failures, the limited role of auditors, the weak link between executive compensation and company performance and several others. It was under these circumstances that the Cadbury Committee was set up by the Financial Reporting Council, London Stock Exchange and the accountancy profession to address particularly the financial aspects of corporate governance. The concern of the sponsors was the low level of confidence both in financial reporting and in the ability of auditors to provide the safeguards which the users of company reports expected. These concerns about the working of the corporate system were heightened, as mentioned earlier, by the unexpected failures of some major companies and by criticisms of the lack of effective board accountability for such matters as directors' pay which had risen to excessive levels unrelated to performance. The cause of their anxiety was not so much that these companies had failed as that their reports and accounts just prior to their failure appeared to give no forewarning of the true state of their financial affairs. Its sponsors feared that if no action was taken to improve standards of financial reporting this could affect London's reputation as a financial centre and the reputation of British accounting firms. Later director's pay became such a live political issue that a study group on director's remuneration was formed under Sir Richard Greenbury to deal with directors' pay. More recently there have been two other Committees – The King Committee and the Hampel Committee – which have examined the issues of corporate governance.

In India the question of corporate governance has come up mainly in the wake of economic liberalisation, de-regulation of industry and business and increasing integration of the Indian economy with the rest of the world. The need to conform to internationally accepted standards of corporate governance has become essential, as stakeholders in the Indian industry are no longer confined to this country alone. Also there have been some important changes in the evolution of the Indian corporate system. Many family owned enterprises have moved from private limited companies to closely held public limited companies and further on to widely held limited companies. The recognition of the need for a code of corporate governance has also moved in line with this trend.

Definition and Content

Corporate governance is not a term which is easy to define. However, the two key elements in corporate governance are first, the enhancement of corporate performance via supervision and monitoring of management performance and second, ensuring the accountability of management to share holders and other stakeholders. Corporate governance is the system by which corporate entities are directed and controlled. Thus it includes the policies and procedures adopted by a company in achieving its objectives. In a normative sense, it means a code of corporate conduct in relation to all the stakeholders, external and internal to which a company commits itself. A framework of effective accountability to all stakeholders is the essence of corporate governance. Competition also needs to be tempered by an appropriate value system so that it works in the long-run interest of the corporate entities themselves. Corporate governance is thus concerned with goals as well as the modalities for achieving the goals.

A major emphasis in the Cadbury Committee Report was on the role of Board of Directors, since the company ultimately makes all its decisions through the Board. The Report touches on such issues as the composition of the board, separation of the post of the chairman and the chief executive, the role of the outside non-executive directors etc. The Report also stresses the role of financial reporting and financial controls. As the Report says "the life blood of markets is information and barriers to the flow of relevant information represents imperfections in the market". The Report adds that "the cardinal principle of financial reporting is that the view presented should be true and fair. Further principles are that boards should aim for the highest level of disclosure consonant with presenting reports which are understandable and with avoiding damage to their competitive position. They should also aim to ensure the integrity and consistency of their reports and they should meet the spirit as well as the letter of reporting standards". Transparency through greater flow of information thus becomes important.

As the Cadbury Committee Report has repeatedly emphasised, openness, integrity and accountability must be the dominant elements of corporate governance. In ensuring effective accountability besides the Board of Directors, external auditors and audit committees, the capital markets, institutional investors and banks also have a role to play. Banks have an important role in corporate governance of companies in as much that strong creditors are as critical to the efficient functioning of enterprises as are strong owners. Creditor monitoring and control become essential at all times.

Financial Reporting and Transparency

Apart from the principles governing the conduct of boards of directors, a major element in corporate governance is reporting. The relevant questions in this regard are what kind of information the markets and public require for the effective governance of enterprises, how this information can be best verified and disclosed and what constitutes internationally best practice with respect to disclosure of governance related information. Disclosure should include material information on corporate objectives, financial and operating results of the company, major share ownership, voting rights, remuneration to the members of the Board, foreseeable major risk factors, material issues regarding the employees and stakeholders and governance structures and policies. Information should be prepared, audited and disclosed in accordance with high quality standards of accounting. Channels for disseminating information should provide for fair, timely and cost efficient access to relevant information by users.

The major gain to a corporate conforming to a code of conduct is the confidence it gives to various stakeholders. It assures the shareholders of a reasonable return, bondholders, banks and other creditors of solvency and employees of growth. It will also help the company to access the capital market and mobilize more resources. Disclosure and other requirements will check undesirable behaviour. In fact, the disclosures that are made must be over and above what are required under law.

Role of Institutional Investors

Shareholders are the owners of a company. That is not how many shareholders regard themselves. Shareholders are considered by companies as sleeping partners. The sleeping partners will continue to sleep so long as they receive a reasonable rate of return. Occasionally some irate shareholders make themselves a nuisance at the annual general meeting. But normally shareholders regard themselves as investors. This may be all right in the case of really small individual shareholders but not necessarily for the large institutional holders.

An important issue regarding the ownership role of shareholders has arisen in the context of the changing structure of shareholding. In U.K., the percentage of equity owned by individuals has come down from 54 per cent in 1963 to less than 18 per cent in 1993. Correspondingly the share of financial institutions has increased to 62 per cent. This phenomenon is true of many countries including India. This poses the question whether such institutional holders should regard themselves as 'investors' or 'owners'. If a large chunk of shareholders of a company refuse to play the role of 'owners', it has serious consequences on the governance of such a company. It must also be recognised that different types of institutions will have varying time frames for their investment portfolio. Cadbury has argued that while 'free riding' may be an option for individual institutional investors, for institutions collectively this may not be a tenable proposition. How intrusive the supervision of institutional investors should be is a matter for discussion. However, they cannot opt out of performing the 'ownership' role, despite some conflict of interest between their role as 'investors' responsible to the contributors of the funds they manage and as 'owners' of the company in which they hold shares. In this context, it may be of interest to note that in the US a group of public and private pension funds have joined together to form the Council of Institutional Investors. The Council has provided a forum for these funds to coordinate and communicate with each other on a variety of matters including activism programs aimed at facilitating solution of problems in underperforming portfolio firms. For a variety of reasons, the institutional shareholding in companies in India is also high. Sometimes they play a dual role, as creditors and shareholders. In the Indian context many of the institutional investors are public owned. The art of improved governance lies in establishing an appropriate relationship between institutions who are shareholders and the management. But the role of institutions particularly pure institutional investors, cannot be wished away.

Function of Company Secretaries

Corporate governance under the new paradigm imposes many responsibilities on professionals. Company Secretaries are an important part of this professional group. Corporate governance goes beyond company law. The company secretary has a key role to play in ensuring that board procedures are both followed and regularly reviewed. The chairman and the board will look to the company secretary for guidance on what their responsibilities are under the rules and regulations to which they are subjected and on how those responsibilities should be discharged. The Institute of company secretaries has made a valuable contribution in developing a cadre of highly competent professionals and I trust that the company secretary will go beyond ensuring compliance with company law and provide necessary support to the board in maintaining high standards of corporate governance and implementing best practices. They must be willing to play the part of an independent professional. The essence of good corporate governance lies in achieving a balance between autonomy for management which is necessary for enterprise and growth and accountability to the organisation's various stakeholders.

Inaugural address at the First National Conference of Company Secretaries in Practice, Hyderabad, August 27, 1999.

V

External Sector

18

Managing External Economic Challenges in the Nineties Lessons for the Future

SHANKAR ACHARYA

The 1990s has been an extraordinarily eventful decade for the Indian economy, especially in regard to the external sector. In my talk I will cover six external economic challenges that confronted the economy and economic policy-makers during the decade. These challenges are the balance of payments crisis of 1991, the surge in foreign capital inflows in 1993 and 1994, trade liberalisation, external debt management, the risks of contagion from East Asian flu, and options and issues in exchange rate management. Quite clearly, each of these topics merits a separate lecture. Indeed, quite a few papers have been written and lectures given on these subjects. Inevitably my treatment of these six topics will be somewhat compressed and selective. I do hope it will not be dull and that variety will compensate for depth of analysis.

Balance of Payments Crisis of 1991

The decade began with a bang; a full-fledged balance of payments crisis which saw foreign currency reserves plummeting to hardly $1 billion (or about 2 weeks of imports) in the summer of 1991, export growth turning negative, access to external

The views expressed in this paper are those of the author and do necessarily reflect the views of the Government of India.

commercial credit markets denied, industrial growth collapsing to negative 1.3 per cent, inflation soaring above 16 per cent in August 1991 and overall economic growth plunging to less than 1 per cent in 1991-92 (Table–1).

The underlying causes of the crisis included a succession of high fiscal deficits in the latter half of the eighties, excessive regulation of industry and trade, foreign trade policies which discouraged exports and fostered high-cost import substitution, growing recourse to external borrowing to finance a series of large trade deficits, a negative approach to foreign investment and a weakening financial sector. Against this backdrop of deep-seated, underlying weaknesses, the Gulf War and associated surge in the oil import bill was the proximate trigger which tipped the external sector and the economy into crisis.

The new Government which took office after general elections in June 1991 quickly realised the gravity of the situation, undertook a strong stabilization programme and launched wide-ranging reforms in fiscal policy, industrial policy, foreign trade, the exchange rate system, foreign investment policy, the tax system, the financial sector, capital markets, agricultural pricing and distribution policies and the public sector. The reforms in each of these areas varied in timing, intensity and comprehensiveness. I will not tax your patience by attempting a lengthy description of all the reform measures. However, I should perhaps give some flavour of reforms pertaining directly to the external sector. These included :

- The exchange rate system was transformed in less than 2 years from a discretionary basket-pegged system to a market-determined unified exchange rate, after a short intermediate period of a dual rate.
- The detailed system of import licensing was virtually abolished for capital goods, raw materials and intermediates. Quantitative restrictions remained in place for most consumer goods.
- A programme for reducing the exceptionally high customs duty structure (ranging up to 300 per cent in 1990-91) was launched, with peak protective duty rates brought down to 85 per cent by March 1993.

- Foreign direct investment approvals up to 51 per cent of equity in a large list of industries was made automatic. The Foreign Investment Promotion Board was constituted for expediting approvals in other sectors and for investments above 51 per cent.
- The Foreign Exchange Regulation Act (FERA) was amended to liberalise the operating environment for firms with foreign equity and also to make it easier for Indian business operating abroad.
- A new policy was begun to promote participation by Foreign Institutional Investors (FIIs) in the secondary market for Indian stocks. Portfolio foreign investment was also encouraged through the medium of GDRs and ADRs floated abroad by Indian firms.

As Tables–1 and 2 and Figure–1 show the rewards to these reforms were quite swift. Overall economic growth revived to 5.3 per cent in 1992-93 and accelerated thereafter. Industrial revival took a little longer but growth accelerated to 9.3 per cent by 1994-95. Export growth in US dollar terms surged to 20 per cent by 1993-94. The current account deficit quickly fell from the unsustainable height of $9.7 billion (3 per cent of GDP) in 1990-91 and remained manageable in the 1.0 to 1.5 per cent GDP range even after import growth recovered after 1993-94. Foreign investment rose rapidly from a negligible base to over $4 billion by 1993-94. Foreign currency reserves also recovered sharply, especially from 1993-94 onwards.

It may also be interesting to note that, by the yardstick of overall economic growth, India's recovery from the 1991 crisis compares very favourably in international comparisons with other developing countries undertaking post-crisis reform programmes. As Table–3 shows average economic growth in the first 3 years after start of the reform/adjustment programme was 6.4 per cent in India as compared to an average of 2.2 per cent for 30 developing countries surveyed in one study.

Managing a Surge in Capital Inflows

The turnaround in the external sector was very welcome as vindication of the economic reform policies. But it brought with it the brand new problem of a surge in foreign capital inflows. For us this was a novel challenge and in responding we had to try and marry textbook prescriptions with practical realities – and that is a marriage which is not made in heaven. Let me give a flavour of the key issues faced, the policy choices made and the ensuing results and lessons.

Between September 1993 and October 1994, foreign currency reserves rose by $12.2 billion, or about $1 billion per month. Another way of looking at this is that reserve build up during those 13 months amounted to about 4 per cent of GDP. Table–2 gives more details.

The surge in inflows of foreign exchange confronted us with three major issues :

- Should the nominal exchange rate be permitted to appreciate in response to these flows or should the money be taken into foreign exchange reserves?
- How could the problem of capital surge be transformed into opportunities for liberalisation of external trade and payments?
- If reserves were going to rise sharply what could monetary authorities do to limit the impact on inflation?

Let me say a few words on each of these issues. You have to remember that in taking decisions we were severely handicapped by ignorance about the future trajectory of capital flows; in particular, whether the phenomenon of surge was temporary or lasting.

On the exchange rate issue, despite contrary advice from the IMF, we decided to build up reserves and not permit the nominal rupee-dollar parity to appreciate. Several reasons informed this key decision. First, in September 1993 our stock of foreign currency reserves, at $7.6 billion (or about 3 months imports) was still quite modest and after the trauma of 1991 we certainly preferred a higher comfort level of forex reserves. Second, at that time we were in the early months of an export boom, which we did not want to choke off through a sharp nominal appreciation in the exchange rate. Third, since we were uncertain about the durability of the capital surge, we were reluctant to ride the possible roller-coaster of a sharp nominal appreciation followed by an equally abrupt nominal depreciation in the currency.

To moderate the monetary impact of reserve accumulation and seize opportunities for liberalisation and strengthening of the external sector, we undertook several initiatives. First, imports of essential consumer goods, such as sugar, edible oils and cotton, were liberalised from quantitative restrictions. Second, we formally moved to current account convertibility in August 1994 by accepting IMF's Article VIII obligations. Third, we took deliberate measures to retire short-term external debt obligations. Fourth, we phased out the category of Foreign Currency Non-Resident Deposits which benefited from exchange guarantee by the Reserve Bank of India. Fifth, we partially liberalised the overseas investment policy for Indian firms.

On the monetary side, we undertook partial sterilisation of the foreign asset cumulation through an increase in reserve requirements and some open market sale of government securities by the RBI. Fuller sterilisation operations were constrained by the lack of depth in the securities market, the sharp increase in *new* government securities because of major fiscal slippage in 1993-94 and a policy choice not to throttle monetary expansion at early stages of an investment boom.

Looking back, the results and lessons of these policy choices appear to have been reasonably favourable :

- Foreign currency reserves did get built up from 3 months import cover to over 6 months by March 1995;
- The export boom continued strong for three successive years between 1993-94 and 1995-96 at about 20 per cent annual growth in dollar terms.
- The environment for foreign capital inflows remained conducive, although the surge in foreign exchange reserves levelled off after 1994-95 as a strong industrial recovery fuelled high import growth and widened the current account deficit.
- Overall economic growth accelerated to over 7 per cent by 1994-95, led by an industrial boom.
- The reduction in short-term external debt led the way for

improvements in external debt indicators.

- On the negative side, both monetary growth and inflation did accelerate in 1994-95. But by the middle of 1995 the annual growth rate of both inflation and broad money had come down to reasonable levels (Figure–2).

The overall lesson I would draw is that while a temporary capital surge does pose a significant challenge, it can be handled. Perhaps the key point is to prevent temporary phenomena from destabilising medium-term objectives of growth in exports, investment and the economy.

Trade Liberalisation

At the beginning of the Nineties decade, India's foreign trade regime was highly restrictive, especially on the import side. Peak customs tariff rates were as high as 300 per cent in June 1991. Quantitative controls and licensing of imports was the norm: it has been estimated that out of a little over 5,000 Harmonised System tariffs lines at the 6-digit level, about 80 per cent were subject to some form of import licensing restriction as of mid-1991. These extraordinarily high tariffs and the widespread prevalence of import restrictions had exacted a heavy toll on productivity and economic efficiency for many years. The liberalisation of trade policy was crucial for increasing industrial productivity, reducing the policy bias against exports and agriculture, and generally reaping greater benefits from a more open economy.

Let me first review the trends in trade liberalisation during this decade with respect to two key yardsticks, namely, import tariffs and quantitative restrictions on imports. Figure–3 shows the trends in peak customs duty between 1990 and 1999. As noted earlier, the peak rate was reduced quite fast from 300 per cent to 85 per cent in 2 years between mid-1991 and March 1993. Further reductions in the peak protective duty followed, at a more moderate rate, bringing it down to 42 per cent by July 1996. After that, due to revenue constraints, there was some back-tracking, taking the peak rate to 45 per cent by the end of 1997. The most recent budget has restored the peak rate down to 40 per cent effective March 1999. Figure–3 also shows the corresponding trend decline in the average customs collection rate, which, of course, has displayed a shallower path of decline than the peak rate.

The trend of liberalisation with regard to quantitative restrictions has also been unidirectional throughout the decade, although year by year comparisons in the licensing regime are somewhat complicated by changes in the system of trade classification undertaken in the early 1990s. Broadly speaking, at the 6-digit level of the Harmonised System of trade classification, about 4,000 lines were subject to import licensing restrictions in mid-1991 out of total of over 5000 lines. In the initial burst of liberalisation in 1991-92, some 3,000 tariff lines, covering raw materials, intermediates and capital goods, were freed from licensing restrictions. The trend of liberalisation continued in subsequent years as shown by more detailed data at the 10-digit level, which is available on a comparable basis from April 1996 (Table–4). This shows that by April 1999, nearly 80 per cent of 10,220 tariff lines were free of licensing restrictions. Another 9 per cent of tariff lines relate to items which could be readily imported through freely tradable Special Import Licenses (SIL), which are earned by various categories of exporters based on export performance. In effect, only about 12 per cent of tariff lines, mostly consumer goods, remain under licensing restrictions at present.

In reviewing this pattern of trade liberalisation, it is interesting to explore the relative roles of (a) unilateral liberalisation initiatives, (b) multilateral trade commitments and (c) regional trade cooperation initiatives. With respect to the trend of reductions in peak customs duty, unilateral liberalising initiatives have been the driving force with very little role for multilateral and regional agreements. Of course, there are separate tariff concessions for specified lists of products under regional trade agreements such as SAPTA and the Indo-Sri Lankan Trade Agreement. But these did not influence the trajectory of the peak customs duty rate during the decade.

Many observers in India have noted that the country's customs tariff rates are often significantly lower than the corresponding "bound" rates stemming from obligations undertaken in GATT/WTO multilateral trade negotiations such as the Uruguay Round.

Some representatives of domestic industry have considered this divergence to be an anomaly and called for a raising of customs duty rates to their GATT/WTO bound levels. Such a demand for greater protection to domestic industry misunderstands the two-track approach to customs duty reform consciously followed by successive Governments during the Nineties. On one track, the level of customs duties have been deliberately reduced through successive budgets because such reductions have been judged to be in the national economic interest for improving productivity, lowering costs and reducing the policy bias against exports and agriculture. On a separate track of multilateral trade negotiations, Government has chosen to bind tariffs at certain levels in multilateral trade agreements in negotiations where customs tariff is only one of a set of issues on the negotiating table. So, the fact that many tariff rates are lower than corresponding bound rates is in no sense an anomaly. However, it does support the view that the trajectory of customs duty reform has been largely driven by national policies for trade liberalisation and not by multilateral obligations.

In the area of quantitative restrictions the story was somewhat different. Here both multilateral agreements and regional cooperation initiatives have played a significant role to complement the autonomous national policy for liberalisation of trade restrictions. In the period 1991 to 1996, and especially in the initial years, unilateral trade liberalisation was the dominant element behind the removal of quantitative restrictions. After 1996 both multilateral and regional commitments reinforced the consistent trend towards reducing the quantitative restrictions on imports. For several decades India had justified quantitative restrictions on imports of a wide range of products (including most consumer goods) on account of balance of payments reasons under Article XVIII-B of GATT. Following the marked improvement in the balance of payments situation after 1993 it became increasingly difficult to deploy the BOP cover for maintaining quantitative restrictions on imports. In 1997, India agreed to a 6-year phase out of these BOP-justified quantitative restrictions with her major trading partners (with the exception of U.S. which did not agree with this phase out and proceeded to file a dispute in WTO). This QR phase out programme, agreed under multilateral auspices, has strengthened the process of trade liberalisation in the arena of quantitative/licensing restrictions.

The process of QR-liberalisation also received a major boost from regional trade cooperation initiatives under SAARC. As you know, the SAPTA agreement was signed in April 1993 at the Seventh SAARC Summit in Dhaka and came into force in December 1995. There have been a number of Rounds of SAPTA negotiations since then focussing on tariff concessions. From the beginning of the SAPTA process several of India's partner countries, especially Sri Lanka and Bangladesh, have been pressing for removal of quantitative import restrictions by India. In the Tenth SAARC Summit held in Colombo last year they got their wish. At one stroke the Indian Prime Minister announced the removal of import restrictions maintained on BOP grounds for SAARC countries with effect from 1st August 1998. Thus, from that date, for about 2300 products (at the 8-digit HS level), licensing restrictions have been removed, if these products come from SAARC countries and subject to their conforming with SAPTA Rules of Origin.

In this way, the SAARC/SAPTA regional trade cooperation framework has played a significant role in helping India meet the challenge of trade liberalisation during the closing years of this decade. For those who worry about Regional Trade Agreements diverting attention and effort from the wider endeavour of Multilateral Trade Liberalisation, here is a clear instance where a regional trade agreement was conducive to strengthening the overall process of trade liberalisation.

External Debt Management

As indicated earlier, one of the underlying causes of the 1991 balance of payments crisis was the rapid growth in external indebtedness in the latter half of the 1980s and the associated deterioration in key external debt indicators. As Table–5 shows, India's total external debt to GDP ratio had risen to a peak of 38 per cent in 1991-92, short-term debt (by original maturity) as a proportion of total debt had also attained a peak of 10.2 per cent by March 1991, debt service payments as a ratio of current receipts had risen above 35 per cent in 1990-91 and the ratio of short-term debt to foreign currency reserves had soared to a perilous high of 382 per cent in March 1991. Against this background, it is quite remarkable that India was able to avoid a full-blown debt crisis. The country was able to continue to meet all her debt obligations through a combination of policies to compress imports and arrange exceptional balance of payments financing from multilateral and bilateral sources in the context of a wide-ranging reform programme.

Following the severe strains on the external debt front, policy makers consciously adopted a multi-pronged strategy to bring the external debt situation into a more comfortable zone. The principal elements of this strategy were :

- Short-term debt was reduced and strict controls put in place to prevent undue expansion in future.
- Even medium-term borrowing from private commercial sources was made subject to annual caps and minimum maturity requirements.
- Non-debt creating flows, notably, foreign direct and portfolio investment, were encouraged.
- Foreign exchange reserves were consciously accumulated to provide higher insurance against external sector uncertainties and stresses.
- The growth of Non-Resident Deposits was moderated through specification of interest rates or interest rates ceilings for different maturities and schemes.
- Foreign trade and payments policies were calibrated to encourage growth of exports and other current receipts.

Table–5 shows that this multi-pronged strategy has paid off handsomely. By 1998-99, the debt service ratio had dropped to 18 per cent, the total external debt to GDP ratio had fallen to 23.7 per cent, the ratio of short-term debt to total debt was down to 4.4 per cent by March 1999 and the ratio of short-term debt to foreign currency reserves had fallen from over 380 per cent in March 1991 to 14.7 per cent in March 1999. Figure–4 shows the profile of dramatic improvements in short-term debt. This is especially important in the light of the East Asian crisis, which has underlined the vulnerability of countries to excessive, short-term external indebtedness. Even after adding long-term debt obligations maturing within one year to the outstanding amount of short-term debt (by original maturity) the resulting total of about $ 10 billion at the end of 1998 amounted to less than one-third of the country's foreign exchange reserves.

A few quick comparisons of India's external debt situation with other developing countries also emphasize the relatively high degree of comfort achieved by 1997. Table–6 gives the basic debt indicators for the top 15 debtor countries and some South Asian countries. Figures–5 and 6 shows that India compares quite favourably with respect to the indicators of debt to GNP and debt service to current receipts. Figures–7 and 8 shows that India does very well on the yardsticks of short-term debts. Figure–9 shows that the addition to total external debt stock between 1991 and 1997 had been very low in India as compared to most other large debtor countries.

I should hasten to add that these sanguine trends in external debt indicators provide no guarantees for the future. Safety and comfort in respect of external debt can only be assured through successful adherence to the *policy* strategy outlined earlier.

Coping with Contagion

The writings on the East Asian crisis, its causes, consequences and lessons have filled reams of paper and felled forests of trees. In contrast, I shall be brief. I shall limit myself to seeking answers to the question: why didn't India catch the East Asian flu? The question is also relevant for Sri Lanka and other South Asian countries. Indeed, even if other South Asian countries followed the best of policies, had India succumbed to the contagion, then her immediate neighbours may well have been found it impossible to ward off serious infection.

At one level, the experience of the last two years has underlined the weaknesses in the international financial architecture in coping with sudden panics in international financial markets and massive swings in cross-border flows of mobile capital. While we should work jointly to strengthen the international financial architecture, here I shall confine myself to some of the lessons of the East Asian crisis for *national* economic management. To my mind, the key lessons include :

- Avoid high levels of short-term external debt. This also assumes fairly complete knowledge of the country's total (including short-term) external liabilities, information on which was found to be woefully incomplete in several East Asian countries at the time of crisis.
- Avoid sustained and substantial appreciation in the real effective exchange rate of the country. In some East Asian countries, the combination of a fixed parity with the dollar, combined with high capital inflows, had laid the basis for the ensuing crisis.
- Avoid massive expenditure of forex reserves in support of unrealistic exchange rate levels.
- Seek to strengthen the domestic financial sector in terms of the capital adequacy, prudential norms, disclosure requirements and a well functioning regulatory environment.
- Consider prudential limits for exposure of the banking system to speculative markets, such as real estate and stocks, where asset bubbles can build-up and deflate with severe consequences for the financial system.
- Keep close watch on the size of the current account deficit in relation to growth of current receipts through exports and invisibles.
- Tread the path towards capital account convertibility cautiously with due regard to the strength of the domestic fiscal and financial situations.

If we accept these as some of the major lessons of the East Asian crisis for emerging countries, it is noteworthy that Indian policy appears to have internalised some of these prudential lessons *before* the onset of the East Asian financial conflagration in mid-1997. Let me list some India-specific points :

- Short-term external debt was, as we have seen, under tight control and at very modest levels.
- The market determined exchange rate system had been managed in a moderately flexible manner in the 5 or 6 years preceding mid-1997. This practice continued during

the period of maximum stress (from the East Asian flu) from August 1997 to December 1998. The rupee-dollar parity depreciated by 16 per cent during this period. Figure 10 compares India's nominal exchange rate trajectory with other Asian countries.

- There was some use of foreign currency reserves, which reduced holdings from $26.4 billion in August 1997 to $ 23.9 billion in June 1998. However, by December 1998 the reserves level had recovered to $27 billion.
- A series of financial sector reforms were undertaken in the period 1992 to 1997 which had helped to strengthen the financial sector.
- Prudential limits on exposure of financial intermediaries to stocks and real estate were quite stiff and helped to reduce systemic risks.
- Although export growth had already begun to slow in 1996-97, the current account deficit remained well within manageable limits.
- While foreign direct and portfolio investors in India and external lenders enjoy complete convertibility, resident firms and individuals are subject to strict capital controls. In June 1997, an official Expert Committee (Tarapore Committee) came out with a report recommending a phased implementation of capital account convertibility. Its timing, virtually coincident with the onset of the East Asian crisis, meant that the recommendations would be treated with more than the normal does of official caution!

Despite these very favourable circumstances, India did not remain completely immune from the gales of financial turbulence roaring through Asian markets. Between August 1997 and January 1998, the foreign exchange market was subject to repeated bouts of speculative pressure. In both spot and forward markets, there were persistent excess demand conditions and considerable volatility. To give just one indicator of persistent pressure, outstanding forward sales of foreign currencies by the Reserve Bank surged from negligible levels in early August 1997 to over $3 billion by January 1998. Despite such massive intervention in the forward market, the six-month forward premium rose from 3.6 per cent in July 1997 to 14.6 per cent in February 1998, before declining thereafter.

To cope with this spillover of East Asian contagion (to some extent compounded by domestic political uncertainty) monetary authorities deployed a range of measures, which included :

- Substantial intervention by RBI in both spot and forward exchange markets to curb excessive volatility.
- Exchange rate flexibility to the tune of 8 per cent depreciation between July 1997 and February 1998, with respect to the US dollar.
- A phased tightening of monetary policy from November 1997, culminating in a mid-January 1998 package which raised the Bank Rate by 2 per cent, increased reserve requirements and raised the interest surcharge on bank credit for imports.

These measures had a salutary effect. By March 1998 foreign currency reserves had climbed back to $26 billion, the six month forward rate had dropped below 10 per cent, and RBI's outstanding forward sales of foreign currencies had been rolled back below $1.8 billion.

Between May and August 1998, there were further bouts of pressure on Indian foreign exchange markets, as the East Asian contagion spread to Russia and Brazil and the situation was compounded by economic sanctions imposed against India's nuclear policy. Once again the authorities responded with a similar mix of counter measures which included flexibility of the exchange rate, judicious intervention by RBI in the foreign exchange markets, and tightening of monetary policy in August 1998. In addition, the new Government's initiative to float Resurgent India Bonds had mobilized 4 billion dollars of additional resources in August and September 1998, which helped calm the markets. By end-December 1998, foreign currency reserves were comfortable at $27 billion, six month forward premia were running around 7 per cent, interest rates were again on a downward path and the antidote to Asian flu appeared to have worked.

Before I am accused of undue complacency, let me assert

straight away that much remains to be done to strengthen India's capability to deal with uncertainty and volatility in international capital markets. In particular, the financial sector needs to be strengthened and made more competitive and flexible, fiscal deficits have to be reduced and far reaching reforms need to be undertaken to strengthen the productivity and competitiveness of the real economy.

Exchange Rate Management: Some Options and Issues

I have already discussed some exchange rate management issues in my remarks on the capital surge problem and the East Asian contagion. I am also rapidly running out of time. Therefore, I will confine myself to three main issues in this section. First, the evolution of the international monetary system over the last couple of decades has squarely confronted developing countries, such as India, with the issue of choice among alternative exchange rate systems. Very broadly speaking, the choice lies between the following three broad categories :

(A) A "nominal anchor" system: this can take the strong form of a Currency Board or a somewhat a weaker version of credible commitment to maintaining a fixed parity with respect to a reserve currency.

(B) An adjustable peg system: the peg can be to a single currency or a basket of currencies and adjustment can be either discretionary or according to some version of an announced crawling-peg mechanism.

(C) A market-determined float, which can either be relatively "clean" or "dirty" depending on the degree and extent of central bank intervention.

As you all know, Brazil for some years in this decade followed a successful "nominal anchor" policy of commitment to a parity with respect to the US dollar. While this was a critical element of Brazil's successful strategy of bringing down inflation from high levels, the nominal anchor had to be abandoned in January 1999 in the face of increasing over-valuation and the international market's growing skepticism about the stability of the anchor. For several years Argentina has been experimenting with the currency board system. Basically, the nominal anchor approach entails giving up all or most of national discretionary authority over monetary policy. Such a decision is more likely to be taken against a background of long periods of high inflation of the kind experienced in earlier decades in Latin America. Since average annual inflation rates have stayed below 10 per cent in the last three decades in India, I see very little appetite for the loss of monetary discretion that "nominal anchor" systems entail. So we can rule out this option for the foreseeable future.

As regards the adjustable peg approach, the system was tried and found somewhat wanting in the years leading up to the crisis of 1991. As long as the peg has to be adjusted through discretionary governmental decisions, the likelihood of delays and distortionary widening of the gap between the pegged rate and a market-equilibrating rate is high. Therefore, it is not recommended, especially since India has made a successful transition early in this decade from a discretionary, adjustable peg system to a market-determined rate. Of course, adjustment to the peg could be made automatic, perhaps linked by some transparent formula to relative rates of inflation and relative rates of productivity increase in the home country versus abroad. However, in a world of growing capital account convertibility and astonishingly mobile capital flows, the sustainability of a credible crawling peg system may require very high levels of forex reserves. But perhaps this alternative needs more fresh thinking and should not be ruled out of court straight away.

In fact, of course, India has opted, since early 1993, for a market-determined exchange rate system, under which the exchange rate is determined by supply and demand in the foreign exchange market. The market includes the Reserve Bank as a major participant, who can be either passive or active in buying and selling foreign currencies. The basic philosophy is for the RBI to intervene to moderate volatility while allowing underlying forces of supply and demand associated with "fundamentals" to be reflected in the market rate. Figure–11 shows trends in India's nominal and real exchange rates during the Nineties.

This leads to the second main issue: in a market-determined exchange rate system of the kind followed in India, how does the central bank distinguish between (i) market rate changes which are due to "fundamentals" of productivity, inflation etc. and (ii) market rate changes due to short-term speculative phenomena including changes in market sentiment? In practice, such a distinction is extremely difficult to make, even with the paraphernalia of indicative guidance from REER indices and so forth. That is why exchange rate management by the central bank is much more an art than a science. The problem is compounded if political authorities perceive political costs in depreciation and none (perhaps political gain) in appreciation.

The third major issue arises from the fact that exchange rate movements according to fundamentals are, in their nature, inter-linked with volatility around a equilibrium path. They are intimately bound through expectations and actions of market agents. To take a concrete example, if fundamentals indicate a depreciation in the exchange rate and the central bank is passive as market forces bring about this depreciation, there is always a danger that market expectations might get out of hand and lead to the type of massive and costly "over-shooting" that occurred in some East Asian countries in 1997-98. This is a real world problem But the alternative of the central bank continuously going "against the market" to shore up an unviable exchange rate is also not a feasible proposition in a world of finite forex reserves.

No wonder exchange rate management is more a matter of art than science. And one might go on to add that successful management requires a delicate mix of technical skill, strategic transparency, tactical opaqueness — and lots of good luck. The bottom line is that in a market-determined exchange rate system both political authorities and the central bank have to learn to live with a great deal of exchange rate flexibility, both in the short and medium-term, if the system is to deliver optimal results.

Challenges for the Next Decade

Since I have drawn the lessons for policy along the way, I will not try to pull them together in my final remarks. Instead, let me close with a few thoughts on what I foresee to be the major challenges that India's external sector is likely to face in the first decade of the new millennium.

The single greatest challenge will be to enhance the productivity and competitiveness of the Indian economy in an increasingly integrated global environment. This is crucial for assuring sustained growth in exports of goods and services, which, in turn, is central to the long-term health and viability of India's external sector. Higher productivity and greater competitiveness will not happen by themselves. It will require strong and sustained commitment to what has been called the second generation of reforms in such difficult areas as fiscal responsibility legislation, labour laws, corporate governance, bankruptcy laws, ownership, pricing and distribution of public utility services, deeper tax reform, effective privatisation of many public enterprises and redirection of scarce public resources towards the valuable social goods of education, health, rural infrastructure, enhanced quality of environment and governance.

Second, the emerging new international financial architecture will impose fresh disciplines and challenges for developing countries, especially in fiscal and financial systems.

Third, progress towards greater capital account convertibility is both desirable and inevitable, but such progress will have to be carefully calibrated to reduce the down side risks that have been brought home so vividly by the recent East Asian crisis.

Fourth, exchange rate management will continue to be a demanding task. The challenge will be to ensure market-responsive flexibility while minimising the risks and costs of "over-shooting".

Fifth, India still has a fair distance to travel on the path of trade liberalisation. This will require a pro-active stance towards multilateral trade negotiations and a workable commitment to "open regionalism", especially in the context of SAPTA, ASEAN and APEC. It will also require fulfillment of commitments given by successive Finance Ministers to bring down India's customs duties to Asian levels within a few years.

Sixth, India, along with all other countries, must be prepared to contend with a possible slowdown in US economy. For the past eight years the world economy has benefited from and been conditioned by the unprecedented American boom. The day might come when the long-predicted slowdown actually occurs and poses a new crop of problems for the world economy.

Finally, India will have to face and surmount the challenges posed by new technologies and market places, such as internet and e-commerce.

Table – 1

Selected Macro Economic Indicators

	Average of (1985-90)	1990-91	1991-92	1992-93	1993-94	1994-95	1995-96	1996-97	1997-98	1998-99
Growth Rates										
1. GDP	6.0	5.4	0.8	5.3	6.2	7.8	7.6	7.8	5.0	6.0
2. GVA (Industry)	7.5	7.2	–1.3	4.2	6.6	9.3	12.2	6.0	5.9	1.1
3. Exports (US $)	11.4	9.0	–1.1	3.3	20.2	18.4	20.3	5.6	4.5	–3.9
4. Imports (US $)	9.4	14.4	–24.5	15.4	10.0	34.3	21.6	12.1	4.6	–7.1
5. Inflation (WPI)	6.7	10.3	13.7	10.1	8.4	10.9	7.7	6.4	4.8	6.9
6. Broad Money (M3)	17.6	15.1	19.3	15.7	18.4	22.3	13.7	16.2	17.9	17.8
As per cent of GDP at current market prices										
7. Gross Domestic Savings	20.6	24.3	22.9	22.0	21.8	24.2	24.1	24.4	23.1	N.A.
8. Gross Domestic Investment	23.1	27.7	23.4	23.9	22.4	25.4	25.8	25.7	24.8	N.A.
9. Current Account Balance #	–2.1	–3.0	–0.3	–1.7	–0.4	–1.0	–1.6	–1.2	–1.3	–0.9
10. GFD (Centre and States)#	8.7	9.2	6.8	6.8	8.1	6.9	6.4	6.2	7.1	8.4

Notes:

GDP : Gross domestic product at factor cost; GVA: Gross value added originating in Industry comprising mining & quarrying, manufacturing, electricity, gas & water supply, and construction; GFD: Gross fiscal deficit

1&2 : Growth rates in GDP & GVA (Industry) upto 1992-93 are based on Old Series (Base: 1980-81) and for the years 1993-94 onwards on New Series (Base: 1993-94)

3&4 : Growth rates based on balance of payments data.

5 : Annual (52 weeks average) inflation rate based on Wholesale Price Index (WPI) Base: 1981-82;

7&8 : Ratios upto 1992-93 are based on Old Series (Base: 1980-81) and from 1993-94 onwards on New Series (Base: 1993-94)

10 : Combined GFD is the GFD of the central government plus GFD of state governments minus lending from the centre to the State governments.

Data in respect of state governments for the years 1997-98 & 1998-99 are provisional

\# GDP at current market prices for earlier years have been interpolated by using an average link factor of 1.0878 obtained from the overlapping years viz., 1993-94 through 1996-97 for which both old series and new series for the GDP at current market prices are available.

Table – 2

External Sector Performance

	Average of (1985-90)	1990-91	1991-92	1992-93	1993-94	1994-95
Export Growth (in US $)	11.4	9.0	–1.1	3.3	20.2	18.4
Import Growth (in US $)	9.4	14.4	–24.5	15.4	10.0	34.3
Trade Deficit (% of GDP)	–2.9	–2.9	–1.0	–2.1	–1.5	–2.7
Current Account Deficit (% of GDP)	–2.1	–3.0	–0.3	–1.7	–0.4	–1.0
Foreign Investment ($ million)		103	133	559	4153	5138
(a) Direct		(97)	(129)	(315)	(586)	(1314)
(b) Portfolio (FIIs+GDR & Others)		(6)	(4)	(244)	(3567)	(3824)
Capital Account Surplus ($ million)	5099	8402	4563	4224	9882	8013
Foreign Currency Reserves ($ million)	5022	2236	5631	6434	15068	20809
Change in Foreign Currency Reserves ($ million)	–423	–1132	3395	803	8634	5741
Exchange Rate (Rs/US $)	13.8	17.9	24.7	29.0	31.4	31.4

Notes: 1. Foreign currency reserves position from 1990-91 onwards is for end of the financial year i.e. 31st March of the respective year

2. Exchange rates are period averages.

Table – 3

Average Economic Growth in First 3 Years after start of Reform/Adjustment Programme

(Per cent)

India (1991-92)	**6.4**
Average of 30 Developing Countries	*2.2*
Kenya (1981)	2.4
Nigeria (1983)	2.1
Mexico (1983)	0.6
Thailand (1983)	5.1
Turkey (1980)	4.1

Note: Year in parenthesis indicates year reform or adjustment programme was launched.

Source: CSO for India. For other countries, "Macroeconomic Performance under adjustment lending" in Thomas, Chhibber, Dailami and de Melo (eds). *Restructuring Economics in Distress, Policy Reforms and the World Bank*, Oxford University Press, 1991.

Table – 4

Different Types of NTBs imposed on India's imports, 1996-97 - 1998-99 (Number of tariff lines, 10 digit level)*

Panel: A

Type of NTB	As on 1.4.1996 No. of Lines	As on 1.4.1996 Percent Share	As on 1.4.1997 No. of Lines	As on 1.4.1997 Percent Share	As on 1.4.1998 No. of Lines	As on 1.4.1998 Percent Share	As on 1.4.1999 No. of Lines	As on 1.4.1999 Percent Share
Prohibited	59	0.6	59	0.6	59	0.6	59	0.6
Restricted	2984	29.6	2322	22.8	2314	22.7	1183	11.5
Canalised	127	1.2	129	1.3	129	1.3	37	0.4
Sil	765	7.6	1043	10.2	919	9.0	886	8.7
Free	6161	61.0	6649	65.1	6781	66.4	8055	78.8
Total	10096	100.0	10202	100.0	10202	100.0	10220	100.0

* As per Harmonised System of India Trade Classification, HS-ITC classification of export and import items.

Source: DGFT, Ministry of Commerce

Panel: B

Status of NTBs Notified to W.T.O. under BOP cover (As on 1.4.1999 at 8 digit level)*

Total number of items notified to WTO	2714
Total number of items in the Free List	1298
Restricted items	702
SIL Items	679
Canalised Items	35

* As per Harmonised System of India Trade Classification. HS-ITC classification of export and import items.

Table – 5

External Debt Indicators

(ratios as per cent)

Year	1991	1992	1993	1995	1997	1999
Total Debt/Gross Domestic Product	28.0	37.7	36.6	30.0	23.8	23.7
Debt Service/Current Receipts	35.3	30.2	27.5	26.2	21.2	18.0
Short term Debt/Total Debt	10.2	8.3	7.0	4.3	7.2	4.4
Short term Debt/Reserves	382.1	125.6	98.5	20.5	30.1	14.7
Interest Payments/Current Receipts	15.5	13.0	12.5	9.7	7.3	8.0

Note: The stock figures (Total Debt, Short term and Reserves) are for 31st March of respective years. Flow figures (Debt Service, Interest, Current Receipts and Gross Domestic Product) are for the financial year i.e. for 1991 it refers to 1st April 1990 - 31st March 1991.

Table – 6

International Comparison of Top Fifteen Debtor Countries, 1997

S.No.	Ranking Country	Total External Debt	Debt to GNP	Short-term to Total Debt	Debt Service to Exports of Goods and Service
		(US $ mn.)	(ratios as per cent)		
1.	Brazil	193663	24	19	57
2.	Mexico	149690	38	19	32
3.	China	146697	17	21	9
4.	Korea	143373	33	38	9
5.	Indonesia	136174	65	26	30
6.	Russian Federation	125645	26	5	7
7.	Argentina	123221	39	15	59
8.	India	94404	25	5	20
9.	Thailand	93416	63	37	15
10.	Turkey	91205	47	25	18
11.	Malaysia	47228	51	32	8
12.	Philippines	45433	53	26	9
13.	Poland	39890	30	10	6
14.	Venezuela	35542	42	12	31
15.	Colombia	31777	35	18	27
	South Asia				
	Pakistan	29665	48	8	36
	Bangladesh	15125	35	1	11
	Sri Lanka	7638	51	6	6

Note: Serial number 1 to 15 is the rank of the country in terms of total indebtedness.

Source: Global Development Finance, 1999, Country Tables, The World Bank.

Figure : 1 Recovery from 1991 Crisis

Panel : A

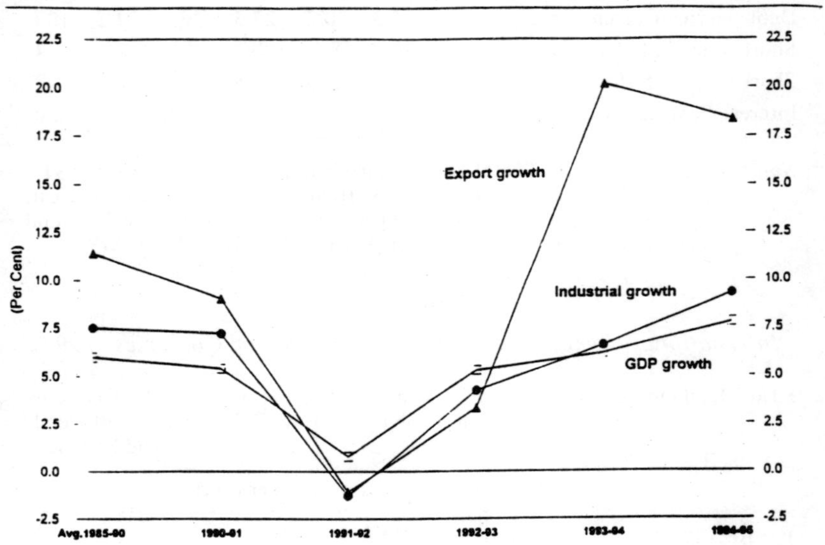

Panel : B

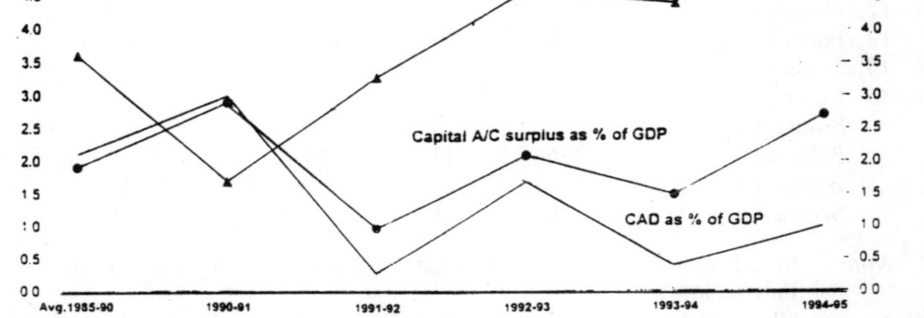

Figure: 2 Month-wise Trends in M3, WPI and FCAs

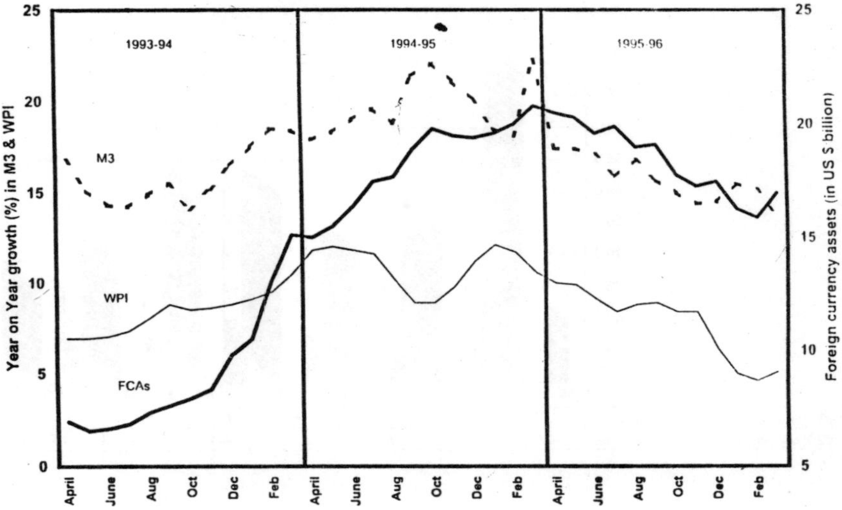

Figure : 3 Peak Customs Duty and Customs Duty collection Rates
1990-91 to 1999-2000

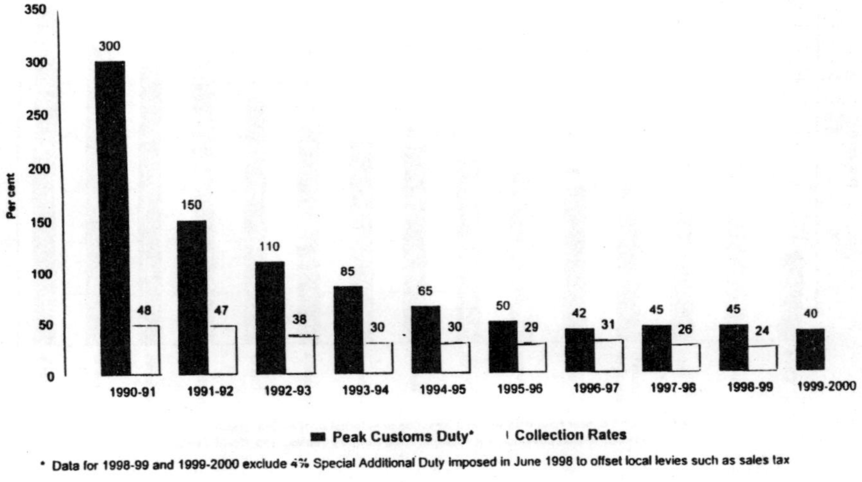

* Data for 1998-99 and 1999-2000 exclude 4% Special Additional Duty imposed in June 1998 to offset local levies such as sales tax

Figure : 4 Short-term Debt Ratios

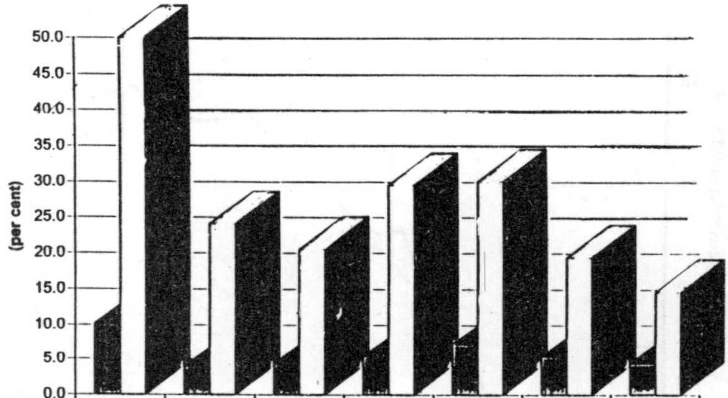

	Mar'1991	Mar'1994	Mar'1995	Mar'1996	Mar'1997	Mar'1998	Mar'1999
■ Short-Term to Total Debt Ratio	10.2	3.9	4.3	5.4	7.2	5.4	4.4
□ Short-Term Debt to Reserves Ratio	382.1	24.1	20.5	29.5	30.1	19.4	14.7

Figure : 5 International Comparison of Debt to GNP Ratio, 1997

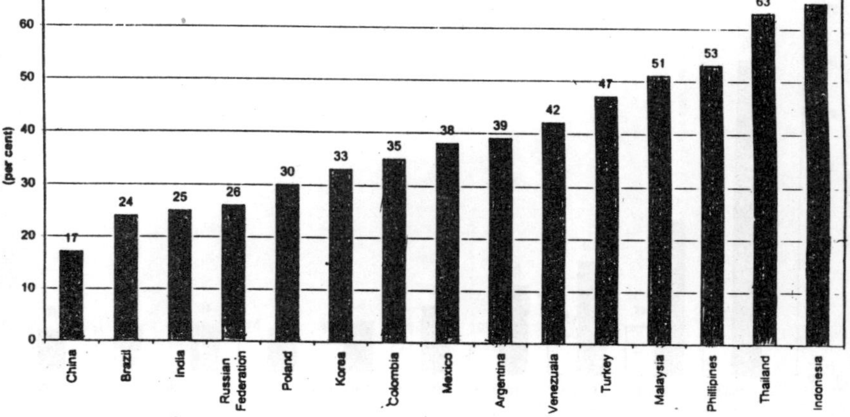

Note : Top 15 debtor countries ordered by ratios of external debt to GNP (ascending order).
Source : Global Development Finance, 1999, Country Tables, The World Bank.

Figure : 6 International Comparison of Debt Service to Exports of Goods and Services Ratio, 1997

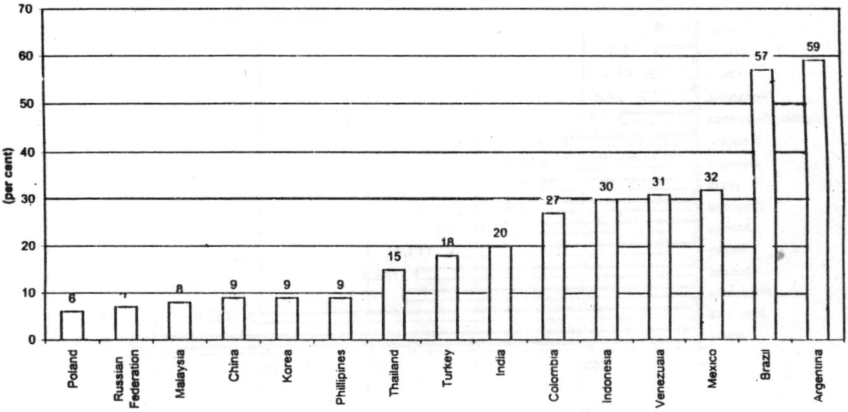

Note : Top 15 debtor countries ordered by ratios of debt service to exports of goods & services (ascending order).
Source : Global Development Finance, 1999, Country Tables, The World Bank.

Figure : 7 International Comparison - Proportion of Short-term to Total External Debt, 1997

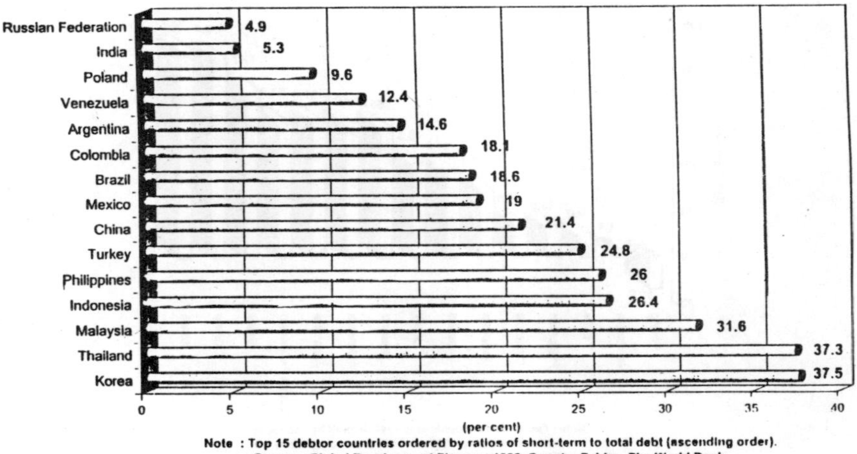

Note : Top 15 debtor countries ordered by ratios of short-term to total debt (ascending order).
Source : Global Development Finance, 1999, Country Tables, The World Bank.

Figure : 8 International Comparison - Proportion of Short-term Debt to Reserves, 1997

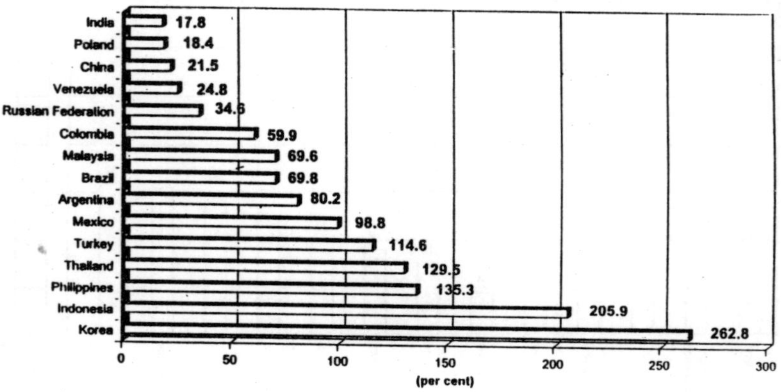

Note : Top 15 debtor countries ordered by ratios of short-term to reserves (ascending order).
Source : Global Development Finance, 1999, Country Tables, The World Bank.

Figure : 9 International Comparison of Change in External Debt Stock between 1991 and 1997

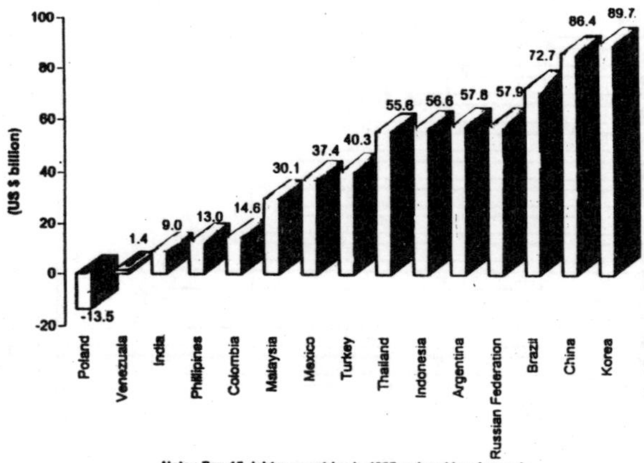

Note : Top 15 debtor countries in 1997 ordered by change in debt stock between 1991 and 1997 (ascending order).
Source : Global Dev. Finance, 1999, Country Tables, The World Bank.

Figure : 10 Indices of exchange rate of South East-Asian Currencies and Indian Rupee
against US $ (monthly average)- US $ per local currency

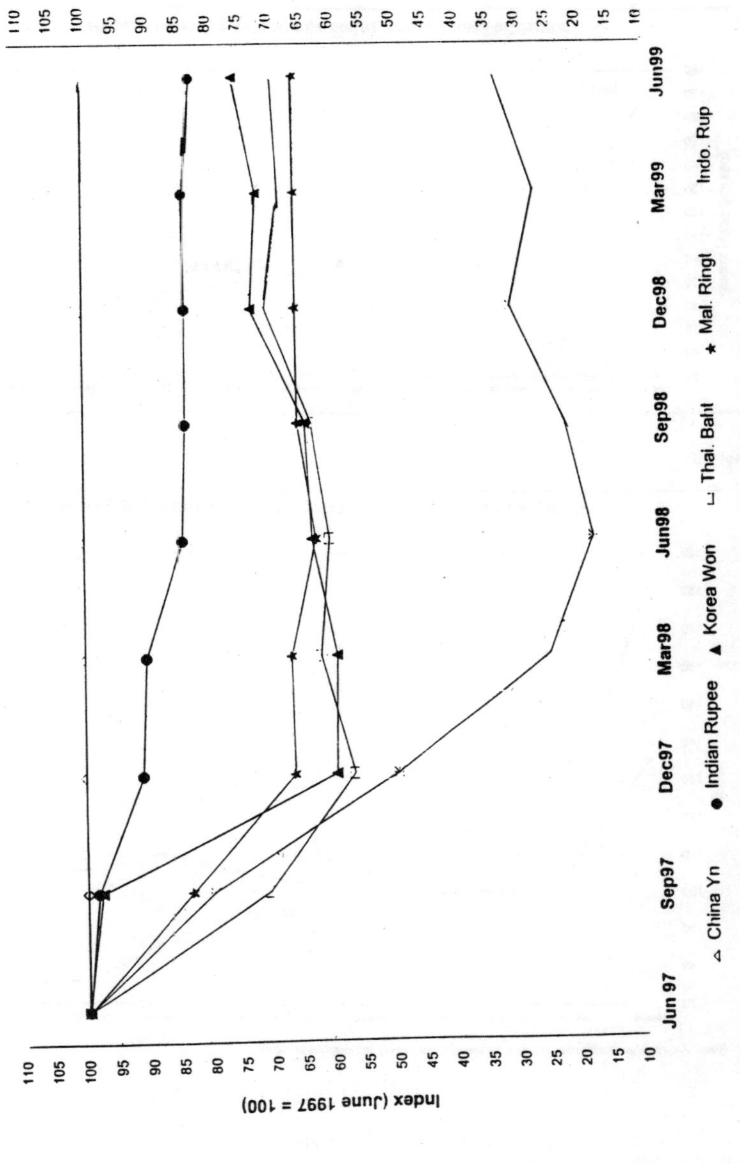

Note : An Increase (decerease) in index means appreciation (depreciation) of local currency against the US dollar.

Figure : 11 Exchange rate trends in the Nineties

Panel : A

Exchange rate of Indian rupee against US $ (period average)

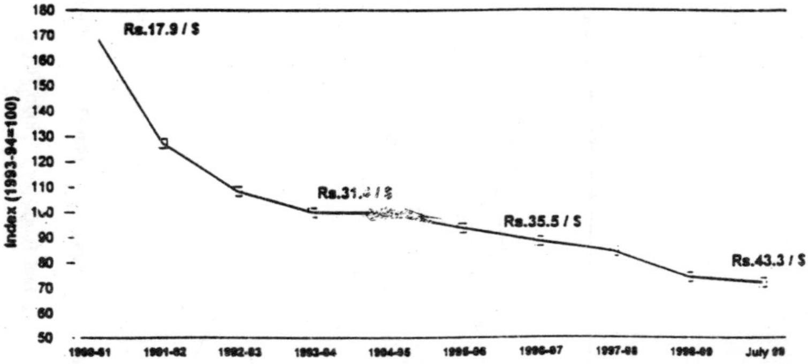

Panel : B

5-Country NEER and REER Index of Rupee with base 1993-94=100

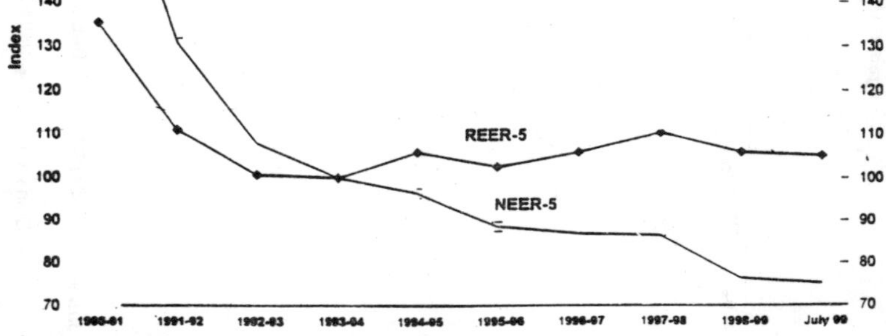

Note : An increase (decrease) in index means appreciation (depreciation) of rupee.

Anniversary Lecture delivered at the Centre for Banking Studies, Central Bank of Sri Lanka, Colombo, September 9, 1999.

19

Liberalisation and Changing Patterns of Foreign Direct Investment

NAGESH KUMAR

I

Introduction

India has sought to increase inflows of foreign direct investment (FDI) with a much liberal policy since 1991 after four decades of cautious, if not always restrictive, attitude to it. The timing of policy liberalisation by India has coincided with the dramatic upsurge in the global FDI outflows from US $ 50 billion a year in the mid-1980s to cross a peak of $ 350 in 1996. The 1990s have witnessed a sustained rise in annual inflows to India. They have grown from a rather small figure of US $ 200 million in 1991 to $ 3.2 billion in 1997 in actual terms. Although they would appear quite small relative to the kinds of magnitudes that some of India's counterparts in south-east or east Asia attract, the rise would appear to be impressive. In a recent analysis of changing patterns of global FDI inflows, Dunning (1998) has found the rate of growth of investment directed to India to be well above average although absolute magnitudes remained very small. It is not clear, however, whether this rise has been provoked by the policy liberalisation alone or has resulted from expansion of scale of global FDI activity. The inflows in the 1990s have also changed from the past patterns in terms of sources, sectoral composition, organisational form. This paper examines the emerging trends and patterns in FDI inflows to India in the recent period. A major objective is to evaluate the role that policy liberalisation has played in shaping these patterns. This is attempted with an analysis of changes in India's shares in FDI outflows from European and other triad sources of FDI as well as by analysing the changes in the shares of major source countries with policy liberalisation. It is concluded with a few remarks for policy.

The structure of the paper is as follows. Section II briefly traces the evolution of India's policy towards FDI to provide a background to trends in FDI inflows. Section III discusses the expansion of FDI inflows to India in the wake of recent liberalisation and emerging sectoral and organisational patterns. Section IV examines the trends in the relative importance of major conventional or triad source countries of FDI to India viz, the US, European countries and Japan, in the FDI stocks and approvals since 1980. Section V follows it up by examining the trends in India's share in FDI outflows from major triad sources over 1985 to 1995 to detect the impact of policy liberalisation in India. Finally, Section VI concludes the paper for some remarks on India's policy.

II

Evolution of Indian Government's Policy Towards FDI since Independence

This section we briefly review the evolution of India's policy towards FDI over the past five decades to provide a background to the subsequent analysis. Four distinct phases in the evolution of India's policy have been observed as follows [Kumar 1994, 1996, for a detailed analysis].

Early Post-Independence Period (1948-67) : Import Protection and Receptive Attitude to FDI

Soon after independence, India embarked on a strategy of import substituting industrialisation in the framework of development planning with a focus on development of local capability in heavy industries including the machinery manufacturing sector. The scope of import substitution extended literally to almost everything that could be manufactured in the country (see Bhagwati and Desai 1970, for more details). The domestic industry was accorded considerable protection in the form of high tariffs and quantitative restrictions on imports. In order to channel country's scarce investible resources (the savings rate was just over 10 per cent in 1950) according to Plan priorities, an industrial approval (licensing) system was put into place in the country that regulated all industrial investments beyond a certain minimum. A number of key industries were earmarked for further development in the public sector either in view of their strategic nature or anticipated lack of initiative in the private sector because of large capital requirements. As a part of the development plans large investments were made in human resources creating activities such as expansion of educational, especially the technical and engineering, facilities and creation of a scientific and technological infrastructure in the form of a network of national and regional laboratories in the country. The government also made investments in development of institutional infrastructure for industrial development such as term lending and capital markets development.

As the domestic base of 'created' assets, viz, technology, skills, entrepreneurship was quite limited, the attitude towards FDI was increasingly receptive. FDI was sought on mutually advantageous terms though the majority local ownership was preferred. Foreign investors were assured of no restrictions on the remittances of profits and dividends, fair compensation in the event of acquisition, and were promised a 'national treatment'. The foreign exchange crisis of 1957-58 led to further liberalisation in the government's attitude towards FDI. In a bid to attract foreign investment to finance foreign exchange component of projects, a host of incentives and concessions were extended. The protection accorded to local manufacture acted as an important locational advantage encouraging market seeking FDI. A large number of foreign enterprises serving Indian market through exports started establishing manufacturing affiliates in the country. This (viz, late 1950s and early 1960s) was the period when western multinational enterprises started showing real interest in India.

From 1968 to 1979: Restrictive Attitude to Protect the Domestic base of 'Created' Assets

Investments made in machinery fabrication facilities, manpower development, scientific and technological infrastructure made in the previous period had led to development of certain 'created' assets in the country. For instance, certain capabilities for process and product adaptations had been built up in the country. A number of local design engineering and project management consultants had accumulated considerable expertise while acting as subcontractors for western prime consultants. A considerable plant fabrication capability had been built up in the country by late 1960s. The share of imported machinery and equipment as a proportion of gross domestic capital formation had gone down from 69 per cent in 1950 to under 25 per cent by 1968-69. However, locally available skills and capabilities were needing some sort of infant industry protection as these were not able to stand competition from more established industrialised country sources. Constraints on local supply of capital and entrepreneurship had begun to ease somewhat. On the other hand outflow on account of remittances of dividends, profits, royalties, and technical fees, etc, abroad on account of servicing of FDI and technology imports from the earlier period had grown sharply and had become a significant proportion of the foreign exchange account of the country.

All these factors together prompted the government to streamline the procedures for foreign collaboration approvals and adopt a more restrictive attitude toward FDI. Restrictions were put on proposals of foreign direct investments unaccompanied by technology transfer and those seeking more than 40 per cent foreign ownership. The government listed industries in which FDI was not considered desirable in view of local capabilities. The permissible range of royalty payments and duration of technology transfer agreements with parent companies were also specified for different items. The guidelines evolved for foreign collaborations required exclusive use of Indian consultancy services wherever available. The renewals of foreign collaboration agreements were restricted. From 1973 onwards the further activities of foreign companies (along with those of local large industrial houses) were restricted to a select group of core or high priority industries. In the same year a new Foreign Exchange Regulation Act (FERA) came into force which required all foreign companies operating in India to register under Indian corporate legislation with up to 40 per cent foreign equity. Exceptions from the general limit of 40 per cent were made only for companies operating in high priority or high technology sectors, tea plantations, or those producing predominantly for exports.

The 1980s: Cautious Deregulation

Towards the end of the 1970s India's failure to significantly step up the volume and proportion of her manufactured exports in the background of the second oil price shock began to worry the policy-makers. It led to the realisation that international competitiveness of Indian goods had suffered from growing technological obsolescence and inferior product quality, limited range, and high cost which in turn were due to the highly protected local market. Another limiting factor for Indian manufactured exports lay in the fact that marketing channels in the industrialised countries were substantially dominated by MNEs. The government intended to deal with the situation by putting emphasis on the modernisation of industry with liberalised imports of capital goods and technology, exposing the Indian industry to foreign competition by gradually liberalising the trade regime, and assigning a greater role to MNEs in the promotion of manufactured exports. This strategy was reflected in the policy pronouncements that were made in the 1980s. These covered liberalisation of industrial licensing (approval) rules, a host of incentives, and exemption from foreign equity restrictions under FERA to 100 per cent export-oriented units. Four more export processing zones (EPZ) were set up in addition to the two existing ones, namely those at Kandla (set up in 1965) and at Santacruz (set up in 1972) to attract MNEs to set up export-oriented units. The trade policies gradually liberalised the imports of raw materials and capital goods by gradually expanding the list of items on the Open General Licence (OGL). Between 1984-85 alone, 150 items and 200 types of capital goods were added to OGL list. Tariffs on imports of capital goods were also slashed. Imports of designs and drawings and capital good were permitted under a liberalised Technical Development Fund Scheme.

The liberalisation of industrial and trade policies was accompanied by an increasingly receptive attitude towards FDIs and foreign licensing collaborations. Approval systems were streamlined. A degree of flexibility was introduced in the policy concerning foreign ownership, and exceptions from the general ceiling of 40 per cent on foreign equity were allowed on the merits of individual investment proposals. The rules and procedures concerning payments of royalties and lump sum technical fees were relaxed and withholding taxes were reduced. The approvals for opening liaison offices by foreign companies in India were liberalised. New procedures were introduced enabling direct application by a foreign investor even before choosing an Indian partner. A 'fast channel' was set up in 1988 for expediting clearances of FDI proposals from major investing countries, viz, Japan, Germany, the US and the UK.

1990s: Full-Scale Liberalisation and Integration with World Economy

In June 1991, the Indian government initiated a programme of macro-economic stabilisation and structural adjustment supported by the IMF and the World Bank. As a part of this programme a New Industrial Policy (NIP) was announced on July 24, 1991 in the parliament which has started the process of full scale liberalisation and intensified the process of integration of India with the global economy. The NIP and subsequent policy amendments have liberalised the industrial policy regime in the country, especially, as it applies to FDIs beyond recognition. The industrial approval system in all industries has been abolished except for 18 strategic or environmentally sensitive industries. In 34 high priority industries FDI up to 51 per cent is approved automatically if certain norms are satisfied. FDI proposals do not necessarily have to be accompanied by technology transfer agreements. Trading companies engaged primarily in export activities are also allowed up to 51 per cent foreign equity. To attract MNEs in the energy sector, 100 per cent foreign equity was permitted in power generation. International companies were allowed to explore non-associated natural gas and develop gasfields including laying down pipelines and setting up liquified petroleum gas projects. A new package for 100 per cent export-oriented projects and companies in export processing zones was announced. A Foreign Investment Promotion Board (FIPB) authorised to provide a single window clearance has been set up in the prime minister's office to invite and felicitate investments in India by international companies. The existing companies are also allowed to raise foreign equity levels to 51 per cent for proposed expansion in priority industries. The use of foreign brand names for goods manufactured by domestic industry which was restricted has also been liberalised. India became a signatory to the Convention of the Multilateral Investment Guarantee Agency (MIGA) for protection of foreign investments. The Foreign Exchange Regulation Act of 1973 has been amended and restrictions placed on foreign companies by the FERA have been lifted. Companies with more than 40 per cent of foreign equity are now treated on par with fully Indian owned companies. New sectors such as mining, banking, telecommunications, highways construction and management have been thrown open to private, including foreign owned, companies. These relaxations and reforms of policies have been accompanied by active courting of foreign investors at the highest level. The international trade policy regime has been considerably liberalised too with lower tariffs on most types of importables and sharp pruning of negative list for imports. The rupee was made convertible first on trade and finally on current account.

III

Liberalisation of Indian Policy Regime and FDI Inflows

The approvals of FDI inflows since the liberalisation of policy in 1991 reveal a dramatic jump as shown in Figure 1. In order to take out the possible effect of exchange rate movements, the US $ figures have been plotted in Figure 1a. Compared to approvals of FDI totalling $ 200 million in 1991, US $ 14.6 billion worth of FDI have been approved in 11 months of the year 1997. The approvals, however, have been slow in materialising into actual inflows and are still much lower than FDI inflows. Actual inflows in 1997 amounted to $ 3.2 billion.

FIGURE – 1

Foreign Direct Investments in India, 1991-97: Approvals and Actual

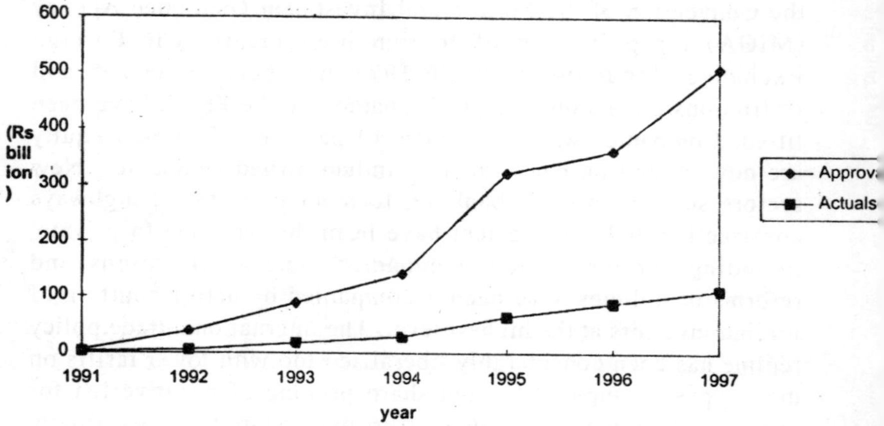

Source: Based on data from India, Ministry of Industry, *SIA Newsletter*, December 1997.

As observed earlier, the years when FDI inflows in India have expanded have also been those when global inflows of FDI have expanded, dramatically. Hence, it is difficult to say if all the increase in FDI inflows to India has been brought about by liberalisation of policy or it results from a global phenomenon. In order to find answers of this question, the emerging patterns of FDI inflows and approvals are analysed below.

FIGURE 1A

Foreign Direct Investments in India, 1991-97: Approvals and Actual

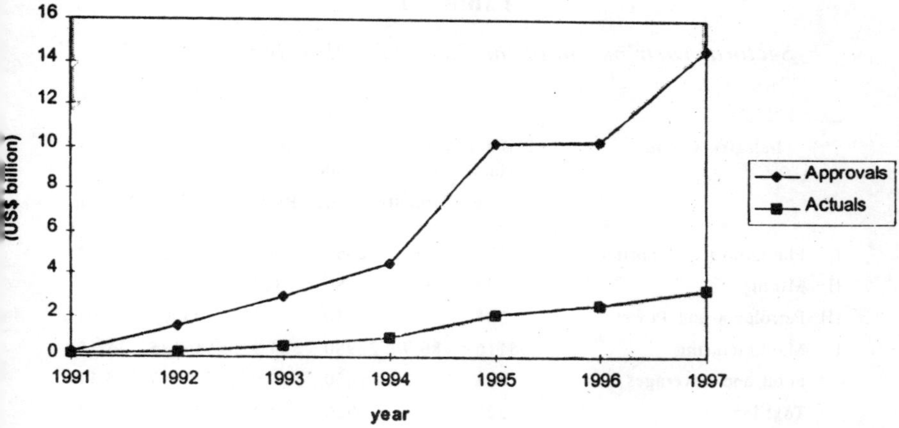

Source: Based on data from India, Ministry of Industry, *SIA Newsletter*, December 1997.

Sectoral Patterns of New Inflows

The government policy pursued until 1990 generally restricted FDI to technology-intensive branches of manufacturing industry. Hence, 85 per cent of FDI stock in 1990 was in manufacturing. Plantations and services accounted for 9.5 and 5 per cent share of FDI stock in 1990. However, the bulk of the inflows in the 1990s have been directed to non-manufacturing infrastructural sectors such as energy (29 per cent) and telecommunication services (20 per cent) as is clear from Table–1. The share of manufacturing has gone down to 37 per cent. Among the manufacturing subsectors, FDI approvals in 1990s are also more evenly distributed between food and beverages, transport equipment, metals and metal products, electricals and electronics, chemicals and allied products, and miscellaneous manufacturing unlike a very heavy concentration in relatively technology-intensive sectors, viz, machinery, chemicals, electricals, and transport equipment up to 1990. The infrastructural sectors which have commanded nearly half of total approved investments in the 1990s had not been open to FDI inflows before and hence, could be attributed to the policy liberalisation.

Table – 1

Sectoral Distribution of the Stock of FDI in India, 1980-97

(Million rupees)

	Industry Group	FDI Stock as in March 1980		FDI Stock as in March 1990		Approvals 1991-97	
		Value	Percent	Value	Percent	Value	Percent
I	Plantations and horticulture	385	4.1	2560	9.5	4901	0.33
II	Mining	78	0.8	80	0.3	15576	1.06
III	Petroleum and Power	368	3.9	30	0.1	423905	28.91
IV	Manufacturing	8116	86.9	22980	84.9	545135	37.18
	Food and beverages	391	4.2	1620	6.0	75748	5.17
	Textiles	320	3.4	920	3.4	23700	1.62
	Machinery and machine tools	710	7.6	3540	13.1	32830	2.24
	Transport equipment	515	5.5	2820	10.4	71082	4.84
	Metal and metal products	1187	12.7	1410	5.2	73225	6.00
	Electrical and electronics	975	10.4	2950	10.9	79702	5.44
	Chemicals and allied products	3018	32.3	7690	28.4	100759	6.88
	Miscellaneous manufacturing	1000	10.7	2030	7.5	88089	6.01
V	Services	385	4.1	1400	5.2	459086	31.31
	Telecommunications	0	0	0	0	296271	20.21
	Finance and Banking	na	na	na	na	63012	4.30
	Hotels and tourism	na	na	na	na	29720	2.03
	Air and sea transport	na	na	na	na	19954	1.36
	Consultancy	na	na	na	na	10068	0.69
	Other services	na	na	na	na	40061	2.73
	Total	**9332**	**100.0**	**27050**	**100.0**	**1466218**	**100.0**

Note : Percentages might not add up to hundred because of rounding off errors.

Sources : 1980 and 1990 figures compiled in Kumar, 1994, on the basis of data from RBI, 'India's International Investment Position', *Reserve Bank of India Bulletin*, April 1985; and RBI, 'India's Foreign Liabilities and Assets as on March 31, 1990', *Reserve Bank of India Bulletin*, August 1993, pp 1031-51; approvals for 1991-97 based on India, Ministry of Industry, *SIA Newsletter*, December 1997.

Liberalisation and Organisational Form of FDI Inflows

With the liberalisation, the policy barriers that were neutralising the internalisation advantages of foreign investors to the country have been removed. Hence, a greater proportion of transactions of Indian enterprises for technology acquisition takes place through internal or FDI mode. Table–2 shows that the proportion of foreign collaborations that are internalised through FDI in total approvals has gone up from just over 16 per cent in the 1970s to nearly 58 per cent during the 1990s. Therefore, liberalisation has shifted the balance between FDI and licensing in favour of FDI. Furthermore, majority foreign ownership, which was restricted to certain exceptional cases during 1970s and 1980s because of regulations, is becoming more popular again. Table–3 shows that majority of approvals over the 1990s have been in the 50-100 per cent foreign ownership range with a third of approvals accounted for by wholly foreign owned subsidiaries. A number of MNEs have taken advantage of new rules to increase their stake in their existing affiliates in the country. The importance of joint venture mode of operations has declined with the liberalisation.

Table – 2

Summary of Foreign Collaboration Approvals, 1948-97

Period	Average Number of Collaborations	Those with Foreign Equity: Average Number per Year Approved per Year	Those with Foreign Equity: Proportion in Total	Average Foreign Investment Involved per Year (Rs Million)
1959-66	297	108*	36.36	na
1967-79	242	39	16.11	53.62
1980-90	738	180	24.44	1165.16
1991-97#	1780	1026	57.64	209605

Note : * On the basis of 1961-66;
up to November 1997

Source : Updated from Kumar (1994), Table 1.4 with more recent data provided by India, Ministry of Industry, *SIA Newsletter*, December 1997.

Table – 3

FDI Approvals by Proportion of Foreign Equity Ownership

	1981-83			1991-97*		
Foreign Ownership (Per Cent)	No of Contracts (Rs. Million)	Investment Involved	Share in Total	No of Contracts (Rs. Million)	Investment Involved	Share in Total
25>	76	260.6	12.49	1077	49462	4.73
25 to 40	160	1683.1	80.65	689	105485	10.09
40 to 50	9	106.5	0.51	1746	305819	29.24
100< >50	27	115.8	5.55	1725	241692	23.11
100	2	13.5	0.65	800	343342	32.83

Note : * On the basis of approvals between August 1991 and May 1997.

Source : Based on foreign collaboration approvals data reported in *SIA Newsletter*, India, Ministry of Industry.

IV

Liberalisation and Changing Sources of FDI in India

European countries had been major sources of FDI inflows to India until 1990. However, their relative importance has steadily declined in the liberalisation period. Table–4 shows that major European source countries (which include the UK, Germany, France, Switzerland, Sweden, Italy and the Netherlands) accounted for 69 and 66 per cent of FDI stock in 1980 and 1990, respectively. However, they accounted for only 18 per cent share of FDI inflows approved between 1991-97. The US has emerged as the most important source of FDI over this period with a share of 27 per cent. The decline in the relative importance of European countries as sources of FDI to India has been made more prominent by diversification of sources of FDI by the country over the 1990s. The traditional sources of FDI in the triad countries, viz, Europe, US and Japan have contributed only 50 per cent of FDI inflows over the 1990s compared to 90 per cent in the earlier periods.

The stock data that has been used for 1980 and 1990 is not strictly comparable with the flow of approvals for the 1990s as the former is biased in favour of large sources in the past as it covers accumulated earnings that are reinvested. However, a similar trend of declining importance of European countries as sources of FDI is discernible from the data on FDI approvals on a comparable basis over the 1981-97 period. Figures–2 and 2a plot the magnitudes of approvals of FDI by major source countries over 1981-97 and for the sub-period 1981-91, respectively. It is clear that approvals of FDI originating in the European countries had been consistently higher than those of US FDI during the period from 1986-1990 (Figure–2a). However, US has established a clear lead over the European sources since 1991.

Table – 4

Relative Importance of Major Source Countries in Inward FDI in India, 1980-97

(In million rupees)

Country	FDI Stock 1980	Per Cent Share	FDI Stock 1990	Per Cent Share	Total Approvals 1991-97	Per Cent Share
UK	5033	54	13210	49	97329.6	7
Germany	650	7	2670	10	57324.5	4
Switzerland	547	6	860	3	20523.8	1
Netherlands			360	1	31650.4	2
Italy					23744.7	2
France					29009.9	2
Sweden	201	2	770	3	12261.3	1
Sub-total Europe (7)	6431	69	17870	66	271844.2	18
US	1964	21	5180	19	398990.3	27
Japan	43	0	1320	5	62733.3	4
Sub-total Triad	8438	90	24370	90	7335678	50
Others	894	10	2680	10	739215.7	50
Total	9332	100	27050	100	1472784	100

Source: Updated from Kumar (1994a), Table 1.5 with more recent data provided by India, Ministry of Industry, *SIA Newsletter*, December 1997.

Figure–3 plots the shares of major triad sources in the total FDI approvals for 1981-97 period on a comparable basis. The overtime trend in the share of European countries as a source of FDI is one of decline most consistently since 1990. Hence, policy reforms in India do not seem to have provoked a greater response of European companies in India. The importance of US has fluctuated wildly but on the whole it is rising especially since

FIGURE – 2

Foreign Direct Investments Approvals, 1981-97

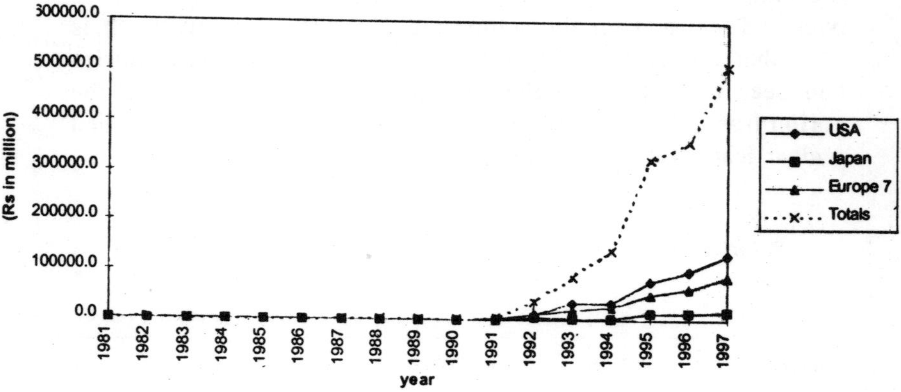

FIGURE 2A

Foreign Direct Investments Approvals for Sub-Period, 1981-91

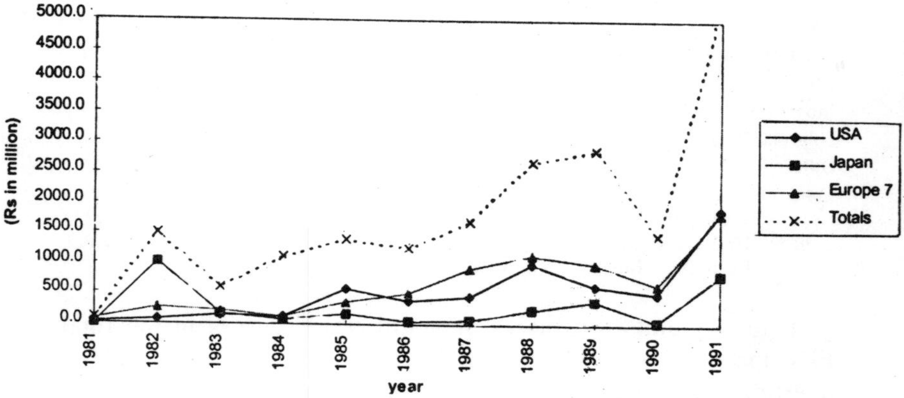

Source: FDI approvals data from India, Department of Scientific and Industrial Research, *A Compilation of Foreign Collaboration Approvals 1995*, New Delhi: 1996, and India, Ministry of Industry, *SIA Newsletter*, December 1997.

FIGURE – 3

Shares of Major Source Countries in FDI Approvals in India, 1981-97

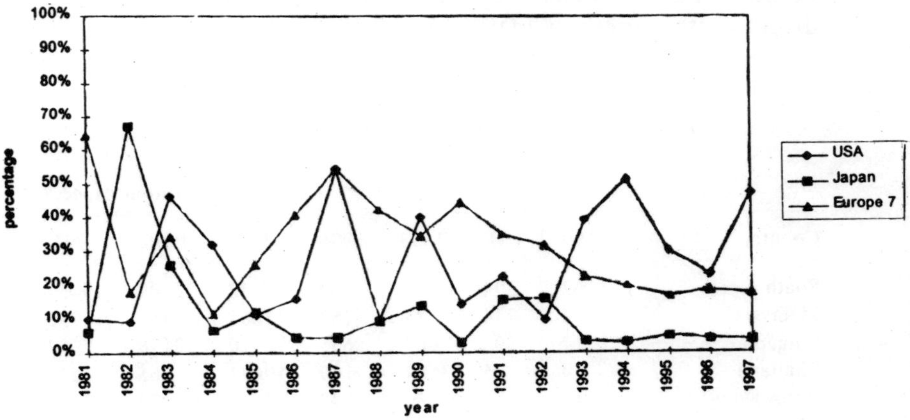

1992. Hence, liberalisation seems to have caught the eye of American enterprises. Japanese MNEs have also not shown any discernible trend in response to the liberalisation of India's FDI and trade regime.

The data arrayed above underscore an important trend of rising importance of non-conventional sources of FDI over the 1990s. A number of emerging sources of FDI such as South Korea, Singapore, Israel, Malaysia, Thailand, among others, have emerged as significant sources of FDI to India in the recent years. As shown in Table–5, these countries together contributed a peak of 18 per cent of all FDI approvals in 1995. In the approvals of 1997, their share was 10 per cent. FDI base of most of these countries other than Korea and Singapore, however, is rather small, as one-shot investments in telecommunications services or similar other projects account for the bulk of their approvals. The non-resident Indians have also contributed a significant, but varying, proportion of FDI approvals which peaked in 1993 with a 12 per cent share of approvals but falling afterwards to 2 per cent in 1997. A considerable proportion of FDI approvals has also been routed through tax haven countries such as Mauritius and Cayman Islands.

Therefore, opening new sectors to FDI as a part of liberalisation of trade and investment regime seems to have helped India to diversify its sources of FDI.

Table – 5

Emerging Sources of FDI in India from East and South-East Asia, 1991-97

(Million rupees)

Country	1991	1992	1993	1994	1995	1996	1997
South Korea	62	394	293	1069	3142	32209	19457
Malaysia	2	744	85	252	13861	423	19955
Singapore	14	602	667	2655	9910	3198	7994
Thailand	0	25	3684	100	19681	765	248
Hong Kong	212	571	880	1648	4072	5079	2572
China	8	0	617	273	5811	140	4
Philippines	0	50	132	41	730	2837	49
Sub-total	296	2386	6358	6037	57206	44651	50278
Total Approvals	5341	38875	88593	141872	320717	361468	510291
Share of Emerging Sources in All Countries (per cent)	6	6	7	4	18	12	10

Source: based on data provided by India, Ministry of Industry, *SIA Newsletter*, December 1997.

V

India's Relative Importance as a Host of FDI Outflows from Triad Source Countries

Because India also liberalised its policy regime during the period of dramatic expansion of global FDI outflows, it is unclear if the rise in absolute inflows to India from major source countries is in response to liberalisation alone. Alternatively, it is not clear if liberalisation has improved India's relative importance as a host for FDI flows originating in the major triad sources.

To find trends in the relative importance of India as a host of FDI, we compiled data on geographical distribution of FDI outflows from major OECD countries for the period 1985-95 reported in the OECD (1997). Among the European countries only the UK, Germany, and France reported detailed data for the entire period. Hence, Italy, Sweden, Switzerland, the Netherlands had to be dropped. This, however, is not a major limitation as the UK and Germany are the most important sources among European countries for India. The national currency-based figures were converted in US $ using exchange rates reported in OECD (1997). The US $ figures for the UK, Germany and France were added to obtain European total on a basis comparable to the US and Japan. The data were used to compute shares of India in outflows of the European countries, the US and Japan going to non-OECD countries. In addition, the share of India in flows directed to prominent Asian countries for which data had been reported separately. These shares have been ploted in Figure–4, 5 and 6, respectively, for European, US and Japanese outflows.

Figure–4 shows that India is a relatively important host for FDI originating in the European countries covered here within Asian region with a share fluctuating around 7 per cent. However, the trends over time in India's share in European FDI directed to developing countries or those going to Asian countries does not reveal an upward or a downward movement over the whole period of past 10 years. However, liberalisation may have helped India to recover her share from a declining trend set in late 1980s and continuing up to 1992.

India has been a marginal host for the US FDI outflows. However, in the second half of 1980s, India received a significant share (around 5 per cent) of US FDI directed to the Asian countries. India's share among the Asian countries in the US FDI tended to decline during 1987-1990. It has recovered since 1990 slightly. The liberalisation of policy in 1991 does not seem to have made a significant difference to India's share. But as with European countries, probably it helped avert a further decline in her share in the US outflows.

FIGURE – 4

*India as a Host of FDI Outflows from Major European Countries, 1985-95**

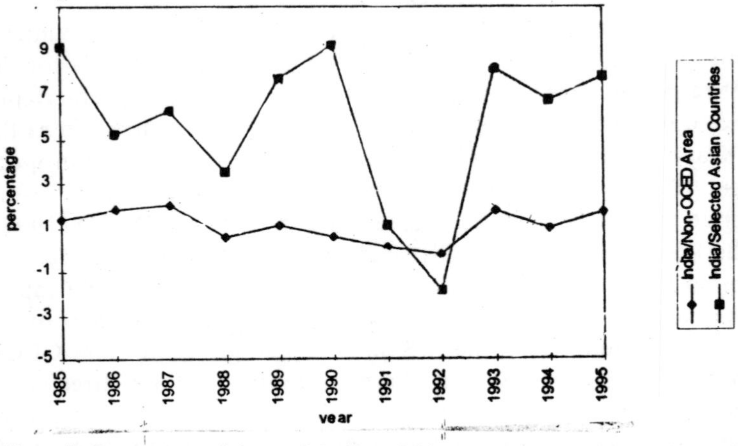

Note :* Represents shares of India within aggregated FDI outflows from UK, Germany and France in US $ going to non-OECD area and to non-OECD Asian countries, respectively.

Source : Based on data compiled from OECD, *International Direct Investment Yearbook 1997*, Paris: OECD..

FIGURE – 5

India as a Host of US FDI Outflows, 1985-95

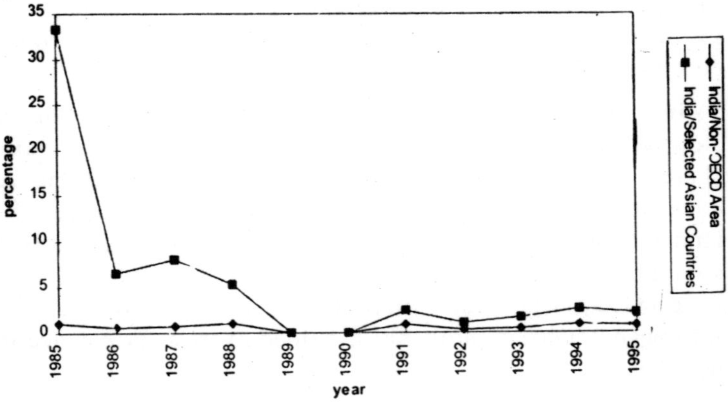

Source: Based on data compiled from OECD, *International Direct Investment Yearbook 1997*, Paris OECD.

Figure–6 shows that India has had an even more marginal share of Japanese FDI outflows until 1991. The liberalisation of trade and investment regime since 1991 appears to have helped India improve her share in Japanese FDI outflows. India's share still remains very small (around 1 per cent inflows to Asian developing countries) but has improved compared to what it was before the policy reform.

FIGURE – 6

India as a Host of Japanese FDI Outflows, 1985-95

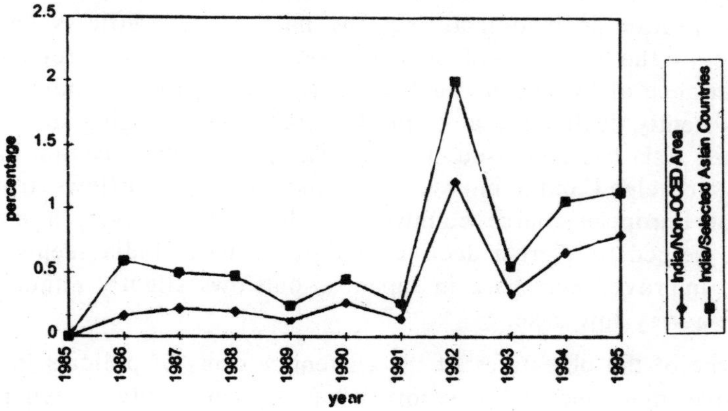

Source: Based on data compiled from OECD, *International Direct Investment Yearbook 1997*, Paris OECD.

Therefore, the liberalisation of policy regime by India since 1991 has not yet led to a significant improvement in India's relative attractiveness as a host of FDI amongst major western source countries. Liberalisation seems to have improved India's attractiveness for Japanese corporations although from a very low base. Liberalisation has also helped India diversify her sources of FDI especially the newly industrialising Asian countries have recently emerged as important sources of FDI for the developing countries [see Kumar et al 1998: chapter 2, for a detailed analysis]. The Asian newly industrialising countries have, however, been affected by the 1997 currency crisis which may affect their ability to sustain outward investments in the coming few years.

VI

Concluding Remarks

In the foregoing, we have summarised the emerging patterns and trends in inflows of FDI in India in the wake of policy reforms initiated since 1991. While the magnitudes of inflows have recorded impressive growth, they are still at a small level compared to the country's potential. The policy reforms have enabled the country to widen the sectoral as well as the source country composition of FDI inflows. Compared to a near total concentration in manufacturing, the bulk of new inflows have come in the energy and services sectors. While the relative importance of European countries as sources of FDI in India has consistently declined, that of the US and some emerging sources in east Asia has increased steadily. The policy liberalisation has not yet helped India improve her share in FDI outflows from major European source countries or the US. However, it may have helped to avert a decline in India's share. India seems to have improved her share in Japanese outflows slightly although from a very low base.

One of the objectives of the current reforms of policies is to remove impediments for export-oriented manufacture in general and to attract MNEs to locate efficiency-seeking FDI in the country. These investments could help India in expanding manufactured exports by using her as an export platform. The majority of the recent approvals of FDI, however, aims to explore India's sizeable and expanding domestic market. The efficiency-seeking FDI have yet to start flowing to the country in a considerable manner. In an era of stiff competition among developing countries to attract export-oriented FDIs, liberalisation of policies alone may not be enough to win the race. More active negotiations and bargaining with MNEs may often be required. As we argued elsewhere at a greater length [Kumar 1994, Postscript], India should use her bargaining advantages such as large domestic markets, abundant supply of trained and low wage labour, vast pool of technical professionals, well developed capital markets, etc, more effectively to attract a greater proportion of efficiency-seeking FDI.

[The initial version of this paper was prepared while the author served on the faculty of the United Nations University Institute for New Technologies (UNU/INTECH), Maastricht, the Netherlands for presentation at a Conference on 'Major Challenges for European Corporations in Asian Globalising Economy', held in Macau, April 3-4, 1998. Leann Chervenic-Poeth of UNU/INTECH provided valuable research assistance in preparation of this paper. Views expressed and any errors should be attributed to me and not to UNU/INTECH or to Research and Information System for Developing Countries, New Delhi, with which I am now affiliated.]

References

Dunning, John H (1998): 'The Changing Geography of Foreign Direct Investment: Explanations and Implications' in Nagesh Kumar et al (eds), *Globalisation, Foreign Direct Investment and Technology Transfers: Impacts on and Prospects for Developing Countries*, Routledge, London and New York, 43-89.

India, Department of Scientific and Industrial Research (1996): *A Compilation of Foreign Collaboration Approvals 1995*, Ministry of Science and Technology, New Delhi.

India, Ministry of Industry, *SIA Newsletter*, December 1997.

OECD (1997): *International Direct Investment Yearbook 1997*, OECD, Paris.

Kumar, Nagesh (1994): *Multinational Enterprises and Industrial Organisation: The Case of India*, Sage, New Delhi (a revised and updated edition of *Multinational Enterprises in India*, Routledge, London and New York, 1990).

—— (1996): 'India: Industrialisation, Liberalisation and Inward and Outward Foreign Direct Investment' in John H Dunning and R Narula (eds), *Foreign Direct Investment and Governments*, Routledge, London, 348-79.

Kumar, Nagesh in collaboration with John Dunning, Robert Lipsey, Jamuna Agarwal and Shujiro Urata (1998): *Globalisation, Foreign Direct Investment and Technology Transfers: Impacts on and Prospects for Developing Countries*, Routledge, London and New York.

Reserve Bank of India (1985): 'India's International Investment Position', *Reserve Bank of India Bulletin,* April.

—— (1993): 'India's Foreign Liabilities and Assets as on March 31, 1990', *Reserve Bank of India Bulletin*, August, 1031-51.

Reprinted with permission from the author; Economic & Political Weekly Vol. 33, No. 22, May 30-June 5, 1998.

20

Capital Account Convertibility Revisited

S. S. TARAPORE

We in India have, over the past four years, gone through an extensive debate on managing the capital account. While initially the authorities were sympathetic to a gradual opening up of the capital account, the East Asian currency crisis of the second half of 1997 resulted in a change in the public posture of the Indian authorities from a commitment to gradually opening up to one of extreme caution. The public posture apart one finds that the gradual opening up of the capital account has continued in India though the authorities are in no way committed to any particular road map or timing.

Influential policy makers in India keep saying that capital account convertibility is a low down priority in the Indian context. Nevertheless, the authorities do have to deal with the central issue of evolving a viable exchange rate policy in the context of a gradual opening up of the capital account. There is an erroneous belief that India avoided the East Asian currency contagion as its capital account was closed. The reason for India not facing turbulence at that time was that it followed a sensible exchange rate policy and that its key external parameters were sound with significant reductions, as compared with the position at the time of the crisis of 1990-91, in the current account deficit, the external debt service ratio and the proportion of short-term debt to total external debt. Furthermore, in the capital flows there was a shift from exclusive debt financing to a blend of debt-equity financing with a significant liberalisation of foreign direct investment and portfolio flows. More importantly, India has had a relatively low medium-term inflation rate.

Now what sort of exchange rate policy did India follow and indeed what kind of policy does it follow at the present time? The avowed policy of the Indian authorities in the mid-1990s was that it had moved to a market determined exchange rate and that it would try to stabilise the real effective exchange rate, using as a reference the base of March 1993, which was the point of unification of the exchange rate (the RBI uses a 5 country model for which information is available contemporaneously and a more elaborate 36 country model for which data is available with a lag). The Committee on Capital Account Convertibility (May 1997) in its report recommended that the authorities should follow an exchange rate policy, intended to stabilise the real effective exchange rate, with an announced base and with a band of ± 5 per cent. Furthermore, there should be clearly set out guidelines as to when the RBI would ordinarily intervene and when it would ordinarily not intervene in the forex market. The recommendation of the Committee was in no way novel and all that it attempted to do was to formalise the *de facto* policy. It is not as if the exchange rate can be based on an REER with a permanent base. Given changes in economic fundamentals it would be desirable to periodically alter the base as also the weights in the basket. In the latter part of 1997 there was considerable hype in the media that the authorities were about to formalise the exchange rate band and as there was considerable turbulence in the exchange market the authorities distanced themselves from the idea of a band. In the middle of 1998 the authorities also distanced themselves from the concept of a REER by releasing elaborate calculations that different base dates could give different results. More recently, the authorities have stressed that the REER has meaning only in the medium-term and that it is not desirable to strictly follow a REER for short-term policy responses and that in the short-run it is necessary to focus policy attention on the nominal exchange rate. Thus, the RBI was freed from any commitment on the exchange rate. It is, however, clear to market participants that the RBI closely monitors the REER with 1993-94 as the base and that large deviations do trigger policy responses. In a lighter vein the RBI's exchange rate policy is rather like a Galileo after the recantation-sound and correct but belief is whispered rather than proclaimed from the roof tops !

Exchange rate Pundits often talk of the two-corner approach i.e. that countries have an option of either a free float or a peg (akin to a currency board) and that intermediate regimes are not viable. By that count the Indian exchange rate policy should be deemed to be unviable but it is acknowledged the world over that India has managed its exchange rate policy in an exemplary manner. In this context we in India should be warned by the recent release of a discussion paper jointly authored by the French and Japanese Finance Ministries entitled *Exchange Rate Regimes for Emerging Market Economies*. The paper argues that a managed or pegged exchange rate – in which the currency moves within a band centred on a basket of currencies – could prove the best method of stabilising volatile exchange rates across Asia. Anglo-Saxon thinking has predictably been against intermediate regimes and felt that the only viable options are a hard exchange rate regime, such as a currency board, or a free float. It is gratifying that the Managing Director of the IMF Horst Kohler recently hinted at a less doctrinaire approach in that no single exchange rate regime is appropriate for all Members in all circumstances, though he rightly warns against the perils of pegs (or bands) which were not backed by unwavering macro economic policies. While recognising the move by major industrial countries to floating exchange rate regimes Horst Kohler stresses that these countries should not practice *benign neglect* and he sees merit in selective and well co-ordinated intervention. The purpose of this somewhat long discussion of the exchange rate issue is to assure Dr. Yoshitomi and Dr. Shirai that their views on exchange rate policy would find great empathy in India.

The question of forex intervention has been debated at great length and while some countries have recognised the need for intervention there are others who see intervention as dangerous. In forex markets which are not fully developed intervention becomes necessary. There is, however, a need to ensure certain safeguards. Thus, intervention should be essentially oriented towards altering *inter-temporal* perceptions and these could take the following forms: (i) sell spot-buy forward, (ii) buy spot, (iii) buy spot-sell forward, (iv) outright forward purchases and (v) forward-to-forward purchases and sales. The authorities should, however, abjure from spot sales or outright forward sales other than for very specific and limited purposes if the authorities are convinced that the movements in the market are out of sync with fundamentals and that it is necessary to squelch speculative forces. But to ensure success of the intervention there should be swingeing increases in interest rates, albeit for short periods. If these measures do not yield the desired results it must be recognised that there is a fundamental disequilibrium and the authorities should let the exchange rate depreciate. In all probability this is what the RBI does but for reasons of not revealing its strategy it does not formally state that this is precisely the stance of the RBI's policy on intervention. Another aspect of forex intervention is that over a period of time the intervention should yield a profit to the central bank. On these considerations the RBI's exchange rate policy could be deemed to be successful. The depreciation of the rupee against the US dollar of a little over 5 per cent per annum, between the end of 1996 and the end of 2000, can be considered as a good performance given the strength of the US dollar and the inflation rate of differentials.

It is recognised that in the context of a gradual opening up of the capital account it is no longer possible to consider the issue of adequacy of reserves only in terms of an import cover. The Indian authorities, for instance, do appear to take note of the fact that as compared with the position upto 1993, volatile flows such as non-resident repatriable deposits, net portfolio flows and the requirements of debt servicing for say a 12 month period would be over US $ 45 billion and in this context the foreign exchange reserves of $ 40 billion do not appear excessive. At the same time it bears stressing that the ratio of reserves to these liabilities for India compares very favourably with other countries. The *Guidotti rule* recommends that reserves should be adequate to cover one year's imports and capital flow requirements. On the Guidotti rule India would probably need somewhat more reserves. This approach to adequacy of reserves is one of abundant caution and it is not as if all non-resident deposits and portfolio investors would exit simultaneously and that there would be a total cessation of capital inflows.

Another way of assessing adequacy of reserves is to track the net-foreign exchange assets-currency ratio (NFA-C ratio). The RBI does not give any credence to this ratio which is somewhat unfortunate. Any sensible portfolio investor would derive comfort from the present NFA-C ratio of 87 per cent. It is not advocated that India should follow a mechanistic currency board system. Nevertheless if the reserves are sizeable in relation to the currency with the public there is a great degree of comfort to the authorities as well as foreign investors. A fall in the foreign exchange reserves *per se* would result in a fall in currency but if the authorities expand currency the NFA-C ratio would start falling and a sharply falling NFA-C ratio would give foreign investors an early warning signal. If for instance, the authorities were to allow the ratio to fall below 40 per cent, which as a rule of thumb, is a *Plimsoll Line* it would only be prudent for foreign investors to exit. Now let me stress that far from allowing a sharp fall in the ratio the net impact of the policy has been that this ratio has been rising quite steadily over the past several years which is indicative of sound macro economic management. The RBI would do well to formally integrate this ratio into its monitoring system.

It is clear that there should be a proper sequencing of capital account liberalisation and that there must be a strong commitment to maintain macro economic stability and strengthen the domestic financial sector. These thoughts pervade the Indian report on capital account convertibility. To facilitate discussions at this Seminar I thought it would be useful to give a brief background to certain unique aspects of the present status of capital account liberalisation in India. Unlike many countries which attempt to control capital inflows the Indian situation is just the opposite. While countries like Chile maintain unremunerated reserves on foreign inflows we in India have the peculiar situation of having abolished reserve requirements on non-resident deposits while there are punitive reserve requirements on domestic deposits. The Indian stance does make sense when there is a pressure on outflows but prescribing no reserve requirements when the foreign exchange reserves position is very comfortable is clearly not viable. At the present time there is a strong case for a gradual increase in the cash reserve requirement on non-resident deposits.

The FDI, FII regulatory framework in India is very liberal both for foreign inflows and outflows. The authorities have also undertaken bold measures to liberalise the policy on gold which is a hybrid between a commodity and a capital asset and this is crucial to the liberalisation of the capital account. Nonetheless, capital outflows by residents are still strictly controlled. In the recent period Indian industry has been provided significantly greater flexibility to invest abroad and some relaxations have been also provided to Indian mutual funds. The controls on banking capital flows are still stringent and the system could benefit from a gradual opening up. The fears of market integration – money, securities and forex – appear to hold up this reform but such integration is inevitable notwithstanding the wedge we endeavor to draw between markets. When an attempt is made to draw a wedge between markets all that happens is that the markets move off-shore. As a basic principle all participants in the spot forex market should have access to the forward market. It needs to be recognised that widening and deepening of the forward market contributes to stability of the overall exchange market.

Under the extant Indian controls there is a total ban on capital outflows by individual residents which is unreasonable, harsh and unsustainable as large seepages can take place through the extremely liberal facilities for individuals in terms of current account outflows. Permission for overseas investments by individuals is being contemplated for certain specific categories of professionals, foreign currency earners, stock options, etc. Such piece-meal liberalisation increases rather than decreases the work load on the Exchange Control. It would be far better to allow capital outflows for all individuals and prescribe modest but reasonable annual ceilings. It would be useful if our speakers could throw light on how the issue of consistency in current and capital accounts is handled for resident individuals in other countries.

There is considerable discussion of exchange rate stability, monetary policy independence and capital account convertibility and this is labelled as the *holy* or *unholy* trinity depending on one's predilection. The issue of reconciling these policies is by no means easy but if sound policies are followed it should be possible to attain a satisfactory resolution of the trinity. If a country uses the inflation rate as a nominal domestic anchor, depending on the inflation rate differentials *vis-a-vis* other major countries, the movements in the exchange rate should be acceptable. Now, if a country then subjects itself to the rigours of capital account convertibility it would make secure its basic policy objectives as with a liberalised capital account regime corrective measures would need to be taken expeditiously. Thus, the question whether it is appropriate for a country to move to capital account convertibility is, in a sense, not the issue. Rather, the question which a country has to ask itself is whether it chooses to have a higher or lower inflation rate relative to major industrial countries. Once this policy choice is made the exchange rate and capital flows will fall into place. A country cannot afford to blame capital account convertibility for the ailments of its economy. It is admittedly true that sometimes capital flows may go against the grain of fundamentals and generate unwarranted instability in the exchange rate. In such a situation forex intervention of the type discussed earlier would be quite apposite.

A final thought I would like to leave with participants is whether there is a real choice for countries between capital account convertibility and capital controls. In an increasingly integrated world, and with current account convertibility, the only choice appears to be between an orderly sequenced capital account liberalisation and a disorderly liberalisation imposed by the international economy. The benefits of a well prepared and gradual integration into the global financial system outweighs the risks; this does not mean that a country should plunge into rapid capital liberalisation without proper preparation to attain the preconditions of fiscal reforms, inflation control and strengthening of the domestic financial system. There is no substitute for sound macro economic policies and it is not as if we can follow imprudent policies and protect ourselves with capital controls.

Inaugural address at the Asian Development Bank Institute and Export-Import Bank of India, February 2, 2001, Mumbai.

21

Globalisation and the Indian Economy

UMA KAPILA

What does Globalisation Mean ?

We are living in the age of technology when distances of time and space have shrunk and the vast big world of ours has become one global village. Globalisation is a process which draws countries out of their insulation and makes them join the rest of the world in its march towards a new world order.

Technological revolution in transport and communication has brought about an enormous reduction in the time needed, as also the costs involved, in covering geographical distances.

When we see this movement of things and people, we realise that we have entered a new phase in development where countries are getting intimately inter-linked and inter-related with each other.

Globalization involves the increasing interaction of national economic systems — more integrated financial markets, economies and trade, higher factor mobility, and spectacular change in information technology leading to the spread of knowledge throughout the world.

Globalisation has witnessed a phenomenal expansion in international trade flows. World exports have increased from US$ 61 billion in 1950 to US$ 315 billion in 1970 and US$ 3447 billion in 1990. Interestingly, growth in world trade is significantly higher than growth in world output. The share of world exports in world GDP rose from about 6 per cent in 1950 to 16 per cent in 1992. International investment flows expanded at an equally amazing scale. Direct financial investment in the world economy increased from US$ 68 billion in 1960 to US$ 1948 billion in 1992. These figures are indeed staggering. Advances in IT technology, capital movements and geographical extension of banking business have become the new engines of global integration.

Globalization: Opportunities and Challenges

Globalization and liberalization bring a variety of changes, presenting opportunities as well as risks both in economies and financial systems throughout the world. One fact is quite clear: the undeniable benefits of globalization are only available to the countries that best manage their economies.

(1) *One obvious benefit of globalization is that active international capital flows* improve the efficiency of the allocation of world financial resources. As the world market economy has become more globalized, we have witnessed rapid growth in *world trade*, leading to a higher standard of living during the 1980s and 1990s. In plain language, competition, productivity gains, lower trade barriers and lower cost of external financing on a worldwide basis are the key factors that have led to growth in world trade and rising standards of living.

(2) *Globalization has also increased and enhanced competition* worldwide. There are several factors behind this consequence.

(a) Firstly, the integration of world markets and rapid technological change led to efficiency gains and growth, driven by the lower transaction and information costs. These in turn increased competition through lower costs and higher market efficiency, higher productivity, lower barriers to entry, and new investment opportunities. Geographic distance is no longer a factor that limits the provision of goods and services.

Hence, *competition both in the industrialized and developing countries has reached almost the same level.* At this point, it is worth noting that many developing countries, particularly emerging market economies, have actively participated in the world trade and global economy over the last two decades. The presence of emerging market countries, particularly the Asian economies, is growing, and their share in world trade has increased significantly.

Therefore, we can say that the higher the level of international competition, the higher the economic growth, the higher the income level, the higher the quality of products and thus the higher the living standards the globalization process would bring.

Risks Arising from Globalization

It is a well-known fact that the process of globalization does not evolve equally worldwide. Some countries obtain great benefit from the process, mainly driven by their rapid integration into the global economy relative to other countries. In other words, the integrated global economy does not guarantee that the benefits of globalization are shared by all countries involved in the process.

More importantly, opportunities provided by the globalization process are not always beneficial, as shown by the recent crises. Hence, the process of globalization always carries social, economic, financial, cultural and even political risks in addition to the risk of contagion.

There are several reasons for this situation. Some of them are beyond the control of the countries involved such as external shocks and other unexpected changes in external environment. Indeed, most of these reasons are due to:

- weak macroeconomic and financial policies;
- inconsistencies in domestic policies;
- increased vulnerability of national economies to external shocks;
- higher international capital mobility (i.e., higher sensitivity of international capital flows among economies);
- higher volatility of exchange rates due to integrated financial markets, which hits real sectors of economies.

As countries' economies become more vulnerable to external changes, they are exposed to shocks and crises with severe consequences both in financial and real sectors, as well as facing heavy social costs.

It is also true that the benefits of globalisation have not been evenly shared between all countries. Inequalities and asymmetries are evident. Some have benefitted more from it, some less and some have remained on the margin. But to think that this unevenness in distribution of the benefits is the return of the old colonial order would be to misread, misunderstand and misconceive this new phenomenon of human history. Globalisation is no longer being driven by a desire to conquer territorial empires. It is science and technology which is generating a new force and speed to the natural urge of human beings to catch up with those ahead of them and conquer new frontiers. We are witnessing a new kind of degree of convergence.

As Abid Hussain remarks[1], "Acceptance of globalisation does not mean that we should passively succumb to any mechanisms, pressures and manoeuvrings engineered by trans-national corporations, international banks or financial intermediaries which may disintegrate the domestic economy. Inequalities, asymmetries and exploitations and other reasons of undesirable practices, associated with globalisation, have to be monitored and managed through persistent political efforts as a nation state cannot lower its guard on sensitive issues. Fair working of multilateral framework, effectively influenced by the nation state, could prevent the harm which the negative side-effects of globalisation could bring about."

Developed countries have, by and large, gained from globalisation, since they already had a head start and so were better prepared to handle the new situation and opportunities, arising out of technological innovations. They have used the fullest advantage of the technologies of communication and transport. The relatively large gains the developed countries have made with the ushering in of globalisation have made developing countries suspect the very opportunities of globalisation to be harmful to their interests. But since borders can no longer be closed, so flows cannot be stopped and ideas cannot be prevented from motivating people in the different parts of the world. We do not

---

1. Abid Hussain, Globalisation of Indian Economy in Economic Developments in India, Vol.10 (Academic Foundation, 1998).

have the option of getting back fearing the bugbear of globalisation. We have to get ready to compete, and make and share gains with others.

Globalisation and Indian Economy

The Fears: It is not that India cannot compete with outsiders or that the foreigners will easily overcome us in an open competition. Those who believe in such a defeatist proposition do not perhaps know the real strength of India. India has talent, assets and the power of its genius to compete with the best in the world. Indians are as good as, if not better than, anybody else in the world.

Perhaps, the origin of our lack of confidence lies in the long conditioning of our minds by the Licence-Control Raj which had kept us away from free market conditions and made our industries work in an over-protected environment. In fact, if we look at the performance of some of our business houses with such exceptional entrepreneurial abilities, we will be convinced that we can compete effectively. Even our labour has done well. Japanese, Taiwanese and others who win labour contracts in West Asia sub-contract their jobs to Indian labour. Not because our labour is cheap but because they are found to be more productive and reliable. Similarly, in the area of new technologies like software, whether it is in America or in Japan or anywhere else, the search is always for Indian expertise to be engaged and success in such a sophisticated area of technology is a clear commentary on our capacities. The view that Indians cannot compete is misconceived.

Indian manufacturing talent has never been under question but Indian products have been found to be defective and not of world quality. This has again been due to the closed Government policies which did not let Indian entrepreneurs have access to the most modern equipment, technologies and investment choices. There is enough evidence that when the Government policies changed in favour of greater free market conditions, Indian manufacturing did come into its own and our products proved equally competitive. The trouble lay in the economic regime rather than in Indian entrepreneurship. Competition is indeed the crux of globalisation. Benefits of globalisation go to those who succeed in competition.

Opposition to globalisation and to certain aspects of its development is not confined to the developing countries alone. There are lobbies in the developed countries as well which are equally hostile to it on grounds that trade with poor countries impoverishes labour by taking away jobs and investments from their countries. This, however, remains unsubstantiated. If labour has lost jobs in America, it has not been due to global trade with developing countries but because it did not acquire the new skills required by industry to achieve a productive edge over others. It is not trade but a paradigm shift in manufacturing to modern information-based technical methods, i.e., replacing unskilled labour by computers that need skilled rather than unskilled labour. It is technological change and not global trade that has hurt labour in the developed countries.

Controversies relating to child labour and environmental standards, raised by the developed countries to prevent the smooth working of globalisation, need to be opposed.

The problems of labour should not be allowed to be mixed up with the problems of trade and should, in all fairness, be looked into by ILO. Similarly, the question of environment deserves deeper study. If pollution is there in India, its source lies in poverty. And unless the matters are set right at the source, the problem will remain. Any refusal to understand the circumstances of poverty in developing countries is betrayal of logic. The point in favour of globalisation is that it would, in fairness, be able to take the economies up rather than damage them.

Was the East Asian Crisis due to Globalisation?

The financial crisis of South-East Asia is also being categorised as one of the crises attributable to globalisation. It is being treated as proof of the fact that the cause of the present misery is globalisation and that it has played havoc with the economies rather than helping them. As Abid Hussain has rightly stated, this accusation is too simplistic. The validity of the facile linkage between the breakdown of South-East Asian economies and globalisation cannot be established. In fact, it was mainly due to factors of globalisation which encouraged flows of technology, investment and opening up of South-East Asian markets that no other group of countries have gained so much in such a short span of time as the South-East Asian countries. Facts and figures are there that speak out as to how the South-East Asian countries have gained from globalisation. Can one deny the fact that the high rates of growth reached by the Republic of Korea and other tiger economies were mainly due to globalisation? Can one deny the fact that the trade balances went up in their favour mainly due to free access provided to their products in American markets? Can it be doubted by anyone that most of the technological improvements which have marked the development of their economies were due mainly to the flows of technology from America, Japan and Germany which could not have been possible but for the forces of globalisation? To say that the present flight of capital was due to international trade would be a false conclusion drawn from the crisis. The South-East Asian crisis has not been due to their close integration with the world economy but because of the distortions in competitive markets creating crony capitalism leading to corruption and inefficiencies in resource allocation, which impeded economic efficiency and competition and reduced the productivity of investment. The crisis manifested itself in the form of overinvestment in unproductive ventures, misdirection of foreign capital inflows, and some other severe problems resulting from relying too heavily on hot money.

With economies booming in these countries, large amounts of foreign capital started pouring in. The money flowed in because the lenders knew that their profits would be a lot more in South-East Asia than by investing them in any other part of the world. With the latest information and communication facilities available, they realised the advantages of investment in these countries. But then as money started accumulating and the economy was booming, the misuse of money became a temptation which the local leadership and hierarchy could not resist. The outside investors also backed the firms and entrepreneurs having close relations of political leaders as Directors; however, it soon became clear that this crony approach leads to skewed investment. Once the outsiders realised the folly of such investments, they started quickly withdrawing them, and thus inadvertently the floodgates got opened and money rushed out like a torrent of gushing water. The moral of the story is that there should have been a better management of money, and, more importantly, greater transparency to prevent unproductive investments. Furthermore, it was not foreseen that hot money thrives on the principle of 'easy come, easy go'. It is, therefore, crony capitalism presided over by the non-democratic authoritarian interests which caused the South-East Asian catastrophe. It was also compounded by the greed of those who pushed their money in these countries to make easy and quick profits. The ailment was due to soft money, the short term money invested in non-productive ventures. South-East Asia had to learn the lessons of its follies. The countries had gained by globalisation where they were careful and cautious. They went wrong where they were careless and where avarice and greed got the better of their judgment. Other countries which would like to benefit from globalisation must be careful when they liberalise their financial systems, and not close down the channels of support which come from outside, but harness and make use of these channels more sensibly to the advantage of their economy.

What measures India needs to take for reaping maximum benefits from globalisation

It is being said that we have to work out a strategy for India to take advantage of globalisation and improve its economy, the living standards of its people and the quality of life itself.

Complete Unfinished Agenda of Economic Reforms

For this first thing to be done is to reinvigorate the process of economic reforms and complete its unfinished agenda. India is losing out since it had slowed down and halted the progress of reforms. More and better market friendly reforms have got to be put through. Controversy relating to capital and consumer goods should be put to rest and more freedom be given to entrepreneurs in terms of choice of technology, products and markets. Free market, however, does not imply the end of State's role in developing the economy. A strong market needs strong State intervention, but the quality and direction of intervention should not be to restrict the freedom of the market but to prevent its going against the fundamentals. The State should also bring radical changes in terms of the technological profile of the product through careful building of technological relations and alliances with other countries. Growing domestic economy ensures suitable policies and having an open mind on economic issues is a prerequisite for reaping maximum benefits from globalisation.

Same Status to Agriculture as to Industry

Second, there is no reason why we should accord a different status to agriculture vis-a-vis industries. Agriculture in India should have been given greater freedom to develop in respect of choices to be exercised by farmers. Farmers cannot produce what they would like to produce. They cannot sell the products as they would wish. They cannot export their products to fetch optimum prices in the international market. The question arises as to why farmers are being denied their rights. Restrictions in exports and imports are being relaxed for industry, why not for agriculture? Advantages of free trade and globalisation are closed for them. If this continues to be the fate of agriculture in India, we would miss out many of the advantages that globalisation can offer to products from this sector. Time has come that the questions of land tenure, land improvement, technological modernization of agriculture on mass scale should be addressed on priority.

Strengthen Scientific base of Research to Development

The third important thing to do is to strengthen and develop the scientific base of research and development, since science and technology would continue to hold the key to future progress. Today, it is not weapons, not army, not even nuclear bombs that constitute the strength of a country. Knowledge represents strength that matters. Today, knowledge and information have the power to enable people face challenges of their lives and spearhead new changes. If the State does not invest adequate resources on development of science and technology, it would lose out to other countries which rely on such a power. Along with strengthening the base of science and technology, education should be imparted to people at large on a mass scale. It is now a well-established fact that literate people are indispensable to a country's development. Else the benefits of science and technology remain confined to a limited section of society, when a large number of people are still outside the orbit of education.

Transparency in Governance

Fourth, we have to realise the importance of transparency in governance. The system of secrecy should end, and measures should be taken to ensure that participants in development are genuinely taken into confidence. We must create a streamlined regime for ensuring quick transactions, which are based on, but not shifted by, rules and regulations. It would be counter-productive if transactions cannot be materialised fast. Delays in transactions and non-transparency of rules together go to create a vicious circle of vacillation, corruption and nepotism, and are the main obstacles in competing effectively in both domestic and global markets.

India to be an effective player at WTO

Fifth, India, should act as an effective member of the WTO and forcefully advocate the interests of the developing world and its own. It should play a vital role in framing fair global rules, regulations and safeguards, and work in harmony with other like-minded countries in the WTO to block unjust practices. This would require a good deal of homework to be done. Genuinely well-informed groups should be set up to examine issues that are of concern to India, and then arrive at the decisions.

Similarly, we have to evolve a much stronger strategy of alliances with regional trading blocs, lest we become their victims or remain outside of their benefits. Regional arrangements are, indeed, welcome milestones in the journey towards a universal open trading system. In the interim, they could harm and restrict free trade and that should be prevented by ensuring the primacy of global rules over regional arrangements, wherever they are detrimental to open free trade. India's efforts to evolve a South Asian global system is welcome. But this should not be and cannot be in lieu of our commitments to a global system.

Stated in simple terms globalisation means integrating the economy of a country with the world economy. The terms globalisation has four parameters: (i) Reduction of trade barriers so as to permit free flow of goods across national frontiers; (ii) creation of an environment in which free flow of capital can take place among nation-states; (iii) creation of environment, permitting free flow of technology; and (iv) last, but not the least, from the point of view of the developing countries, creation of an environment in which free movement of labour can take place in different countries of the world. The advocates of globalisation, more especially from developed countries, limit the definition of globalisation to only three components, viz., unhindered trade flows, capital flows and technology flows. They insist on the developing countries to accept their definition of globalisation and conduct the debate on globalisation within the parameters set by them. However, several economists in the developing world believe that this definition is incomplete and in case the globaliser's ultimate aim is to look upon the world as a 'global' village, then the fourth component, unlimited movement of labour cannot be left out. But the entire issue whether debated at the World Trade Organisation (WTO) or at other forums blacks out the 'labour flows' as an essential component of globalisation.

WTO and Related Issues

The World Trade Organisation (WTO) as contained in the Final Act was established on 1st of January 1995 and India became a founder member of WTO by ratifying the WTO agreement on 30 December 1994. According to the Estimates prepared by the World Bank, OECD and GATT Secretariat, the overall trade impact as a consequence of Uruguay Round Package will be addition to the merchandise good by $ 745 billion by the year 2005. The GATT Secretariat further projects that the largest increases will be in the area of clothing (60%), agriculture, forestry and fishery products (20%) and processed food and beverages (19%). According to the Economic Survey (1994-95), "since India's existing and potential export competitiveness lies in these product groups, it is logical to believe that India will obtain large gains in these sectors. Assuming that India's market share in world exports improves from 0.5% to 1%, and that we are able to take advantage of the opportunities that are created, the trade gains may conservatively be placed at US$ 2.7 billion extra exports per year. A more generous estimate will range from 3.5 to 7 billion US$ worth of extra exports.

India attaches utmost importance to the rule-based trading system, predicated on equitable principles, with avoidance of linkage of trade with extraneous issues.

The fourth WTO Ministerial Conference was held at Doha, Qatar from 9-14 November, 2001 to decide upon the future work programme of the WTO. In view of the failure of the third Ministerial Conference (Seattle, 1999) to take any decision, and in the context of the concerted efforts of certain developed countries to seek endorsement of expanded agenda for WTO, the Conference assumed considerable importance and attracted wide publicity. While there were strong pressures to launch a comprehensive round of negotiations including multilateral regimes on investment, competition policy, trade facilitation, Government procurement and environment, India was opposed to any such overburdening of the multilateral trading system with non trade or new issues in the agenda. It felt that WTO already had a sufficiently large agenda consisting of mandated negotiations and mandated reviews and therefore, India underlined the need for resolving the implementation issues, arising from the current agreements in a time bound manner before addressing new issues for negotiations.

India played a proactive role in the deliberations at the fourth Ministerial Conference at Doha. It wanted a genuine resolution of implementation related concerns, increased market access in agriculture, sufficient flexibility and clarity under TRIPS for public health policies and was strongly opposed to introduction of non-trade issues like labour in the agenda. It was able to ensure adoption of an agenda that emphasised not only trade but also the developmental goals and priorities of developing countries. The outcome of the Conference (Box) takes into account a number of concerns expressed by India. India along with other developing countries would work to ensure that their interests and concerns are adequately taken care of in the work programme. The opportunity also needs to be used for hastening the pace of domestic reforms to further strengthen the country's competitiveness in global trade.

BOX

The Doha Declaration

The Doha Declaration – comprising of a main Declaration, a Declaration on TRIPS Agreement and Public Health and a decision on Implementation related issues and concerns- launches the future work programme of the WTO and includes elaboration and timetables for the current negotiations in agriculture and services and negotiations/possible negotiations in a range of other issues.

Implementation Issues: A number of implementation issues have been addressed in the Decision on implementation related issues and concerns including longer time frame (of six months) for compliance with new SPS and TBT measures, moratorium of two years on non-violation complaints under the TRIPS Agreement, need for special care for initiation of back to back antidumping investigations within a year and co-operation and assistance by members in investigations relating to declared values. The declaration agrees that negotiations on all other outstanding implementation issues shall be an integral part of the work programme. Where specific negotiations are mandated, relevant implementation issues shall be addressed under that mandate and other outstanding implementation issues shall be addressed as a matter of priority by the relevant WTO bodies, which shall report to the Trade Negotiating Committee by the end of 2002 for appropriate action.

Agriculture: The Declaration commits to comprehensive negotiations aimed at: substantial improvements in market access for developing countries; reductions of, with a view to phasing out, all forms of export subsidies; and substantial reductions in trade distorting domestic support being given by the developed countries. It also takes note of non trade concerns of developing countries and their development needs including food security and rural development. Special and differential treatment for developing countries would be an integral part of the negotiations.

Services: The Negotiating Guidelines and Procedures adopted by the Council for Trade in Services would form the basis for continuing negotiations in Services with a view to achieving the objectives of GATS. The declaration recognises the large number of proposals submitted by the members on various sectors including on movement of natural persons.

Industrial tariffs: The negotiations under industrial tariffs would aim at reducing or as appropriate eliminating tariffs, including the reduction of tariff peaks, high tariffs and tariff escalations, as well as non tariff barriers, in particular on products of export interest to developing countries. Product coverage shall be comprehensive and without a priori exclusions with negotiations taking into account the needs and interests of the developing countries including through less than full reciprocity in reduction commitments.

TRIPS: The Work programme mandates negotiations on

establishment of a multilateral system of notification and registration of geographical indications for wines and spirits by the 5th session of the Ministerial Conference. The issues related to extension of the higher level of protection of geographical indications to products other than wines and spirits, examination of relationship between the TRIPS Agreement and the Convention on Biological Diversity (CBD), the protection of traditional knowledge and folklore and other relevant new developments would be addressed by the TRIPS Council as part of the Implementation issues. Further, the Declaration on

TRIPS and Public Health is one of the most significant outcomes of the Doha Conference. It recognises that the TRIPS Agreement can and should be interpreted and implemented in a manner supportive of WTO members' right to protect public health and to promote access to medicines for all.

WTO Rules: The Declaration mandates negotiations aimed at clarifying and improving disciplines under the Agreement on Implementation and Subsidies and Countervailing Measures while preserving the basic concepts, principles and effectiveness of these Agreements and taking into account the needs of developing countries. It also includes negotiations aimed at clarifying and improving disciplines and procedures under the existing WTO provisions applying to regional trade agreement (keeping into view the developmental aspects of these Agreements). Negotiations are further mandated on improvements and clarifications of the Dispute Settlement Understanding. Addressing outstanding implementation issues on these subjects would be an integral part of these negotiations.

Special and Differential Treatment (S&D): The negotiations shall fully take into account the principle of special and differential treatment for developing countries. It has also been agreed to review all special and differential treatment provisions with a view to strengthening them and making them more precise, effective and operational.

Electronic Commerce: The Work Programme declares that Members will maintain their current practice of not imposing customs duties on electronic transmissions until the Fifth Ministerial Session.

Singapore issues: The issues relating to Trade and Investment, interaction between Trade and Competition, Transparency in Government

Procurement and Trade Facilitation will continue to be pursued in the Working Group Study process. Negotiation on these subjects, according to the Work Programme, will take place after the Fifth session of the Ministerial Conference on the basis of a decision to be taken, by explicit consensus, at that session on modalities of negotiations.

Environment: Negotiations on limited aspects of trade and environment (relationship between existing WTO rules and specific trade obligations set out in Multilateral Environmental Agreements, procedures for regular information exchange between MEA and WTO and reduction/elimination of tariff and non tariff barriers to environmental goods and services) has been mandated, along with instructions to the Committee on Trade and Environment to pursue its work on all items on its agenda, giving particular attention to the issues of market access, the relevant provisions of the TRIPS Agreement and labeling.

Labour: The Declaration recognises that ILO is the appropriate forum to address the issue of core labour standards.

Working Groups: The Work Programme has also set up two Working Groups. One to examine the relationship between Trade, Debt and Finance for suggesting solutions, within the WTO mandate, to the problem of external indebtedness of developing countries and to strengthen the coherence of international trade and financial policies, with a view to safeguarding the multilateral trading system from the effects of financial and monetary instability. The other Working group will examine the relationship between Trade and transfer of Technology and to facilitate, within the WTO mandate, increased flow of technology to developing countries. Negotiations under the Work Programme are to be concluded not later than 1 January 2005 (except negotiation on improving and clarifying the Dispute Settlement Understanding which is to be concluded by end of may 2003). The conduct, conclusion and entry into force of the outcome of negotiations will be treated as parts of a single undertaking (except for DSU). The overall conduct of the negotiations is to be supervised by a Trade Negotiations Committee under the authority of the General Council.

Source: Economic Survey 2001-02.